MILTON

MILTON

by E. M. W. TILLYARD

LITT. D., F. B. A.

Late Master of Jesus College, Cambridge

Revised Edition

With a Preface by

PHYLLIS B. TILLYARD

COLLIER BOOKS, NEW YORK

Library of Congress Catalog Card Number: 67–22733

FIRST COLLIER BOOKS EDITION 1967

This Collier Books Edition is published by arrangements with Chatto & Windus Ltd

The Macmillan Company, New York

Printed in the United States of America

Contents

CONTENTS

Editor's Preface

THIS book was first published in 1930, and though there have been numerous subsequent impressions, the author was unable to make any alterations of importance, owing to the pressure of other work. In his preface to the Third Impression he wrote: 'So much has happened in Milton scholarship since 1930 that to take it all into account would mean rewriting. But to rewrite would be to spoil such merits as the original possesses. Moreover, I should not wish to go back on my main propositions. I prefer to alter nothing and instead to remind the reader that no account is taken of anything published after 1930.' This applies even more forcibly to any later edition.

In the present edition, therefore, references have been brought up to date as far as possible, and some, noting recently discovered evidence, have been added. Remarks no longer applicable have been deleted, and omissions (such as some of Cowper's translations of the Latin poems) have been made good. A few slips have been corrected. But no major works of criticism after 1930 have been taken into consideration.

The monumental Columbia edition (*The Works of John Milton*, ed. Patterson, Columbia University Press, New York, 1931–40), containing all Milton's works, is of course indispensable to the specialist. But for the ordinary reader the antique orthography interrupts the course of the argument and hinders easy reading. This applies also to the Yale edition (*Milton's Complete Prose Works*, ed. Wolfe, Yale University Press, Newhaven, 1953 – in progress). The versions in the Bohn edition (J. A. St John, *The Prose Works of John Milton*, Bohn's Standard Library, George Bell and Sons, 1848–51) have, therefore, been retained for quotations from the prose works. The Bohn edition, however, does not include the *Defensio pro Se* or the *Prolusions*. For the latter, and for the letters, my own translation (Milton, *Private Correspondence and Academic Exercises*, translated by Phyllis B. Tillyard, with an Introduction and Commentary by E. M. W. Tillyard, Cambridge University Press, 1932) is used.

This not being available when the present book was written, the author made his own translations of the *Prolusions* and gave the somewhat unsatisfactory Bohn edition versions of the letters. But as he used my version in his later writings it seemed best to substitute it here, for the sake of uniformity, and to enable readers to follow up the contexts of the quotations if they wish to do so.

PREFACE

For quotations from Milton's poems and for Cowper's translations of the Latin and Italian verse the Oxford editions have been used, by kind permission of the Oxford University Press. Appendix E is a letter to *The Times Literary Supplement*, by courtesy of The Times Publishing Co.

To Dr Rosemary Freeman I owe many thanks for her advice, help with the proofs, and several valuable references; these are marked with her initials. And I am very grateful to Mr Herbert Rees for checking all quotations, and for reading the final proofs for press.

Phyllis B. Tillyard.

December 1965

Introduction

No ONE reading through *Paradise Lost* with any degree of seriousness can help asking with what the poem as a whole is most truly concerned, what were the feelings and ideas that dominated Milton's mind when he wrote it. Such was my own experience, and when I found the question difficult to answer, I sought help from the books on Milton that are most read in England. But they helped very little. The majority, however good on other topics, made no attempt at all to answer this particular question; or what they did say went no further than to summarize Milton's own professions as to the true subject of his poem. The only critics who seemed to tackle the problem in the right kind of way were the Satanists, namely those who invested the character of Satan with all that Milton felt and valued most strongly. But the more I considered the Satanic explanation, the more inadequate it seemed: far too simple to solve so complicated a problem. And so I was led to work out my own solution, the results of which attempt are the central part of this book. I found in due course that more had been written on the subject than I had known, especially in America, where opinion had already reacted against the Satanists; but nothing I have read has convinced me that there is not room for several more attempts to find out with what *Paradise Lost* as a whole is most truly concerned.

Paradise Lost was some years in the writing, and its origins go back in part to still earlier years. It is not surprising that Milton should have changed somewhat during its composition. In fact, a change of mentality seemed to me the only solution of some of the problems the poem presents. The subject of *Paradise Lost*, then, led quite naturally to that of how Milton's mind developed. And this, Milton's mental development, is broadly the subject of this book. I do not mean that I am at all competing with M. Saurat's work on Milton's dogma and philosophy.[1] It is Milton's literary development I have mainly in mind, but illumined as far as possible by his mental experience. I have had of course to touch on Milton's thought; but only as a means to some other end, not with the idea of contributing to the knowledge of his philosophy.

The book has been divided into three parts, corresponding with the three well-marked epochs of Milton's life: the early poems, covering the period from his birth till his return from Italy and the

1. *Milton, Man and Thinker*, 2nd ed., 1944.

writing of *Epitaphium Damonis*; the period of the prose, 1639–60; the later poems, from the Restoration to his death. Owing to the varying material that has survived, treatment of Milton's mental growth has had to be different in each of these three periods.

In studying Milton's formative years I found that the known facts of his life had never been closely applied to his poems. Something here remained to be done. There is therefore a certain amount of biography in the first part: more than in the rest. While I was writing, Professor J. H. Hanford published his *Youth of Milton*, a study much on the lines I had been following. But his matter is more biographical and less literary than mine, and though there may be a little overlapping, my version, which reaches some rather different conclusions, need not be taken to compete with his more detailed analysis. Another fact that became evident from studying Milton's early years was that his Latin poems and Latin academic exercises had not usually been stressed enough, and certainly had not been inserted in their proper order in Milton's writings. Professor Grierson has registered a practical protest against this manner of treatment by printing, in his edition of Milton's verse, English, Latin, and Italian poems in their chronological order, not in linguistic groups. Milton wrote Latin as readily as he did English; and to understand him we must give each language impartial treatment. This, at the risk of tedium (for Milton's Latin verses are not particularly easy), I have tried to do. In themselves some of the Latin verses are extremely interesting and some beautiful; and the slight additional trouble (for those whose Latin is not very ready) of reading them in the original is well rewarded. But although what we know of Milton's life in his early years had, before Professor Hanford's study, not been exploited properly, it is, even when exploited, annoyingly patchy. There are blank years besides well-illumined moments; and the reader must be warned against expecting the impossibility of symmetrical treatment.

In the middle period external biographical fact seems to help comparatively little, but there is ample compensation in the personal avowals found so richly in the pamphlets. As far as I know, Milton's prose has never been examined in strictly chronological order. It has usually been taken in isolated groups, or studied as a whole without the slightest reference to development. For instance, how many books on Milton make their readers aware that *Areopagitica* and the *Tractate on Education* were written in the middle of his pamphlets on divorce? And yet this order has a good deal of bearing on Milton's state of mind during these years. I hope through having studied Milton's prose in its chronological sequence to have pointed out certain changes in Milton's mind and certain crises in his experience not hitherto detected.

In the third period biography does not help at all. There is only the rather problematic evidence of the poems themselves. Mental change is detected between the first part of *Paradise Lost* and the last part, with which *Paradise Regained* is to be associated, and also between *Paradise Regained* and *Samson Agonistes*. But generally it is the mentality, not the change of mentality, that has concerned me in my third part. The criticism is more purely literary.

Though having in mind, as the connecting subject of the book, Milton's literary and mental development, I have commented on many poems as isolated works of art, have tried to assess their individual value. For instance, I have tried to explain not only how *Lycidas* is a landmark of Milton's mental growth, but in what its poetical greatness lies and why it is easily the most valuable of his early poems. Similarly I have sought to fill part of the curious lack of literary criticism on *Paradise Regained*. A good deal therefore of what has been written may not be very closely linked with the main subject.

In some ways Milton is a romantic, and there are signs that recent opinion is setting against him as well as against the avowed romantic school of the nineteenth century. Anyhow, it is not safe to assume that his reputation will continue to stand as high as it has done for the last two hundred years. I cannot myself see that Milton's value is superannuated, and in the epilogue I have stated very simply why I hold this opinion.

A very little experiment showed that all but briefest references to the literature, history, and thought of Milton's day must be excluded to keep the book within the limits designed. I have therefore kept, on the whole, very closely to Milton's text. As a compromise I have added, in the first two parts, tables showing the dates of Milton's writings, of events in his life, and of current political events; and I would like to ask readers to consider these tables as part of the book, to associate them with the chapters to which they are prefixed.

It is extremely difficult, in a book like this which tries to combine a certain amount of scholarship with an appeal to the general literary public, to know how much knowledge to assume in the average reader. To assume little is insulting; to assume much has the disgusting taint of academic snobbery. Roughly I have assumed some knowledge of Milton's English poems, and an acquaintance with the facts of his career obtainable in such books on Milton as those published in the Home University Library or Macmillan's Literature Primers.

PART I

THE EARLY POEMS

CHAPTER ONE

Childhood and School

Date	Milton's age	Writing or event in Milton's life	Contemporary event
1605			Gunpowder Plot
			Bacon's *Advancement of Learning*
			Sylvester's translation of Du Bartas
1608, Dec. 9		Milton born	
1620	11	Enters St Paul's	Beginnings of religious animosity
1624	15	Paraphrase of Psalms cxiv and cxxxvi	
1625, Feb.	16	Enters College	

MILTON's father, the child of comparatively wealthy Catholic parents, early forsook the paternal religion, was disinherited, and forced to earn his own living. It is likely that he had small taste for the scrivener's profession, into which a relative had introduced him; but he accepted the necessity, made a competence, and retired when conditions allowed. Music was his chief delight; and he would probably have liked to make this, his lifelong hobby, into his main business in life. Thwarted himself of full indulgence in the arts, he seems to have attempted the nearest compensation, and 'destined' his eldest son, the poet Milton, 'from a child to the pursuits of literature'. Milton responded with precociousness, and in the eleventh year of his age had become (so Aubrey tells us) already a poet. His appetite for knowledge was so voracious that after he was twelve he hardly ever left his studies or went to bed before midnight. One of the maids had to sit up with him. Not considering the ordinary school teaching at St Paul's sufficient, the elder Milton supplemented it with a tutor.[1] He caused his son (who remembered it later with gratitude)[2] to be taught French, Italian, and Hebrew, as well as the usual Latin and Greek. In sum, he was as anxious to instil learning into his son as Lord Chesterfield to inculcate the

1. For a note on Thomas Young, Milton's tutor, see Appendix A, p. 315.
2. In the Latin poem, *Ad Patrem*, 78–85.

7

graces. He did not omit the question of a profession, and chose the Church; not, it would seem, because he was set on his son being a clergyman, but because in that profession his learning would find the widest scope.

The effect of all this concentrated care and unremitted pressure on Milton's powerful, sensitive nature was to make him believe from a very early age, to make him assume indeed axiomatically, that he was no ordinary person, but destined to some high achievement in one of the fields of learning.

Three years before Milton's birth, in 1605, the year of the Gunpowder Plot, were published two books which made a great impression on contemporary England: Bacon's *Advancement of Learning* and Sylvester's translation of Du Bartas. The first exercised a steady and ever-increasing influence in England during the years of Milton's nonage. The second was extremely popular, especially among the Puritans, and must have been one of the books of English verse with which Milton first became acquainted. It is easy enough to see why the translation of this enormous pseudo-epic on the Creation, written by a French Protestant, should have been so popular in the early seventeenth century. Published in the year of the Gunpowder Plot, it ministered to the anti-Catholic animus that rose steadily throughout the reign of James I. It had too the great advantage, unlike some contemporary drama and the poems of Donne (at that time known to a few in manuscript), of being extremely easy to understand. Yet it had a sort of modernity. Science was in the air, and Sylvester's Du Bartas was full of the popular science of the day.

Milton, like Dryden, must have read Sylvester with enthusiasm in his early school-days. His first extant poem, a version of the 114th Psalm, written at the age of fifteen, is in the metre and manner of Sylvester. Witness especially the violence of the two lines:

> That glassy flouds from rugged rocks can crush
> And make soft rills from fiery flint-stones gush.

The companion piece, the version of the 136th Psalm beginning 'Let us with a gladsom mind', though still reminiscent of Sylvester, is different. It is simple and it is dignified:

> He with his thunder-clasping hand,
> Smote the first-born of *Egypt* Land.

And it is in places original: there is nothing in the Psalm to suggest the image in

> The floods stood still like Walls of Glass,
> While the Hebrew Bands did pass.

Milton at fifteen had already gone beyond Sylvester.

Still it would be wrong to ignore Sylvester in estimating what Milton owed to other writers. Sylvester's fame as a noble didactic poet probably worked on his imagination and guided his ambition. He would outdo Sylvester, as Spenser had sought to outdo Ariosto. Again, when the time came for him to choose a subject for his epic he may have been more influenced than he knew by his school-boy ambition to write a rival poem on the Creation.

There is no indication that the rebelliousness which was part of Milton's character was aroused at St Paul's. He seems to have liked his school: which implies that he accepted the mental nourishment provided and that his own talents were appreciated. The Headmaster, Alexander Gill, belonged like his predecessor Mulcaster to the race of schoolmasters who taught the literary canons of the Renaissance. Milton must have learnt to revere the Greek and Latin classics as the source of all humane knowledge, and to read them as living languages, to look on poetry as a means of teaching and as a vehicle of learning. But Gill's literary interests were not confined to the classics. He was the author of a manual of English grammar entitled *Logonomia Anglica*, written in Latin but freely illustrated by English quotations. Jonson, Campion, Sidney, and a few others, are very rarely drawn on, but the bulk of the passages comes from the *Faerie Queene*. Spenser is assumed to be the English Virgil, the one undoubted English classic, international by his learning and his constant recourse to classical models, domestic by his having set the standard of English versification. During his school-days Milton would have come to believe in serious literature as belonging to one great humane tradition, whatever language it was written in. If it was modern, it should still be international: for it might be written in Latin, the common tongue of European culture; or if it was written in the vernacular, it should conform to a no less common tradition of literary imitation. Milton never departed from the critical canons he learnt at school: it will be shown in a later chapter how, reinforced by his residence in Italy, they gave a definite turn to his literary production. Even his school-boy versions of the Psalms, usually assumed to owe their origin to the Puritan temper of his home, are in the larger Renaissance tradition. Milton, like Wyatt many years before, is not less international in translating the Psalms into the vernacular than he was later in writing Latin elegies after the model of Horace and Ovid.

In composition Milton was probably encouraged to write Latin rather than English. The younger Gill, usher in his father's school, with whom Milton grew very familiar and for whom he retained a great admiration, was an adept at original Latin verse and must have incited him to excel in that art. Another incitement was his love for the Latin elegiac poets, 'the smooth elegiac poets, whereof the schools are not scarce, whom, both for the pleasing sound of their numerous writing, which in imitation I found most easy and most agreeable to nature's part in me, and for their matter, which what it is there be few who know not, I was so allured to read that no recreation came to me better welcome'.[1] None of these imitations survives from before his second year at college, but these later verses show a familiarity with Ovid's elegiac writings so thorough that it must have begun a number of years before.

Outside school Milton is certain to have read widely in English, but before going to Cambridge he is not likely to have come into contact with the rivalries and ambitions of modern literary circles. The bias at school would have been towards Spenser, at home towards a Puritan poet like Sylvester and naturally towards Spenser too. How much Milton frequented the theatre, whether he frequented it at all, is still a matter of doubt.[2]

As well as acquiring a proficiency in various languages, Milton, he tells us himself,[3] had made considerable progress in philosophy before going up to Cambridge. *Philosophy* is vague enough, but it may imply that he was acquainted with the ideas of Bacon, whose *Novum Organum* was published while Milton was still at St Paul's. This is likely enough in view of his immediate dissatisfaction with Cambridge, where the Baconian philosophy had not penetrated into the curriculum.

It was to his school-days that Milton owed his only intimate friend, Diodati. The basis of this friendship was the admiration felt by a simple, quick, and unselfish nature for another of superior power. Masson gives a translation of two letters, written in Greek by Diodati to Milton, probably soon after Milton left school, which bear out this assumption. The second ends as follows:

Live, laugh, enjoy youth and the hours as they pass, and desist from those researches of yours into the pursuits, and leisures, and indolences of the wise men of old, yourself a martyr to overwork all the while. I, in all things else your inferior, both think myself and am superior to you in this, that I know a measure in my labours.[4]

1. *Apology for Smectymnuus*, Bohn, iii. 116–17.
2. On this matter see especially W. H. Garrod's remarks in *Essays and Studies of the English Association*, xii. 1926, 20–3.
3. In *Defensio Secunda*, Bohn, i. 254.
4. Masson, *Life of Milton*, i. 2nd ed. 163.

The friendship was not one-sided; there is no reason to doubt Milton's affection: but the basis was the homage of the weaker to the stronger.[1]

It seems likely that when Milton left school at the age of sixteen he was extremely learned and inexperienced, confident and ambitious, that he combined a high sense of his own parts with a totally false idea of the value that would be placed on them by a world that did not consist of admiring parents and encouraging schoolmasters.

1. This letter has now been published in the Columbia edition, xii. 295–6, and Yale edition, I. 33 [P.B.T.].

CHAPTER TWO

First Years at Cambridge

Date	Milton's age	Writing or event in Milton's life	Contemporary event
1625, Feb.	16	Enters College	
1625, March	16	First Letter to Thomas Young	Accession of Charles I
1625–26 (winter)	17	*Elegy on Death of Fair Infant*	
1626, April or May	17	*Elegia Prima* (to Diodati) Quarrel with Tutor	
1626, Sept.?	17	*Elegia Secunda* (on death of Esquire Bedell)	
1626, Sept.	17	*Elegia Tertia* (on death of Bishop of Winchester)	
1626, Oct.	17	*In Obitum Praesulis Eliensis*	
1626, Oct.	17	*In Obitum Procancellarii Medici*	
1626, Nov.	17	*In Quintum Novembris* (Gunpowder Plot)	

MILTON has told us a good deal about himself at college, but, as he usually did this in Latin, his remarks have not been very widely heeded. The references in his later pamphlets are well enough known, although it remained for Hanford[1] to work out the implications in the autobiographical passage from the *Apology for Smectymnuus*. But few people read Milton's Latin poems, and still fewer the *Prolusiones Oratoriae*, or academic exercises, composed from time to time at college to satisfy the requirements for obtaining the usual degrees. Portions of them deserve to be as well known as the three autobiographical passages, in *Reason of Church Government*, *Apology for Smectymnuus*, and the *Defensio Secunda*.[2]

It was at Cambridge that Milton's uncommon powers of resistance and of controversy seem first to have been aroused. He was for a

1. In *The Youth of Milton*, in University of Michigan Publications (Language and Literature), *Studies in Shakespeare, Milton and Donne*, vol. i., 87–163.

2. On the *Prolusions* see my Introduction to P. B. Tillyard's translation (*Milton, Private Correspondence and Academic Exercises*) reprinted in *Studies in Milton*, 113–36. (For the Latin of the *Prolusions* and letters see Columbia edition, xii [P.B.T.].)

time unpopular with his fellow-undergraduates, he got into trouble with the dons, and he was hostile to the system of education then in vogue. And though he lived down his unpopularity and became reconciled with the authorities, he never gave up his less personal hostility.

The education in Milton's day was still based on the medieval system of disputation. And the disputation was based on the practice of the scholastic philosophy. In order to qualify for his degrees a candidate had to uphold or to attack from time to time, both in his college and in the public schools, certain usually very abstract theses; and his education would be directed to fitting him to conduct his argument according to the rules of scholastic logic or to weight it with a sufficiently impressive mass of learning. Cambridge was of course very much smaller than it is now; there was far less liberty, though a good deal of breaking bounds; and in the first years at least there was no choice of study. The course may have provided a good mental discipline, but it had little pretension to what Arnold understood by culture. Now although the system continued many years after Milton left Cambridge, opposition to it had already arisen, and this opposition was connected with the ideas of Bacon. Bacon had kept in touch with his old University and was extremely anxious that his conception of learning and education should gain an entry into it. He left money (which proved not to be there) for founding a lectureship in Natural Philosophy. The Baconians or educational reformers must have been a small but important minority in the Cambridge of Milton's day.

Milton began his career of radicalism by declaring with great emphasis for reform. He considered the intensive training in scholastic logic a waste of time, and favoured subjects like History, Geography, or Astronomy, that were concerned with man and the universe. His *Third Prolusion, Contra Philosophiam Scholasticam,* is an open attack on the Cambridge system of education and a plea for reform. It is in addition a very interesting personal document. Milton, after the manner that distinguished him throughout his life, argues from the personal to the general. Here is his description of how he himself fared with the scholastic philosophers.

Many a time, when the duty of tracing out these petty subtleties for a while has been laid upon me, when my mind has been dulled and my sight blurred by continued reading – many a time, I say, I have paused to take breath, and have sought some slight relief from my boredom in looking to see how much yet remained of my task. When, as always happened, I found that more remained to be done than I had as yet got through, how often have I wished that instead of having these fooleries forced upon me I had been set to clean out the stable of Augeas again, and I have envied Hercules his luck in having been spared such labours as these by a kindly Juno.[1]

Not merely is the scholastic philosophy inhuman and unpleasant, it is useless too; and he recommends that experimental knowledge should be substituted for it.

But how much better were it, gentlemen, and how much more consonant with your dignity, now to let your eyes wander as it were over all the lands depicted on the map, and to behold the places trodden by the heroes of old, to range over the regions made famous by wars, by triumphs, and even by the tales of poets of renown, now to traverse the stormy Adriatic, now to climb unharmed the slopes of fiery Etna, then to spy out the customs of mankind and those states which are well-ordered; next to seek out and explore the nature of all living creatures, and after that to turn your attention to the secret virtues of stones and herbs. And do not shrink from taking your flight into the skies and gazing upon the manifold shapes of the clouds, the mighty piles of snow, and the source of the dews of morning; then inspect the coffers wherein the hail is stored and examine the arsenals of the thunderbolts. And do not let the intent of Jupiter or of Nature elude you, when a huge and fearful comet threatens to set the heavens aflame, nor let the smallest star escape you of all the myriads which are scattered and strewn between the poles.[2]

And throughout the *Prolusions* Milton loses no opportunity of showing his contempt for the studies he is forced to take up. For instance, in the *Fourth Prolusion*, supporting the scholastic thesis that no dead thing resolves itself into primordial matter, he punctuates his discourse by saying he may be boring his audience because he knows he is boring himself. Nor did he let the matter rest in later life. He speaks of Bacon as being among 'the greatest and sublimest wits in sundry ages',[3] while in the *Tractate on Education* (to mention one passage out of a number) he accuses the Universities of being 'not yet well recovered from the scholastic grossness of barbarous ages', and speaks of the undergraduates as being 'mocked and deluded with ragged notions and babblements, while they expected worthy and delightful knowledge'.

Bearing in mind how extremely stubborn a controversialist Milton later showed himself, and how bold in saying what he

1. P. B. Tillyard, *Milton, Private Correspondence and Academic Exercises*, 68–9.
2. ibid., 72. Although this passage shows Milton to be supporting the Baconians, it is also much influenced by the popular science of Sylvester's Du Bartas.
3. *Apology for Smectymnuus*, Bohn, iii. 108.

14

thought, we can readily understand the quarrel with his tutor and his unpopularity among the undergraduates. Chappell, his first tutor, was, according to Fuller, 'a most subtle disputant'; his strength lay in the very studies Milton hated. Chappell probably confined Milton to the scholastic beat, till Milton became exasperated and told his tutor what he thought of the Cambridge educational methods.[1] For the undergraduates' hostility the *First Prolusion*, the date of which is unknown but written presumably fairly early in his University career, is the authority. Before coming to the subject of disputation he addressed his audience as follows:

> How can I hope for your good-will, when in all this great assembly I encounter none but hostile glances, so that my task seems to be to placate the implacable? So provocative of animosity, even in the home of learning, is the rivalry of those who pursue different studies or whose opinions differ concerning the studies they pursue in common. . . . Yet to prevent complete despair, I see here and there, if I do not mistake, some who without a word show clearly by their looks how well they wish me. The approval of these, few though they be, is more precious to me than that of the countless hosts of the ignorant, who lack all intelligence, reasoning power, and sound judgment, and who pride themselves on the ridiculous effervescing froth of their verbiage.[2]

The wording is vague. But the 'different studies' and the 'rivalry' are likely to refer respectively to those who favoured the strict adherence to the old curriculum and those who tried to work in all the new matter they could. Be this as it may, the passage is interesting in showing us Milton with a completely realized personality. He is proud, intolerant of mediocrity, and with an aristocratic preference for the intelligent few. But he is also extremely simple-minded and candid: there is not a trace of personal rancour in his attack. Even later, when he was on better terms with the undergraduates, he continued to be distressed at their low level of intelligence. It looks as if he had suffered something of a shock when he came up. Prone, as he later showed himself, to expect too much from normal humanity, he doubtless expected to find himself in company with other Miltons under the tuition of men more remarkable for piety and learning than even Young and the Gills. And of course he found that his companions were not at all like other Miltons and that the dons fell short of his high expectations. This passage from a letter to the

1. For Milton's quarrel with his tutor see Keightley, *Life, Opinions, and Writings of John Milton*, 119; Hanford, op. cit., 102–3.
2. P. B. Tillyard, op. cit., 53–4.

younger Gill, written at Cambridge on 2 July, 1628, shows what he thought of the undergraduates in his fourth year.

Whenever I call to mind your almost constant conversations with me, the like of which I vainly seek even in the very seat of learning, the University itself, I realize at once, to my sorrow, of how much profit my absence deprives me. For I never quitted your company without some clear increase or *crescendo* of learning, just as if I had paid a visit to some mart of erudition. At any rate, so far as I know, there are but one or two among us who do not take their flight to theology before ever they are fledged, almost untrained and uninitiated in literature and philosophy alike. And even of theology they are content with a mere smattering, if it be but enough to enable them to piece together after a fashion some little homily and patch it up as it were out of scraps of other men's rags. So much so, that there is a serious risk of our clergy gradually falling into the popish ignorance of former ages. As for myself, since I find here hardly any congenial fellow-students, I should turn my eyes straightway back to London, if I were not planning this Long Vacation to bury myself deep in literary retirement, and so to speak take cover in the precincts of the Muses.[1]

The sentences about the clergy show that the seeds of the denunciatory passage in *Lycidas* had been sown many years before. They show too, I think, that Milton had already abandoned the idea of taking Orders. It is evident from the end that he was irked by the limitations of the University studies and could only be satisfied by a long stretch of undisturbed reading.

It is hazardous to connect any of the known events of Milton's college years with his poetical remains, but it is at least worth noting that his first productive period begins about the time when the quarrel with Chappell took place. That Milton destroyed any valuable early poems seems extremely unlikely; and we are fairly entitled to claim that his eighteenth year, to which one English and eleven Latin poems belong, is a landmark in his poetical development. Possibly his disillusionment about Cambridge and the reaction against his studies there may have awakened his powers, as his transfer in the Easter Term of 1626 to another tutor, implying a semblance of victory, may have induced a certain propitious serenity.

Critics sometimes forget that before the *Nativity Ode* Milton wrote more Latin than English, and, one may suggest, that the best of the Latin is at least as good as the best of the English. At any rate it is wrong to isolate the English poems; and his elegy *On the Death of*

1. P. B. Tillyard, op. cit., 8.

a Fair Infant must be considered as the first of a series of five elegies,[1]
written during the first ten months of his eighteenth year. They are
all of them exercises, and yet, as Longinus would say, the exercises
of Milton. There is in them a sense of deliberate apprenticeship, of
which Milton was clearly not in the least ashamed and of which, as
will be pointed out later, there are signs even in *Comus*. Only he
varies his models, choosing the Elizabethans for the English poem,
Ovid and Horace for the Latin. But all alike contain common
Miltonic qualities: an unusual assurance of tone, which might easily
verge on arrogance, the beginnings, generally rather blurred, of
serene grandeur and of grave sweetness, and a very rigorous sense of
form.

On the Death of a Fair Infant, though often said to imitate Spenser,
is rather in the tradition of the Ovidizing Elizabethans, of poems like
Hero and Leander and *Venus and Adonis*. The opening,

> O fairest flower no sooner blown but blasted,
> Soft silken Primrose fading timelesslie,

was probably suggested by the fragment in *The Passionate Pilgrim*
beginning

> Sweet Rose, fair flower, untimely pluckt, soon faded,
> Pluckt in the bud, and vaded in the spring.
> Bright orient pearl, alack too timely shaded,
> Fair creature killed too soon by Death's sharp sting.

But the effect of the poem is individual. The bright staccato quality
of the Elizabethan conceits has been resolved into something
slower, more hesitating, but more gravely sonorous. Once at least
the verse breaks into stateliness. After the lines describing how
Boreas, spying the infant,

> with his cold-kind embrace
> Unhous'd thy Virgin Soul from her fair biding place,

comes the soar-up of

> Yet art thou not inglorious in thy fate,

somewhat spoiled by the amateurish repetition of rhythm in the
next verse,

> Yet can I not perswade me thou art dead.

1. *Elegia Secunda, Elegia Tertia, In Obitum Praesulis Eliensis, In Obitum Procancellarii
Medici* are the other four.

The assurance of tone is very marked in the last stanza. He orders the child's mother to cease grieving, to learn wisely 'to curb her sorrows wild', with the instinctive certainty of a commanding nature, but forgetful that the lady he addresses may have more experience of life than himself. But against this tactlessness may be set the line (so prophetic of the *Nativity Ode*)

Let down in clowdie throne to do the world some good,

which exhibits a touch of the engaging innocence that often redeems Milton's less amiable qualities.

Of the Latin elegies two are in the elegiac metre, two in Horatian metres. The example of Ovid, whom Milton admired to excess in his early years, was unfortunate. He copies Ovid's elegiacs with great skill and thoroughly enjoys the Ovidian game of mythological circumlocution, but his ardent temperament could not possibly find proper expression in so narrow a form, or, to vary the metaphor, he cannot really accommodate his huge stride to the twinkling little steps of the Ovidian metre. Horace was really a more effective model; and the Alcaics *In Obitum Procancellarii Medici* contain lines as good as any we have before the *Nativity Ode*. These are the concluding verses:

> At fila rupit Persephone tua
> Irata, cum te viderit artibus
>   Succoque pollenti tot atris
>   Faucibus eripuisse mortis.
>
> Colende praeses, membra precor tua
> Molli quiescant cespite, et ex tuo
>   Crescant rosae, calthaeque busto,
>   Purpureoque hyacinthus ore.
>
> Sit mite de te judicium Aeaci,
> Subrideatque Aetnaea Proserpina,
>   Interque felices perennis
>   Elysio spatiere campo.[1]

The last verse has a dignity very remarkable in a writer only seventeen years of age.

1. *For translations of the Latin poems I use Cowper's version:*
  37–48:

But resentful Proserpine,	Wise and good! untroubled be
Jealous of thy skill divine,	The green turf that covers thee!
Snapping short thy vital thread	Thence, in gay profusion, grow
Thee too numbered with the dead.	All the sweetest flowers that blow!

> Pluto's consort bid thee rest!
> Aeacus pronounce thee blest,
> To her home thy shade consign,
> Make Elysium ever thine!

There remain to be mentioned two more poems belonging to Milton's eighteenth year: *Elegia Prima* and *In Quintum Novembris.* The first, written shortly after the poem *On the Death of a Fair Infant,* is his earliest surviving Latin poem. As literature it is very immature and redundant, but it shows a mastery over an alien tongue extraordinary in a young man of seventeen. Its very redundance too betrays the exuberance of Milton's nature, which can only be seen fully in his prose and which he strove so hard to hide beneath the severity of his versification. Biographically, *Elegia Prima* is one of Milton's most interesting poems. Addressing himself to Diodati, he refers to his trouble at college and says that he is quite happy to be in London, where he is surrounded by books and can vary his studies by visiting the theatres or by walking in the suburbs and looking at the young ladies; whose beauty he praises with great fervour, making it plain that by seventeen he was susceptible to female charm.

> Ah quoties dignae stupui miracula formae
>   Quae possit senium vel reparare Jovis;
> Ah quoties vidi superantia lumina gemmas,
>   Atque faces quotquot volvit uterque polus;
> Collaque bis vivi Pelopis quae brachia vincant,
>   Quaeque fluit puro nectare tincta via,
> Et decus eximium frontis, tremulosque capillos,
>   Aurea quae fallax retia tendit Amor.
> Pellacesque genas, ad quas hyacinthina sordet
>   Purpura, et ipse tui floris, Adoni, rubor.[1]

1. 53–62:
> Here many a virgin troop I may descry
> Like stars of mildest influence, gliding by.
> Oh forms divine! Oh looks that might inspire
> Even Jove himself, grown old, with young desire!
> Oft have I gazed on gem-surpassing eyes,
> Outsparkling every star that gilds the skies,
> Necks whiter than the ivory arm bestow'd
> By Jove on Pelops, or the Milky Road!
> Bright locks, Love's golden snare! these falling low,
> Those playing wanton o'er the graceful brow!
> Cheeks too, more winning sweet than after shower
> Adonis turned to Flora's favorite flower.

The Gunpowder Plot poem, *In Quintum Novembris*, which has perhaps been a little over-admired,[1] is a mixture of some genuine power and a good deal of melodrama. Milton describes how Satan, seeing and hating the Protestant bliss of England under the pious James, journeys to Rome and instigates the Pope to engineer the Gunpowder Plot. Satan is a crude monster, breathing 'Tartarean fire' and 'lurid sulphur', while his 'adamantine teeth' clash together like smitten armour. Milton warms up in describing Satan's journey to Rome, but cannot sustain his ardour, and he wearies so rapidly that he never describes the actual plot at all but ends with seven hurried lines on the discovery of the plot and the punishment of the conspirators. Besides being a vigorous failure, the poem has the slight interest of showing that Milton had been reading Phineas Fletcher. Not only is it probable that Fletcher's *Locustae*, a Latin poem dealing with the Gunpowder Plot with similar machinery, was Milton's general model, but a passage such as that describing the Cave of Phonos in Milton's poem is extremely like some of the numerous passages in *The Purple Island* describing the abode of some personified quality. It may be guessed that the brothers Giles and Phineas Fletcher had a considerable following in Cambridge. They had both been dons there, and though they retired to livings in the eastern counties they never severed connection with their old University. Their poems were printed at Cambridge and were valued as the productions of local talent. Giles had died four years before Milton came up, but Phineas published his poems during Milton's residence. Another recommendation of the brothers' poems was their sultry Protestant fervour. Coupled with the *Nativity Ode*, whose 'pathetic fallacies' owe something to Giles, *In Quintum Novembris* is a faint indication that Milton was temporarily attached to the admirers of the two Fletchers.

Something may be conjectured from the remarkable literary production of Milton's eighteenth year, a production all the more remarkable because we have but one poem belonging to his next year. First, I believe, from the extraordinary accent of assurance with which he writes, he had already made up his mind that he was going to be a great poet. Secondly, having thus made up his mind, he had deliberately set himself to practise, the idea of practising the elegy being suggested to him by the Latin poets he most loved and by the prevalence of the plague that had caused the death of his infant niece. That he was much moved by any of the deaths he

1. By Masson, *Life of Milton*, and E. K. Rand in 'Milton in Rustication,' *Studies in Philology*, 1922, 109–35.

celebrates I doubt, but with him practice was a very serious thing, and he puts into his pieces the very best work he is capable of. After writing five elegies, the latest (*In Obitum Procancellarii Medici*) being the best, he turns in the Gunpowder Plot poem to the small-scale epic, a literary type sanctioned by classical example. After a resolute effort, producing some two hundred lines, he finds, as on a later occasion, 'the subject to be above the years he had, when he wrote it', finishes the poem in a hurry, and gives up writing till further study shall fit him for, or some special occasion exact, a further poetical trial. The process was repeated later.

CHAPTER THREE

Middle Years at Cambridge

Date	Milton's age	Writing or event in Milton's life	Contemporary event
1628, May	19	*Elegia Septima* (amorous adventure)	
1628, May 26	19	Letter to Gill (political reference)	Petition of Rights
1628, July 2	19	Letter to Gill (verses for one of dons)	
July 21		Second Letter to Thomas Young	
1628, July	19	*Naturam non pati Senium*	
1628, July	19	The Vacation Exercise: prose (=*Sixth Prolusion*), and verse	Aug. Murder of Buckingham
1628–29?	19–20	De Idea Platonica	
1629, March	20	Takes B.A. Degree	The Three Resolutions of Parliament. No Parliament till 1640
1629, April	20	*Elegia Quinta, in Adventum Veris*	

NEARLY two years separate *In Quintum Novembris* from Milton's next effective composition. The *Elegia Septima*, probably written in May 1628, is Milton's first love poem. In the *Elegia Prima* he had praised the girls of England for their beauty: now he relates in a formal and elaborate way how Cupid at last has subdued him. One day, when he was walking out to look at the young ladies, he notices one far surpassing the rest in beauty. He quickly loses sight of her, but not before he has fallen in love. There is little doubt that Milton is narrating an actual experience; and one is glad to think that at the age of nineteen he was not in every way unlike other young men of that age. But later he judged unkindly of his hasty passion, for when he collected his minor poems for publication he attached to the *Elegia Septima* the following lines, in which he contrasts his present indifference to love with his late foolish susceptibility:[1]

> Haec ego mente olim laeva, studioque supino,
> Nequitiae posui vana trophaea meae.
> Scilicet abreptum sic me malus impulit error,
> Indocilisque aetas prava magistra fuit.
> Donec Socraticos umbrosa Academia rivos
> Praebuit, admissum dedocuitque iugum.
> Protinus extinctis ex illo tempore flammis,
> Cincta rigent multo pectora nostra gelu.
> Unde suis frigus metuit puer ipse Sagittis,
> Et Diomedeam vim timet ipsa Venus.[2]

About the time Milton wrote the *Elegia Septima* he makes the one reference to politics that belongs to his college days; which uniqueness may remind us how patchy is our knowledge of Milton during his early years. For it cannot be doubted that his political views had then been forming or were already formed. The reference is in a letter to Gill, dated 26 May, 1628, a little over a fortnight before Charles accepted the Petition of Rights presented to him by both Houses of Parliament. After praising Gill's Latin verses on a Dutch victory over the Spaniards, he conjectures what a poem will be forthcoming from Gill if domestic affairs take the right turn, in other words if Charles accepts the Petition. Milton's remark is the more interesting because it may indicate that he too had at that time the ambition of being the poetical celebrator of his country's deeds, an ambition he explicitly claims in the first days of the Revolution.[3]

1. It has been suggested that these lines refer to all the seven Latin elegies in the elegiac metre, which are printed consecutively in the 1645 edition, not to the *Elegia Septima* alone. This is doubtful; the lines certainly do not provide an apposite comment on (for instance) the ascetic resolutions of *Elegia Sexta*. I think Milton referred them to the one poem, about which he felt in a peculiar way. When exactly he wrote the lines, whether in 1645 or earlier, is a matter for guessing alone.

2. Such were the trophies that, in earlier days,
   By vanity seduced, I toiled to raise,
   Studious, yet indolent, and urged by youth,
   That worst of teachers! from the ways of truth;
   Till learning taught me, in his shady bower,
   To quit love's servile yoke, and spurn his power.
   Then on a sudden, the fierce flame supprest,
   A frost continual settled on my breast,
   Whence Cupid fears his flame extinct to see,
   And Venus dreads a Diomede in me.

3. See below, p. 101.

With this fleeting reference to politics may be connected Milton's
next Latin poem, *Naturam non pati Senium*, proclaiming the undecayed vigour of nature. It is interesting, not because Milton treats
the subject with any uncommon poetic power, but because it refers
to a controversy that was current at the time. Many men in the
seventeenth century were dominated by the idea (which received
its best-known expression in Donne's *Anniversaries* and Browne's *Urn
Burial*) that the world was in an advanced stage of physical decay. It
was probably most powerful in those writers and thinkers over
whom the Middle Ages retained the strongest hold. Contrariwise it
would be most repugnant to the type of reforming Protestant who
had (consciously or unconsciously) substituted a belief in progress
for the other-worldliness of the Middle Ages. Divergence of opinion
was turned into controversy by the appearance in the year before
Milton's poem of a book written by George Hakewill entitled *An
Apologie or Declaration of the Power and Providence of God in the Government of the World*.[1] Hakewill, who believed that the Reformation had
made the world a better place than it ever had been, maintains,
with the usual apparatus of seventeenth-century learning, that the
fabric of the universe has suffered no decay since creation; further,
that Scripture foretells signal improvements in the lot of man before
the final conflagration of the world: and he suggests that the con-
version of the Jews may even now be imminent. A few quotations
from the Epistle Dedicatory will make plain Hakewill's general
temper. The following shows how firmly he links his thesis with the
Reformation:

Together with the reviving of the *Arts* and Languages, which for sundry
ages lay buried in barbarisme, the rust of *superstition* was likewise in many
places scowred off from Religion, which by degrees had crept upon it, and
fretted deepe into the face of it, and the *Arts* being thus refined, and Religion
restored to its primitive brightnesse, manners were likewise reformed even
among them, a foule shame were it then for us who possesse a thorow
reformation in matter of *Doctrine*, to bee thought to grow worse in matter
of manners. *God* forbid it should be so, I hope it is not so, I am sure it
should not be so.

Inseparable from his belief that the fabric of the world is undecayed
and that civilisation has not declined is his faith that man's future
is in his own power, that he can progress if he wishes:

The first step to inable a man to the atchieving of great designs is to bee
perswaded that by endeavour hee is able to atchieve, the next not to be
perswaded that whatsoever hath not yet bin done, cannot be done. . . . If

1. See J. B. Bury, *The Idea of Progress*, 88–92.

we excell not all ages that have gone before us, it is only because we are wanting to our selves.

If we fail to equal our ancestors, it is because we are lazy, not because conditions are against us.

If then we come short of our *Ancestors* in *Knowledge*, let us not cast it upon the deficiencie of our wits in regard of the *World's decay*, but upon our own *sloth*; if we come short of them in *vertue*, let us not impute it to the *declination of the World*, but to the malice and faintness of our owne wills.

Milton's lines were supplied (so he writes to Gill) to one of the Fellows of Christ's, who was to take part in a public disputation on the subject of Hakewill's book. They are concerned with the natural world alone, not with the fate of mankind, but the fact that Milton wrote them at all suggests that he was on Hakewill's side in the whole matter. And the real point of interest is that Hakewill's ideas are nearly identical with those that dominate the whole of Milton's early prose. I do not wish to imply that Milton got his notions of human progress, of man's destiny being in his own power, from Hakewill; they could not have been confined to Hakewill, rather they were in the air at the time: but that Milton had embraced these notions as early as 1628, that he was already the young reformer, may reasonably be concluded; and that he connected progress with contemporary political events may not unreasonably be guessed. It looks as if in politics and religion Milton at college was not very different from the Milton of 1641 we know so much better.

If the summer of 1628 gives glimpses of Milton as the lover and less certainly as the radical, it reveals him plainly as a person of importance at Cambridge. The lines just discussed were written by Milton not for his own use but for that of one of the dons. He would hardly have been asked unless by now a person of some importance in college. He was chosen, too, to deliver a *Vacation Exercise* or speech designed to enliven a holiday celebration, attended by most of the University and held after the end of the Easter Term 1628. This *Vacation Exercise* consists of the *Sixth Prolusion* together with the lines of verse entitled *At a Vacation Exercise*. It is to be regretted that the two are usually read apart, or rather that the verses only are widely known: together they are the most interesting personal document of Milton's college years.

The whole composition is divided into three: an introduction on the theme that it is wise at times to interrupt serious studies with mirth, a comic address full of local allusions, and the verses *At a Vacation Exercise*. The first is chiefly interesting for a reference to a recent change in college opinion towards Milton and for the fine compliment he pays his former enemies. He writes:

> I was further strongly induced and persuaded to undertake this office by the new-found friendliness towards me of you who are fellow-students of my own college. For when, some months ago, I was to make an academic oration before you, I felt sure that any effort of mine would have but a cold reception from you, and would find in Aeacus and Minos a more lenient judge than in any one of you. But quite contrary to my expectation, contrary indeed to any spark of hope I may have entertained, I heard, or rather I myself felt, that my speech was received with quite unusual applause on every hand, even on the part of those who had previously shown me only hostility and dislike, because of disagreements concerning our studies. A generous way indeed of displaying rivalry, and one worthy of a royal nature! For while friendship itself is often wont to misinterpret what is really free from faults, on this occasion keen and biting enmity was kind enough to construe in a more gentle and lenient spirit than I deserved both my mistakes, which may have been many, and my rhetorical failures, which were doubtless not a few.[1]

The passage confirms one's natural surmise about Milton: that though aloof, sensitive, and proud, he was not in the least vindictive if he was let alone, and responded quickly to a little kindness. His fellow-undergraduates would come to realise this, and knowing his abilities would end by allowing him their admiration.

Much more interesting as a whole is the comic address. After admitting that he has no aptitude for mirth and wit he proceeds to do his duty, to try to make his audience laugh. His indomitable will carries him through, and somehow he forces out an extraordinary medley of bad puns, extravagant bawdry, and comic references to college rags. But he cannot lose himself in his task; and lest his hearers should taint his own private niceness with the dirt that issues from his lips he interposes the passage (famous out of its context) referring to his nickname of 'Lady'. With a vigour of contempt faintly prophetic of later pamphleteering invective he both maintains his own purity and defends himself against the evil implications the nickname might possess.

> Some of late called me 'the Lady'. But why do I seem to them too little of a man? Have they no regard for Priscian? Do these bungling grammarians attribute to the feminine gender what is proper to the masculine, like this? It is, I suppose, because I have never brought myself to toss off great bumpers like a prize-fighter, or because my hand has never grown horny with driving the plough, or because I was never a farm-hand at seven

1. P. B. Tillyard, op. cit., 86.

or laid myself down full length in the midday sun; or last perhaps because
I never showed my virility in the way these brothellers do. But I wish they
could leave playing the ass as readily as I the woman.[1]

None but a very sensitive man would have troubled to slip in this
apology at such a time. Nor, it can be added, would any but an
extremely simple-minded egotist have confided to a large assembly
of dons and undergraduates ('concurrente tota fere Academiae
juventute' is the heading of the *Prolusion*), with very few of whom he
would be familiar, his plans for writing poetry, which occupy the
central portion of his verses, *At a Vacation Exercise*.

This poem has a double interest: it contains the earliest passage
of Milton's verse in which the rhythm is sustained with the peculiar
Miltonic sublimity; and it shows Milton critically aware of contemporary English poetry. Marking his contrast with the word *yet*,
he turns from describing the task for which he must now use his
native language to describing that to which his genius prompts him.
And the verse that has kept the ground now takes wing.

> Yet I had rather if I were to chuse,
> Thy service in some graver subject use,
> Such as may make thee search thy coffers round,
> Before thou cloath my fancy in fit sound:
> Such where the deep transported mind may soare
> Above the wheeling poles, and at Heav'ns dore
> Look in, and see each blissful Deitie
> How he before the thunderous throne doth lie,
> Listening to what unshorn *Apollo* sings
> To th' touch of golden wires, while *Hebe* brings
> Immortal Nectar to her Kingly Sire:
> Then passing through the Spheres of watchful fire,
> And mistie Regions of wide air next under,
> And hills of Snow and lofts of piled Thunder,
> May tell at length how green-ey'd *Neptune* raves,
> In Heav'ns defiance mustering all his waves;
> Then sing of secret things that came to pass
> When Beldam Nature in her cradle was;
> And last of Kings and Queens and Hero's old,
> Such as the wise *Demodocus* once told
> In solemn songs at King *Alcinous* feast,
> While sad *Ulisses* soul and all the rest
> Are held with his melodious harmonie
> In willing chains and sweet captivitie.
> But fie my wandring Muse how thou dost stray![2]

1. ibid., 98–9.
2. 29–53.

If Milton had not already in his eighteenth year decided to become
a poet, this passage makes it tolerably plain that by now he had
decided; and in his native tongue. But if the poem shows Milton
decided to be a poet, it shows him undecided how to write. The
passage quoted may be individual, but in the rest he falls into whatever current style he thinks best suits his subject. In writing of the
rivers he imitates Spenser through Browne:

> Or sullen *Mole* that runneth underneath,
> Or *Severn* swift, guilty of Maidens death,
> Or Rockie *Avon*, or of Sedgie *Lee*,
> Or Coaly *Tine*, or antient hallowed *Dee*.[1]

But when discussing the way he means to write he falls into the
contemporary extravagance of sustained metaphor too loosely
named metaphysical. He speaks of his native language as

> Driving dum silence from the portal dore,
> Where he had mutely sate two years before.[2]

And later he says:

> I have some naked thoughts that rove about
> And loudly knock to have their passage out;
> And wearie of their place do only stay
> Till thou have deck't them in thy best aray.[3]

Those passages show Milton, as I said, critically aware of the different modes of contemporary verse: as too does another passage in
which he disclaims a certain literary mode. He begs his native
language to bring out the richest dresses from its store and

> Not those new fangled toys, and trimming slight
> Which takes our late fantasticks with delight.[4]

Who are 'our late fantasticks'? Euphuists and Metaphysicals have
been suggested. Euphuists are not in court because Milton speaks of
poets; and if Metaphysicals, why *late* fantasticks, when the metaphysical movement was in its first vigour? Had a group of 'fantasticks' clustered round George Herbert, till about a year before
Public Orator at Cambridge, and become the 'late fantasticks' now
he had gone? At any rate English models have begun to compete
with Ovid far more seriously than two years before.

Milton had, however, not yet finished Ovidizing, for his next
poem is in Latin elegiacs, the *Elegia Quinta, in Adventum Veris*,
written in April 1629, eight months before the *Nativity Ode*. He
wrote it soon after completing his exercises for the B.A. degree, a
time when he may have felt justified in taking a holiday. At any

1. 95–8.   2. 5–6.   3. 23–7.   4. 19–20.

rate, whether he was writing in a holiday mood or not, the tone of the poem is, for Milton, surprising. Masson in describing it as 'a laborious Latin anticipation of the sentiment of Tennyson's lines:

> In the spring a livelier iris changes on the burnish'd
> dove:
> In the spring a young man's fancy lightly turns to
> thoughts of love,'

gives a completely wrong implication. It is one of the least laborious, one of the least crammed with learning, of all the Latin pieces. But it is curiously turgid and swift, and pulsates like not a single other in the elegiac metre. Masson obviously thinks that Milton is simulating a conventional vernal frenzy, but to an unbiassed reader the poem is as full of sex as it pretends to be and faithfully expresses Milton's restlessness in spring time. The content is mainly a description of how the season spreads love over the universe: a description tedious because overlong, but never lacking in vitality on account of the throb of the verse.

> Nunc etiam Satyri cum sera crepuscula surgunt,
>   Pervolitant celeri florea rura choro,
> Sylvanusque sua Cyparissi fronde revinctus,
>   Semicaperque Deus, semideusque caper.
> Quaeque sub arboribus Dryades latuere vetustis
>   Per juga, per solos expatiantur agros.
> Per sata luxuriat fruticetaque Maenalius Pan,
>   Vix Cybele mater, vix sibi tuta Ceres,
> Atque aliquam cupidus praedatur Oreada Faunus,
>   Consulit in trepidos dum sibi Nympha pedes,
> Jamque latet, latitansque cupit male tecta videri,
>   Et fugit, et fugiens pervelit ipsa capi.[1]

There is nothing laboured in this: only it shows the strange phenomenon of Milton writing for once in the vein of Swinburne or of the *Pervigilium Veneris*.

1. 119–30:
> Now too the Satyrs, in the dusk of eve,
> Their mazy dance through flowery meadows weave,
> And neither god nor goat, but both in kind,
> Silvanus, wreathed in cypress, skips behind.
> The Dryads leave their hollow sylvan cells
> To roam the banks and solitary dells;
> Pan riots now, and from his amorous chafe
> Ceres and Cybele seem hardly safe;
> And Faunus, all on fire to reach the prize,
> In chase of some enticing Oread, flies;
> She bounds before, but fears too swift a bound,
> And hidden lies, but wishes to be found.

And Pan by moon and Bacchus by night,
  Fleeter of foot than the fleet-foot kid,
Follows with dancing and fills with delight
  The Maenad and the Bassarid;
And soft as lips that laugh and hide
The laughing leaves of the trees divide,
And screen from seeing and leave in sight
  The god pursuing, the maiden hid.

The items of information that have been collected in this and the
last chapter are too scrappy and scattered to create anything like a
coherent picture of Milton, but to those who see him as a soul that
dwelt apart and no more, they should give material for reflection
and perhaps surprise. They have shown him rebellious when unduly
restricted, ambitious of scope, probably a radical in politics (from
which religion cannot be disconnected), far too sensitive of others'
opinions to be said to dwell apart, with a normal susceptibility to
feminine charm, quickly responsive to a little kindness, and public-
spirited enough to oblige his fellows by doing a job for which he had
no natural aptitude; as a poet not at all aloof but a patient experi-
menter in the manner of the masters. In his next poem, the *Nativity
Ode*,[1] many of the above qualities joined to make a pattern.

1. I do not wish to state dogmatically that this was his next poem. For the
chronology of Milton's poems at this period see Appendix B, p. 316.

CHAPTER FOUR

The Nativity Ode

Date	Milton's age	Writing or event in Milton's life	Contemporary event
1629, Dec. 9	21	Comes of age	
1629, Dec. 25	21	*Nativity Ode*	
1629, Dec.	21	*Elegia Sexta* (to Diodati concerning *Nativity Ode*)	

In his *Apology for Smectymnuus* Milton recounts how he came to prefer above the 'smooth elegiac poets' (who had hitherto been the models for the bulk of his verse) 'the two famous renowners of Beatrice and Laura, who never write but honour of them to whom they devote their verse, displaying sublime and pure thoughts, without transgression'.[1] Milton may have begun reading the Italians some years before he slackened his Ovidizing, but, if the order of his poems is the one suggested, the *Nativity Ode* is the first written in an Italianate manner. There are resemblances to Petrarch, to Tasso's *Canzone sopra la Cappella del Presepio*;[2] and there is something distinctly baroque about the ornate figure of Peace in the third stanza of the hymn: meek-eyed, crowned with green olive, she divides the amorous clouds with turtle wing, and waves a myrtle wand. And over the whole there are shed warm colours, new in Milton's verse, that suggest Italy.

The merits of the *Ode* have been variously judged. The eighteenth century gave it little praise, and Warton's opinion that except for one or two stanzas 'the *Ode* chiefly consists of a string of affected conceits, which his early youth, and the fashion of the times, can only excuse', went little counter to contemporary taste. The nineteenth century grew enthusiastic but did not answer Warton's charges; it merely ignored them, treating the *Ode* as sacrosanct, something too inspired to be argued about. Hallam considered it as 'perhaps the most beautiful ode in the language'; and Keightley remarks loftily, 'We offer no particular criticism on it, for it is, in

1. Bohn, iii. 117.
2. See Grierson, *Metaphysical Lyrics and Poems of the Seventeenth Century*, xlviii.

effect, nearly all beauty.' But Warton was a close and sympathetic student of Milton, and we are not likely to understand the poem if we ignore his remarks. Was he right in characterizing it as full of conceits? and, if he was, in condemning it on their account?

No impartial judge can doubt that the *Ode*, or at least the hymn, is sown with the startling comparisons and 'pathetic fallacies' common in Giles Fletcher and other seventeenth-century poets. It is in this vein that the hymn begins.

> It was the Winter wilde,
> While the Heav'n-born-childe
>   All meanly wrapt in the rude manger lies;
> Nature in aw to him
> Had doff't her gawdy trim,
>   With her great Master so to sympathise:
> It was no season then for her
> To wanton with the Sun her lusty Paramour.
>
> Onely with speeches fair
> She woo's the gentle Air
>   To hide her guilty front with innocent Snow,
> And on her naked shame,
> Pollute with sinfull blame,
>   The Saintly Vail of Maiden white to throw,
> Confounded, that her Makers eyes
> Should look so neer upon her foul deformities.[1]

The ideas are far-fetched, and the earth is given the feelings of a person. Not all the verses of the hymn are conceited in just this degree. Some are quite simple: others, like the penultimate stanza with the grotesque comparison of the rising sun to a man waking up in a curtained bed,

> So when the Sun in bed,
> Curtain'd with cloudy red,
>   Pillows his chin upon an Orient wave,[2]

suggest the graver excesses of the seventeenth century; the 'congies lowe' of Giles Fletcher's lion for instance, or the tearful little pimples that mourned in Dryden's poem the death of their author Lord Hastings. But on the whole the opening stanzas of the hymn are typical of Milton's normal vein in the *Nativity Ode;* and the general tissue of conceit must either be justified or condemned. For it is not enough to invoke with Saintsbury 'the peculiar stateliness which redeems even conceit from frivolity or frigidity'. The conceit is

1. 29–44.   2. 229–31.

organic, not to be redeemed by the mere superaddition of stateliness: it must mean something, must correspond to some mental state in the author, not otherwise to be expressed, if it is to be anything but a blemish.

The truth is that the conceits cannot be spared from the *Ode*, for it is partly through them that is created the quality that gives it its unique charm: the clean exuberance of the best primitive art. A fifteenth-century Italian picture of the Nativity gives the simplest comparison. Here the absurdities – the rickety shelter, the far from new-born physique of the child, the cows peering with imbecile faces over a broken wall, and the rest – unite with the simple brilliant colouring to create a most captivating sense of youthfulness and simplicity. The essence of the poem is not stateliness excusing conceit, but homeliness, quaintness, tenderness, extravagance, and sublimity, harmonized by a pervading youthful candour and ordered by a commanding architectonic grasp. The homely picture of

> The Shepherds on the Lawn,
> Or ere the point of dawn,
>   Sate simply chatting in a rustick row,[1]

is somehow made to blend with such lines as

> The wakefull trump of doom must thunder through
>   the deep.[2]

The architectonic grasp, rather quaintly manifested, takes longer to illustrate. In the opening stanzas Milton pictures himself present at Bethlehem and hastening to offer his hymn, before the Wise Men, who have just appeared in sight, can arrive with *their* offering. It is a quaint idea, which most poets, had they thought of it, would have dropped when once stated. Not so Milton: his artist's conscience is too strong, and in the last stanza of the hymn he refers to the opening by stating (obliquely) that the Wise Men have arrived and that hence he must stop.

> Time is our tedious Song should here have ending,
> Heav'ns youngest teemed Star,
> Hath fixt her polisht Car,
>   Her sleeping Lord with Handmaid Lamp attending.

'Heav'ns youngest teemed Star' is the latest addition to the firmament, the guiding star of the Wise Men, which has now halted over the stable.

The combination of qualities found in the *Ode* implies a state of mind in the author both desirable and rare. Milton's mind as re-

1. 85–7.   2. 156.

vealed in his other poems was deep rather than varied, powerful rather than swift. But when he wrote the *Nativity Ode* he seemed to write with a pulse beating quicker, with a mind more alert, more varied, more susceptible to fancy as well as to imagination, less censorious, tenderer, less egotistical, than when he wrote any other poem before or since. There is much in the *Ode* that looks forward, the grandeur of language, the delight in names, the introduction of heathen gods, an apparent theological rigidity, the metrical virtuosity – all these and more have been remarked – but there is also much that Milton never repeated. We cannot help wondering what inspired him to write this poem, not his greatest but his poem least resembling his other compositions.

Help may be got from Milton's next poem, and his last essay in Ovidizing, the *Elegia Sexta*, written but a few days after the *Ode*, referring to it, and presumably in some way sharing its mood. Diodati, to whom it is written, had, Milton implies, sent him some verses, excusing their poor quality by the distraction of Christmastide, in the midst of which they were written. Milton begins by commending the verses, saying that they give a lively picture of the festivities; and goes on to praise the inspiration which wine works in the lyric poet. There follow learned references to Anacreon, Pindar, and Horace. Music, too, and dancing and the company of pretty girls are an added inspiration. All sorts of festal cheer inspire the Elegy.

> Namque Elegia levis multorum cura deorum est,
>   Et vocat ad numeros quemlibet illa suos;
> Liber adest elegis, Eratoque, Ceresque, Venusque,
>   Et cum purpurea matre tenellus Amor.[1]

Milton seems to be speaking both of Diodati's and of his own elegies. Then he suddenly changes his tone and says that for the writer of the Heroic Poem the conditions are different.

> At qui bella refert, et adulto sub Jove caelum
>   Heroasque pios, semideosque duces,
> Et nunc sancta canit superum consulta deorum,
>   Nunc latrata fero regna profunda cane,
> Ille quidem parce Samii pro more magistri
>   Vivat, et innocuos praebeat herba cibos.

.   .   .   .   .   .

1. 49–52:
> For numerous powers light Elegy befriend,
> Hear her sweet voice, and at her call attend;
> Her Bacchus, Ceres, Venus, all approve,
> And, with his blushing mother, gentle Love.

Additur huic scelerisque vacans, et casta juventus,
   Et rigidi mores, et sine labe manus.
Qualis veste nitens sacra et lustralibus undis
   Surgis ad infensos augur iture Deos.[1]

It was in such ascetic manner that the old Greek poets and prophets lived, Tiresias, Linus, Calchas, and Orpheus. Homer too fasted when he sent Odysseus on his voyages through the sea, to the palace of Circe

et vada foemineis insidiosa sonis.[2]

Then follows at once the news that he, Milton, has written a poem on the Nativity, implying that this poem is an essay in the heroic style.

It was the happy idea of Hanford[3] to connect a passage from the *Apology for Smectymnuus* with the qualifications of the writer of heroic poetry in the *Sixth Elegy*. After describing in that pamphlet his devotion to the Latin elegiac poets, then to Dante and Petrarch, Milton goes on:

And long it was not after, when I was confirmed in this opinion, that he who would not be frustrate of his hope to write well hereafter in laudable things, ought himself to be a true poem; that is, a composition and pattern of the best and honourablest things; not presuming to sing high praises of heroic men, or famous cities, unless he have in himself the experience and the practice of all that which is praiseworthy.[4]

Taken together, the passages from the *Sixth Elegy* and the *Apology for Smectymnuus* make it highly probable that about Christmas 1629 Milton made a mental dedication of himself to the high calling of epic poet. On 9 December of the same year he came of age. In view of the stock-taking fervour of the sonnet he wrote on reaching the

1. 55–60, 63–6:
      But they, who demi-gods and heroes praise,
      And feats performed in Jove's more youthful days,
      Who now the counsels of high heaven explore,
      Now shades that echo the Cerberean roar,
      Simply let these, like him of Samos, live;
      Let herbs to them a bloodless banquet give.

      .   .   .   .   .   .

      Their youth should pass in innocence, secure
      From stain licentious, and in manners pure,
      Pure as the priest, when robed in white he stands,
      The fresh lustration ready in his hands.
2. 74: and shoals insidious with the siren train.
3. op. cit., 123.   4. Bohn, iii. 117–18.

age of twenty-three what more probable than that he should have made some great decision on his twenty-first birthday?

This experience of Milton may help our quest. The serenity that comes from a deep committal, fervently and whole-heartedly made, has entered into the *Nativity Ode*: there is something neophytic about it. Milton is the 'young Probationer and Candidate of Heav'n', and the suggestion in 'candidate' of the white toga and of the aspirant for office should not be forgotten. But if self-dedication provided the mental excitement that unified Milton's experience into a poem, it was itself but a portion of the experience. An extremely important sentiment is hope, the hope of human progress. Milton indulges in the fancy of a Golden Age:

> For if such holy Song
> Enwrap our fancy long,
>   Time will run back, and fetch the age of gold,
> And speckl'd vanity
> Will sicken soon and die,
>   And leprous sin will melt from earthly mould,
> And Hell it self will pass away,
> And leave her dolorous mansions to the peering day.[1]

This is what he would have:

> But wisest Fate sayes no,
> This must not yet be so.[2]

Events must proceed as theology dictates. Only when the world has been destroyed can all good be consummated, but there is hope of something: with the coming of Christ our bliss has begun, and may spread almost indefinitely:

> And then at last our bliss
> Full and perfect is,
>   But now begins; for from this happy day
> Th' old Dragon under ground
> In straiter limits bound
>   Not half so far casts his usurped sway.[3]

As well as hope there has entered in, I feel obstinately convinced, something of sex. It does not disturb and irritate as it had done shortly before in *Elegia Quinta*, the poem on spring: on the contrary it animates, not usurping the mind but stimulating many other feelings into delightful activity. For this statement there is no authority in the *Ode;* it is merely an impression derived from the run

---

1. 133–40.   2. 149–50.   3. 165–70.

of the verse, the dance of that incomparable stanza; it cannot be argued about. All that can be pleaded is that Milton wrote *Elegia Quinta* not long before, his Petrarchian love sonnets probably but little after, and that for sex to be entirely absent from the poem into which a man of twenty-one emptied the contents of his mind would be extremely surprising.

If self-dedication helps to explain why the *Nativity Ode* is what it is, it may help also to explain why no later poem has just the *Ode*'s qualities. Up till now Milton's life at college seems to have been well diversified by various social events: he had been forced to mix with his kind and prevented from indulging himself in the studious retirement he was constantly seeking. And he may have benefited. With the self-dedication seems to have begun the process of austere sacrifice of anything that appeared to hinder the work for which he believed himself to have been chosen, the process which may have intensified some qualities in his mind but which could not but curtail the beautiful diversity of the *Nativity Ode*.

CHAPTER FIVE

Between the Nativity Ode and Comus

Date	Milton's age	Writing or event in Milton's life	Contemporary event
1630, Lent	21	*The Passion*	
1630?, May	21	*Song on May Morning*	
1630?	21	Sonnet, *O Nightingale*	
1630?	21	Italian Sonnets and Canzone	
1630	21	*On Shakespear*	
1631, Jan.	22	*Epitaphs on Hobson*	
1631, April	22	*Epitaph on the Marchioness of Winchester*	
1631–2	22–3	*Seventh Prolusion*	
1632, July	23	Takes M.A. Degree	
1632, Dec.	23	Sonnet, *How soon hath Time*	Death of Eliot in Tower
1633	23	Letter to unknown friend	
1632–4?	23–5	*Arcades*	1633. Laud becomes Primate
1632–4?	23–5	*On Time, Upon the Circumcision, At a Solemn Music*	
1632–4?	23–5	*L'Allegro and Il Penseroso*	

AFTER he became a B.A. Milton tells us little of his life at Cambridge. Custom would now permit him to be laxer in keeping his terms, and possibly he took advantage of it. Anyhow, in examining his life one is conscious of little change of conditions, from the last years at Cambridge to the first years at Horton.

The success of the *Nativity Ode* and the ambition shown in the *Sixth Elegy* seem to have prompted that incomplete attempt at high poetry *The Passion*, written almost certainly in the Lenten season of 1630. Like *In Quintum Novembris* it seems to be an over-ambitious attempt, inspired by a less ambitious success but ending in failure; for the Latin poem was brought to a hurried and patched-up close, the English poem never completed. In *The Passion* Milton attempts to recapture, and in accordance with the more tragic theme to deepen, the mood that prompted the *Nativity Ode*. The failure is complete. It is as full of conceits as the earlier poem: but these call a dreadful attention to themselves; puerility has supplanted youthfulness. Milton seems to have forsaken the Italians and in his poverty of invention to have resorted to the common stock of English seventeenth-century extravagance. Todd gives a page of parallels to the lines:

> The leaves should all be black whereon I write,
> And letters where my tears have washt a wannish white.

They are indeed derivative and valueless. Similarly

> Most perfect *Heroe*, try'd in heaviest plight
> Of labours huge and hard, too hard for human wight,

is Giles Fletcher, somewhat watered. How ill Milton succeeded in animating extravagance can be seen by comparing his seventh stanza with a passage of Crashaw[1] expressing a similar sentiment. Milton imagines himself standing to weep over the Holy Sepulchre and says:

> Yet on the softned Quarry would I score
> My plaining vers as lively as before;
>   For sure so well instructed are my tears,
> That they would fitly fall in order'd Characters.

And this is from Crashaw's *Upon the Death of a Gentleman*:

> Eyes are vocal, tears have tongues,
> And there be words not made with lungs;
> Sententious showers, O, let them fall,
> Their cadence is rhetorical.

Milton's drowsy Alexandrine sounds absurd compared with the tightness of

> Their cadence is rhetorical.

Crashaw's critical intelligence is all alert and we feel it: Milton's intelligence here seems confined to counting the feet and seeing that the grammar is right. Still there are a few fragments of worth to be

---

1. Noted by Warton.

gleaned from the wreckage of *The Passion*, a line like

> But headlong joy is ever on the wing;

and Keats in a greater ode was to give the 'viewless wing' of the last verse a vitality not originally its own.

After *The Passion* the poems cannot any longer be accurately dated, but it is probable that the next in order of time are the *Song on May Morning*, the sonnet *O Nightingale*, and the six Italian love poems (five sonnets and one canzone) that follow the English sonnet in the 1645 edition of the minor poems. All these may be tentatively assigned to the same year, when Milton was aged twenty-one.[1]

If, as is probable, the *Song on May Morning* was written for May Day 1630, it shows a significant change from the mood in which a few weeks earlier *The Passion* was composed. The note appended to *The Passion*, 'This subject the Author finding to be above the years he had, when he wrote it, and nothing satisfi'd with what was begun, left it unfinish't', shows that such a change was possible. Milton had realized that his age was not yet ripe for the highest themes, that he must resume his apprenticeship, and, presumably, that he might legitimately turn his thoughts to lighter things. And so he writes:

> Hail bounteous *May* that dost inspire
> Mirth and youth, and warm desire.

There is nothing in the *Sixth Elegy* to suggest that a return to a less serious vein was for him impossible, for he allows to the smaller forms of verse a certain function. Nor does his reference to *casta juventus* in the same poem imply that he had taken a vow to keep away from all female society or to refuse to be attracted by any woman; it implies that Milton believed premarital chastity to be part of the discipline the writer of epic should undergo. He had taken no vow to abstain from writing love poetry.

The sonnet, *O Nightingale*, must be considered along with the six Italian poems, a conjunction by which it gains greatly in significance. Allowing all we can for the conventional extravagance of the sonneteer, we must admit that these poems tell of an actual experience[2]

1. On the dating of these poems see Appendix B, p. 316–17.

2. See J. S. Smart, *The Sonnets of Milton*, 133–55. Smart's elucidation of these Italian poems is one of the most important recent pieces of Milton scholarship. He was, however, not the first to see that they did not belong, as had always been assumed, to Milton's Italian journey. See D. H. Stevens in *Modern Philology*, 1919, 25–33.

and that Milton, towards the end of his college career, and probably at the age of twenty-one, was paying some kind of court to a lady. We even know a little about her and about Milton's feelings towards her. He begins a sonnet to Diodati as follows:

> Diodati, e te 'l dirò con maraviglia,
>> Quel ritroso io ch' amor spreggiar solea
>> E de suoi lacci spesso mi ridea
>> Gia caddi, ov'huom dabben talhor s'impiglia.
> Nè treccie d'oro, nè guancia vermiglia
>> M'abbaglian sì, ma sotto nova idea
>> Pellegrina bellezza che 'l cuor bea;[1]

and in the rest describes her charms. The lady is dark and of foreign extraction, a linguist and a singer; and from the opening lines of the first Italian sonnet we know that her name was Emilia. But Milton does not pursue love single-hearted: it is delightful that love should have come his way, but more important seems the stimulus it gives him for conducting serious experiments in the manner of the Italian sonneteers. He laments, as if thinking of his failure in *The Passion*, that his slow heart and hard bosom are better soil for Love than for God; and the most heartfelt lines of all are those in which he describes to Emilia his own steadfast and sensitive nature. True, he proffers his heart, but with little sign of the sacrifice that would mark a mastering passion.

> Giovane piano, e semplicetto amante
>> Poi che fuggir me stesso in dubbio sono,
>> Madonna a voi del mio cuor l'humil dono
>> Farò divoto; io certo a prove tante
> L'hebbi fedele, intrepido, costante,
>> De pensieri leggiadro, accorto, e buono;
>> Quando rugge il gran mondo, e scocca il tuono,
>> S'arma di sè, e d'intero diamante,
> Tanto del forse, e d'invidia sicuro,
>> Di timori, e speranze al popol use
>> Quanto d'ingegno, e d'alto valor vago,

1. Charles – and I say it wondering – thou must know
   That I, who once assumed a scornful air,
   And scoffed at love, am fallen in his snare,
   (Full many an upright man has fallen so)
   Yet think me not thus dazzled by the flow
   Of golden locks, or damask cheek; more rare
   The heart-felt beauties of my foreign fair;

E di cetra sonora, e delle muse:
    Sol troverete in tal parte men duro
    Ove amor mise l'insanabil ago.[1]

The canzone shows that Milton's friends were surprised at his courtly attentions and even more that he should write in a new language. 'Why', they ask him, 'do you forsake your promised means of immortality and lay this new burden on your shoulders?' I fancy this indicates that Milton had by this time told his friends (perhaps after the *Nativity Ode* and before the unsuccessful *Passion*) what he had already hinted at in the *Lines written at a Vacation Exercise*, namely that he had resolved to write a great work in his native language.

The sonnet *O Nightingale* is the first and *Il Penseroso* the last of what I should call Milton's poems of early maturity. With the exception of the Italian experiments and the Hobson epitaphs the poems in the group are all marked by a new sureness of touch, a knowledge of what can be achieved, and a resolve not to go beyond the clearly achievable. A serenity pervades them that doubtless had its counterpart in Milton's life at the time. The *Nativity Ode* had brought confidence, *The Passion* soberness; and Milton, with a clear mind, could settle down to serene, unhurried preparation. His last years at college and his early years at Horton were probably very happy. Yet for all their new sureness these poems, except *L'Allegro* and *Il Penseroso*, are in the nature of experiments, their very diversity suggesting that Milton was anxious, whenever he interrupted his studious preparations by composing, to try some new mode.

1. Before giving Cowper's version it must be remarked that the words *on foreign ground* have no warrant in the original and were inserted on the false assumption that Milton was writing from Italy:

    Enamoured, artless, young, on foreign ground,
        Uncertain whither from myself to fly,
        To thee, dear Lady, with an humble sigh
    Let me devote my heart, which I have found
By certain proofs, not few, intrepid, sound,
        Good and addicted to conceptions high:
        When tempests shake the world, and fire the sky,
    It rests in adamant self-wrapt around,
As safe from envy, and from outrage rude,
        From hopes and fears that vulgar minds abuse,
        As fond of genius and fixt fortitude,
Of the resounding lyre, and every muse.
        Weak you will find it in one only part,
        Now pierced by Love's immedicable dart.

The sonnet *O Nightingale*, though so close probably in time to the *Nativity Ode*, marks a new stage in Milton's poetical growth.

> O Nightingale, that on yon bloomy Spray
>   Warbl'st at eeve, when all the Woods are still,
>   Thou with fresh hope the Lovers heart dost fill,
>   While the jolly hours lead on propitious *May*,
> Thy liquid notes that close the eye of Day,
>   First heard before the shallow Cuccoo's bill
>   Portend success in love; O if *Jove's* will
>   Have linkt that amorous power to thy soft lay,
> Now timely sing, ere the rude Bird of Hate
>   Foretell my hopeles doom in some Grove ny:
>   As thou from yeer to yeer hast sung too late
> For my relief; yet hadst no reason why,
>   Whether the Muse, or Love call thee his mate,
>   Both them I serve, and of their train am I.

The inspiration that created the *Ode* was not recoverable, was a sudden fire-up: but the sonnet springs from a mind that has won a certain degree of force as its permanent possession; Milton, had he wished, could have written other poems as good. There is in it the sense of deliberateness, of the exercise of the conscious will, united with the primary inspiration, that marks all Milton's mature poetry but which is not so conspicuous in the *Nativity Ode*. He has already imposed his peculiar Latinized arrangement of words on the English poetical sentence and with no hesitating hand:

> Thy liquid notes that close the eye of Day,
> First heard before the shallow Cuccoo's bill
> Portend success in love.

The poem is not, of course, one of Milton's greatest, but it is faultless in structure and has much verbal felicity. The climax, coming in line 9 with the words, 'Now timely sing', is led up to with cunningly delayed expectation; and the epithet 'shallow' applied to the cuckoo in line 6, criticizing at once the song and the manners of that irresponsible bird, is rich in meaning. The poem reflects a mind exquisitely alert, eager for experience, but gravely master of itself. And the eagerness and mastery do not conflict: they are balanced or even help each other. Some writers feel very differently about the sonnet. To Sir Walter Raleigh *O Nightingale* was Milton's 'earliest and poorest sonnet';[1] Mark Pattison held in singular

---

1. *Milton*, 30.

detestation 'its frigid and far-fetched ingenuities'.[1] But Raleigh by his error in calling it Milton's only love poem, and Pattison by complaining that it contains no real experience, show that they approached it in a prejudiced mood. Milton to them had no knowledge or experience of youthful love or courtship: hence any poem he wrote on this theme could never succeed. It is through neglect of the Latin and Italian poems that these wrong assumptions came to be made.

Milton's lines *On Shakespear* are his one successful venture in the more extravagant, and at that date (1630) more vital, type of seventeenth-century verse. Often referred to as illustrating Milton's early liberality of taste, they have not been sufficiently admired as a poem. Here is the earliest version, that of the original publication in the second folio of Shakespeare.[2]

ON SHAKESPEAR. 1630

What neede my *Shakespear* for his honour'd bones
The labour of an age in piled Stones,
Or that his hallow'd reliques should be hid
Under a Starr-ypointing *Pyramid*?
Dear son of memory, great heir of Fame,
What need'st thou such weak witnes of thy Name?
Thou in our wonder and astonishment
Hast built thy self a live-long Monument:
For whilst to th' shame of slow-endevouring art
Thy easie numbers flow, and that each heart
Hath from the leaves of thy unvalu'd Book
Those Delphick lines with deep impression tooke,
Then thou, our fancy of it self bereaving,
Dost make us Marble with too much conceaving;
And so Sepulcher'd in such pomp dost lie
That Kings for such a Tomb would wish to die.

1. Pattison (*Milton's Sonnets*, 84–5) makes a curious onslaught on the 'baldness of the opening', and lays down the rule that a sense of disappointment will always be felt when 'O' is merely the sign of the vocative, when it is prefixed to a substantive standing alone. Similarly with 'Ah'. He does not however say whether 'O God, our help in ages past' or 'Ah Sunflower, weary of time' are bad openings too.

2. For an exhaustive discussion of the different readings of the poem and of possible sources see Garrod in *Essays and Studies of the English Association*, xii. 1926. 72–3. Milton himself dated the lines 1630.

The chief variant here from the usual (1645) version is *part* for *heart* in line 10, a reading which makes the encomium more explicit though it gives a less quickly obvious sense. Shakespeare would appeal not to the hearts of all his readers but to the reader's every part or faculty: a tribute to the 'myriad-minded man' that anticipates Coleridge. Milton's praise is indeed extremely reverential, far more so than the politeness of a verse tribute absolutely demanded. To judge from his habit of generalizing from the personal it is quite reasonable to think that he was modestly comparing Shakespeare'-'easie numbers' and 'Delphick lines' with his own 'slow-endevouring' art, his own 'late spring' which showed 'no bud or blossom'. This is but a detail; what matters is that Milton for once should have grown interested in so extravagant an analogy as that of men's wonder with a monument; that he should have elevated, as he so painfully failed to do in *The Passion*, a conceit to sublimity. Moreover the conceit is complicated. Not merely does he say that our wonder, because it will not change, is a monument: he must explain with great exactness the nature of the process. Shakespeare's art prints itself on all our faculties, but it goes further, it robs our fancy of its active power, including that of effacing the impression. In this monument, frozen into marble yet covered with the impression of his verses, Shakespeare may meetly be interred. Displaying as it does an impassioned critical intelligence, this is the one poem of Milton that can be called metaphysical. Why this uniqueness? Perhaps because, having strong views concerning the proprieties of various literary *genres*, he admitted to the epitaph though not to other *genres* an intellectual subtlety. Perhaps in this his first published poem he wished to write strictly in the current manner, not yet feeling strong enough to stand in isolation. But I fancy he was interested in the effect the reading of Shakespeare had on his own creative powers, and in analysing that effect. As a model Shakespeare was discouraging; and Milton is interested in setting forth the reason.

There is a metaphysical tinge in the second set of verses on Hobson: for instance in

> Made of sphear-metal, never to decay
> Untill his revolution was at stay;[1]

while punning, of which the verses most consist, was not unexploited by the metaphysical school. But the poem has not the combination of elements that marks that school. Milton is entirely occupied with

1. 5–6.

being ingenious. Not that his puns are bad (as they are often said to be): indeed the line

> Yet (strange to think) his wain was his increase

is quite up to Hood's standard. But in the poem Milton shows what was to be his chief poetic weakness: an inability to do a large number of things at the same time.

Like the Shakespeare lines, the *Epitaph on the Marchioness of Winchester* bears the marks of its age. But it is quieter and less ambitious, recalling not Donne but the funerary art of Jonson or Browne or Herrick. Nothing could belong more centrally to the early seventeenth century than the lines

> And those Pearls of dew she wears
> Prove to be presaging tears
> Which the sad morn had let fall
> On her hast'ning funerall.[1]

The willing acquiescence in contemporary ways of writing argues that Milton was contented with his age in a way in which later he was never to be. There is of course no question of mere imitation; the poem is primarily Miltonic: and lines like those quoted are blended with something as purely individual as

> Far within the boosom bright
> Of blazing Majesty and Light.[2]

The *Seventh Prolusion*, on the thesis that Art makes men happier than Ignorance, written probably about the time of the poems just discussed, is easily the most important personal document of Milton's late years at college. Taken in comparison with the poems it is particularly instructive, because it puts them in their place as minor products of Milton's mind, small experiments executed when he relaxed from his main object, now clearly stated, of universal knowledge. But the whole *Prolusion* is so little known, epitomizes Milton's thoughts on life and defines his ambitions so clearly, that I had better give a brief summary of his argument.

Milton begins in the personal vein one has now grown familiar with when he addresses an academic audience. He is reluctant to interrupt the serene pursuit of learning with composing an oration. Has he not been taught that in poetry and rhetoric alike mediocrity is to be abhorred, while excellence can only be attained by a man 'omnium Artium omnisque Scientiae circulari quodam subsidio instructum et consummatum', or as one might now say, 'with a complete knowledge of every art and science as a background'?

1. 43-6.   2. 69-70.

And it is this background of knowledge for which he longs every day more ardently. The previous summer he had indulged this desire; and he calls to witness the woods and streams near which he lost himself in his learned meditations with the Muses. (Milton, it must be remembered, had never learnt the modern notion of isolating the different Muses; Poetry and Learning were of the same divine origin.)

In stating his plea for meditation Milton uses the lore of Plato. The great creator of the world planted a divine spark in the breast of mortal man, which having inhabited mortality for a time, seeks to return to its own heavenly abode. Our happiness concerns the visit of this divine spark and its future fate. To foster this spark we must gain a knowledge of Plato's 'ideas', and this we can only do through learned contemplation; for no other end have we been endowed with the thirst to know sublime things. There is nothing remarkable in this Platonizing, but it may be mentioned here that the whole body of *Prolusions* (especially the present one and the early *De Sphaerarum Concentu*) provide conclusive proof of Milton's early and deep devotion to Plato. As well as to the poetic appeal that Plato would naturally make, Milton must have been sympathetic to the Platonic notion that the science of mathematics was a prime aid to contemplating divine things. Here was something to set against the purely logical or metaphysical tendencies of the Aristotelians. For the single subject of mathematics, however, Milton wished to substitute the whole range of knowledge. Milton's Platonizing, in itself not remarkable, is interesting in bringing him into close relations with the Cambridge Platonists. To investigate these relations would be to go too far afield; but it can be said dogmatically that Milton's religious and ethical ideas, as gathered from the body of his prose works, are in their outlines close to those of the Cambridge Platonists. He even altered his views on Predestination at precisely the time when owing to the Platonists' influence the Arminian doctrine began to dominate Cambridge.[1] Henry More was Milton's younger contemporary at Christ's, and Milton may have been loosely associated with the Cambridge Platonists for many years of his life.[2]

1. See F. J. Powicke, *The Cambridge Platonists*, 54.

2. Milton's relations with his English contemporaries, Hobbes, the Cambridge Platonists, etc., have been very ably dealt with by Marjorie H. Nicolson in the following articles: 'The Spirit World of Milton and More,' *Studies in Philology*, 1925, 433–52; 'Milton and Hobbes,' ibid., 1926, 405–33; 'Milton and the Cabbala,' in *Philological Quarterly*, 1927, 1–18.

To return to the *Prolusion*, Milton proceeds in the conventional Protestant manner to put down the barbarism of the Middle Ages to monkish ignorance. Ignorance, he admits, does not necessarily create vice; but the intellect, the master of knowledge, gives light to the will, the parent of virtue, for the will can rarely do right unaided. Here Milton states the notion so strong in *Paradise Lost* that virtue consists in the will doing what is right in full knowledge of the issues, the belief in deliberate not instinctive valour. The next topic is the effect of learning on man as a social being, for Milton takes it as an axiom that the greatest earthly happiness is found in human society and the making of friends. He admits that many learned men can commune better with gods than with their kind and that they lack the quicker social graces: but the true philosopher fosters friendship with the most reverent care; witness Plato, whose works are the conversations of friends. Earthly happiness, as well as in friendship, consists in the free satisfaction of mental desires, and Art or Learning is their natural good. And learning for Milton is what he meant by it when earlier in his college career he attacked the University curriculum: it includes every kind of natural science. And when once the soul has completed its circle of knowledge, it will grow tired of its fleshly prison and reach out to things beyond the sensible world. The study of history too conduces enormously to earthly felicity: for to know history is to live in all ages, to be coeval with time; almost, by extending life indefinitely backwards, to achieve an immortality.

And then for a moment Milton reveals his own ambitions, not this time of reform but of fame, in words curiously suggestive of his later pathetic boastings in the *Defensio Secunda* of the glory brought to him by the *Pro Populo Anglicano Defensio*.

I pass over a pleasure with which none can compare – to be the oracle of many nations, to find one's home regarded as a kind of temple, to be a man whom kings and states invite to come to them, whom men from near and far flock to visit, while to others it is a matter for pride if they have but set eyes on him once. These are the rewards of study, these are the prizes which learning can, and often does, bestow upon her votaries in private life.[1]

In public life the rewards are more doubtful: learning does not usually procure office. But it procures the rule of oneself, far more glorious than that of the whole world. (So early has Milton found in his mind the doctrine of the 'Paradise within' that dominates the last books of *Paradise Lost* and *Paradise Regained*.)

1. P. B. Tillyard, op. cit., 112–13.

48

Moreover learning is easier to acquire than is often thought. If only our students could be spared scholastic metaphysics and other superfluities, they would learn so quickly that before their life was done they would sigh for more worlds of learning to conquer (the germ of the *Tractate on Education*). But there is the question of fame. Why seek fame on earth, when the world may be so near its final conflagration that this fame can last at best but a few years? And Milton replies exactly as he was to reply in *Lycidas*, that fame in heaven is the proper reward for good deeds on earth.

Then comes his peroration. The happiness of ignorance is at best animal, not proper to humanity. Let those who uphold ignorance drink of Circe's cup and walk prone on the ground: lower in the scale of being than beasts or plants or stones, who at least answered the music of Orpheus which ignorance would affect to despise.

There is probably not a thought in this *Prolusion* that is not a commonplace of the Renaissance, but that a man in the midst of the doubts that had by now beset the movement could utter these commonplaces with such a thrust of energy is a sort of miracle. Milton speaks like a cultured Tamburlaine. We have to wait till *Lycidas* for a comparable display of power.

Whenever it was that Milton wrote the *Seventh Prolusion*, he had made up his mind with all the fixity of which it was capable to spend his best energies in acquiring the background of universal knowledge he thought necessary. Yet it was not to be expected that even he could settle down to a prolonged extension of his education, giving up his intention of entering the Church and sacrificing any immediate fruits of his studies at Cambridge, without some qualms of conscience. These qualms are revealed in his sonnet *How soon hath Time*, written on his twenty-third birthday, that is in the winter before he took his M.A. degree. The sonnet is too well known to need comment, but there exists another document, written on the same subject, which is both less known and more explicit. In the Milton manuscript at Trinity College, Cambridge, there is a letter[1] he wrote to an unknown friend enclosing a copy of the sonnet, which he calls 'my nightward thoughts somewhile since'. The words 'somewhile since' are too vague to fix a date for the letter; but as Milton's correspondent seems to have accused him of 'having given up himself to dream away his years in the arms of studious retirement like Endymion with the moon', we can guess that it was

1. Given in full by Masson, i. 2nd ed., 323–5, in part by Hanford, *Handbook*, 3rd ed., 23–9 (not to speak of the facsimile of the MS. edited by Aldis Wright). Also in the Columbia edition, xii. 320–5 and Yale edition, I. 319–21 [P.B.T.].

written not before Milton retired to Horton, that is after taking his degree in July 1632. Although Milton's correspondent is unknown, the impression one gets is that he was an older man. The letter opens:

> SIR, – Besides that in sundry respects I must acknowledge me to profit by you whenever we meet, you are often to me and were yesterday especially as a good watchman to admonish that the hours of the night pass on (for so I call my life, as yet obscure and unserviceable to mankind) and that the day with me is at hand wherein Christ commands all to labour while there is yet light.

It is likely that this man was a friend of Milton's father put up by him to urge his son to adopt a profession. Whoever he was, he had suggested that Milton's backwardness was due to too much love of learning. Milton was acutely touched by the charges, and with a mixture of earnestness and scholastic pedantry argues that it is not an excessive love of learning for learning's sake, but the desire to do his very best even at the price of beginning late, that is holding him back. He argues that the 'mere love of learning . . . may proceed from a principle bad, good or natural', but that none of these three types is sufficient in itself to account for his withdrawing from action. The bad type would weigh nothing against the natural vanity and ambition of youth urging him to some sort of action; and this bad type he calls

> a poor regardless and unprofitable sin of curiosity . . . whereby a man cuts himself off from all action and becomes the most helpless, pusillanimous, and unweaponed creature in the world, the most unfit and unable to do that which all mortals must aspire to, either to defend and be useful to his friends or to offend his enemies.

Here for the first time Milton states the very essence of his personal creed, which animates above all other themes his *Paradise Lost,* namely his belief in the virtue of high action. Further he implies, if indeed he had already decided to be a poet, his belief that poetry was a mode of action. The spirit of the passage is that of the *Third Prolusion*; there is common to both a hatred of mere antiquarianism, of isolated dialectical subtleties, of the unrelated fact generally: but the direct mention of action is new and the more remarkable as being at the beginning of a prolonged period of studious retirement. It comes, too, as a sort of postscript to the *Seventh Prolusion*, where he may have felt that he had spoken in too unqualified praise of learning, not having had time to deal with the kind of learning he considered pernicious.

The 'natural' proneness to study he does not define – mere curiosity was apparently quite bad, not even neutral – but, whatever it is, it could not compete with

a much more potent inclination inbred, which about this time of a man's life solicits most: the desire of house and family of his own: to which nothing is esteemed more helpful than the early entering into creditable employment, and nothing more hindering than this affected solitariness.

It is interesting to see Milton aged twenty-three deciding against marriage. Further, one may from this letter gather the reason for this decision; which is nothing more than that he cannot allow any alien desire or occupation to interrupt his immediate business of self-preparation. If he is to make the best of his gifts, he must have leisure: marriage would mean that he must sacrifice his time to a profession, and that he cannot do. There is no hint whatever of the mystical idea of chastity found in *Comus*, and nothing to suggest that two years earlier, when enjoying the society of Emilia, he could not have had the intention of making her his wife.

Milton's intentions as explained in the *Seventh Prolusion* seem to have been put into execution when he left Cambridge and retired to Horton, in a very businesslike way. Hanford in his analysis of Milton's Commonplace Book[1] has concluded that when at last he was free from University obligations he settled down, among other things, to a comprehensive study of world-history from the original authorities, beginning from the beginning as he conceived it and proceeding in chronological sequence. This is a valuable discovery and may help us to replace the conventional picture of Milton placidly studious in his country retreat by something more credible. We should picture him rather in a concentrated and delighted fury of study, striving to gain a knowledge of all known human events in order that he may learn the causes of things also; but for all his eagerness too well-disciplined in mind to admit of hurry, and, from what little we know, too sensible of social obligations to cut himself off from a reasonable amount of human intercourse. But the concentrated study was the main thing, nor could any of the poems of the Horton period have been considered by Milton as more than interludes (though often experimental interludes) in the sequence of more serious occupations.

The dates of the other poems to which I shall refer and which precede *Comus*, namely *Arcades, On Time, Upon the Circumcision, At a*

1. *Chronology of Milton's Private Studies,* in *Publications of the Modern Language Association,* 1921, 288–9.

Solemn Music, L'Allegro, and *Il Penseroso,* are uncertain; some of them may have been written before Milton's twenty-third birthday: but they all belong to what I am calling Milton's early maturity. My feeling is that they are later than any of the poems previously discussed.

Arcades shows Milton the master of a new form, the song, and again illustrates an acquiescence in contemporary taste. The heading in the 1645 edition, 'Part of an entertainment', has spread the mistaken idea that the poem is a mere fragment, whereas it is complete in itself. It is very simply but very well constructed, and as a masque is quite effective. It is often read, I fancy, as an unrelated series, of a song, a speech in couplets, and two songs; but it helps much to bear in mind a picture of the setting and what slight plot can be gathered from the verses. The Countess of Derby, in whose honour the masque was written, was seated in state. At some distance a group of young persons of her family appear disguised as nymphs and shepherds. They sing a song in praise of the Countess, as if they had not seen her before, had come expressly now to visit her, and were amazed to find how far she exceeds her fame. As they approach nearer, the Genius of the place, that is of the Harefield estate, stops them. He knows their quest: they have come from Arcadia on a solemn search; and he will lead them up himself. But not before he has described his functions in tending the woods and plants, thereby complimenting the magnificence of Harefield. Then as a climax he describes the heavenly music of the spheres to which he listens at night when his duties are done, adding that if he could but utter such music himself he might praise his mistress fitly. He will try, and breaks into the song 'O're the smooth enameld green', as he leads the nymphs and shepherds forward to salute the object of their quest. They come forward, salute, and overcome by admiration sing the beautiful choric song 'Nymphs and Shepherds dance no more', whose fuller music contrasts exquisitely with the more fragile song of the Genius, exhorting the other nymphs and shepherds to forsake Arcadia for a better soil and Syrinx for a nobler mistress. The piece is pretty well perfect; the tact with which Milton subordinates his material, not merely to the poem as a whole but to the poem as a masque, is remarkable. The noble passage about the music of the spheres – the one place where Milton allows his imagination to rove from the courtly vein of compliment he had been commissioned to exploit – is not too long to tire the ordinary listener, must have added a pleasing touch of solemnity to the minds even of those who did not understand it, thereby forming an effective climax, and is perfectly linked to the main theme. The sense of powerful imagination joyfully controlled is here as in the *Nightingale* sonnet, and on a larger scale. Milton must have written *Arcades* in a mood of serene and hopeful endeavour, on the whole well contented with his lot and the England he intended some day to glorify with a great poem. It is not surprising that he was asked to write a second masque, nor, we may add, that after *Comus* he is not known to have been asked for a third.

The three kindred pieces, *On Time*, *Upon the Circumcision,* and *At a Solemn Music,* are a new departure. They are experiments on high themes and in novel metres, but like the rest of the poems of Milton's early maturity they are the work of a master. It would seem that Milton, the failure of *The Passion* being a thing of the past, felt himself once more able to deal with the matters which might one day be his chief poetic concern, but he carefully limits his ambitions and produces three quite short pieces. But, short though they are, they are important in Milton's poetic development, both in technique and in idea. Technically they mark a new departure in his metrical paragraphing: he is deliberately aiming at and achieving a new kind of sustained music. The first and third poems are concerned with ideas of good and evil that have a direct bearing on *Paradise Lost*.

Upon the Circumcision

Ye flaming Powers, and winged Warriours bright,
That erst with Musick, and triumphant song
First heard by happy watchful Shepherds ear,
So sweetly sung your Joy the Clouds along
Through the soft silence of the list'ning night;
Now mourn, and if sad share with us to bear
Your fiery essence can distill no tear,
Burn in your sighs, and borrow
Seas wept from our deep sorrow,
He who with all Heav'ns heraldry whileare
Enter'd the world, now bleeds to give us ease;
Alas, how soon our sin
  Sore doth begin
    His Infancy to sease!
O more exceeding love or law more just?
Just law indeed, but more exceeding love!
For we by rightfull doom remediles
Were lost in death, till he that dwelt above
High thron'd in secret bliss, for us frail dust
Emptied his glory, ev'n to nakednes;
And that great Cov'nant which we still transgress
Intirely satisfi'd,

53

And the full wrath beside
Of vengeful Justice bore for our excess,
And seals obedience first with wounding smart
This day, but O ere long
Huge pangs and strong
　　Will pierce more neer his heart.

Of the three poems this is the least good, but it reaches considerable grandeur and has hardly received due credit. It suffers from two plain defects. First, the angels, to whom the opening lines are addressed, are left, as it were, suspended in air unheeded; secondly, there is something very unsatisfactory in a poem consisting of two stanzas of equal length. A third stanza seems needed; or if there are to be two divisions only they should be of unequal length, as in the lines *At a Solemn Music*. Nor had Milton learnt to turn the scholastic question, how angels weep, into poetry. Donne might have made poetry of the idea; later Milton wisely avoids both competition with Donne and an answer to the question at issue by writing

　　　　　Tears such as angels weep.

But the second verse is full of power, and its opening lines have the accent of the more dialectical speeches of *Paradise Lost* as none of the other early poems have.

The other two pieces are more evenly good. Metrically they would seem to be the fruit of Milton's Italian studies and to be modelled on the canzone, but he may have got the idea of the long metrical paragraph from Spenser's *Epithalamium*. Even if he was indebted to Spenser for the idea, the slow concentrated stateliness of his verse is utterly different from the ample swell of his model's. The skill shown in the two pieces is consummate and suggests a greater mental power in the author than perhaps is found, except for a passage or two in *Comus*, till the writing of *Lycidas*.

ON TIME

Fly envious *Time*, till thou run out thy race,
Call on the lazy leaden-stepping hours,
Whose speed is but the heavy Plummets pace;
And glut thy self with what thy womb devours,
Which is no more then what is false and vain,
And meerly mortal dross;
So little is our loss,
So little is thy gain.
For when as each thing bad thou hast entomb'd,
And last of all, thy greedy self consum'd,
Then long Eternity shall greet our bliss
With an individual kiss;

54

And Joy shall overtake us as a flood,
When every thing that is sincerely good
And perfectly divine,
With Truth, and Peace, and Love shall ever shine
About the supreme Throne
Of him, t' whose happy-making sight alone,
When once our heav'nly-guided soul shall clime,
Then all this Earthy grosnes quit,
Attir'd with Stars, we shall for ever sit,
    Triumphing over Death, and Chance, and thee O Time.

These lines are divided into two paragraphs: lines 1–8 and 9–22. The first deals with Time, the second with Eternity. The rhythm of the first is slow, and dwindles grudgingly till the short last lines. The second paragraph, in superbly simple contrast, swells, after cunning little temporary ebbings, to the magnificent final Alexandrine.

The rhythm is sustained longest of all in *At a Solemn Music.*

Blest pair of *Sirens*, pledges of Heav'ns joy,
Sphear-born harmonious Sisters, Voice, and Vers,
Wed your divine sounds, and mixt power employ
Dead things with inbreath'd sense able to picrce,
And to our high-rais'd phantasie present,
That undisturbed Song of pure concent,
Ay sung before the saphire-colour'd throne
To him that sits theron
With Saintly shout, and solemn Jubily,
Where the bright Seraphim in burning row
Their loud up-lifted Angel trumpets blow,
And the Cherubick host in thousand quires
Touch their immortal Harps of golden wires,
With those just Spirits that wear victorious Palms,
Hymns devout and holy Psalms
Singing everlastingly;
That we on Earth with undiscording voice
May rightly answer that melodious noise;
As once we did, till disproportion'd sin
Jarr'd against natures chime, and with harsh din
Broke the fair musick that all creatures made
To their great Lord, whose love their motion sway'd
In perfect Diapason, whilst they stood
In first obedience, and their state of good.
O may we soon again renew that Song,
And keep in tune with Heav'n, till God ere long
To his celestial consort us unite,
To live with him, and sing in endles morn of light.

The poem consists of only two sentences, the first containing the first twenty-four lines, the second the last four. But the first sentence is divided into two by a change (though not an interruption) of rhythm corresponding to a change of sense. This change is almost the reverse of the change noted in *On Time*, for the first sixteen lines, beginning slowly, work up to the ecstatic description of the 'Cherubick host' and their heavenly music and end with the trochaic beat of

> Hymns devout and holy Psalms
> Singing everlastingly;

In contrast, but still within the same sentence and verse-paragraph, follows in sober couplets a description of the earthly answer to this heavenly music, spoiled by the entry of sin into the world. The last four lines, couplets also, are a prayer that heavenly and earthly music may once again be in harmony. The skill with which Milton sustains the verse of the first sixteen lines is remarkable and deliberate. The gradual quickening of rhythm to the final trochaics is managed with extreme skill: compare, for example, the slowness of line 4:

> Dead things with inbreath'd sense able to pierce,

with the impetus in line 10

> Where the bright Seraphim in burning row

Wherever there is any danger of the voice resting as if at the end of a verse-paragraph, Milton obviates it by some skilful means. For instance it would be possible, as far as the rhythm goes, to make a longish pause at the end of lines 6 and 9. But the word *that* in line 6

> That undisturbed Song of pure concent

suggests that the song is to be further described; while the last word of line 9, *Jubily*, being a new rhyme-sound, impels us to go on to find its rhyme-fellow, which is carefully kept back till *everlastingly* in line 16.[1]

L'Allegro and *Il Penseroso* are the most finished products of what I have called Milton's early poetic maturity. They have been praised lavishly and justly; and they have probably pleased more readers than anything else Milton wrote. But this popularity is not without danger to a properly proportioned appreciation of Milton, for they might easily be taken, with a view either to praise or censure, as typical of him. But if typical, they are typical of only a part, and not

1. The meaning of this poem with its Platonic and Apocalyptic references is discussed in the course of Appendix C, pp. 320–1.

a large part, of his mind. They are poems of escape, of fancy; and to take them too seriously is most unjust. They are a delightful recreational interlude in the comprehensive studies undertaken at Horton. And it is these studies, with the ambitions that prompted them, that held the chief place in Milton's thoughts.[1]

1. Since I wrote this paragraph I have found reasons for assigning *L'Allegro* and *Il Penseroso* to Milton's college days. These reasons and a detailed criticism of the poems are given in Pamphlet no. 82 of the English Association, reprinted in my *Miltonic Setting*, 1–28.

CHAPTER SIX
Comus

READERS of *Comus* have usually failed to see that it is an experiment, not entirely unsuccessful, in drama.[1] Johnson wrote as follows:

> As a drama it is deficient. The action is not probable. A Masque, in those parts where supernatural intervention is admitted, must indeed be given up to all the freaks of imagination; but, so far as the action is merely human, it ought to be reasonable, which can hardly be said of the conduct of the two Brothers; who, when their Sister sinks with fatigue in a pathless wilderness, wander both away together in search of berries too far to find their way back, and leave a helpless Lady to all the sadness and danger of solitude. ... The discourse of the Spirit is too long; an objection that may be made to almost all the following speeches; they have not the sprightliness of a dialogue animated by reciprocal contention, but seem rather declamations deliberately composed, and formally repeated, on a moral question.

The usual answer to this charge is that Johnson was looking for what is not there, that Milton does not intend to be dramatic. 'We must not read *Comus* with an eye to the stage', wrote Warton, 'or with the expectation of dramatic propriety. ... *Comus* is a suite of speeches, not interesting by discrimination of character; not conveying a variety of incidents, nor gradually exciting curiosity: but perpetually attracting attention by sublime sentiment, by fanciful imagery of the richest vein, by an exuberance of picturesque description, poetical allusion, and ornamental expression.' And the general opinion would be that such blemishes as the improbability of the plot and the singular dramatic ineptitude of the Elder Brother's discourse on chastity can easily be forgiven for the sheer splendour of the poetry.

All such criticism rests on a fallacy, because not a little of *Comus* is deliberately and successfully dramatic. Johnson and Warton overlook the really dramatic portions altogether; and those elements that are usually regarded as blemishes would not be blemishes at all, had not Milton, by writing dramatically in parts, forced us to exact in the other parts a kind of probability new in his writing. The fact is that Milton is not always certain whether or not he is in Arcadia. The Elder Brother's speech on chastity, beautiful in itself, would be

---

1. On the dramatic element in *Comus* see the essay on the action of *Comus* in my *Studies in Milton*, 82–99.

perfectly in place in the unalloyed Miltonic Arcadia; but a few
lines later Milton begins writing in the vein of the Elizabethan
dramatists and arouses a new set of expectations.

> *Eld. Bro.* List, list I hear
> Som far off hallow break the silent Air.
> *2 Bro.* Me thought so too; what should it be?
> *Eld. Bro.* For certain
> Either som one like us night-founder'd here,
> Or els som neighbour Wood-man, or at worst,
> Som roaving Robber calling to his fellows.
> *2 Bro.* Heav'n keep my sister, agen agen and neer,
> Best draw, and stand upon our guard.
> *Eld. Bro.* Ile hallow,
> If he be friendly he comes well, if not,
> Defence is a good cause, and Heav'n be for us.
>
> *The attendant Spirit habited like a Shepherd*
>
> That hallow I should know, what are you? speak;
> Com not too neer, you fall on iron stakes else.
> *Spir.* What voice is that, my young Lord? speak agen.
> *2 Bro.* O brother, 'tis my father Shepherd sure.

Whereupon, with a sudden relapse into Arcadianism, the Elder
Brother says

> *Thyrsis?* Whose artful strains have oft delaid
> The huddling brook to hear his madrigal,
> And sweeten'd every muskrose of the dale.[1]

Indeed, the mixture of styles[2] in *Comus* has never been sufficiently
recognized. But until it is, one cannot put *Comus* in its right place
among the early poems of Milton. Let us examine the fluctuations
of style at the beginning.

The opening speech of the Attendant Spirit is a Euripidean
prologue in which drama is not looked for, and the opening,

---

1. 480–96.

2. It will be noticed in what follows that I say nothing of Spenser. This does not
mean that I disagree with Hanford, who (*Youth of Milton*, 136–43) argues that
during the first years at Horton, and in *Comus* especially, there are signs that Milton
had been reading Spenser. In *Comus* the influence is confined to the subject-
matter: it does not affect the style much. And as the subject had not Milton's
whole-hearted interest, the influence though wide is not of the first importance in
helping us to judge the poem.

rhymed, section of Comus's first speech leaves the sequel in doubt;
but as soon as he begins speaking blank verse with

> Break off, break off, I feel the different pace
> Of som chast footing neer about this ground,[1]

we see that Milton has definitely ventured beyond the undramatic
couplet-writing he had used for *Arcades*. The rest of the speech is
vigorous and, though not particularly reminiscent in style of any
of the Elizabethan dramatists, yet dramatic enough to interest one
in the action as well as in the poetry. And the Lady in the opening
lines of her speech,

> This way the noise was, if mine ear be true,
> My best guide now,[2]

fulfils the interest Comus's words have raised. But not for long. In
spite of her plight, she exchanges the language of feeling for the
exquisite circumlocutions of the pastoral. She cannot say plainly
that her brothers left her when it was growing dark, but

> They left me then, when the gray-hooded Eev'n
> Like a sad Votarist in Palmers weed
> Rose from the hindmost wheels of *Phoebus* wain;[3]

and from this she falls into a delightful conceit (betokening an
ordered and leisurely exercise of the wits):

> els O theevish Night
> Why shouldst thou, but for som fellonious end,
> In thy dark lantern thus close up the Stars,
> That nature hung in Heav'n, and fill'd their Lamps
> With everlasting oil;[4]

from which she rises into lines which in their self-contained beauty
can be detached with no loss of value from their histrionic setting:

> What might this be? A thousand fantasies
> Begin to throng into my memory
> Of calling shapes, and beckning shadows dire,
> And airy tongues, that syllable mens names
> On Sands, and Shoars, and desert Wildernesses.[5]

When the Lady speaks such poetry, we heed only the poetry and
forget her desperate plight. Then follows a strain of rapturous

1. 145. 2. 170. 3. 188–90. 4. 195–9. 5. 205–9.

meditation, and only the last few lines of the speech have a cadence faintly dramatic:

> I cannot hallow to my Brothers, but
> Such noise as I can make to be heard farthest
> Ile venter, for my new enliv'nd spirits
> Prompt me; and they perhaps are not far off.[1]

Then follows the Echo Song, and with Comus's enthusiastic appreciation of it the dramatic interest rises again, for by now he is much more anxious than before to capture the Lady. In passing it may be noted that Comus is easily the livest character in the masque. There is a fullness and an opulence in his speeches not found in any of the others. Warburton and Newton object to Comus's hyperbolic description of what would happen to the world if strict temperance reigned:

> Th' earth cumber'd, and the wing'd air dark't with plumes,
> The herds would over-multitude their Lords,
> The Sea o'refraught would swell, and th' unsought diamonds
> Would so emblaze the forhead of the Deep,
> And so bestudd with Stars, that they below
> Would grow inur'd to light, and com at last
> To gaze upon the Sun with shameless brows.[2]

Here the case is very different from what it was in the Lady's first speech: we need the dramatic context to justify the sentiments. Comus has worked himself up (he has been drinking too) and the hyperboles match the excited flashing of his eyes. To return from the digression, after describing with rapture the beauty of the Lady's song Comus hails her as if she were the Miranda of the desert; the Lady replies, and the two fall into a most curious stichomythia, that sounds like a very indifferent translation from Greek tragedy, ending

> *Co.* Imports their loss, beside the present need?
> *La.* No less then if I should my brothers loose.
> *Co.* Were they of manly prime, or youthful bloom?
> *La.* As smooth as *Hebe's* their unrazor'd lips.[3]

In strange contrast to this classicizing interlude there follows Comus's description of when he saw the two brothers, a description whose Elizabethan character Raleigh has already noted. And after a few lines the Lady, wondering whether the spot can now be found, slips back for a moment into the manner of the stichomythia:

1. 226–9. 2. 730–6. 3. 287–90.

To find out that, good Shepherd, I suppose,
In such a scant allowance of Star-light,
Would overtask the best Land-Pilots art
Without the sure guess of well-practiz'd feet.[1]

Comus replies in the vein of *A Midsummer Night's Dream*:

I know each lane, and every alley green

In the next speech the Lady thinks good to be more dramatic and ends in the style of the post-Elizabethan drama:

In a place
Less warranted then this, or less secure
I cannot be, that I should fear to change it.
Eie me blest Providence, and square my triall
To my proportion'd strength. Shepherd lead on.[2]

An examination of the rest of the play before the lyrical close reveals much the same mixture of styles.

It is all the more noteworthy that Milton should have tried to be really dramatic in parts, because there was no apparent need for the attempt. He had written a very good masque in *Arcades* and he did not need to alter his style to write another. In fact, had he stuck to the earlier style, the masque, as a masque, would have been very much better. The inference is that Milton, in writing *Comus* as he did, had motives other than those of supplying a suitable entertainment for the Bridgewater family; and it would seem that he used *Comus* as a private experiment in dramatic style, in preparation for the great tragedy or Morality he at that time intended should be the end or one of the ends of his years of preparation.[3] Although in *The Reason of Church Government* he states that it was in Italy he decided to use his life for writing a great poem, there can be no doubt that such had been his *hope* from much earlier years.[4] In his poem to Manso, written in 1639, he is meditating an epic; in his schemes preserved in the Trinity College Manuscript and dating in the next year he is planning a tragedy. In his earlier years, too, he

1. 307–10.   2. 326–30.

3. A. H. Gilbert, 'The Cambridge MS. and Milton's Plans for an Epic,' in *Studies in Philology*, 1919, 172–6, gives reasons for thinking that Milton meant his plans for epic and tragedy to be concurrent, not alternative. *Samson* would be not an after-thought but the fulfilment of what he had meant to do all along in addition to his epic.

4. The passages quoted from *At a Vacation Exercise* and *Elegia Sexta* are sufficient warrant. See pp. 27 and 34 above.

probably had not made up his mind between the claims of these two great forms, if indeed he did not intend to use both; and it was inevitable that at some time he should have considered writing in the dramatic form that was the inheritance of the Elizabethan age. In *Comus* his dramatic aspirations are reflected.

That Milton was peculiarly conscious of the imperfections of *Comus* is made likely by the motto he prefixed to the first edition, published in 1637, and perhaps by the first lines of *Lycidas*. The motto, which runs

> Eheu, quid volui misero mihi! floribus austrum
> Perditus,

is part of a sentence from Virgil's second Eclogue completed by the words

> et liquidis immisi fontibus apros.

'Alas, what was I thinking of; unhappy man, I have let the wind blow on my flowers.' Milton would hardly have expressed his fear of public opinion had he felt satisfied with what he had written. If the opening lines of *Lycidas* refer to *Comus*, as in all probability they do, there is additional proof that Milton was not satisfied with his dramatic experiment.

One of the passages, found in the Egerton and Trinity Manuscripts but omitted in the printed editions, shows how tentatively Milton could write in *Comus*. The Elder Brother's speech beginning at line 407 runs

> I do not, brother,
> Inferr, as if I thought my sisters state
> Secure without all doubt,

and in the manuscripts it continues thus,

> or question, no;
> I could be willing though now i' th' darke to trie
> A tough encounter with the shaggiest villain
> That lurks by hedge or lane of this dead circuit
> To have her by my side, though I were sure
> She might be free from perill where she is.

Moreover for 'I could be willing' Milton first wrote 'Beshrew me but I would', and for 'encounter' 'passado'. Clearly he felt he had pushed his experiment too far towards realism and the language of men, and backed out before publication.

To bring a fresh unprejudiced judgment to bear on a poem so familiar as *Comus* is exceedingly difficult. During the years one has known it all sorts of extraneous and personal prejudices, whose origin is altogether forgotten, must have crept in. But the attempt is worth making. The final impression I get from *Comus* viewed as a whole is that when Milton wrote it he was not inspired by any compelling mood to give it unity. But this impression is not shared by all readers. Saurat writes: 'The theme of *Comus* is no artificial choice; it corresponds to one of the deepest needs in the poet: the need to triumph over sensuality, which in itself implies sensuality.'[1] Hanford seems to agree when he writes: 'The intensity with which Milton seized upon this virtue [chastity] as the center and test of his ethical idealism is explained by the strength of his own romantic passion, a passion which is still the chief force of his imaginative life.'[2] Both statements seem to me greatly exaggerated. Of course Milton was concerned personally in the doctrine of chastity, but I cannot see that it had this great, almost exclusive, hold on his imagination. There were several other topics that held his mind at this time: such as ambition, the craving for knowledge, the desire for personal perfection (which would include other things than chastity), and absorption in poetic experiment. Milton may have been sufficiently interested in the question of chastity to choose it (in accordance with the example of Spenser and Fletcher) as the subject of his poem; but he did not feel strongly enough about it, he was not enough in earnest, to make it the instrument of a true poetic unity, the instrument for evoking and fusing a considerable portion of what most occupied his mind. *Comus* remains a by-product of his total activity. And as an artistic unity it cannot compare with the *Nativity Ode, L'Allegro* and *Il Penseroso,* and *Lycidas.*

This does not mean that the parts are not superlatively good. There is in *Comus* finer poetry than anything Milton wrote earlier. Sir Henry Wotton was perfectly justified in writing, 'Wherein I should much commend the Tragical part, if the Lyrical did not ravish me with a certain Dorique delicacy in your Songs and Odes, whereunto I must plainly confess to have seen yet nothing parallel in our Language.' We do not know what Sir Henry Wotton really thought of the tragic part – the compliment he pays it is doubtful enough – but he certainly chooses to praise the parts of the poem rather than the whole.

1. op. cit., 16.

2. *Youth of Milton,* 143.

By reason of the experiments it contains *Comus* corresponds to *In Quintum Novembris* and the fragment of *The Passion*, but by the nature of those experiments it is far more interesting and important. Though the more dramatic passages may be stitched onto the smooth Arcadian texture of the rest, they go, some of them, to prove that Milton, had he persisted, could have compassed a style lively enough for a certain kind of tragedy. The meeting of the two Brothers and the Attendant Spirit, already quoted, is tense and exciting. Of a striking and dramatic opening to a speech Milton is already master: indeed several of the least dramatic speeches give good examples; like the Lady's first speech, the Elder Brother's which opens so splendidly with

> Unmuffle ye faint stars,

and Comus's

> Why are you vext Lady? why do you frown?

And once or twice a character will detach itself from its author and create for a moment the genuine dramatic illusion. When the Lady, imprisoned in Comus's magic chair, begins her final speech with

> I had not thought to have unlockt my lips
> In this unhallow'd air,

the reader is transported in imagination to the enchanter's bower and watches the drama rather than listens to the melody of the speech. Such examples suffice to prove my contention. Milton was not a man to let slip what he had acquired. In *Comus* he had mastered the elements of drama, and had he thought good he might later have combined them to make a great tragedy. But he put off his attempt till too late in life. By the time he wrote *Samson Agonistes* his style had hardened: it could never be suppled to the degree of flexibility necessary for the writing of authentic drama.

More remains to be said of the manner in which Milton was concerned with the doctrine of chastity as set forth in *Comus*.[1] Did he choose the subject because it happened to be sanctioned by Spenser and John Fletcher, or because self-expression was a relief or a necessity? Although the subject was far from occupying the whole of his attention, I think it had some relation to his recent experience.

---

1. This paragraph is a dogmatic statement of what depends on a number of pieces of evidence. Full discussion would overweight the text, and has been placed in Appendix C, pp. 318–21.

In his letter to an unknown friend[1] he had admitted his inclination to marriage but had chosen celibacy for the time being, in order to devote his whole attention to self-discipline. But in his studious retirement this curbing of inclination would tend to irk him more than in the fuller social life of Cambridge. His thoughts would run on questions of chastity and marriage. Having in the first instance chosen celibacy purely as a matter of expediency, he is gradually impelled by the force of his feelings to seek a stronger justification for his abstention. By a process of compensating fiction he would invest chastity with some unusual power, turning a negation into an active principle. There are signs of this mystical notion of chastity in *Comus*. Chastity is a 'sublime notion and high mystery', it is a hidden strength and a protection against all perils.

> So dear to Heav'n is Saintly chastity
> That when a soul is found sincerely so,
> A thousand liveried Angels lacky her,
> Driving far off each thing of sin and guilt,
> And in cleer dream, and solemn vision,
> Tell her of things that no gross ear can hear.[2]

In Milton, who believed in, or came later to believe in, the natural goodness of the flesh, the notion was unhealthy. It lasted perhaps in his mind till his journey to Italy; anyhow all traces of it have vanished in *Paradise Lost*,[3] where not merely is human love exalted, but the angels enjoy some higher physical mingling. Milton was no mystic, and his dallying in *Comus* with a magical view of chastity was no more than an interlude.

1. See pp. 49–51, 319.   2. 453–8.   3. viii. 622–9.

CHAPTER SEVEN

Later Horton Period and Lycidas

Date	Milton's age	Writing or event in Milton's life	Contemporary event
1634	25	*Comus*	
1634, Dec. 4	25	Letter to Gill	
1636, Aug.			Festivities of Charles I and Laud at Oxford
1637?	28	*Ad Patrem*	Prynne in the pillory.
1637, Sept. 7	28	Letter to Diodati from London	Hampden refuses to pay Ship Money. Attempt to
1637, Sept. 23	28	Letter to Diodati from London	force Laudian Prayer Book on Scotland
1637, Nov.	28	*Lycidas*	

IN THE years between *Comus* and *Lycidas* Milton continued his plan of comprehensive study. About this time, according to Hanford,[1] he began dealing with more modern history, from the later Roman Empire. There are signs too that he was making up his mind on various political and religious questions, settling in fact many of the principles which subsequently were stated in his prose pamphlets. To have the leisure to master a great mass of what he thought the most important learning must have brought satisfaction and serenity; a serenity that may help to account for the happiness already noted in the poems belonging to the early Horton period. But (quite apart from the causes of unrest mentioned in the last chapter) the strain was severe (he mentioned later 'the wearisome labours and studious watchings, wherein I have spent and tired out almost a whole youth'[2]); nor could the occasional journeys to London which are recorded have completely mitigated the monotony of his studies. Milton must in the later Horton period have experienced the satisfaction of feeling that his powers were growing, that he had it in him to write greatly, and anxiety because he still had to wait before he could put these growing powers to the test. What survives of Milton's writings in these years shows this double tendency of mind: the Latin poem *Ad Patrem* expressing confidence

---

1. See *Youth of Milton*, 155–6, and for the whole analysis of Milton's Commonplace Book (Hanford's authority), *Chronology of Milton's Private Studies*, in *Publications of the Modern Language Association*, 1921, 288 ff. (See also the Yale edition, I. 344–513 [R.F.].)

2. In the *Apology for Smectymnuus*, Bohn, iii. 96.

in his mastery over verse and in his future fame; the long letter to
Diodati dated 23 September, 1637, ambition and restlessness.

The poem *Ad Patrem*, which I should date not earlier than 1636,
not later than the date of Milton's departure for Italy, and probably
some time in 1637,[1] goes with the two other poems in hexameters,
Mansus and *Epitaphium Damonis*. The three poems show a mastery
and an individuality of phrase that put them in quite a different
class from the earlier Latin poems, whose interest was more biographical than literary. They can rank on their purely poetical
merit with the body of Milton's English lyrics. Though inferior to
Lycidas they are the Latin counterpart of that poem, for common to
all four is the sense that Milton has passed a turning-point in his progress to greatness, a sense which is not present in *Comus*. It is not at all
easy for a modern to read aright original Latin verse which is neither
classical nor frankly medieval. Most people who have enough Latin
to read Milton's Latin poems with ease find it difficult to keep out of
their judgment the question of correctness. Milton imitates Ovid and
Virgil freely, reminding us of the 'fair copy'; and it is difficult to prevent the question, *Yes, but is this Latin?* from intruding, when we
should be asking *Is this Milton?* In *Ad Patrem*, certainly the least good
of the three and uneven in quality, there are paragraphs whose
noble sound and phrases whose felicity make the question of correct
Latinity frivolous. Here is the passage in which, after defending the
sanctity of song on earth, he speaks of music in the heavens:

> Nos etiam patrium tunc cum repetemus Olympum,
> Aeternaeque morae stabunt immobilis aevi,
> Ibimus auratis per caeli templa coronis,
> Dulcia suaviloquo sociantes carmina plectro,
> Astra quibus, geminique poli convexa sonabunt.
> Spiritus et rapidos qui circinat igneus orbes
> Nunc quoque sydereis intercinit ipse choreis
> Immortale melos et inenarrabile carmen.[2]

1. For discussion of the date of *Ad Patrem* see Appendix D, p. 327.

2. 30–7:
> We too, ourselves, what time we seek again
> Our native skies, and one eternal now
> Shall be the only measure of our being,
> Crown'd all with gold, and chaunting to the lyre
> Harmonious verse, shall range the courts above,
> And make the starry firmament resound.
> And, even now, the fiery spirit pure
> That wheels yon circling orbs, directs, himself,
> Their mazy dance with melody of verse
> Unutt'rable, immortal.

The second line, quite clear and quite untranslatable, is mature and perfect Milton: tense, serene, and, as befits the subject, trance-like; unequalled till the description of heavenly beatitude in *Lycidas*. As in *Lycidas* too, so here Milton can change his tone suddenly according to his mood. There is a contrast between the tones in which he speaks of the past and of the future. To the future belong his hopes of poetic fame, and of these[1] and of the high functions of poetry[2] he speaks with eagerness. His dealings with his father belong to the past, and he speaks of them in a tone of quiet and tender reminiscence.[3]

Ad Patrem has been praised for its kindly display of filial affection. And justly: but is it realized with what consummate (and probably unconscious) firmness Milton puts his father in his place? The poem shows that the elder Milton had protested to his son that it was time for him to do something to earn his living. Milton's real reply, easily detected through his sincere thanks for past kindness, is with easy confidence to ignore his father's suggestions as not meant seriously at all. His father had said something against the Muses: to which he replies:

> Tu tamen ut simules teneras odisse Camoenas,
> Non odisse reor.[4]

How could his father object to his turning poet, when he had had him so 'curiously and plentifully' educated? But though Milton really tramples on his father, he expresses his gratitude for past favours with a charming candour. For all his strength of mind he would seem to have responded very sensitively and sweet-naturedly to kindness; and this poem helps us to understand how it was that Milton, in spite of the deterrent of political controversy, was so plentifully befriended to the end of his life.

About two months before *Lycidas*, in September 1637, Milton wrote two letters to Diodati. In the first he mentions how exacting and unintermitted his studies have been: the idea that his excursions to London were much relaxation cannot be allowed. He writes:

Your method of study is, as I know, such as to allow of frequent breathing-spaces, visits to friends, a good deal of writing and not infrequent journeys; while my own disposition is such that no delay, no rest, no thought or care

1. 101–10.   2. 17–55.   3. 56–92.

4. 67–8:
> No! howsoe'er the semblance thou assume
> Of hate, thou hatest not the gentle Muse.

for anything else, can divert me from my purpose, until I reach my goal and complete some great cycle of my studies.[1]

The second letter[2] gives other and more definite information. First, and this is important as showing the state of mind out of which *Lycidas* grew, he is struck by the longing for immortality. He writes:

What am I thinking about? you ask. So help me God, of immortality. What am I doing? Growing wings and learning to fly; but my Pegasus can only rise on tender pinions as yet, so let my new wisdom be humble.[3]

Of the restlessness or rather mental anguish which *Lycidas* proves to have resulted at times from this longing he indeed states nothing; but he admits that he is tired of Horton and is thinking of a move to London.

To be serious, my plan is to take rooms in one of the Inns of Court, where I hope to find a pleasant and shady spot in which to stroll, and which may afford a more convenient dwelling-place, among congenial companions, when I wish to stay at home, and a more suitable *point d'appui* if I prefer to roam abroad; here my life is, as you know, obscure and cramped.[4]

A cause of restlessness, particularly in the mind of one who had nearly finished a long period of preparation for some great work, was that in 1636 and 1637 the plague had been bad in England. In the latter year it spread to Horton, and a number of people there died of it. This is a fact to be remembered in reading *Lycidas*.

Lycidas is the last and greatest English poem of Milton's youth. Though shorter, it is greater than *Comus*, written with newly-won but complete mastery and expressing a mental experience both valuable and profound.

Most criticism of *Lycidas* is off the mark, because it fails to distinguish between the nominal and the real subject, what the poem professes to be about and what it is about. It assumes that Edward King is the real, whereas he is but the nominal subject. Fundamentally *Lycidas* concerns Milton himself;[5] King is but the excuse for one of Milton's most personal poems. This cannot be proved: it can only be deduced from the impression the poem leaves. Most readers agree that Milton was not deeply grieved at King's death, as they agree that the poem is great. If it is great, it must contain

1. P. B. Tillyard, op. cit., 11.
2. See also mention of it in Appendix C, p. 324.
3. P. B. Tillyard, op. cit., 14.
4. ibid., 14–15.
5. 'Ce n'est pas King qu'il faut y chercher, c'est Milton lui-même.' E. Legouis, in Legouis et Cazamian, *Histoire de la Littérature anglaise*, 567.

deep feeling of some sort. What then is this deep feeling all about?

From the circumstances in which *Lycidas* was written and from the two obviously personal passages the question can be answered. When Milton wrote *Lycidas* in 1637 he was twenty-nine years of age, and early in the next year he set out for Italy with perhaps the intention of going on to Greece. Whether the last line of the poem,

> To morrow to fresh Woods, and Pastures new,

refers to this intended journey is doubtful; it may well do so. Anyhow at the time of writing *Lycidas* Milton must have had the Italian and possibly the Greek journey in his mind. When he heard of King's death, and still more when by consenting to write the elegy he had to make his mind dwell on it, he cannot but have felt the analogy between King and himself. Milton and King had been at the same college in the same University. Their careers and interests had been similar there. Milton was a poet, King had written verse too. King had made a voyage on the sea, Milton was about to make voyages. How could Milton have missed the idea that *he* might make the analogy complete by getting drowned, like King, also? At a time when, through plagues and what not, life was less secure than in modern times of peace, Milton, having sacrificed so much to his great ambition, must anyhow, as the time of preparation drew to an end, have dwelt on the thought that it might be all for nothing. Not that he was a coward: but the fear that his ambitions might be ruined at the last moment must have been at times difficult to endure. Those who had experience of the late war must have known the miserable anxiety suffered immediately before going on leave. It was not that people feared to die more then than at other times, but the thought of being baulked by death of their desire for home was peculiarly harrowing. Milton's state of mind must at times have been somewhat similar, and in considering King's fate his fears must have come crowding on him. That he was at least partly thinking of his own possible fate is made clear by the reference in the first paragraph to his own destined urn and sable shroud. As a reason for his singing of Lycidas he writes:

> So may som gentle Muse
> With lucky words favour my destin'd Urn,
> And as he passes turn,
> And bid fair peace be to my sable shrowd.
> For we were nurst upon the self-same hill,
> Fed the same flock, by fountain, shade, and rill.[1]

1. 19–24. For a note on the paragraphing of this passage – paragraphing here affects the connotations – see Appendix E, p. 328.

In other words, 'If I die, some one will requite me with a requiem, for in other ways the analogy between us was complete.' And much more agonizingly does the thought of premature death start in his mind when he writes of poetic fame and 'the blind *Fury* with th' abhorred shears'. Why should he have submitted himself to rigorous self-denial, if to no end?

But his fears of premature death, though part of the subject, are not the whole. The real subject is the resolving of those fears (and of his bitter scorn of the clergy) into an exalted state of mental calm. The apotheosis of Lycidas in the penultimate paragraph has a deeper meaning: it symbolizes Milton's own balanced state of mind to which he won after the torments he had been through. This is the secret of the strength of *Lycidas* and the reason why it is a greater poem than *Comus:* in the one calm after struggle, in the other calm of a kind but without the preliminary struggle. To prove that the deepest and most satisfying calm is that which follows on mental struggle one has only to point to the greatest tragedies.

If the above idea is accepted, it is possible to see in *Lycidas* a unity of purpose which cannot be seen in it if the death of King is taken as the real subject of the poem. In particular the outburst against the clergy, usually regarded as a glorious excrescence, will be found perfectly in keeping with the profounder and less elegiac significance of the whole. Let me try to explain this harmony by describing how the purpose of the poem develops.

Milton begins with characteristic egotism. His first lines do not concern King but his own reluctance to write a poem before he is mature. But he must write, for Lycidas died prematurely – '*Young* Lycidas' – and for a premature death he must be willing to risk premature poetry. Moreover, if he writes an elegy for Lycidas, some other poet may reward him when he dies with an elegy too. The introduction, lines 1 to 24, thus ends on Milton's possible death.

The first section, beginning 'Together both, ere the high Lawns appear'd', consists of lines 25 to 84. It contains a lament for the death of Lycidas, regret that the Muse could not protect her son, and leads up to the first great cause of pain in Milton's own mind: the risk of death before his great work is completed. What has been the use of all his laborious preparation, his careful chastity (for doubtless he means this by his references to Amaryllis and Neaera), if fame, for whose sake he has denied himself, is to escape him, anticipated by death? Earthly fame, he replies to himself in the person of Phoebus, has nothing to do with heavenly fame: it depends on deeds, not on what those deeds effect. So he argues, but one does not get the impression of emotional conviction yet: the final impression of the first section is that it would be a cruel shame and a wicked waste, if he were to die. It should be noted with what consummate skill Milton in this section works the subject from King to its climax in himself.

In the second section, lines 85 to 131, beginning 'O Fountain *Arethuse*', he does exactly the same thing. In the elegiac tradition various persons come to visit the body. It is perfectly natural that St Peter should come to visit a priest, and equally natural that he should proceed from lamenting the death of a good priest to denouncing the bad. But this denunciation reveals the second great cause of mental pain in Milton: his quarrel with contemporary England, typified by the rottenness of the clergy. Thus St Peter's outburst is not an excrescence but strictly parallel with Milton's earlier outburst about the blind Fury. One can even see a close connection of ideas between the two grievances. One grievance is that 'the hungry Sheep look up and are not fed'; England has bad or useless teachers: the other is that he, Milton, whose ambition was to teach by writing a great epic, to feed the hungry sheep of England, may easily be cut off before it can be realized. It should be noted too that the second grievance, like the first, is answered at the end of the second movement. Punishment is waiting; the two-handed engine[1] stands ready to smite. But even less than at the end of the first section has mental calm been attained. The end of the second section marks the climax of the poem. Milton has stated his quarrel with life: we await the conclusion.

Of the third section, lines 132 to 164, beginning 'Return *Alpheus*', it is more difficult to describe the function. Some quieter interlude is clearly necessary between St Peter's bitter outburst and the heavenly triumph of the final movement. But it is more than an interlude, it has value as a transition too. The sudden change from the terror of the two-handed engine to the incredible beauty of the description of the flowers contains an implication that somehow the 'Dorique delicacy', of which the description of the flowers is the highest example in Milton, is not irreconcilable with the sterner mood, and hence is able to insinuate some comfort. So too from the dallying with a false surmise, the escape into a region of pure romance

> Where the great vision of the Guarded Mount
> Looks toward *Namancos* and *Bayona's* hold,

1. For an addition to the already too numerous explanations of this riddle see Appendix F, p. 330.

some comfort is allowed. But these sources of comfort are but minor, leading up to the greater solution.

The fourth section purports to describe the resurrection of Lycidas and his entry into heaven. More truly it solves the whole poem by describing the resurrection into a new kind of life of Milton's hopes, should they be ruined by premature death or by the moral collapse of his country. The loss or possible loss of human fame is made good by fame in heaven, the corrupt clergy are balanced by

> all the Saints above
> In solemn troops and sweet Societies[1]

and the harsh forebodings of Peter, the pilot of the Galilean lake, are forgotten

> Through the dear might of him who walk'd the waves.[2]

But above all the fourth section describes the renunciation of earthly fame, the abnegation of self by the great egotist, and the spiritual purgation of gaining one's life after losing it.

Some people might call *Lycidas* a religious poem, for Milton appears to found his comfort on his hopes of heaven: others might object that his grounds of comfort are extraordinarily flimsy and that the pessimism of *Paradise Lost* is truer to the facts of life than the optimism of *Lycidas*. But the question of beliefs is unimportant; what matters and what makes *Lycidas* one of the greatest poems in English is that it expresses with success a state of mind whose high value can hardly be limited to a particular religious creed. Milton by ridding himself of his inhibiting fears, by subordinating the disturbing ambition to have done a thing to the serene intention of doing it as well as possible, had proved his mettle and issued from the ordeal a great man. *Lycidas* expresses a mind of the keenest sensibility and most powerful grasp acutely aware of a number of most moving sensations, but controlling these sensations so that they do not conflict but rather by contrast reinforce one another: a mind calm after struggle but keyed up to perform heroic deeds, should they need to be done.

1. 178–9.   2. 173.

74

CHAPTER EIGHT
Visit to Italy

Date	Milton's age	Writing or event in Milton's life	Contemporary event
1638, April	29	Leaves for Italy	
1638, Sept. 10	29	Letter written in Florence to Benedetto Buonmattei	
1638–39 (winter)	29–30	Poems to Leonora at Rome	
1638–39 (winter)	29–30	*Mansus* written at Naples	
1639, March 30	30	Letter to Holstenius from Florence	War with Scotland (first Bishops' War)
1639, Aug.	30	Reaches home	
1639	30	*Epitaphium Damonis*	

FROM the terms in which Milton refers to his visit to Italy we can gather that he put a very high value on the experience. His account in the *Defensio Secunda*, though mainly concerned with events, the places he visited, the friends he made, the way he stood up to the Jesuits, is yet written with a fervour which suggests that he relished after his five years of study at Horton all the various activities he pursued in Italy. We have too his explicit statement in a letter written some years after his return home to one of his Italian friends, the Florentine noble Carlo Dati. After affectionate greetings Milton complains how

Those who are so greatly endeared to me by sympathy of manners, disposition and tastes, are almost all separated from me either by death or by the cruel accident of distance, and are as a rule snatched from my sight so swiftly that I am compelled to spend my life in almost perpetual loneliness. It gives me great satisfaction to hear that since I left Florence you have always been anxious about my health and have never forgotten me, and to find that the feelings which I had, perhaps perversely, imagined to be mine alone, were in fact fully reciprocated. I can assure you that my departure gave real pain to myself as well, and that it left a sting which I still feel acutely whenever I recollect all the kind and congenial friends and companions I left behind me in that one city, so distant but so well beloved. It was with the utmost reluctance that I tore myself away.[1]

1. P. B. Tillyard, op. cit., 22–3. Letter dated 21 April, 1647.

There is therefore no doubt of Milton's liking for Italy. Equally certain is the liking the Italians had for him. The number and rank of his acquaintance, the compliments addressed to him by the Italian men of letters and prefixed to his Latin poems, and, most convincing of all, the entries in the minute-books of certain Italian academies,[1] prove that he enjoyed a success both social and literary. And after the heart-searchings of *Lycidas* appreciation not opposition was what he needed. The appreciation too must have been very solid and satisfying, because it was of his early efforts in Latin verse; and these, he must have realized, were very inferior to what he had already written in English, still more to what he felt he could write. In sum he seems to have been warmed and matured by the actual sunshine of the country[2] and the figurative sunshine of men's applause.

How he matured we have his explicit statement in *Reason of Church Government*; a statement which helps to explain the few writings that survive from Milton's Italian visit, besides being of exceptional importance in the history of his mental development.

But much latelier in the private academies of Italy, whither I was favoured to resort, perceiving that some trifles which I had in memory, composed at under twenty or thereabout, (for the manner is, that every one must give some proof of his wit and reading there,) met with acceptance above what was looked for; and other things, which I had shifted in scarcity of books and conveniences to patch up amongst them, were received with written encomiums, which the Italian is not forward to bestow on men of this side the Alps; I began thus far to assent both to them and divers of my friends here at home, and not less to an inward prompting which now grew daily upon me,[3] that by labour and intense study (which I take to be my portion in this life,) joined with the strong propensity of nature, I might perhaps leave something so written to aftertimes, as they should not willingly let it die. These thoughts at once possessed me, and these other; that if I were certain to write as men buy leases, for three lives and downward, there ought no regard be sooner had than to God's glory, by the honour and instruction of my country. For which cause, and not only for that I knew it would be hard to arrive at the second rank among the Latins, I applied myself to that resolution, which Ariosto followed against the persuasions of Bembo, to fix all the industry and art I could unite to the adorning of my native tongue; not to make verbal curiosities the end, (that were a toilsome vanity,) but to be an

1. See Masson, i. 2nd ed. 782.

2. Those who consider Milton a sun-shy albino will have to explain how he urvived and enjoyed the glare of Florence in summer.

3. Note once more how Milton insists on self-reliance rather than reliance on others' advice.

interpreter and relater of the best and sagest things among mine own citizens throughout this island in the mother dialect. That what the greatest and choicest wits of Athens, Rome, or modern Italy, and those Hebrews of old did for their country, I, in my proportion, with this over and above, of being a Christian, might do for mine; not caring to be once named abroad, though perhaps I could attain to that, but content with these British islands as my world; whose fortune hath hitherto been, that if the Athenians, as some say, made their small deeds great and renowned by their eloquent writers, England hath had her noble achievements made small by the unskilful handling of monks and mechanics.[1]

I think it clear from the context that Milton was in Italy when he came to the conclusions referred to; and, if this is true, it may be said that as in writing *Lycidas* he harmonized the different impulses of his own mind, it was during his Italian visit that he settled his relations with the world. But before enlarging on what the passage just quoted implies, I wish to speak of the actual writings that belong to the Italian visit.

The only writing of the first importance is the Latin hexameter poem *Mansus*, but they all have this in common: that they contain or consist of compliments at once polished and sincere. Milton plainly had the art of behaving himself gracefully abroad. If Selvaggi in a crudely fulsome epigram states that England may be proud of Milton, who is worth Homer and Virgil together, Milton shows himself an equal master of hyperbole by saying of Leonora, the matchless Roman singer (to the scandal of Charles Lamb), 'Tua praesentem vox sonat ipsa Deum.' But even as a mere complimentary piece *Mansus* is easily the best.

Manso, to whom the poem is addressed, the patron of Tasso and Marini, was clearly a very impressive and distinguished old man. Milton speaks thus of him in *Defensio Secunda*:

There [at Naples] I was introduced by a certain recluse, with whom I had travelled from Rome, to John Baptista Manso, marquis of Villa, a nobleman of distinguished rank and authority, to whom Torquato Tasso, the illustrious poet, inscribed his book on friendship. During my stay, he gave me singular proofs of his regard: he himself conducted me round the city, and to the palace of the viceroy; and more than once paid me a visit at my lodgings. On my departure he gravely apologized for not having shewn me more civility, which he said he had been restrained from doing, because I had spoken with so little reserve on matters of religion.[2]

1. Bohn, ii. 477–8.
2. Bohn, i. 256.

Milton may not really have thought less of Manso for his religious prejudices, for one can imagine him in his old age acting in exactly the same manner had he been visited by a gifted and ardent young Catholic[1] from Italy. The poem praises Manso for his patronage of Tasso and Marini, through whose immortality Manso's name too will be remembered, but not without reminding him that the northern island has had its poets too and that he, Milton, is meditating a great poem about his own native land. The two themes are blended with a perfect tact. Milton's insisting (quite simply and calmly) on his own merit raises the importance of Manso's attention to him and is really but an added compliment. His tact prevents him from direct statement. After saying, 'You have been fortunate in having acquired immortality through patronizing Tasso and Marini', he might so easily have added, 'And your immortality is further assured by having befriended me'; but he refrains. Indeed we see Milton here in his most charming mood, responding with sweetness and courtesy and a grave warmth to Manso's kind attentions.

But *Mansus* is more than a mere compliment. Its sustained sweetness and dignity, rising at times to positive grandeur, make it the best of all Milton's Latin poems (the *Epitaphium Damonis* included), and the one which as a whole can seriously compete with say *L'Allegro* or *Arcades*. To be more definite I would say that it is certainly a good deal less important than *Lycidas* but more important than the *Epitaph on the Marchioness of Winchester*. No wonder if after such a poem Milton again considered the question of writing his great works in Latin. Certainly the way in which he here writes – with complete grasp of his medium and with hardly a falter from beginning to end – is quite astonishing. Here are examples of what seems to be excellent. The line,

Quin et in has quondam pervenit Tityrus oras,[2]

closing a paragraph has almost precisely the same effect as

And old *Damaetas* lov'd to hear our song,

closing a paragraph in *Lycidas*. For dignity take these three lines:

1. In his latest prose work, *Of True Religion*, published 1673, he is still uncompromisingly hostile to Catholics. He cannot allow them the use of their conscience: that is if they are English citizens. But he expressly extends a courteous tolerance to visitors: the embassies of Catholic powers are of course to be allowed their private chapels.

2. 34.

Ergo ego te Clius et magni nomine Phoebi,
Manse pater, jubeo longum salvere per aevum
Missus Hyperboreo juvenis peregrinus ab axe.[1]

For grandeur the lines, so well known biographically, telling of the projected Arthuriad are a sufficient illustration. Speaking of how lucky the Italian poets have been in the cherishment of Manso, he says:

O mihi si mea sors talem concedat amicum
Phoebaeos decorasse viros qui tam bene norit,
Si quando indigenas revocabo in carmina reges,
Arturumque etiam sub terris bella moventem;
Aut dicam invictae sociali foedere mensae,
Magnanimos Heroas, et (O modo spiritus adsit)
Frangam Saxonicas Britonum sub Marte phalanges.[2]

There is great power in the crash of *frangam* after the hushed parenthesis of *O modo spiritus adsit*.

The plan for an epic shadowed in these lines may bring us back to the passage in *Reason of Church Government*, quoted above, in which Milton recounts how he decided to 'fix all the industry and art I could unite to the adorning of my native tongue'. It was perfectly natural and fitting that Milton's Italian visit should have incited him to write an English poem. People are inclined to feel most warmly about their country when they are away from it, and in the Italian academies Milton would have encountered or rather have had revived in him the peculiar patriotic theory of poetry which marked the literary ideas of the sixteenth century. The whole autobiographical passage in *Reason of Church Government* is saturated with this theory, but, as critics have only recently begun to see how

1. 24–6 :
I therefore, though a stranger youth, who come
Chill'd by rude blasts, that freeze my Northern home,
Thee dear to Clio, confident proclaim,
And thine for Phoebus' sake, a deathless name.

2. 78–84:
Oh might so true a friend to me belong,
So skilled to grace the votaries of song,
Should I recall hereafter into rhyme
The kings and heroes of my native clime,
Arthur the chief, who even now prepares,
In subterraneous being, future wars,
With all his martial Knights, to be restored,
Each to his seat around the federal board,
And Oh, if spirit fail me not, disperse
Our Saxon plunderers, in triumphant verse!

completely in his ideas on poetry Milton belongs to the Renaissance, it is worth while saying in what the theory mainly consists.[1]

In speaking of his resolution to adorn his native tongue Milton mentions Ariosto, who wrote his heroic poem in Italian against the advice of Bembo. This act is held to mark a new phase in the poetry of the Renaissance. The theory of rigid imitation, that the best literature strictly imitated in Latin the prose of Cicero and the verse of Virgil, was abandoned; and there arose the idea of cultivating through imitation of the best models the potentialities of the mother tongue. Not merely did this use of the vernacular ensure a greater vitality, it got connected with the idea of patriotism, and at the time when the spirit of nationalism was growing in western Europe. The Pléiade in France, whose manifesto is du Bellay's *Deffense et Illustration de la Langue françoise*, shows perfectly the theory put into practice. In England Wyatt was the first practitioner.[2] He set himself to show the world that the English tongue could cope with the sonnets of Petrarch and the paraphrased Psalms of Aretino, and seems to have been more admired for these patriotic but dismal ventures than for the vigorous beauty of his lyrics. Spenser, however, is the great English example.

The two sides of the theory, the patriotic use of the native tongue and the imitation of the best models, may now be applied in turn to Milton. It is often stated that Milton hesitated between English and Latin as a poetic medium; and I think rightly, for otherwise his statement in *Reason of Church Government* would have little force. Further, one may guess with some plausibility at the history of this hesitation. Whether in his college days Milton ever really contemplated making Latin his definitive medium is, though sometimes assumed, uncertain. His Latin verses may have been to him mere exercises from the first. Anyhow he makes it quite clear when

1. The most comprehensive account I know is in Renwick's *Edmund Spenser*, chapter i.; but much more of the book, which deals largely with the literary ideas in which Spenser grew up, could apply to Milton. Renwick considers Mulcaster the chief English source for the theory; and if Spenser learnt it from Mulcaster's lips at Merchant Taylors, Milton must have read it in the *Elementarie*.

2. Renwick does not seem to recognize this. But Leland's *Naeniae in Mortem Thomae Viatae* and Surrey's *Wyatt resteth here* prove it. Leland writes:

Anglica lingua fuit rudis et sine nomine rhythmus;
Nunc limam agnoscit, docte Viate, tuam.

And Surrey speaks of Wyatt's head
where that some work of fame
Was dayly wrought to turne to Britaines gayn.

See my *Sir Thomas Wyatt* (Scholartis Press), 22.

addressing his native language in the lines written *At a Vacation Exercise* that henceforward English is to be his medium. And that he so resolved is confirmed by the bulk of his early work after that date being written in English. There is no hint that he revised his resolve till he went to Italy, but there, I fancy, the applause that greeted his early Latin pieces made him hesitate. Avid of fame, he could hardly help asking himself whether he had better not after all write in a language which all men understood, and not confine himself to a tongue which to continental ears was not so very far this side barbarism. Much as Milton loved his country's language, there is yet no doubt that as an instrument of culture he classed it perhaps with French and certainly below Italian, not to say Latin and Greek. It had been natural to him to write in Italian as well as in the two dead languages. In a letter written in Florence on 10 September, 1638 (that is early in his Italian visit and some months before he wrote *Mansus*) to Benedetto Buonmattei, who had written a book on the Italian tongue, he says:

> Among them (*sc.* foreigners) there is no one with any pretensions to superior intellect or to culture and elegance but counts the Tuscan language among his chief delights, and even considers it an essential part of his serious studies.[1]

He makes no mention of French or of his own tongue. It was impossible for him not to have reflected how provincial he would have felt himself had he been unable to write freely in the Latin and Italian tongues to impress the Italian academies. Moreover there was the powerful precedent of the great Buchanan. A younger man than Ariosto, and frequenter of France in the full flowering of the Pléiade, he had yet refused to use his native dialect and had won a vast international reputation by writing plays and lyrics in Latin. How many educated Italians had read Spenser, how many had not read Buchanan?

It was not then without a struggle that Milton, when in Italy, 'applied himself to that resolution, which Ariosto followed against the persuasion of Bembo, to fix all the industry and art I could to the adorning of my native tongue'. There is good evidence too in the *Epitaphium Damonis*, when he speaks of his own plans for an English poem. The context shows Milton's mind full of memories of the Italian tour, and when speaking of his poetical plans he treats them as springing from that tour. He says he will write an English epic, and goes on:

1. P. B. Tillyard, op. cit., 17.

O mihi tum si vita supersit,
Tu procul annosa pendebis fistula pinu
Multum oblita mihi, aut patriis mutata camoenis
Brittonicum strides, quid enim? omnia non licet uni
Non sperasse uni licet omnia, mi satis ampla
Merces, et mihi grande decus (sim ignotus in aevum
Tum licet, externo penitusque inglorius orbi)
Si me flava comas legat Usa et potor Alauni,
Vorticibusque frequens Abra et nemus omne Treantae,
Et Thamesis meus ante omnes, et fusca metallis
Tamara, et extremis me discant Orcades undis.[1]

One can paraphrase as follows: 'If life lasts me to undertake my great design, my Latin pastoral strain will either cease or be exchanged for the harsher English tongue. Well, what of that? One man cannot excel in everything: he must make his choice. I shall have sufficient reward if, after giving up my hopes of lasting worldwide fame, I am known throughout the length of England and Scotland.' Regret at having to give up his hopes of international fame is most apparent in these lines.

In *Mansus* it is clear that the choice has been made, that patriotism has won the day. *Mansus* is indeed one of the noblest and least offensive patriotic poems written by an Englishman. There is in it even an exquisite hint of *Home Thoughts from Abroad* when he recalls England with its

Flaventes spicas, et lutea mala canistris
Halantemque crocum.[2]

1. 168–78:

and Oh, if Fate
Proportion to these themes my lengthened date,
Adieu my shepherd's reed – yon pine-tree bough
Shall be thy future home, there dangle thou
Forgotten and disused, unless ere long
Thou change thy Latian for a British song;
A British? – even so, – the powers of man
Are bounded; little is the most he can:
And it shall well suffice me, and shall be
Fame, and proud recompence enough for me,
If Usa, golden-haired, my verse may learn,
If Alain bending o'er his chrystal urn,
Swift-whirling Abra, Trent's o'ershadowed stream,
Thames, lovelier far than all in my esteem,
Tamar's ore-tinctured flood, and, after these,
The wave-worn shores of utmost Orcades.

2. 41–3:

the golden ear,
The burnish'd apple, ruddiest of the year,
The fragrant crocus,

But for our present purpose it is Milton's account of the English claim to poetical culture that is of main interest. Though not thinking fit to name any English poet, he claims firmly but unostentatiously that England too has had her poets and that one of them has already visited Italy.

> Nos etiam in nostro modulantes flumine cygnos
> Credimus obscuras noctis sensisse per umbras,
> Qua Thamesis late puris argenteus urnis
> Oceani glaucos perfundit gurgite crines.
> Quin et in has quondam pervenit Tityrus oras.[1]

It cannot be proved how many poets Milton is referring to, but I think he means (as Hurd and Warton guessed) Chaucer, Spenser, and no more. Tityrus is certainly Chaucer, because that was Spenser's name for him and because he only of England's great poets before Milton had visited Italy. The Thames suggests Spenser before all other English poets both because of his referring to it as his birthplace and of the refrain of *Prothalamium* (*Sweete Themmes! runne softly, till I end my Song*). Further, by choosing to refer to Chaucer by Spenser's name for him, *Tityrus*, Milton seems to be indicating Spenser as the other poet he has in his mind. I think the passage implies that Milton saw himself (as Mackail chose to see him in *The Springs of Helicon*) the third great English poet in the tradition of the Renaissance. He also makes the patriotic implication that he is not without worthy objects of imitation in his own language. When Milton told Dryden that he was Spenser's poetical son, he was perhaps thinking of Spenser as his immediate predecessor in the poetical tradition of his choosing. But the mention of Spenser leads to the second part of the poetical theory we have been applying to Milton: the use of the best models.

The theory on which the Pléiade worked was that although it was right and patriotic to use the native tongue, it was necessary to go to classical literature for the best models. Other subsidiary models like Petrarch were admitted, but they could only supplement, never supersede, the great authors of Greece and Rome. And so we find it with Milton. Although he may hint that Chaucer and Spenser

1. 30–4:

> We too, where Thames with his unsullied waves
> The tresses of the blue-haired Ocean laves,
> Hear oft by night, or slumbering seem to hear,
> O'er his wide stream, the swan's voice warbling clear,
> And we could boast a Tityrus of yore ,
> Who trod, a welcome guest, your happy shore.

are not to be overlooked, the first objects of imitation are the classics. The passage in *Reason of Church Government* immediately following the account of how he resolved to write in English enumerates the models he considers the most suitable: Homer, Virgil, and Tasso, for the long epic; the *Book of Job* for the brief epic; Sophocles and Euripides for the drama, also the *Song of Solomon* and *Revelation*; Pindar and Callimachus, but above all the writers of the Old Testament for lyric. There is no mention of any English writer, which may warn us that we need not take Milton's poetical sonship to Spenser too seriously.

Not only was the theory of the best models something that connected Milton with the chief writers of epic in the sixteenth century, it was also an incentive, for it implied a further theory that goes far to explain the intense seriousness with which Milton undertook the writing of his epic. There is an excellent account of this theory in Ker's introduction to Dryden's Essays,[1] from which I cannot do better than quote.

There were exact patterns of different kinds of poetry laid up in some heaven to which the true scholar might rise in his contemplations, and from which he might bring down his knowledge for the instruction of modern poetical artificers. . . . What influence those ideal patterns had, what reverence they evoked, is scarcely conceivable now, and is seldom thought of by historians. The 'Heroic Poem' is not commonly mentioned in histories of Europe as a matter of serious interest: yet from the days of Petrarch and Boccaccio to those of Dr. Johnson, and more especially from the sixteenth century onward, it was a subject that engaged some of the strongest intellects in the world. . . . There might be difference of opinion about the essence of the Heroic Poem or the Tragedy, but there was no doubt about their value. . . . [Certain poets] undertook to show by their example how the rules and principles of the Heroic Poem might be carried out in practice. *Paradise Lost* is one of those experiments. . . . No small part of Milton's motive was the learned ambition to embody the abstract form of Epic in a modern vernacular work.

The reason of course why this theory of the abstract form of Epic is connected with the theory of models is that these models are a fairly close approximation to this abstract form. If a modern wished to write a good epic he would have to study both the theoretical nature of the Epic and the best embodiments of that nature, in Milton's judgment the *Iliad, Odyssey, Aeneid,* and *Gerusalemme Liberata.*

As well as this quasi-mystical value attached to the great forms of literature there was another which Milton and the body of

1. Oxford, 1920, i. xv-xix.

literary thought he was familiar with attributed to them; and that was the sheer didactic value. It was a strongly held Renaissance doctrine that a country which had produced a great poem was the more likely to breed virtuous citizens. How earnestly Milton believed this is proved by the passage in *Reason of Church Government* following his words about fitting models:

These abilities [*sc.* to write poetry], wheresoever they be found, are the inspired gift of God, rarely bestowed, but yet to some (though most abuse) in every nation; and are of power, beside the office of a pulpit, to imbreed and cherish in a great people the seeds of virtue and public civility, to allay the perturbations of the mind, and set the affections in right tune; to celebrate in glorious and lofty hymns the throne and equipage of God's almightiness, and what he works, and what he suffers to be wrought with high providence in his church; to sing victorious agonies of martyrs and saints, the deeds and triumphs of just and pious nations, doing valiantly through faith against the enemies of Christ; to deplore the general relapses of kingdoms and states from justice and God's true worship. Lastly, whatsoever in religion is holy and sublime, in virtue amiable or grave, whatsoever hath passion or admiration in all the changes of that which is called fortune from without, or the wily subtleties and refluxes of man's thoughts from within; all these things with a solid and treatable smoothness to paint out and describe. Teaching over the whole book of sanctity and virtue, through all the instances of example, with such delight to those especially of soft and delicious temper, who will not so much as look upon truth herself, unless they see her elegantly dressed; that whereas the paths of honesty and good life appear now rugged and difficult, though they be indeed easy and pleasant, they will then appear to all men both easy and pleasant, though they were rugged and difficult indeed. And what a benefit this would be to our youth and gentry, may be soon guessed by what we know of the corruption and bane which they suck in daily from the writings and interludes of libidinous and ignorant poetasters.[1]

It is impossible to stress this passage too strongly. It explains how Milton was willing to give up world-wide fame: enough if he could mould the morals of his countrymen. The naïve belief in the immediate didactic efficacy of great poetry working on the sensitive, passionate, and credulous substance of Milton's brain encouraged his belief in himself as the agent of great national good. And only if we realize how strong and deeply rooted this confidence was, can we understand how great was the shock when he learnt at last that he was powerless to make the English nation pay him appreciable heed or can we understand at once the humiliation and the strength which caused him to say 'fit audience though few'.

1. Bohn, ii. 479–80.

It may be thought that this last topic, Milton's didactic purpose, would more fittingly concern a later chapter, but I believe Milton reached his conclusions as stated in *Reason of Church Government* during his visit to Italy. Certainly all the ideas I have mentioned would have been the commonplaces of the learned academies he frequented; and, freed temporarily from the exhaustive programme of study which he had pursued at Horton and stimulated by the praise of the learned, what more natural than that he should have thought out definitively the principle by which he meant to guide his future career?

Milton composed *Epitaphium Damonis*, his elegy on Diodati's death, very soon after his return from Italy, and probably at Horton. He speaks in pastoral language of coming home and of feeling as soon as he sat beneath the accustomed elm the full sorrow of his loss. Though containing perhaps the most beautiful passages, the *Epitaphium* is not the best of Milton's Latin poems. And the reason is that it reveals a troubled, disunited mind. A quite successful poem dealing with painful experience will not reveal a troubled state of mind: it will derive its success precisely from expressing a state of mind that has found equilibrium after and in spite of sorrow. *Lycidas*, Shelley's *Lines written in Dejection in the Bay of Naples*, even Coleridge's *Ode to Dejection* (where the equilibrium may be perilous enough) are such poems. The *Epitaphium Damonis* suffers from the defect of Meredith's *Modern Love*: the pains that made up the experiences described have not been resolved; however moving and interesting, both poems suffer from this unsurmountable defect.

I get the impression from *Epitaphium Damonis* that Milton is suffering from a mental reaction after his return from Italy. Not merely does he suffer sincerely from the loss of his friend, but he finds Horton tame after his active social life in Italy. Moreover in Italy his thoughts all turned to the future: now in piety he must needs spare 'a night of memory and sighs' for what is with tragic obviousness something that belongs to the past. Indeed I cannot help feeling that there is something a little forced about the poem as a whole. Is it an accident that *Lycidas* has 193 lines, the *Epitaphium Damonis* 213? Did Milton feel he must draw out the latter to a superior length in order not to slight Diodati's memory? And would this conscientious enlargement explain Milton's lapse of taste in dwelling at such length on his own future instead of confining himself to the subject of the elegy?[1] Certainly it is with the paragraph

1. This criticism does not at all apply to *Lycidas*, where the chief subject is plainly Milton himself. The subject of *Epitaphium Damonis* is primarily regret at Diodati's death.

beginning at line 124 that the poem begins to flag, and here he begins speaking of his own experiences in Italy. Nor can I feel enthusiastic about the final description, Diodati's reception in heaven. It shows extraordinary power over the Latin language and is striking in the extreme, but there is something hyperbolical and morbid about it: it does not ring quite true. Milton seems to recall with a false ardour feelings which he has outgrown and which scarcely concern him now.

Still, though the poem does not succeed as a whole, it shows as masterly and individual a use of Latin as *Mansus*, and the grave sweetness of Milton is present throughout. Moreover the first 123 lines are almost faultless, and unique in Milton from the peculiar tenderness of tone in which they are written. Here is the description of Thyrsis and Damon (Milton and Diodati) talking away the night:

> Pectora cui credam? quis me lenire docebit
> Mordaces curas, quis longam fallere noctem
> Dulcibus alloquiis, grato cum sibilat igni
> Molle pyrum, et nucibus strepitat focus, at malus auster
> Miscet cuncta foris, et desuper intonat ulmo.[1]

And there is in these lines a piercing sense of his desolation:

> At jam solus agros, jam pascua solus oberro,
> Sicubi ramosae densantur vallibus umbrae,
> Hic serum expecto; supra caput imber et Eurus
> Triste sonant, fractaeque agitata crepuscula silvae.[2]

The last four words may not be good Latin, but they are certainly good poetry.

Epitaphium Damonis is the epilogue to the period of Milton's life that has been dealt with up to now. In it he takes leave not merely of his dead friend but of habits of mind or composition he had out-

1. 45–9:
> In whom shall I confide? Whose counsel find
> A balmy med'cine for my troubled mind?
> Or whose discourse with innocent delight
> Shall fill me now, and cheat the wint'ry night,
> While hisses on my hearth the pulpy pear
> And black'ning chestnuts start and crackle there,
> While storms abroad the dreary meadows whelm,
> And the wind thunders thro' the neighb'ring elm.

2. 58–61:
> Where glens and vales are thickest overgrown
> With tangled boughs, I wander now alone,
> Till night descend, with blustering wind and show'r
> Beat on my temples through the shatter'd bow'r.

grown. He chose to write in Latin because he had used it in all his
other writings addressed to Diodati, but henceforward he has done
with the conventional modes of Latin versifying. And in the final
lines, the description of Damon in heaven, he culminates in a mystical
rapture, that looks back to the apocalyptic fury of his early model,
Giles Fletcher, and to his ascetic experiences at Horton, but of
which with the writing of this poem he took a lasting farewell:

> Quod tibi purpureus pudor, et sine labe juventus
> Grata fuit, quod nulla tori libata voluptas,
> En etiam tibi virginei servantur honores;
> Ipse caput nitidum cinctus rutilante corona,
> Laetaque frondentis gestans umbracula palmae
> Aeternum perages immortales hymenaeos;
> Cantus ubi, choreisque furit lyra mista beatis,
> Festa Sionaeo bacchantur et Orgia Thyrso.[1]

1. 212-19:
> Thy blush was maiden, and thy youth the taste
> Of wedded bliss knew never, pure and chaste,
> The honours, therefore, by divine decree
> The lot of virgin worth, are given to thee;
> Thy brows encircled with a radiant band,
> And the green palm-branch waving in thy hand,
> Thou in immortal nuptials shalt rejoice,
> And join with seraphs thy according voice,
> Where rapture reigns, and the ecstatic lyre
> Guides the blest orgies of the blazing quire.

PART II

THE PERIOD OF THE PROSE

CHAPTER ONE

Introductory

Date	Milton's age	Writing or event in Milton's life	Contemporary event
1639, Aug.	30	Reaches home from Italy	
1639	30	*Epitaphium Damonis*	Strafford returns from Ireland
1639–40 (winter)	31	Moves to London. Begins teaching nephews	
1640–41	31–2	Plans for tragedies in Trinity MS.	1640. Short Parliament. Second Bishops' War. Summons of Long Parliament. Arrest of Strafford
1640–41 (winter)	32	Begins teaching more seriously. Plans for poem now probably give way to decision to enter controversy	Root-and-Branch petition
1641, May-June	32	First pamphlet, *On Reformation in England*	

THE *Epitaphium Damonis* brings to an end one period of Milton's poetical career, but by speaking of his plans for a great poem, perhaps an Arthuriad, in the English language it also looks to the future. It therefore leads on directly to the next important fact of Milton's poetical career, the entries in the Trinity Manuscript relating to a proposed tragic poem. Soon after he arrived in England (August 1639) Milton took lodgings in London and began teaching his two nephews. It is about this time that the above entries in the Trinity Manuscript are thought to begin. They would extend over perhaps two years, ending probably during the time in which he was engaged in his first series of pamphlets, that directed against the Episcopacy, dating from May 1641 to about April 1642.

It is sometimes stated on the ground of the Trinity Manuscript that Milton at this time definitely intended to make his great poem a tragedy. It has even been suggested[1] that he changed his mind only when the theatres were closed and all chance of his play's being

1. By Sir Arthur Quiller-Couch, *Studies in Literature,* Second Series, 140.

acted was gone. The date of the closing of the theatres (1642) suits
well enough, but the evidence is strong, not only that he had the
epic in mind just before the theatres were shut, but that he had
never had any idea of substituting the tragic for the epic form. A. H.
Gilbert[1] has very sensibly pointed out that the entries in the Trinity
Manuscript have been misunderstood: we have no right to assume
that they represent the sum of Milton's plans in the years 1640–42;
it is an accident that this particular set of papers has survived rather
than others. Gilbert suggests that parallel plans for an epic (possibly
for lyrics too) may have existed, of which the arguments prefixed
to the books of *Paradise Lost* may be an adaptation. If the evidence
of the Trinity Manuscript is dubious, there is no proof whatever
that Milton at this time was meditating the tragic form for his chief
poem; and all the other evidence makes for the continuity of
Milton's epic plans. First, there are passages in the anti-episcopal
pamphlets of the year 1641 (the very central period of the Trinity
Manuscript entries) which show that Milton pictured himself as
the celebrator of the new order of things so soon to be brought about
by the action of Parliament. Such a picture would suggest anything
rather than tragedy and any subject rather than that of Paradise
Lost, preferred in the Trinity Manuscript. Next, the setting forth of
Milton's literary plans in *Reason of Church Government* (1642) includes
first the epic, second the tragedy, third the lyric. What he says there
about epic harmonizes perfectly with the lines in *Mansus* and *Epitaphium Damonis* and suggests a continuity of intention from the
time of those poems. True, the manner in which he sets forth these
plans is mainly reminiscent; he is referring to his resolutions in Italy:
but had he changed his mind in the interval, he could hardly have
written as he did. The evidence favours Milton's having kept to the
Arthuriad plan from the time of his Italian tour till *Reason of Church
Government* (if not later). The Trinity Manuscript, then, gives but a
partial account of Milton's literary projects and will refer to a plan
for a tragedy parallel with the greater plan for an epic.

That Milton was in earnest about his projected tragedy is proved
by Edward Phillips's stating that at this time Milton wrote some of
the lines Satan addresses to the sun, near the beginning of *Paradise
Lost*, Book Four,[2] as the opening of a drama on the same theme. Can
this indicate something more than that Milton was experimenting?
Could it be that in the early stages of the struggle between King and

1. *Studies in Philology*, 1919, 172–6.
2. *P.L.*, iv. 32 ff.

Parliament, while still in a mood for writing poetry, he planned first a tragedy as something less exacting than the bulk of a whole epic and not impossible of execution in these troubled times? What more fitting for Milton in his early hopefulness than a poem on Paradise Lost to be the prelude to the greater poem on the Paradise regained in England by the victories of Parliament? But this is a conjecture that must not be taken too seriously.

When did Milton transfer the favourite subject of his tragedy to his heroic poem? The latest piece of evidence for the national subject, whether Arthur or not, is in the *Apology for Smectymnuus* (1642), the last of the anti-episcopal tracts. Here again Milton speaks of himself as the future poet of his country's glory. Between 1642 and 1655, when the serious planning of *Paradise Lost* probably began,[1] there is no evidence. But I cannot believe that he settled on the tragic subject till his political hopes had been partly disappointed. I should conjecture that till about 1644 or 1645 he clung to the Arthuriad.

But if Milton intended to supplement his great epic by a tragedy, perhaps too by a brief epic, of which *Samson Agonistes* and *Paradise Regained* may have been the execution (tardy but according to plan), it is probable that he meant to write in prose also. Critics usually assume tacitly or explicitly that Milton was diverted to prose, a medium which he acknowledges to be not fully congenial, by the events of the time, and that but for them he would not have written in prose at all. Further still, some assume that these events provided Milton's mind with most of the material for his prose works. To disprove this last assumption has been one of Hanford's chief efforts in his studies on Milton;[2] and although every one may not be ready to go the whole way with him, there is little doubt that he is often right. In fact, each fresh occasion in the prose period evoked rather than created ideas in Milton's mind. His first prose writing

1. See pp. 165–6 below.

2. See especially 'The Date of Milton's *De Doctrina Christiana*', in *Studies in Philology*, 1920, 314. 'Beside the ambition born of the aesthetic idealism of his youth to leave a work in poetry which posterity would not willingly let die, Milton came also to cherish the coördinate aim of instructing his contemporaries on all the great issues of public and private life. His prose works are not, as they have sometimes been held to be, merely or even primarily partisan or occasional, though they do for the most part attach themselves to immediate events. The truth is rather that Milton saw in the conditions of the revolutionary period an unrivalled opportunity to promote several great reforms, hitherto impossible of realization, by bringing the public mind to envisage in practical form the ideals which had become a part of his own thinking as a result of the meditative study of his early years.'

attacked the Bishops, but it cannot be doubted that for years Milton had nursed his fury against the doings of Laud. There is even a hint that he held unorthodox opinions on marriage before his own particular case forced them into the public view.[1] Moreover the special occasion could not possibly explain a work of personal satisfaction like the *De Doctrina Christiana*, the uncontroversial histories of Britain and Muscovia, or even so faintly topical a work as the *Tractate on Education*. Milton regarded himself as a teacher and the epic the highest mode of teaching; but it is highly improbable, even if there had been no political crisis in his lifetime, that he would have kept unpublished the sum of the comprehensive studies he imposed on himself as a condition of writing a heroic poem. True, the tone of his prose works would have been quieter, and they might have followed not preceded his epic or epics; but that they would never have been written I cannot believe.

In trying to settle this question we cannot neglect Milton's own statements about his prose. At the end of the autobiographical passage in the *Defensio Secunda*[2] he speaks of his pamphlets hitherto published as if they were an ordered consecutive exposition of the idea of liberty in the various spheres of life. That they were called forth by specific events he ignores, and beyond doubt conveys a false impression in so doing. This is how he introduces his pamphlets on divorce:

> When, therefore, I perceived that there were three species of liberty which are essential to the happiness of social life – religious, domestic, and civil; and as I had already written concerning the first, and the magistrates were strenuously active in obtaining the third, I determined to turn my attention to the second, or the domestic species. As this seemed to involve three material questions, the conditions of the conjugal tie, the education of the children, and the free publication of the thoughts, I made them objects of distinct consideration. I explained my sentiments, not only concerning the solemnization of the marriage, but the dissolution, if circumstances rendered it necessary.

That Milton conveys a false impression by saying nothing about his own marriage and its effect on his ideas on divorce is obvious; I doubt if any one could be persuaded that Milton would have written his divorce pamphlets just when he did, but for this disaster: but I do not think we need conclude that the whole passage concerning the pamphlets is false. He may suppress a large portion of the truth,

---

1. Same reference: footnote. But here Hanford goes too far in underestimating the shock to Milton of his unsuccessful marriage.
2. Bohn, i. 258–9.

94

but we need not therefore conclude that what he did say was a mass of lies. On the contrary, it is reasonable to accept his statement that they express a coherent body of ordered thought, which could only have been formed in the meditative period before the Civil War. If, then, we remember that Milton's prose contains the substance of much quiet meditation which would have been published, though in a different form, quite apart from political events, we may perhaps be less reluctant to spend our time in reading it.

'Milton's prose works', wrote Dowden in his interesting study of them,[1] 'form the true complement of the poems.' With this, after what has been said above, I shall hardly disagree. But the prose works are so very much more. They are a very interesting, one might say tragic, display of the changes that took place in Milton's mind; and in a blurred way they preserve fragments of the epic Milton would have written, had political events been otherwise. As far as I know, these two sides of Milton's prose have not been sufficiently dealt with, and it is to them that I shall mainly keep.

But there is another introductory question to be answered before I come to the pamphlets themselves: the old question whether Milton did or did not benefit by entering into religious and political controversy. It is a question that has received conflicting and rather confused answers: chiefly because it is not one but several questions.

First, did Milton gain by living when he did, at a time when religious excitement had such a large relative importance in men's minds, rather than at the time of Spenser or of Pope? This is a question that needs stating so that it may not confuse the other questions, rather than answering.

Secondly, was Milton right in concerning himself with religious and political controversy? Undoubtedly he was. Like other great artists he could not afford to cut himself off from the main sources of the mental activity of his age. It was as necessary for Milton to be interested in the Episcopacy as for Homer to be interested in battles, or Virgil in Roman Imperialism.

Thirdly, was he right not merely in thinking about religious and political controversy but in taking an active part in it? The answer is somewhat equivocal. Granted his character, he was right: but this very fact argues in his character a sort of defect. Certainly he would have been, as he himself explained, false to himself had he held aloof. Holding that poetry was not an end in itself but a means to good and in particular to national good, he could not but measure it with other methods of promoting the same end. He was also aware

1. In *Puritan and Anglican* (1900), 133–96.

95

that poetry more often concerned posterity than the present. When therefore a revolution had begun, likely (as he thought) to achieve at a blow the very ends he had hoped to further by the slow process of poetry, it would have been criminal to prefer his own glory as poet to the end now more likely to be reached by direct action. All his efforts must go to encouraging the deeds of others. The argument is perfectly sound, and most writers have justly praised Milton for the way he behaved. Yet this behaviour, though creditable to the Milton of fact, indicates a defect of character. A man of a more capacious mind and a better knowledge of human nature would have known that the premises on which Milton argued were false, that no revolution could change men's hearts in the way Milton imagined, and that the exhortations and denunciations which Milton indulged in would be powerless to affect the issue in any large degree. To have kept aloof in the controversy would have required great strength of mind, but Milton had sufficient. It was his judgment, not his strength of mind, that was at fault. A Shakespeare would have had the sense to keep out of active controversy.

The fourth question is whether Milton gained by having his Arthuriad upset by a violent political event interrupting his plans just when it did? Would he have been luckier if the Civil War had occurred ten years later? There are two chief reasons why he may have gained: one that a sudden crisis exercised and brought out his character; the other that without the Civil War *Paradise Lost*, as we have it, simply could not have existed. The first seems quite false. *Lycidas*, as I understand the poem, is in itself sufficient proof of a mental strength so trained as to be in no need of unusual exercise. Exercise indeed would be rather dangerous than otherwise, apt to develop the mental muscles unduly. Mental strength had been the most obvious of Milton's native gifts, and he had never omitted to foster it: it was the balancing quality of sympathy that needed developing. The other reason is more cogent and leads to a more interesting question. Of course *Paradise Lost* could not have been what it is without Milton's entry into politics and the disappointment of his hopes; perhaps it would not have been written at all: but can we be certain that something preferable would not have resulted? For it is not as if the case were between *Paradise Lost* and a possible Arthuriad: more truly it is between *Paradise Lost* and two possible long poems. When Milton entered politics he was of all things most plainly an idealist, a young man with a passion for reforming the world and with the high and quite irrational hope of

effecting some great reform. But the trend of politics ruined his hopes
before he could turn them into literature. The fire of his early hope
is, in the pamphlets, obscured by smoke; in *Paradise Lost* it is recognized only in the embers. It may be useless but not unreasonable to
regret that in no work does it burn with a powerful, bright, and
steady flame. For, had the promise of *Lycidas* been fulfilled, had his
ardour received no untimely check, he might have written, perhaps
near the date of *Areopagitica*, a poem of hope, whose hero had the
power of action without the dubious morality of Satan, and the
impetus of whose verse matched throughout the first two books of
Paradise Lost. As things are we have his songs of disillusionment, his
Songs of Experience; his Songs of Innocence are quite over-
shadowed. In this he is the very opposite of Shelley, who had he
lived might have given us not only his Song of Innocence, *Prometheus
Unbound*, but his Song of Experience, of which the *Triumph of Life*
may give us a faint hint. The analogy of Shelley may serve too to
show that an ardent young idealist may awake to the realities of life
without the stress of political disappointment. It was an awakened
and disillusioned Shelley who, referring to Emilia Viviani and
Epipsychidion, spoke of the error of 'seeking in a mortal image the
likeness of what is, perhaps, eternal'. Similarly, Milton would have
become disillusioned, would have learnt that mankind is not swiftly
or easily altered; and I cannot think that he would have failed to
embody that disillusionment in a second great poem.

If *Paradise Lost* presented a complete unity, not merely of construction but of tone, then the above remarks would be futile. But,
as I shall point out, the tone changes during the course of the poem,
and the later books ally themselves more closely to *Paradise Regained*
than to the activity of the opening. It would be possible to imagine a
division of form better corresponding to Milton's change of feeling
than the present division into *Paradise Lost* and *Paradise Regained*.

Finally, it is well that the uncommon exuberance of Milton's
prose style[1] should be stressed. People are still in the habit of contrasting the richness of Shakespeare's vocabulary with the confined-
ness of Milton's. It is perfectly true that Milton's verbal range in his
poems is considerably smaller than Shakespeare's in his plays. But it
should be evident that if Milton was deficient, it was from choice not
necessity. As Raleigh said of *Paradise Lost* and *Samson Agonistes*, 'For
the material of those palaces whole provinces were pillaged, and the

---

1. Raleigh in his *Milton*, chapter 2, has an admirable account of Milton's prose
style.

waste might furnish forth a city.' And the proof lies in the prose, with its extraordinary range of diction from simplest Saxon to most elaborate Latinization. Moreover, there is a bloom on the prose diction that is somehow absent from all Milton's verse except perhaps the *Nativity Ode*, a bloom he deliberately sacrificed to the sterner qualities of power and concentration. Here is a passage, typical of a large number, illustrating both the richness of vocabulary and the freshness of phrase. It comes from the pamphlet *Of Prelatical Episcopacy*.

Notwithstanding this clearness, and that by all evidence of argument, Timothy and Titus (whom our prelates claim to imitate only in the controlling part of their office) had rather the vicegerency of an apostleship committed to them than the ordinary charge of a bishopric, as being men of an extraordinary calling; yet to verify that which St. Paul foretold of succeeding times, when men began to have itching ears, then, not contented with the plentiful and wholesome fountains of the gospel, they began after their own lusts to heap to themselves teachers, and, as if the divine scripture wanted a supplement and were to be eked out, they cannot think any doubt resolved and any doctrine confirmed, unless they run to that indigested heap and fry of authors which they call antiquity. Whatsoever time, or the heedless hand of blind chance, hath drawn down from of old to this present in her huge drag-net, whether fish or sea-weed, shells or shrubs, unpicked, unchosen, those are the fathers. Seeing therefore some men, deeply conversant in books, have had so little care of late to give the world a better account of their reading than by divulging needless tractates stuffed with specious names of Ignatius and Polycarpus, with fragments of old martyrologies and legends, to distract and stagger the multitude of credulous readers and mislead them from their strong guards and places of safety under the tuition of holy writ; it came into my thoughts to persuade myself, setting all distances and nice respects aside, that I could do religion and my country no better service for the time than doing my utmost endeavour to recall the people of God from this vain foraging after straw and to reduce them to their firm stations under the standard of the gospel, by making appear to them, first the insufficiency, next the inconveniency, and lastly the impiety of these gay testimonies that their great doctors would bring them to dote on.[1]

In this passage there is combined the richness of the Elizabethans with the wit of the Metaphysicals. The wealth of phrase-making, of new, vital conjunctions of words is amazing; and the element of wit, of surprise, is most evident. What could be simpler and yet more

1. Bohn, ii. 421-2.

satisfyingly unexpected than 'these gay testimonies'? Milton's prose, then, is the direct evidence of what might be inferred from the poems: that he possesses a mind not merely powerful and sublime but of uncommon wealth and diversity.

CHAPTER TWO

Pamphlets against Episcopacy:

I. GENERAL

Date	Milton's age	Writing or event in Milton's life	Contemporary event
1641, May-June	32	*Reformation in England*	Death of Strafford. Discussions in Parliament between Root-and-Branch men and moderate Episcopalians
1641, June-July	32	*Of Prelatical Episcopacy*	
1641, July-Aug.	32	*Animadversions upon the Remonstrant's Defence*	Root-and-Branch Bill introduced
1641, Nov.	32		Irish Rebellion. Grand Remonstrance
1642, Jan.	33		Attempted impeachment of five members of Parliament. Flight of Charles from London
1642, Jan.-March	33	*Reason of Church Government*	
1642, March-April	33	*Apology for Smectymnuus*	Preparations for war

To ANY one who has studied the works of Milton in the order in which they were written it will be clear enough, first, that there is a gradual but highly important change of tone in the prose; second, that the early pamphlets connect quite naturally with what Milton had last written. Far too often Milton's prose has been treated as a static, an alien mass, a kind of obstructing rock in the stream; which can be commented on as a whole and without reference to dates or developments. How Milton changed during the prose period I shall try to point out as I go; the connections between the last poems of his youth and the early pamphlets must be mentioned here.

The final group of Milton's previous writings had begun with *Ad Patrem* or *Lycidas* and ended with *Epitaphium Damonis:* it includes anything written in Italy. There are three very important elements in that group which reappear in the anti-episcopal pamphlets: literary ambition, patriotism, and a distinctly Renaissance mentality.

Literary ambition is plain from the references to future projects in *Mansus* and the *Epitaphium Damonis*; it is, as I pointed out, at the very centre of the real meaning of *Lycidas*. In a different form it is no less apparent in the pamphlets. I refer, not to the discussion of poetry in *Reason of Church Government* (which has little contemporary application but gives an account of the poetical plans Milton had formed when he was in Italy), but to one or two passages in which Milton attaches his poetical ambitions to the imagined religious and political rebirth of his country. He had planned an Arthuriad, a national poem: now its application is to be made topical. Here are the important passages. Set in that extraordinary prayer, the freest outburst of passion in all Milton's works, which ends his first pamphlet, *Reformation in England*, comes the sentence beginning:

> Then [that is, when the work of reformation is complete] amidst the hymns and hallelujahs of saints, some one may perhaps be heard offering at high strains in new and lofty measure to sing and celebrate thy divine mercies and marvellous judgments in this land throughout all ages.[1]

The 'some one' referred to at the beginning of this passage is of course Milton himself. The same thought occurs in a passage in the *Animadversions upon the Remonstrant's Defence*, to which I shall have to refer again:

> And he that now for haste snatches up a plain ungarnished present as a thank-offering to thee, which could not be deferred in regard of thy so many late deliverances wrought for us one upon another, may then perhaps take up a harp, and sing thee an elaborate song to generations.[2]

And finally in the *Apology for Smectymnuus*, in his panegyric on the ruling majority in the Long Parliament, he expresses his hope that he may celebrate their deeds more worthily in the future, that is, clearly, through the medium of poetry.[3]

There is, indeed, in these early pamphlets no idea that the plans for a great poem are to be postponed unduly.[4] In politics the incredible was happening and would be fulfilled with godsent swiftness, and Milton sees himself now the poet, not of the slower

---

1. Bohn, ii. 418.   2. Bohn, iii. 72.   3. ibid., 145.

4. When, in *Reason of Church Government* (Bohn, ii. 481), he writes, 'Neither do I think it shame to covenant with any knowing reader, that for some few years yet I may go on trust with him toward the payment of what I am now indebted', he is referring to his own present unpreparedness, not to any interruption likely to result from political events.

inscrutable ways of Providence (hopefully as he might have treated that theme), but of a grand culminating reformation of his so much loved country.

The second link between the previous group of writings and the early pamphlets is patriotism: both the love of country and the desire to serve it. In *Mansus* love of country had shown itself: in the pamphlets it is so frequently expressed that there is no need to emphasize its presence. But like his poetic dreams his desire to serve his country has somewhat altered. His first idea, as pointed out above, included the notion that it was patriotic to write an important poem in your mother tongue; you automatically glorified your country by doing this. But now a more obviously patriotic task has presented itself: that of trumpeting abroad the achievements of his own generation of Englishmen. He will be the mouthpiece, rather than the creator, of honour in England.

As to the third link, the presence of ideas springing from the Italian Renaissance, that Milton had them in the front of his mind at the time of his Italian tour is evident from the ease with which he entered the cultured society of that country, while in the more philosophical of the anti-episcopal tracts, *Reformation in England* and *Reason of Church Government* especially, much of the background of thought is of the Renaissance. Take for instance the stately panegyric of the art of government at the beginning of the second book of *Reformation in England*:

It is a work good and prudent to be able to guide one man; of larger extended virtue to order well one house: but to govern a nation piously and justly, which only is to say happily, is for a spirit of the greatest size, and divinest mettle. And certainly of no less a mind, nor of less excellence in another way, were they who by writing laid the solid and true foundations of this science. . . .[1]

Nothing could be more centrally of the Renaissance than this with its exaltation of the great individual, its faith in theory and in pre-cept, and its freshness redeeming platitude. The idea is expanded in the splendid first chapter of *Reason of Church Government*,[2] while the autobiographical passage in the same pamphlet contains a little Renaissance treatise on literary criticism. I do not mean to say that in the earliest pamphlets there is not much alien matter, much topical argumentation which cannot be dignified by the name of

1. Bohn, ii. 390.

2. Liljegren (*Studies in Milton*, xl.) sees the influence of Machiavelli in a passage in this pamphlet.

any great trend of thought, but a great deal of the residue belongs without doubt to Renaissance habits of mind.

These elements common to the last poems of Milton's youth and the earliest group of pamphlets make us feel that the Milton of the prose is far from being a temporary intruder on the poet with his garland and singing robes about him, but a man with the same basic aims, the same hopes of poetic fame to be realized quickly. But there is one big difference. In the passage of *Lycidas* denouncing the clergy, a passage often quoted as foreshadowing the controversial prose, the accent of national hope is missing. Vengeance indeed will fall, but the 'two-handed engine' is too vague to be interpreted as the minister of immediate earthly retribution. There is no hint of a shortly expected paradise on earth. In the early pamphlets Milton has abandoned his whole mind to such an expectation. Doubtless he had always been the fervent ingenuous idealist, but the full extent of his sanguine inexperience is hidden till the prose begins. Stronger than all the controversial bluster, the juggling with Scripture, the immediate anti-prelatical fury, is this dazzling hope of a new and purified England. 'To Milton', wrote J. W. Hales,[1] 'when the Long Parliament met in the autumn of 1640, it had seemed that a new day was dawning for England and mankind.

> The world's great age begins anew,
> The golden years return'.

And Hales goes on to add the Wordsworth of the early days of the French Revolution to the comparison:

> Bliss was it in that dawn to be alive,
> But to be young was very heaven.

This idea of Milton's feelings when he began pamphleteering needs propagating;[2] for, unless it is thoroughly grasped and given scope, his character is misunderstood and the disillusionment of *Paradise Lost* cannot be estimated.

In speaking of Milton's enormous hopes I do not mean to imply that it was unreasonable for a man who valued liberty to be elated at the summoning of the Long Parliament, the collapse of the Laudian machinery, and the execution of Strafford; even the most sober might indulge their hope of many solid political reforms. But there was in the nature of Milton's hopes, as revealed in the anti-

1. In his introduction to *Areopagitica* (Clarendon Press), viii-ix.

2. This Grierson has been doing both in his preface to the Florence Press edition of Milton's poems and in *The Criterion* for September 1928, 20.

episcopal pamphlets, something the very reverse of sober. Allowing for the exaltation natural in the years 1640 to 1642, we have to admit that Milton had an unusually sanguine temperament exaggerated by an unusual ignorance of the nature of common humanity. It is not for nothing that he speaks so warmly in the *Apology for Smectymnuus* of the Utopia form, calling it

that grave and noble invention, which the greatest and sublimest wits in sundry ages, Plato in Critias, and our two famous countrymen, the one in his Utopia, the other in his New Atlantis, chose, I may not say as a field, but as a mighty continent, wherein to display the largeness of their spirits, by teaching this our world better and exacter things than were yet known or used.[1]

As to human nature in England, it may suffer from ignorance, but given proper instruction it is full of virtuous possibilities. Of the Englishman he says:

And verily if we look at his native towardliness in the roughcast without breeding, some nation or other may haply be better composed to a natural civility and right judgment than he. But if he get the benefit once of a wise and well-rectified nurture, which must first come in general from the godly vigilance of the church, I suppose that wherever mention is made of countries, manners, or men, the English people, among the first that shall be praised, may deserve to be accounted a right pious, right honest, and right hardy nation.[2]

Whether Englishmen are, compared with other nations, naturally prone to instruction we need not discuss: the point is that Milton seemed to think that it was possible to impose a 'wise and well-rectified nurture' by a few Acts of Parliament. In another passage he says that when superstition has been defeated (in other words, when prelacy has been abolished) 'all honest and legal freedom of civil life cannot be long absent.'[3] He had no conception of the intractability of the human mind.

And so, overrating the effect of institutions on the fabric of human nature, he is in a furious hurry to complete with utter thoroughness the reformation that has just begun.

Speedy and vehement were the reformations of all the good kings of Judah, though the people had been nuzzled in idolatry ever so long before.[4]

1. Bohn, iii. 108–9.
2. *Reason of Church Government*, Bohn, ii. 470.   3. ibid., 503.
4. *Reformation in England*, ibid., 410.

And thus I leave it as a declared truth, that neither the fear of sects, no, nor rebellion, can be a fit plea to stay reformation, but rather to push it forward with all possible diligence and speed.[1]

Moreover, if we are not careful to seize God's gifts, we may lose them.

The door of grace turns upon smooth hinges, wide opening to send out, but soon shutting to recall the precious offers of mercy to a nation: which, unless watchfulness and zeal, two quicksighted and ready-handed virgins, be there in our behalf to receive, we lose: and still the oftener we lose, the straiter the door opens, and the less is offered. This is all we get by demurring in God's service.[2]

But though there may be danger if God's gifts are rejected, Milton cannot believe but that a new age is at hand. He speaks of 'our time of parliament, the very jubilee and resurrection of the state', and again of 'the present age, which is to us an age of ages wherein God is manifestly come down among us, to do some remarkable good to our church or state'.[3] It is the hand of God that is plainly guiding the Parliament in their acts:

And indeed, if we consider the general concourse of suppliants, the free and ready admittance, the willing and speedy redress in what is possible, it will not seem much otherwise, than as if some divine commission from heaven were descended to take into hearing and commiseration the long and remediless afflictions of this kingdom;

. . . And whereas at other times we count it ample honour when God vouchsafes to make man the instrument and subordinate worker of his gracious will, such acceptation have their prayers found with him, that to them he hath been pleased to make himself the agent, and immediate performer of their desires; dissolving their difficulties when they are thought inexplicable, cutting out ways for them where no passage could be seen; as who is there so regardless of divine Providence, that from late occurrences will not confess? . . . Whence only it is that I have not feared, though many wise men have miscarried in praising great designs before the utmost event, because I see who is their assistant, who is their confederate, who hath engaged his omnipotent arm to support and crown with success their faith, their fortitude, their just and magnanimous actions, till he have brought to pass all that expected good which, his servants trust, is in his thoughts to bring upon this land in the full and perfect reformation of his church.[4]

1. *Reason of Church Government*, Bohn, ii. 472.
2. ibid., 470.   3. *Animadversions*, Bohn, iii. 47 and 69.
4. *Apology for Smectymnuus*, ibid., 149–50.

Finally, expressing the fullest vehemence of his hope, there are the two passages in the course of which Milton refers to his personal aspiration of being the poet of the new age. I quote first from *Animadversions upon the Remonstrant's Defence.*

O perfect and accomplish thy glorious acts! for men may leave their works unfinished, but thou art a God, thy nature is perfection: shouldst thou bring us thus far onward from Egypt to destroy us in this wilderness, though we deserve, yet thy great name would suffer in the rejoicing of thine enemies, and the deluded hope of all thy servants. When thou hast settled peace in the church and righteous judgment in the kingdom, then shall all thy saints address their voices of joy and triumph to thee, standing on the shore of that Red Sea into which our enemies had almost driven us. And he that now for haste snatches up a plain ungarnished present as a thank-offering to thee, which could not be deferred in regard of thy so many late deliverances wrought for us one upon another, may then perhaps take up a harp, and sing thee an elaborate song to generations. In that day it shall no more be said as in scorn, this or that was never held so till this present age, when men have better learnt that the times and seasons pass along under thy feet to go and come at thy bidding: and as thou didst dignify our fathers' days with many revelations above all the foregoing ages, since thou tookest the flesh; so thou canst vouchsafe to us (though unworthy) as large a portion of thy Spirit as thou pleasest: for who shall prejudice thy all-governing will? seeing the power of thy grace is not passed away with the primitive times, as fond and faithless men imagine, but thy kingdom is now at hand, and thou standing at the door. Come forth out of thy royal chambers, O Prince of all the kings of the earth! put on the visible robes of thy imperial majesty, take up that unlimited sceptre which thy Almighty Father hath bequeathed thee; for now the voice of thy bride calls thee, and all creatures sigh to be renewed.[1]

Such lyrical fervour for a changed world joined with so blind a belief in its immediate possibility can be matched in English literature in Shelley alone. 'Thy kingdom is now at hand, and thou standing at the door': one thinks of Asia ready to be united at last with Prometheus. And 'all creatures sigh to be renewed' reminds one of the longing of the earth in Shelley's poem to be made perfect and of 'the unpastured sea hungering for calm'. Here is the second passage, from *Reformation in England*:

O how much more glorious will those former deliverances appear, when we shall know them not only to have saved us from greatest miseries past, but to have reserved us for greatest happiness to come! Hitherto thou hast but freed us, and that not fully, from the unjust and tyrannous claim of thy foes; now unite us entirely, and appropriate us to thyself, tie us everlastingly in willing homage to the prerogative of thy eternal throne. . . . Then, amidst

1. Bohn, iii. 72.

the hymns and hallelujahs of saints, some one may perhaps be heard offering at high strains in new and lofty measures to sing and celebrate thy divine mercies and marvellous judgments in this land throughout all ages; whereby this great and warlike nation, instructed and inured to the fervent and continual practice of truth and righteousness, and casting far from her the rags of her whole vices, may press on hard to that high and happy emulation to be found the soberest, wisest, and most Christian people at that day, when thou, the eternal and shortly expected King, shalt open the clouds to judge the several kingdoms of the world, and distributing national honours and rewards to religious and just commonwealths, shalt put an end to all earthly tyrannies, proclaiming thy universal and mild monarchy through heaven and earth; where they undoubtedly, that by their labours, counsels, and prayers, have been earnest for the common good of religion and their country, shall receive above the inferior orders of the blessed, the regal addition of principalities, legions, and thrones into their glorious titles, and in supereminence of beatific vision, progressing the dateless and irrevoluble circle of eternity, shall clasp inseparable hands with joy and bliss, in over-measure for ever.[1]

Such was the height of apocalyptic ecstasy to which Milton's hopes carried him. Except for one moment[2] he will allow no possibility of disappointment to enter his mind, but this single moment is thereby all the more significant: it occurs in the *Animadversions* about a page before the passage above quoted. Milton speaks of the original Reformation as an 'early thaw' and pictures the sun in his own day to stand at noon. Dreadful indeed if it should freeze once more with the sun at the zenith!

O if we freeze at noon after their early thaw, let us fear lest the sun for ever hide himself, and turn his orient steps from our ingrateful horizon, justly condemned to be eternally benighted. Which dreadful judgment, O thou the everbegotten Light and perfect Image of the Father! intercede, may never come upon us.

It was this dreadful, unthinkable judgment that came upon the England to which at that time Milton had attached all the fervour of hope of which his mind was capable. It is from the prose works that we can see this fervour of hope, and hence measure the disappointment that lies at the back of *Paradise Lost*.

1. Bohn, ii. 418–19.

2. In the autobiographical passage in *Reason of Church Government* (Bohn, ii. 475) he does indeed mention the possibility of the church being brought under heavy oppression, but he is here clearly reminiscent, referring to a time previous to the earliest pamphlets when the issue appeared much more doubtful than in the year when the anti-episcopal pamphlets were written.

Milton inspires too much awe, as a rule, to appear ludicrous. He suffered too much for it to be seemly to laugh at him. Still, a smile may be allowed at the thought of him raising his voice, not only among the true fighters for liberty, but among facile Millennarian fanatics and the mob of so-called Puritans screaming 'No Popery' and 'Reformation'. It is not so much because he raised his voice that we may be permitted to smile, but because he believed in that rabble as in himself, imagining it to know what it was shouting for and to have feelings as noble as his own.

CHAPTER THREE

Pamphlets against Episcopacy:

2. SEPARATE WORKS

MILTON's first prose work, *Reformation in England*, is, more purely than any other, the creation of a scholar and a poet. It is in the light of his long programme of historical studies that he argues against episcopacy. He seeks to prove that the original Reformation in England remained for various reasons incomplete: now is the time for its consummation. Episcopacy would have no historical ground in antiquity, being but a corruption of the earliest Christian practice. In the poetical quality of parts of its prose this pamphlet yields to none. There is an indication in it too that Milton was writing with his mind on his early poems. The degrading influence of superstition and ritual on the religious mind is described in language very like what he uses in *Comus* to describe the degradation of the moral mind through lust.

The superstitious man by his good will is an atheist; but being scared from thence by the pangs and gripes of a boiling conscience, all in a pudder shuffles up to himself such a God and such a worship as is most agreeable to remedy his fear; which fear of his, as also is his hope, fixed only upon the flesh, renders likewise the whole faculty of his apprehension carnal; and all the inward acts of worship, issuing from the native strength of the soul, run out lavishly to the upper skin, and there harden into a crust of formality.[1]

Compare this with

>   but when lust
> By unchaste looks, loose gestures, and foul talk,
> But most by leud and lavish act of sin,
> Lets in defilement to the inward parts,
> The soul grows clotted by contagion,
> Imbodies and imbrutes, till she quite loose
> The divine property of her first being.[2]

'*Lavish* act of *sin*' suggesting '*lavishly* to the upper *skin*' is an amusing example of how the unconscious mind of an author can work.

I seem to detect in the opening of the pamphlet something absent from any other: a tremor in Milton's mind of eagerness to begin, of excitement at having embarked on a task which, if not the work he had specially prepared for, was at least one which he considered

1. Bohn, ii. 365–6.   2. *Comus*, 463–9.

of the greatest weight and greater than any he had yet undertaken. One's mind goes back to *Lycidas* and the emotional strain therein expressed of being unready and unable to begin to be articulate.

In this earliest pamphlet there are very evident some of the unchanging features of Milton's mind, just as the main features of the prose style are there, fully formed. There is first of all an emotional integrity: never the slightest suspicion that Milton in any way tampers with his emotions. But there is also a very indifferent sense of the relative importance of facts. The whole discussion about the episcopacy is animated by the conviction, one of the essentials of Milton's emotional constitution, of the dignity and importance of the individual: the conviction which in the end drove him from all forms of institutional religion to a position where he thought himself to be alone with his God. But he exaggerates the importance of the fact of the episcopacy. For the moment nothing but the episcopacy matters: it is nothing but the episcopacy that is hindering the new heaven on earth. Doubtless Milton was emotionally right in attacking the Laudian system, but how wrong in seeing in it the only impediment! Centring all his wrath on the prelates, he sees nothing but good in his future abhorrences, the monarchy and the Scottish form of church government.

What greater debasement can there be to royal dignity, whose towering and steadfast height rests upon the unmovable foundations of justice, and heroic virtue, than to chain it in a dependence of subsisting, or ruining, to the painted battlements and gaudy rottenness of prelatry, which want but one puff of the king's to blow them down like a pasteboard house built of court-cards?[1]

The second pamphlet, *Of Prelatical Episcopacy*, dealing with the single point that episcopacy cannot be deduced from the apostolical times, is of small importance.

From the *Animadversions upon the Remonstrant's Defence against Smectymnuus* one fine passage has already been quoted. There are a few other pieces of eloquence in it, but the bulk is in the most curious and most tedious of Milton's styles, that of heavy, hectoring jocularity. Bishop Hall, the 'Remonstrant', had attacked the Smectymnuan writings; and Milton proceeds to quote fragments of Hall's attack and, isolating them from their context, to load them with scorn. Here is a typical passage. The Remonstrant, wishing to call attention to the good works of the Church of England under the Bishops' guidance, asks a series of rhetorical questions, to which Milton insists on giving the least desired answers:

1. Bohn, ii. 397.

Remonstrant. Could you see no colleges, no hospitals built?

Answer. At that primero of piety, the pope and cardinals are the better gamesters, and will cog a die into heaven before you.

Rem. No churches re-edified?

Ans. Yes, more churches than souls.

Rem. No seduced persons reclaimed?

Ans. More reclaimed persons seduced.

Rem. No hospitality kept?

Ans. Bacchanalias good store in every bishop's family, and good gleeking.

Rem. No diligence in preaching?

Ans. Scarce any preaching at all.

Rem. No holiness in living?

Ans. No.

Rem. Truly, brethren, I can say no more, but that the fault is in your eyes.

Ans. If you can say no more than this, you were a proper Remonstrant to stand up for the whole tribe!

Rem. Wipe them and look better.

Ans. Wipe your fat corpulencies out of our light.[1]

The whole passage from which this extract comes shows energy, but its manners are deplorable. Why was it that Milton behaved so discourteously in controversial writing? Not that in this particular pamphlet he attacks the character of his opponent: he confines himself mostly to bishops in general. But he was very soon to resort to personal abuse; and the whole question of his controversial methods may conveniently be discussed at this point.

It is sometimes thought that the unpleasantness which appears to mark Milton's method of controversy extended to all his relations with men and women; that he was a proud, isolated, and vindictive man, who not only pursued his political opponents with flagrant abuse, but flogged his nephews, victimized his daughters, treated his wives like domestic servants, and naturally died friendless. This notion (which I have put in its extreme form) is quite false. It is true that Milton, like other schoolmasters of that age, was free with the rod. But Aubrey records of him that 'as he was severe on one hand, so he was most familiar and free in his conversation to those to whom most sowre in his way of education'. And one of those very nephews speaks of Milton's 'generous nature, more inclinable to reconciliation than to perseverance in anger and revenge'. That he made his daughters read to him in languages they did not understand seems undoubted, but the old notion that he used them as his amanuenses has been exploded. Still, he probably expected a great deal from the members of his household. When it comes to manners,

1. Bohn, iii. 89–90.

to the way Milton treated his friends and acquaintances, all the evidence points to refinement, courtesy, and generosity. Of these qualities his relations with his fellow-undergraduates and with his Italian hosts have already given illustrations; his reconciliation with Mary Powell and his good nature in harbouring her many relations in their distress are later instances. And the evidence is strong that he never lacked abundant friends. Aubrey tells us that he was 'of a cheerful humour' and 'extreme pleasant in his conversation'. Further, he showed no personal spite against political opponents. His brother Christopher, though a Royalist, found refuge in Milton's house when the Royalist cause was lost. His earliest biographer, too, is quite explicit concerning his political toleration.

And as hee was not link'd to one Party by self Interest, so neither was hee divided from the other by Animosity; but was forward to do any of them good offices, when their particular cases afforded him ground to appeer on thir behalf. And especially, if on the score of Witt or learning, they could lay claim to his peculiar patronage. Of which were instances, among others, the Grandchild of the famous Spencer, a Papist suffering in his concerns in Ireland, and Sir William Davenant when taken Prisoner, for both whom he procur'd relief.

At the very time, too, of his writing the *Animadversions* Milton was in the habit of frequenting a fashionable society that could hardly have agreed with his passionate support of 'Smectymnuus'; for Phillips recounts how in 1641 Milton moved to Aldersgate Street,

he himself giving an example to those under him . . . of hard study, and spare diet; only this advantage he had, that once in three weeks or a month, he would drop into the society of some young sparks of his acquaintance, the chief whereof were Mr. Alphey and Mr. Miller, two gentlemen of Gray's-Inn, the beaus of those times, but nothing so bad as those now-a-days; with these gentlemen he would so far make bold with his body, as now and then to keep a gawdy-day.[1]

Evidence of Milton's good manners in society could be multiplied. But the puzzle is: how can they be squared with his deplorable methods of controversy? It is true that rudeness in conducting a written dispute was general at the time, and had been made respectable by classical precedent. But this is not sufficient explanation:

1. 'J'ay ouy dire à Silvius, excellent medecin de Paris, que, pour garder que les forces de nostre estomac ne s'aparessent, il est bon, une fois le mois les esveiller par cet excez, et les picquer pour les garder de s'engourdir. (Montaigne, *Essais*, ii, 2, *De l'Yvrongnerie*). For possible links between Milton and Montaigne see my *Studies in Milton*, 130–1.

first, because Milton is much ruder than custom positively demanded; secondly, because he was quite capable of breaking a custom, and his extreme rudeness was probably a deliberate choice. The true answer is that in controversy Milton was really quite impersonal. Something of the sort has already[1] been detected in the comic portions of his Vacation Exercise at Cambridge. There he set himself with a kind of abstract fury to his task of making fun. It was with a similar abstraction that he approached controversy. Believing passionately in the cause he was advocating, he set himself to advance it by any means, personal abuse included, that came handy. Aubrey records an interesting piece of information imparted by Edward Phillips.

> Whatever he wrote against monarchie was out of no animositie to the King's person, or out of any faction or interest, but out of a pure zeale to the Liberty of Mankind, which he thought would be greater under a free state than under a monarchiall government. His being so conversant in Livy and the Roman authors, and the greatnes he saw donne by the Roman commonwealth, and the vertue of their commanders induc't him to it.

Even when Milton seems most virulently personal, for instance in attacking Salmasius or Morus, he is really just as abstract. These personages are hypotheses who have to be damaged by every possible means. And damage them he does with the most brutal and virulent pertinacity; but he never envisages them as human beings.

This method of abstract controversy explains, though it does not excuse, the somewhat discreditable circumstances in which the *Defensio Secunda* was published. Milton had written this pamphlet on the supposition that the author of *Regii Sanguinis Clamor*, his object of attack, was one Alexander More, or Morus. Before publication it turned out that Morus had not written, only encouraged, the book. But Milton was not to be put off, and published his attack on Morus all the same. Aubrey's note on the incident is illuminating.

> *Memorand.* His sharp writing against Alexander More, of Holland, upon a mistake, notwithstanding he had given him by the Dutch ambassador all satisfaction to the contrary: *viz.* that the booke called *Clamor* was writt by Peter du Moulin. Well, that was all one; he having writt it, it should goe into the world; one of them was as bad as the other.

In other words, the genuine facts of personality mattered nothing in comparison with the abstract theme of dispute – and Milton's own masterful nature.

1. See p. 26 above.

I am not defending Milton's methods. On the contrary, this habit of bastraction is singularly productive of bitterness and misunderstanding. But if we realize Milton's extreme impersonality of approach, we may understand, and, as far as his own integrity goes, we may pardon. His whole mentality in a controversy is one more illustration of the strange ingenuousness of his nature. He fought without rancour, and assumed that his abuse would arouse no rancour in his opponents. When he discovered his mistake, as he did after his divorce tracts, he was pained and disappointed; but I do not believe that he ever allowed his disappointment to prompt him to personal spite.

Between the publication of *Animadversions* and *Reason of Church Government* intervened a period of over half a year, in which time a Bill had received Charles's consent excluding Bishops from the House of Lords. Whether because this signal victory for the Root-and-Branch party induced a temporary calm in Milton's mind, or merely because he was less hurried and was answering no particular piece of writing, *Reason of Church Government* is the stateliest and most philosophical of the five anti-episcopal tracts. It is also one of the noblest of the whole body of pamphlets, inferior to none in weightiness though not containing any passage whose gorgeous eloquence can equal the end of *Reformation in England* or parts of *Areopagitica*. As in all Milton's prose, there is a proportion of waste matter; but the introduction, the first, sixth, and seventh chapters of the first book, and the introduction and third chapter of the second book, form a fine bulk of weighty writing.

Milton's feeling for the importance of the individual is expressed even more clearly than in *Reformation in England*. Witness for instance the third chapter, in which he asserts with stately fervour the equality of the layman to any priest or dignitary of the church.

But when every good Christian, thoroughly acquainted with all those glorious privileges of sanctification and adoption, which render him more sacred than any dedicated altar or element, shall be restored to his right in the church, and not excluded from such place of spiritual government, as his Christian abilities, and his approved good life in the eye and testimony of the church shall prefer him to, this and nothing sooner will open his eyes to a wise and true valuation of himself.[1]

And he holds that 'the functions of church government ought to be free and open to any Christian man, though never so laic, if his capacity, his faith, and prudent demeanour, commend him'.

1. Bohn, ii. 496.

But *Reason of Church Government* expresses other beliefs fundamental in Milton, not found or at least not nearly so evident in *Reformation in England:* beliefs in self-reverence, in discipline, and in action. Proud and intensely conscious of his own personality, he had a natural reverence for himself and advocated self-reverence as a quality of the first importance in others. On its purely ethical side the belief must have been confirmed in his mind by education in classical and Renaissance literature. But, being the child of Puritan as well as of Renaissance thought, Milton had to invoke the sanction of theology; and he is easily able to argue that as sons of God we owe ourselves respect. Here is his double plea: the theological first, the purely personal at the end:

But he that holds himself in reverence and due esteem, both for the dignity of God's image upon him, and for the price of his redemption, which he thinks is visibly marked upon his forehead, accounts himself both a fit person to do the noblest and godliest deeds, and much better worth than to deject and defile, with such a debasement, and such a pollution as sin is, himself so highly ransomed and ennobled to a new friendship and filial relation with God. Nor can he fear so much the offence and reproach of others, as he dreads and would blush at the reflection of his own severe and modest eye upon himself, if it should see him doing or imagining that which is sinful, though in the deepest secrecy.[1]

As to discipline, no one looking back on the manner of Milton's past life can doubt the value he put on it. But although it controls his pride and individualism, it does not counter it. Discipline is for him primarily self-discipline, not external discipline: it is consonant with, and necessary to, liberty. Moreover, it is a control that gives the individual greater power than he had without it. It is this belief in discipline that is the theme of a passage near the beginning of *Reason of Church Government*; a passage not unlike Wordsworth's *Ode to Duty* in its sentiments, and of an equal though different beauty.

And certainly discipline is not only the removal of disorder; but if any visible shape can be given to divine things, the very visible shape and image of virtue, whereby she is not only seen in the regular gestures and motions of her heavenly paces as she walks, but also makes the harmony of her voice audible to mortal ears. Yea, the angels themselves, in whom no disorder is feared, as the apostle that saw them in his rapture describes, are distinguished and quaternioned into their celestial princedoms and satrapies, according as God himself has writ his imperial decrees through the great provinces of heaven. The state also of the blessed in paradise, though never so perfect, is not therefore left without discipline, whose golden surveying

1. Bohn, ii. 495.

reed marks out and measures every quarter and circuit of the New Jerusalem. Yet is it not to be conceived, that those eternal effluences of sanctity and love in the glorified saints should by this means be confined and cloyed with repetition of that which is prescribed, but that our happiness may orb itself into a thousand vagancies of glory and delight, and with a kind of eccentrical equation be, as it were, an invariable planet of joy and felicity; how much less can we believe that God would leave his frail and feeble, though not less beloved church here below, to the perpetual stumble of conjecture and disturbance in this our dark voyage, without the card and compass of discipline?[1]

Here Milton does not, as he did before in speaking of self-reverence, seek divine justification of his belief; rather he imposes his personal belief in discipline on heaven itself and with magnificent fallacy argues back from his own assumption. A second point of importance is found at the end: the reference to scriptural authority. Although Milton trusted his own inclinations he professed complete belief in the Bible. These inclinations were, broadly, humanistic; and as the Bible is not primarily a humanistic book, there was bound to be a conflict. In the passage quoted concerning self-reverence there was no conflict, for none was necessary: scriptural authority could easily be found for what Milton wanted. But this could not always be the case; notably when he dealt with the question of divorce. The question of Milton and the Bible will be discussed in the later chapter on Milton's beliefs.

Of the desire for action I shall say as little as possible beyond quoting, as I shall not be able to avoid mentioning it very frequently in the rest of the book: for the reason that it is perhaps the most important element in the sum of impulses that make up Milton's character. In action must be included of course the purely mental: activity might be in some ways a better word. The two passages quoted below are in the section of the pamphlet that deals with schisms. It had been argued that with the removal of episcopacy sects and schisms would arise. Milton replies that they may mean healthful activity and that their mere absence may mean torpor. Do the bishops, he asks, keep away schism?

If to bring a numb and chill stupidity of soul, an unactive blindness of mind, upon the people by their leaden doctrine, or no doctrine at all; if to persecute all knowing and zealous Christians by the violence of their courts, be to keep away schism, they keep schism away indeed: and by this kind of discipline all Italy and Spain is as purely and politicly kept from schism as

1. ibid., 442.

England hath been by them. With as good a plea might the dead-palsy boast to a man, It is I that free you from stitches and pains, and the troublesome feeling of cold and heat, of wounds and strokes: if I were gone, all these would molest you. The winter might as well vaunt itself against the spring, I destroy all noisome and rank weeds, I keep down all pestilent vapours; yes, and all wholesome herbs, and all fresh dews, by your violent and hide-bound frost: but when the gentle west winds shall open the fruitful bosom of the earth, thus overgirded by your imprisonment, then the flowers put forth and spring, and then the sun shall scatter the mists, and the manuring hand of the tiller shall root up all that burdens the soil without thank to your bondage.[1]

The passage is prophetic of *Paradise Lost* again. A 'numb and chill stupidity of soul, an unactive blindness of mind' were the besetting sins of Adam and Eve at the time of their fall. The other passage exhorts in the tone of a more famous one in *Areopagitica*.

Let us not therefore make these things [sects and errors] an incumbrance, or an excuse of our delay in reforming, which God sends us as an incitement to proceed with more honour and alacrity: for if there were no opposition, where were the trial of an unfeigned goodness and magnanimity? Virtue that wavers is not virtue, but vice revolted from itself, and after a while returning. The actions of just and pious men do not darken in their middle course; but Solomon tells us, they are as the shining light, that shineth more and more unto the perfect day.[2]

I cannot help feeling that in some of these words a fragment of the never-written epic has found its way into utterance. About the following passage, too, the same might be said. In describing the man fit to establish civil discipline he calls him

such a one as is a true knower of himself, and in whom contemplation and practice, wit, prudence, fortitude, and eloquence, must be rarely met, both to comprehend the hidden causes of things, and span in his thoughts all the various effects that passion or complexion can work in man's nature; and hereto must his hand be at defiance with gain, and his heart in all virtues heroic.[3]

Is this man merely the ideal Renaissance statesman, or can he be the hero of the projected Arthuriad?

The *Apology for Smectymnuus*, although containing one of the great autobiographical passages and a noble encomium on the members of Parliament, is mainly controversial, being an answer to the charges and arguments of Bishop Hall and his son. It is interesting because, though extremely hopeful, it shows signs of petulance at

1. Bohn, ii. 462–3.   2. ibid., 468–9.   3. ibid., 443.

the delay of complete reformation. In the opening paragraph Milton is perfectly clear that the plain authority of Scripture makes against episcopacy, but he detects in most men 'a carelessness of knowing what they and others ought to do'. He seems a little bewildered (as later he was to be very greatly bewildered) at the way men refused to see what to him was so plainly the truth. Doubtless he had hoped a complete and speedy victory for the party he favoured. But in spite of the Exclusion Bill men still wrote in support of the Bishops, and though the King had fled from London he had split the Parliament and was gathering his armies in the North at the time Milton was writing his pamphlet. And Milton himself, rather than meditating his song of victory, was exercising his body, so he tells, in the event of civil war:

with useful and generous labours preserving the body's health and hardiness to render lightsome, clear, and not lumpish obedience to the mind, to the cause of religion, and our country's liberty, when it shall require firm hearts in sound bodies to stand and cover their stations, rather than to see the ruin of our protestation and the inforcement of a slavish life.[1]

1. Bohn, iii. 112.

CHAPTER FOUR

Milton's Marriage: First Divorce Tract

Date	Milton's age	Writing or event in Milton's life	Contemporary event
1642, Oct.	33		Edgehill
1642, Oct.-Nov.	33	Sonnet, *Captain or Colonel*	Royalist forces advancing on London
1643			Period of Cavalier successes
1643?, May-June	34?	Marriage	Printing Ordinance (leads to *Areopagitica*)
1643?, July or Aug.	34?	Wife leaves him. Father comes to live with him. More pupils	
1643, Aug. 1	34	*Doctrine and Discipline of Divorce* (1st ed.)	Peace agitation in London. Then Gloucester crusade, relief of Gloucester (Sept. 5). Alliance of Parliament with Scots
1644, Feb.	35	Ditto (2nd ed.)	

ONE sonnet, that written 'when the assault was intended to the city', intervenes between the anti-episcopal tracts and those occasioned by Milton's marriage. It gains when its position is remembered. Topical like the prose, it is yet detached, reflective, slightly humorous in tone, as if Milton sought to prove that, when the affair was one to which he could contribute nothing practical, he could remain unsoiled by controversy and show the coolness proper to a scholar and an English gentleman.

Milton's first marriage is unfortunately the subject of more conjecture than of certain comment, but it was or may have been so important in determining his character and beliefs that it is impossible to pass it over shortly.

It is sometimes assumed that Milton married in a great hurry, having never seen his bride before the journey to Oxfordshire which Phillips tells us he made about Whitsuntide 1643. But this is not at all certain. In the *Apology for Smectymnuus*, written rather over a year earlier, not only does he make it clear that he no longer considers marriage a defilement (as in some sort he appears to have considered it in *Comus*), but in reply to the Halls' accusation of being ready to marry a rich widow for her fortune writes a sentence that may conceivably have a directly personal application:

And that he may further learn how his astrology is wide all the houses of heaven in spelling marriages, I care not if I tell him thus much professedly, though it be the losing of my rich hopes, as he calls them, that I think with them who, both in prudence and elegance of spirit, would choose a virgin of mean fortunes, honestly bred, before the wealthiest widow.[1]

Whether the 'virgin of mean fortunes' was Mary Powell or not, at least Milton seems from this passage to have contemplated marriage over a year before he committed himself.[2] It is quite probable that he had made other journeys to the Powells, had liked the look of Mary as a child, and had determined to marry her when she was of suitable age. Anyhow, there is no need to assume that Milton was suddenly swept away by an overwhelming wave of physical passion.

The problems concerning the dates of Milton's marriage, his wife's desertion of him, and the first divorce tract, first discussed by Masson, are very lucidly put by Pattison, from whose book they must be widely known; but it may be well to state them again briefly. On Phillips's authority we learn that about Whitsuntide 1643 (21 May) Milton 'took a journey into the country, nobody about him certainly knowing the reason or that it was any more than a journey of recreation'. After a month (*i.e.* about 21 June) he returns home bringing his bride Mary Powell and some of her nearest relations. A few days were spent in feasting, after which the relations departed (about the end of June). Finally, after leading 'a philosophical life' for a month, Mary is allowed to return to her parents on condition that she returns at Michaelmas. According to Phillips's account, therefore, Mary left Milton about 1 August. When Michaelmas came she refused to return, and this refusal, according to Phillips, evoked from Milton his divorce tracts. Masson, however, discovered that the first edition of the *Doctrine and Discipline of Divorce* was in print on 1 August, or just about the time of the separation. Allowing for hasty writing and printing (of which there is evidence), it is difficult to avoid the conclusion that Milton wrote his tract a very

1. Bohn, iii. 151.

2. This reference would fit in well with the suggestion, plausibly made by Burns Martin in *Studies in Philology*, 1928, 457–61, that the date of Milton's marriage was a year earlier than Phillips said. Milton's anonymous biographer gives the earlier date. Being not completely convinced, I have retained what I had written before reading the above article. The alteration of date would affect only a small proportion of my remarks.

few weeks after he had married and while his wife was still in his house. We have our choice of facing this (to some people) very unpleasant fact or believing Phillips to be wrong in his dates. I do not think we are justified in doubting Phillips. Being Milton's pupil at the time, he was certain to have observed and remembered the domestic happenings, while his remarks about the divorce pamphlets are perfectly plausible, as far as dates go, when applied to the second edition of the *Doctrine and Discipline* and to the subsequent tracts on the subject. It must be remembered that the first edition was published anonymously and that Phillips may have been quite unaware of Milton's having written on divorce till February 1644, when the second edition, addressed by the author to the houses of Parliament and weighted by many additional arguments, was published. True, Phillips in his *Life* mentions the two editions, but that does not prove that the second edition did not principally affect his impressions as a boy: the fact of there having been the two may have been a stray piece of information casually added, without thought of the implication of dates, in middle age. I do not think, therefore, that we are justified in upsetting Phillips's chronology. More important, the tone of the *Doctrine and Discipline of Divorce*, as originally written, if anything, leads us to suppose that the cause of Milton's misery was not absent from the house. Certainly the following sentence suggests it:

But here the continual sight of his deluded thoughts, without cure, must needs be to him, if especially his complexion incline him to melancholy, a daily trouble and pain of loss, in some degree like that which reprobates feel.[1]

Feeling that Milton's surprising conduct needs an unusual explanation, Pattison very nearly adopts the suggestion made by an anonymous writer in the *Athenæum*, that Mary refused him the consummation of the marriage:

Then the pamphlet, however imprudent, becomes pardonable. It is a passionate cry from the depths of a great despair; another evidence of the noble purity of a nature which refused to console itself as other men would have consoled themselves; a nature which, instead of an egotistical whine for its own deliverance, sets itself to plead the common cause of man and of society.[2]

Saurat goes further. He offers an elaborate proof of the suggestion and makes Milton's experience almost the central point of his life. He writes:

1. Bohn, iii. 188.   2. *Milton*, 58.

121

But the young woman's refusal gave Milton the first great shock of his life. He saw at once his irreparable mistake. He found himself placed in a dilemma intolerable both to his purity and to his pride. Physical passion had been roused in him, and then thwarted; he was not really married, and he was now forbidden to get married. His highest ideal, that of love as a harmony between body and spirit, was at once shattered and soiled. And the cause of this painful degradation was the blind impulse of the flesh. Hence the anger against, the mistrust of, the flesh which remained, under his more liberal general ideas, all through his life. The flesh will play an essential part in the Fall.[1]

If, as Saurat thinks, Milton's domestic relations affected the central event of his chief poem, they seem to demand further examination. Briefly, though I believe Milton's marriage was a great shock, I see no proof that it was not consummated or that the Fall as recounted in *Paradise Lost* was due chiefly to sensuality.

To deal with every passage Saurat brings in proof of his opinion would take too long. Suffice it to say that the passage which suggested the original idea seems to me, to say the least, ambiguous. Milton has been saying that 'the soberest and best governed men are least practised in these affairs' of marriage, while the less strict have by their greater experience a better chance of making a success of it.

Whenas the sober man honouring the appearance of modesty, and hoping well of every social virtue under that veil, may easily chance to meet, if not with a body impenetrable, yet often with a mind to all other due conversation inaccessible, and to all the more estimable and superior purposes of matrimony useless and almost lifeless; and what a solace, what a fit help such a consort would be through the whole life of a man, is less pain to conjecture than to have experience.[2]

The passage is ambiguous in its connotations, though it seems to me to suggest that Milton found no joy in physical union with a wife who was afraid of him and (at that time) heartily disliked him. All the other passages Saurat quotes seem to me to be equally inconclusive, if not actually to make against his idea. His most significant argument seems to me this. Milton in one passage speaks of the 'base and brutish condition to be one flesh, unless where nature can in some measure fix a unity of disposition', and Saurat comments:

'A base and brutish condition', 'two carcasses chained unnaturally together', 'a brutish congress': did Milton ever apply such words to anything he was in the remotest way concerned in? I think we can safely answer: Never.[3]

1. op. cit., 47.   2. Bohn, iii. 190.   3. op. cit., 45.

Saurat's quotations are not quite fair, as after 'two carcases chained unnaturally together' come the words 'or, as it may happen, a living soul bound to a dead corpse', by which I should understand 'Milton and Mary Powell'. And anyhow his remark seems to me exactly wrong. Milton *was* speaking of himself, and that he should so speak reveals the dreadfulness of the shock he had suffered. Hitherto he had never committed any act that seriously shook his self-esteem: now he has committed one; he has done the most hateful thing it was possible for him to do.

The issue is really one between two possible motives in Milton's nature: sensuality and pride. I happen to disagree with Saurat in thinking pride the stronger. And one cannot help colouring the evidence according to one's basic reading of Milton's character. In Milton's protests that mere lust can be kept under by 'strict life and labour, with abatement of full diet', Saurat sees only evidence of physical disappointment: for myself I am ready to accept them at their face-value. And here may I suggest that the power of sex in Milton has of recent years been exaggerated? Why this should have been so is easy to see. The discovery that he was not devoid of sexual instinct was made while it was still assumed that he was a Puritan; and when desire becomes apparent in spite of a Puritan distrust of the flesh, it is not unreasonable to suppose that such a desire is unusually strong. But Milton was a man of the Renaissance as well as a Puritan, and was not obliged to be reticent in these matters. There is therefore no need to magnify the importance of the passages in his works that deal with love: they again may be considered at their face-value. And if they are, I cannot see any signs that Milton was over-sexed: that, granted his whole ardent nature, the propensity to love was unduly powerful.

But that his normal instincts, unguided by experience, hoodwinked his reason cannot be doubted: and that he very quickly realized his mistake is equally apparent. The virtues he hoped for under the 'bashful muteness of a virgin' turned out to be 'all the unliveliness and sloth which is really unfit for conversation': he had chanced on 'a mute and spiritless mate'. And the mental tumult following the self-admission that he had made a mistake which was legally irreparable seems to me quite sufficient to account for his writing his pamphlet before his wife left him.

It is unfortunate that the first edition of the *Doctrine and Discipline of Divorce* is inaccessible except in its original publication.[1] Uncom-

1. The Yale edition, II (1959), 217–356, now provides a combined text of both editions, noting where they differ [P.B.T.].

plicated by the preface addressed to Parliament and much of the
reference to learned authorities found in the second book of the later
edition, it bears many marks of haste and of overwhelming personal
feeling. It is distinctly more moving than its revised form. The chief
feelings to be detected in it seem to me to be the admission of having
made a huge mistake, loss of self-respect and despair countered by
courage, and the desire for action. I do not mean to imply that
thwarted passion and hatred (he admits it[1]) of his wife are absent,
but I cannot see them as the chief feelings.

In saying that Milton admitted he had made a mistake, I do not
mean that he cried *Peccavi* from the house-tops. People naturally
differ in the ways they admit they are wrong and in what they mean
by professions of error. Milton was the very reverse of the sort of
person who cheerfully confesses a fault without the slightest inner
regret: from him the merest hint signifies a great deal. But some-
where very deep in his mind he confessed that he had acted at
variance with the personal standards he considered of the utmost
importance, and that the fault was ultimately his. The opening of
the pamphlet by itself seems to indicate as much.

Many men, whether it be their fate or fond opinion, easily persuade themselves, if God would but be pleased a while to withdraw his just punishments
from us, and to restrain what power either the devil or any earthly enemy
hath to work us wo, that then man's nature would find immediate rest and
releasement from all evils. But verily they who think so, if they be such as
have a mind large enough to take into their thoughts a general survey of
human things, would soon prove themselves in that opinion far deceived.
For though it were granted us by divine indulgence to be exempt from all
that can be harmful to us from without, yet the perverseness of our folly is
so bent, that we should never cease[2] hammering out of our own hearts, as it
were out of a flint, the seeds and sparkles of new misery to ourselves, till all
were in a blaze again. And no marvel if out of our own hearts, for they are
evil.[3]

The moral of this is that men have contrived foolish and unnecessary
divorce laws, but surely there is the voice of Milton beneath saying
'*I* have been perverse', and '*mine* is the responsibility'. And the tone
of the opening: how different in its suffering from the hopeful eagerness of *Reformation in England* or the philosophical confidence of
Reason of Church Government. Shaken in the confidence of himself, he

1. 'Then enters Hate; not that hate which sins, but that which only is natural
dissatisfaction, and the turning aside from a mistaken object'.
2. Milton's actual word is 'lin'.
3. Bohn, iii. 180.

thinks of the perverseness of the whole human race. Other passages reveal the despair into which he had fallen.

And yet there follows upon this a worse temptation: for if he be such as hath spent his youth unblamably, and laid up his chiefest earthly comforts in the enjoyments of a contented marriage, nor did neglect that furtherance which was to be obtained therein by constant prayers; when he shall find himself bound fast to an uncomplying discord of nature, or, as it oft happens, to an image of earth and phlegm, with whom he looked to be the copartner of a sweet and gladsome society, and sees withal that this bondage is now inevitable; though he be almost the strongest Christian, he will be ready to despair in virtue, and mutiny against Divine Providence.[1]

And in the following we are shown Milton's sensitive nature and the extent of suffering which it underwent.

As no man apprehends what vice is so well as he who is truly virtuous, no man knows hell like him who converses most in heaven; so there is none that can estimate the evil and the affliction of a natural hatred in matrimony, unless he have a soul gentle enough and spacious enough to contemplate what is true love.[2]

Milton's plight (and there are many more passages that could be quoted in illustration) is pitiful enough, but the speed and power of his recovery compel our admiration.

We pray, 'Lead us not into temptation'; a vain prayer, if, having led ourselves thither, we love to stay in that perilous condition. God sends remedies as well as evils, under which he who lies and groans, that may lawfully acquit himself, is accessory to his own ruin; nor will it excuse him though he suffer through a sluggish fearfulness to search thoroughly what is lawful, for fear of disquieting the secure falsity of an old opinion.[3]

This is the epitome of the feelings I have described as fundamental in this pamphlet: 'having led ourselves hither' – admission of error; temptation – that of despair; courage – in refusing to be passive in this extremity but in seeking an outlet in action however unconventional or bold. And when once Milton was roused to action, it could not be but high action. I cannot do better than quote from Raleigh.

Most men in Milton's position, married to 'a nothing, a desertrice, an adversary', would have recognised that theirs was one of those exceptional cases for which the law cannot provide, and would have sat down under their unhappy chance, to bear it or mitigate it as best they might. Some poets of the time of the Romantic Revival would have claimed the privilege of genius to be a law unto itself; the law of the State being designed for the

1. Bohn, iii. 194.   2. ibid., 254.   3. ibid., 261.

common rout, whose lesser sensibilities and weaker individuality make them amenable to its discipline. Milton did neither the one thing nor the other. The modern idolatry of genius was as yet uninvented; he was a citizen first, a poet and an unhappy man afterwards. He directed his energies to proving, not that he should be exempted from the operation of the law, but that the law itself should be changed. He had entered into marriage, with full ceremonial ushering, by the main door; he would go out the same way, or not at all. Thus even in this most personal matter he pleads, not for himself, but for the commonweal. He cannot conceive of happiness as of a private possession, to be secretly enjoyed; it stands rooted, like justice, in the wise and equal ordinances of the State; and the only freedom that he values is freedom under the law.[1]

Such then are the main feelings in the pamphlet, not of course expressed in the order I have given, for Milton may often in his courage fall into a fit of despair or in his plans for public reform be overcome by the bitterness of his own private fortune.

It is worth remembering that Milton's marriage took place when the fortunes of Parliament in the war were at their lowest point. Possibly we may see here a contributory cause of Milton's feeling despondent about the nature of man. By the time the second edition had been prepared, Gloucester had been relieved and the Parliament had secured the alliance of the Scots.

The second edition is interesting chiefly by its fervent and stately address to Parliament. While his wife was with him, Milton had the decency not to put his name to the pamphlet: when she refused to return, there was less reason to remain anonymous. He therefore signs himself John Milton in this address delivered, with what in a smaller man would be called effrontery, to the Parliament whose licensing order he is in the act of transgressing by the publication. The style of the address is steadier, carefuller, and more dignified than that of any parts of the first edition. Milton has calmed down somewhat. Moreover, something of the old hopefulness has returned. Instead of stressing the natural perverseness of mankind even in the best of conditions, he believes that after all wrong institutions may be responsible for a great deal. We must not neglect the saving freedom of the Mosaic law of divorce, he argues; for

the ignorance and mistake of this high point hath heaped up one huge half of all the misery that hath been since Adam.[2]

1. *Milton*, 55.
2. Bohn, iii. 175. This quotation and the next are from the preface addressed to Parliament, in the second edition.

And again with the patriotic notion added:

> Doubt not, worthy senators! to vindicate the sacred honour and judgment
> of Moses your predecessor, from the shallow commenting of scholastics and
> canonists. Doubt not after him to reach out your steady hands to the mis-
> informed and wearied life of man; to restore this his lost heritage, into the
> household state: wherewith be sure that peace and love, the best subsistence
> of a Christian family, will return home from whence they are now banished;
> places of prostitution will be less haunted, the neighbour's bed less attemp-
> ted, the yoke of prudent and manly discipline will be generally submitted to;
> sober and well-ordered living will soon spring up in the commonwealth.
> . . . Whatever else ye can enact, will scarce concern a third part of the British
> name: but the benefit and good of this your magnanimous example, will
> easily spread far beyond the banks of Tweed and the Norman isles. . . . Let
> not England forget her precedence of teaching nations how to live.[1]

Although in part so personal a document, the *Doctrine and Discipline of Divorce* (even in its first edition) contains enough argument to
make acceptable the assertion of Milton's anonymous biographer[2]
that the lawfulness of divorce 'had upon full consideration and
reading good Authors bin formerly his Opinion'. The passages
concerning man's rights over woman, the exaltation of companion-
ship over mere physical satisfaction, and his protest against forced
and arranged marriages, were probably founded on earlier thought.
It is now fairly widely recognized, I should guess, that Milton
tempered a Hebraic belief in the superiority of man with ideas remarkable in his day for their enlightenment. If Milton has no sympathy with the adoration, sincere or feigned, current among the
Cavaliers for their womankind, at least he believes that the chief
end of marriage is 'the apt and cheerful conversation of man with
woman, to comfort and refresh him against the evil of solitary life'.[3]
And this is how he speaks of forced marriages:

> As for the custom that some parents and guardians have of forcing
> marriages, it will be better to say nothing of such a savage inhumanity, but
> only thus; that the law which gives not all freedom of divorce to any crea-
> ture endued with reason so assassinated, is next in cruelty.[4]

But the most interesting of Milton's beliefs is that which concerns
'nature' and the Scriptures. Although he makes out that the Scrip-

1. Bohn, iii. 177–8.   2. *English Historical Review*, 1902, 103.

(Helen Darbishire, *Early Lives of Milton* [1932] gives a reprint and shows that
this biography was written by John Phillips [R.F.].)

3. Bohn, iii. 181.   4. ibid., 210.

tures are really on his side, he must have realized the extreme difficulty of explaining away to the satisfaction of his compatriots the
words of Christ on the subject of marriage and divorce; and he
is constantly reinforcing his plea by the argument from 'nature'.
Here are some examples. Speaking of the strictness of the marriage
tie in the reformed churches, he says it is iniquitous as

> crossing a law not only written by Moses, but charactered in us by nature,
> of more antiquity and deeper ground than marriage itself; which law is to
> force nothing against the faultless proprieties of nature, yet that this may be
> colourably done, our Saviour's words touching divorce are as it were con-
> gealed into a stony rigour, inconsistent both with his doctrine and his office.[1]

Milton does not actually say that man's mental requirements weigh
heavier than the word of Scripture, but he gives them great weight.
In the following passage humanism is certainly put above authority:

> Yet thus much I shall now insist on, that whatever the institution were, it
> could not be so enormous, nor so rebellious against both nature and reason
> as to exalt itself above the end and person for whom it was instituted.[2]

Nature again enters into one of Milton's most flagrant sophistries,
that the momentous saying of Christ may have been a supernatural
law, not binding us as we are now.

> This saying of Christ, as it is usually expounded, can be no law at all, that
> a man for no cause should separate but for adultery, except it be a super-
> natural law, not binding us as we now are. Had it been the law of nature,
> either the Jews, or some other wise and civil nation, would have pressed it:
> or let it be so, yet that law, Deut. xxiv. 1, whereby a man hath leave to part,
> whenas for just and natural cause discovered he cannot love, is a law
> ancienter and deeper engraven in blameless nature than the other.[3]

Unhappy Milton! at one moment clutching at Scriptural authority
and seeking to upset it at another. Finally there is a noble passage
in which, saying nothing of the Bible, he protests that the ways of
God never cross the just and reasonable desires of men – his paraphrase of what in other passages he called nature.

> If any, therefore, who shall hap to read this discourse, hath been through
> misadventure ill engaged in this contracted evil here complained of, and
> finds the fits and workings of a high impatience frequently upon him; of all
> those wild words which men in misery think to ease themselves by uttering,
> let him not open his lips against the providence of Heaven, or tax the ways
> of God and his divine truth; for they are equal, easy, and not burdensome;

1. Bohn, iii. 182.   2. ibid., 187.   3. ibid., 252.

nor do they ever cross the just and reasonable desires of men, nor involve this our portion of mortal life into a necessity of sadness and malcontent, by laws commanding over the unreducible antipathies of nature, sooner or later found, but allow us to remedy and shake off those evils into which human error hath led us through the midst of our best intentions, and to support our incident extremities by that authentic precept of sovereign charity, whose grand commission is to do and to dispose over all the ordinances of God to man, that love and truth may advance each other to everlasting.[1]

This is the best Milton, free from the degradation of text-grubbing, refusing to complain, and confident that there was nothing in the nature of things that need defeat the human spirit. It was a confidence he never lost, however much his confidence in the fighting power of the human spirit was destined to be shaken.

The general Miltonic idea of nature and the Bible has a curious resemblance to Neo-classic ideas about nature and Aristotle. And just as literary critics differed in the precise degree of authority with which Aristotle was to be invested, so Milton is not quite consistent in the degree of reverence he gives the Bible. It was possible to hold that Aristotle was authority absolute; or that he had to be supplemented by nature, both agreeing; or that nature was the primary authority and that if Aristotle differed from nature, as sometimes owing to insufficient data he may have done, to nature he must in the last resort give way. There are traces of all three shades of opinion (the Bible of course substituted for Aristotle), if not in the pamphlet under discussion, at least in the body of Milton's work; and I cannot help suspecting some influence, conscious or unconscious, of current literary critical ideas on Milton's beliefs concerning nature and the Bible.

1. Bohn, iii. 262-3.

CHAPTER FIVE

Tract on Education and Areopagitica

Date	Milton's age	Writing or event in Milton's life	Contemporary event
1644, June	35	*On Education*	Parliament and Scots besiege York
1644, July	35	*Judgment of Martin Bucer concerning Divorce*	Rupert relieves York, engages in battle of Marston Moor. First decisive victory for Parliament. Lack of enthusiasm on both sides
1644, Aug.	35	First signs of failing sight about this time	Palmer's sermon against divorce tracts
1644, Nov.	35	*Areopagitica*	Quarrel between official Puritans (Presbyterians) and Tolerationists. Cromwell attacks Manchester. Independents get footing in army

IT is well to realize that the divorce tracts are punctuated by the tract *On Education* and *Areopagitica*. Milton seems to have made a good recovery from his matrimonial disappointment and to have reverted to a state of mind not so very unlike that in which he wrote his tracts against the Bishops. True, in his *On Education* he speaks to Hartlib of his occupation with the divorce theme:

I had not yet at this time been induced, but by your earnest entreaties and serious conjurements; as having my mind for the present half diverted in the pursuance of some other assertions, the knowledge and the use of which cannot but be a great furtherance both to the enlargement of truth, and honest living with much more peace.[1]

But the whole tone of *On Education* is serene and hopeful. It is too, perhaps more than any other prose writing of Milton, a document of the Renaissance. In the following passage the charms of learning are described in the tones of Sidney, and the ideal of manhood is the many-sided one of the Renaissance:

1. Bohn, iii. 462.

I shall detain you now no longer in the demonstration of what we should not do, but straight conduct you to a hill-side, where I will point you out the right path of a virtuous and noble education; laborious indeed at the first ascent, but else so smooth, so green, so full of goodly prospect, and melodious sounds on every side, that the harp of Orpheus was not more charming. I doubt not but ye shall have more ado to drive our dullest and laziest youth, our stocks and stubs, from the infinite desire of such a happy nurture, than we have now to hale and drag our choicest and hopefullest wits to that asinine feast of sowthistles and brambles, which is commonly set before them as all the food and entertainment of their tenderest and most docible age. I call therefore a complete and generous education, that which fits a man to perform justly, skilfully, and magnanimously all the offices, both private and public, of peace and war.[1]

And if evidence is wanted for Milton's still sanguine hopes for human nature the sentence following those just quoted is sufficient:

And how all this may be done between twelve and one-and-twenty, less time than is now bestowed in pure trifling at grammar and sophistry, is to be thus ordered.

And then follows the account of all the varied sciences and humanities which the scholars will so easily master. The impossible demands Milton makes of ordinary human nature in his educational scheme are too well known to need further comment: enough that they reveal to perfection his sanguine temperament.

The educational ideas carry on quite naturally the statement of the *Third Prolusion* and the hints contained in the letter to the unknown friend about the time of Milton's twenty-third birthday (see pp. 13–14, 49–51, 66 above). There is the same hatred of mere antiquarianism, of irrelevant dialectical subtleties, of the unrelated fact in general, and of the state of learning at the Universities. His contempt for mere linguistic knowledge is typical of his whole way of thinking.

And though a linguist should pride himself to have all the tongues that Babel cleft the world into, yet if he have not studied the solid things in them, as well as the words and lexicons, he were nothing so much to be esteemed a learned man, as any yeoman or tradesman competently wise in his mother dialect only.[2]

Of special interest are passages showing Milton's ideas at this time about the Fall and the state and potentialities of human nature.

The end of learning is to repair the ruins of our first parents by regaining to know God aright, and out of that knowledge to love him, to imitate him,

1. Bohn, iii. 466–7.   2. ibid., 464.

to be like him, as we may the nearest by possessing our souls of true virtue, which being united to the heavenly grace of faith, makes up the highest perfection.[1]

The Fall, then, is by this time an essential in Milton's idea of things: human nature is not purely good in origin; he is no Rousseauist. But how vast are the possibilities of improvement another passage makes clear.

> But here the main skill and groundwork will be, to temper them such lectures and explanations, upon every opportunity, as may lead and draw them in willing obedience, inflamed with the study of learning and the admiration of virtue; stirred up with high hopes of living to be brave men, and worthy patriots, dear to God, and famous to all ages. That they may despise and scorn all their childish and ill-taught qualities, to delight in manly and liberal exercises, which he who hath the art and proper eloquence to catch them with, what with mild and effectual persuasions, and what with the intimation of some fear, if need be, but chiefly by his own example, might in a short space gain them to an incredible diligence and courage, infusing into their young breasts such an ingenuous and noble ardour, as would not fail to make many of them renowned and matchless men.[2]

Reading this passage I find it difficult to believe that Milton's first marriage was the greatest shock of his life. It certainly caused him to fall momentarily into despair, but despair had not been absent from the passion that revealed itself in *Lycidas* nor was it destined to be absent from his blindness. His ultimate disappointment in human nature was far more serious, and the traces of that, seen in the first edition of the *Doctrine and Discipline of Divorce*, have by the time of the tract *On Education* been pretty effectively effaced, nor do they appear in *Areopagitica*.

Of all the prose works *On Education* is the only one that could be called charming. But the Sidneian freshness is not confined to the passage first quoted; it pretty well pervades the piece and comes out in its fullest charm when the beauties of music and the season to range the country are Milton's topics.

> The interim of unsweating themselves regularly, and convenient rest before meat, may, both with profit and delight, be taken up in recreating and composing their travailed spirits with the solemn and divine harmonies of music, heard or learned; either whilst the skilful organist plies his grave and fancied descant in lofty fuges, or the whole symphony with artful and unimaginable touches adorn and grace the well-studied chords of some choice composer; sometimes the lute or soft organ-stop waiting on elegant voices, either to religious, martial, or civil ditties; which, if wise men and prophets be not

1. Bohn, iii. 464.   2. ibid., 468.

extremely out, have a great power over dispositions and manners, to smooth and make them gentle from rustic harshness and distempered passions.[1]

and

> Besides these constant exercises at home, there is another opportunity of gaining experience to be won from pleasure itself abroad; in those vernal seasons of the year when the air is calm and pleasant, it were an injury and sullenness against nature, not to go out and see her riches, and partake in her rejoicing with heaven and earth.[2]

There is something in these two passages that takes us back to the early poems; to *L'Allegro* very obviously in the first, in the second perhaps to the candour of the *Nativity Ode*. Nor are such reminiscences improbable; for in thinking of education in general Milton would naturally cast his mind back to the time of his own education and the poems he wrote in it.

Very soon after the tract *On Education* Milton published his second divorce tract, *The Judgment of Martin Bucer concerning Divorce*. Mostly translation or adaptation from another author, it need not concern us, and we can pass on at once to *Areopagitica*.

Areopagitica is the best of Milton's English prose works, because it expresses more of his mind than any other. It is also the summit of one period of his development, comparable to *Lycidas*, which was at once the crowning poem of Milton's youth and the promise of what ought to have followed. Not only does *Areopagitica* express more of Milton's mind: it is more economical in the expression; there is relatively little waste. Fortunately few Scriptural passages bear on the question of the liberty of the press; and Milton was spared the uncongenial task of text-hunting. *Areopagitica* is an organism through most of which the blood circulates freely.

In one way *Areopagitica* is Milton's chief song of hope: in it he has uttered most of the few surviving fragments of the epic which I have supposed him to have contemplated as the beginning of the struggle between Parliament and Royalists, the Song of Innocence that never got written. But in another way it shows a maturity of experience quite new in Milton: a definite development of ideas towards *Paradise Lost*. Although pieces of the Arthuriad may have got themselves expressed, it must have been about the time Milton wrote *Areopagitica* that he abandoned any idea of writing such a poem. *Areopagitica* is thus of special interest in looking both back and forward.

1. Bohn, iii. 475–6. 2. ibid., 477.

133

There is much in common between *Areopagitica* and the anti-episcopal pamphlets: the Renaissance tone, the instinct for action, the defence of schisms, and the immense hope of speedy national reformation. The flowery comparison of himself to Isocrates[1] and the appeal to the authority of Plato,[2] who is this time explained away as he happens to be on the wrong side, are in a typically Renaissance manner. The whole plea that the free publishing of books is founded on freedom and width of choice is instinct with the notion that life is worthless without activity, and the more valuable as it is more active.

Well knows he who uses to consider, that our faith and knowledge thrives by exercise, as well as our limbs and complexion. Truth is compared in scripture to a streaming fountain; if her waters flow not in a perpetual progression, they sicken into a muddy pool of conformity and tradition. A man may be a heretic in the truth; and if he believe things only because his pastor says so, or the assembly so determines, without knowing other reason, though his belief be true, yet the very truth he holds becomes his heresy.[3]

And the idea stated in its purest and grandest form:

I cannot praise a fugitive and cloistered virtue, unexercised and un-breathed, that never sallies out and seeks[4] her adversary, but slinks out of the race, where that immortal garland is to be run for, not without dust and heat.[5]

This same passage suggests the lost Arthuriad, displaying as it does what would have been the dominant spirit of that poem. It is, however, near the end of the pamphlet, in the most famous portion, where I feel this suggestion best applies and where we may hear the voice of Milton praising, in never-to-be-fulfilled anticipation, the glory of his reformed country. The whole is to the point, but two pieces can be chosen. Here is Milton's opinion of the English nation – so soon to be revised:

Lords and commons of England! consider what nation it is whereof ye are, and whereof ye are the governors: a nation not slow and dull, but of a quick, ingenious, and piercing spirit; acute to invent, subtile and sinewy to discourse, not beneath the reach of any point the highest that human capacity can soar to.[6]

1. Bohn, ii. 52, 'him who from his private house wrote that discourse to the Parliament of Athens'.

2. ibid., 72.   3. ibid., 85.   4. 'sees' is now the recognized reading.

5. ibid., 68.   6. ibid., 90.

And here is Milton's hope of the immediate future:

> Methinks I see in my mind a noble and puissant nation rousing herself like a strong man after sleep, and shaking her invincible locks: methinks I see her as an eagle mewing her mighty youth, and kindling her undazzled eyes at the full midday beam; purging and unscaling her long-abused sight at the fountain itself of heavenly radiance; while the whole noise of timorous and flocking birds, with those also that love the twilight, flutter about, amazed at what she means, and in their envious gabble would prognosticate a year of sects and schisms.[1]

Sects and schisms: as in *Reason of Church Government*, the thought that they are the signs of a great awakening of spiritual activity rouses Milton to eloquence. But in *Areopagitica* beneath the excitement of hope there can be detected the whisper of doubt. Some men, he says,

> fret, and out of their own weakness are in agony, lest these divisions and subdivisions will undo us. The adversary again applauds, and waits the hour: when they have branched themselves out, saith he, small enough into parties and partitions, then will be our time. Fool! he sees not the firm root, out of which we all grow, though into branches; nor will beware, until he see our small divided maniples cutting through at every angle of his ill-united and unwieldy brigade.[2]

Yet for all this protest I feel he feared, as he had not feared before, lest the adversary might be right.

Nor was such a fear unreasonable, for since the anti-episcopal pamphlets affairs had altered in the Parliamentary camp. To the delay in the fulfilment of his earliest and highest hopes, caused by the resistance and early successes of the Cavaliers, Milton would soon become reconciled: he had sufficient control for that. But the stiffness and intolerance of the Presbyterians[3] was a more serious matter. Sects within the reformed fold might be a sign of vitality, but Presbyterian intolerance was quite a different matter. And so this accent of doubt (if really to be detected) may be connected with the passages where Milton turns his invective against the Presbyters.

> If some who but of late were little better than silenced from preaching, shall come now to silence us from reading, except what they please, it cannot be guessed what is intended by some but a second tyranny over learning: and

1. Bohn, ii. 94.   2. ibid., 93.

3. It was at the time of the writing of *Areopagitica* that Cromwell attacked the Presbyterians for their intolerance of the Independents.

will soon put it out of controversy, that bishops and presbyters are the same to us, both name and thing.[1]

This shows Milton much grown in experience since the anti-episcopal pamphlets. He has learnt that the mere removal of an institution will not bring the millennium.

It is not the unfrocking of a priest, the unmitring of a bishop, and the removing him from off the presbyterian shoulders, that will make us a happy nation.[2]

He is now less trustful of Utopias.

To sequester out of the world into Atlantic and Utopian politics, which never can be drawn into use, will not mend our condition; but to ordain wisely as in this world of evil, in the midst whereof God hath placed us unavoidably.[3]

He disclaims the notion of unqualified human perfectibility. Truth has been, like the God Osiris, 'hewed into a thousand pieces, and scattered to the four winds'.

From that time ever since, the sad friends of Truth, such as durst appear, imitating the careful search that Isis made for the mangled body of Osiris, went up and down gathering up limb by limb still as they could find them. We have not yet found them all, . . . nor ever shall do, till her Master's second coming.[4]

The process of disillusionment has begun, though as yet it is in its early stages and hope remains dominant.

Hostility to the Presbyterians may have suggested another very important development in Milton's ideas. In *Areopagitica* he definitely adopts the doctrine of free will and turns against the pre-destination of the Presbyterians. It is surprising that he could ever have believed differently, his whole nature demanding the utmost liberty of choice, however drastically controlled the actual choice had to be. Anyhow, he was mentally stimulated by his change of doctrine, and some of the most vigorous passages in *Areopagitica* deal with the liberty of choosing widely and the impossibility of segregating the good from the bad. These are the passages that best illustrate the way in which *Areopagitica* looks at once backwards and forwards. The acceptance of free will is more a fulfilment of past promise than anything new: but the kindred problems of good and evil suggest *Paradise Lost* rather than the hypothetical Arthuriad.

1. Bohn, ii. 83.   2. ibid., 90.   3. ibid., 74.   4. ibid., 89.

Good and evil we know in the field of this world grow up together almost inseparably; and the knowledge of good is so involved and interwoven with the knowledge of evil, and in so many cunning resemblances hardly to be discerned, that those confused seeds which were imposed upon Psyche as an incessant labour to cull out, and sort asunder, were not more intermixed. It was from out the rind of one apple tasted, that the knowledge of good and evil, as two twins cleaving together, leaped forth into the world. And perhaps this is that doom which Adam fell into of knowing good and evil; that is to say, of knowing good by evil.

As therefore the state of man now is; what wisdom can there be to choose, what continence to forbear, without the knowledge of evil?[1]

And again:

Many there be that complain of divine Providence for suffering Adam to transgress. Foolish tongues! when God gave him reason, he gave him freedom to choose, for reason is but choosing; he had been else a mere artificial Adam, such an Adam as he is in the motions.[2]

And finally here is a passage stressing less the need of being able to choose than the breadth of choice, the glorious variety of life on this earth.

Suppose we could expel sin by this means; look how much we thus expel of sin, so much we expel of virtue: for the matter of them both is the same: remove that, and ye remove them both alike. This justifies the high providence of God, who, though he commands us temperance, justice, continence, yet pours out before us even to a profuseness all desirable things, and gives us minds that can wander beyond all limit and satiety.[3]

The last sentence reminds not only of 'those thoughts that wander through Eternity' in *Paradise Lost*, Book Two, but of some of Comus's speeches. It proves his intense belief in a full life as well as the belief that for a life truly full and not merely squandered wise control is necessary.

Milton's main beliefs at the time of *Areopagitica* may be outlined as follows. Man is born with the seeds of good and evil in him: mere environment cannot determine his character: in the most favourable environment evil might come out. But man has the power of choice, and knowing both good and evil it is possible for him to choose good. The present world may not ever be perfect, but it may be very much better. It is reasonable to have very high hopes; and it still seems likely that, in spite of set-backs, some great good is to happen to England in the immediate future. There is therefore every incentive for the noblest and most strenuous action.

1. Bohn, ii. 67–8.   2. ibid., 74.   3. ibid., 75.

CHAPTER SIX

Last Divorce Tracts: Tetrachordon
and Colasterion

Date	Milton's age	Writing or event in Milton's life	Contemporary event
1645, March	36	Last divorce tracts: *Tetrachordon* and *Colasterion*	Fairfax in command of Parliamentary Army. New Model Army under central not local control
1645	36	Sonnets, *On the detraction which followed upon my writing certain treatises*	Presbyterianism made State religion

To say, as some do, that *Tetrachordon* is a continuation of the *Doctrine and Discipline of Divorce* is scarcely correct. It may continue the mood and arguments of the portions added when the earlier pamphlet was published in its second edition; but with the poignant personal revelations of the first edition (and it is for these that the *Doctrine and Discipline of Divorce* is chiefly remembered) it has little in common. The success with which in *Tetrachordon* Milton sinks the personal in the social issue is indeed remarkable. Not merely does he put the case for divorce in grand tones and with measured emphasis: he actually describes with an exquisite lyrical fervour the very joys of harmonious wedlock of which he had been so utterly, and as it then seemed so irrevocably, deprived; like Satan watching the joys of Adam and Eve in Paradise, yet without envy.

We cannot, therefore, always be contemplative, or pragmatical abroad, but have need of some delightful intermissions, wherein the enlarged soul may leave off a while her severe schooling, and, like a glad youth in wandering vacancy, may keep her holidays to joy and harmless pastime; which as she cannot well do without company, so in no company so well as where the different sex in most resembling unlikeness, and most unlike resemblance, cannot but please best, and be pleased in the aptitude of that variety. Whereof lest we should be too timorous, in the awe that our flat sages would form us and dress us, wisest Solomon among his gravest proverbs countenances a kind of ravishment and erring fondness in the entertainment of wedded leisures; and in the Song of Songs, which is generally believed, even in the jolliest expressions, to figure the spousals of the church with Christ, sings of a thousand raptures between those two lovely ones far on the hither side of carnal enjoyment. By these instances, and more which might be brought, we may imagine how indulgently God provided against man's loneliness; that he approved it not, as by himself declared not good; that he approved the remedy thereof, as of his own ordaining, consequently good; and as he ordained it, so doubtless proportionably to our fallen estate he gives it; else were his ordinance at least in vain, and we for all his gifts still empty handed.[1]

Milton batters with terrible and shattering persistence at the weak point of the divorce laws: that they take nothing into account but the bodily act, ignoring all other human functions.

This I amaze me at, that though all the superior and nobler ends both of marriage and of the married persons be absolutely frustrate, the matrimony stirs not, loses no hold, remains as rooted as the centre: but if the body bring but in a complaint of frigidity, by that cold application only this adamantine Alp of wedlock has leave to dissolve; which else all the machinations of religious or civil reason at the suit of a distressed mind, either for divine worship or human conversation violated, cannot unfasten. What courts of concupiscence are these, wherein fleshly appetite is heard before right reason, lust before love or devotion? They may be pious Christians together, they may be loving and friendly, they may be helpful to each other in the family, but they cannot couple; that shall divorce them, though either party would not. They can neither serve God together, nor one be at peace with the other, nor be good in the family one to other; but live as they were dead, or live as they were deadly enemies in a cage together: it is all one, they can couple, they shall not divorce till death, no, though this sentence be their death. What is this besides tyranny, but to turn nature upside down, to make both religion and the mind of man wait upon the slavish errands of the body, and not the body to follow either the sanctity or the sovereignty of the mind, unspeakably wronged, and with all equity complaining? what is this but to abuse the sacred and mysterious bed of marriage to be the compulsive sty of an ingrateful and malignant lust, stirred up only from a carnal acrimony, without either love or peace, or regard to any other thing holy or human?[2]

This is but one example of many which make the first part of *Tetrachordon*, dealing with the relevant texts in *Genesis*, the weightiest piece of invective in Milton's prose.

If in the second edition of the *Doctrine and Discipline of Divorce* Milton is bold in setting up 'nature' as a rival to the Scriptures, he is bolder in *Tetrachordon*. At the opening of his discussion, beginning

1. Bohn, iii. 331.   2. ibid., 333.

with the text that God created man in his own image, he complains that 'nothing now-a-days is more degenerately forgotten than the true dignity of man'. Man, forgetting the dignity of his origin, binds himself with petty rules, whereas he should follow that which

makes us holiest and likest to [God's] immortal image, not that which makes us most conformable and captive to civil and subordinate precepts: whereof the strictest observance may ofttimes prove the destruction not only of many innocent persons and families, but of whole nations: although indeed no ordinance, human or from heaven, can bind against the good of man.[1]

The 'good of man' is what in other places Milton calls 'nature'. But what an astonishing sentence for one who is supposed to believe in the ultimate authority of the Bible! And it is still more astonishing when to all appearances we find Milton taking quite literally the story of Eve's creation out of Adam's rib.

That there was a nearer alliance between Adam and Eve, than could be ever after between man and wife, is visible to any. For no other woman was ever moulded out of her husband's rib.[2]

And when it comes to the point, Milton shrinks from applying the full significance of the rebellious words. In discussing the crucial and awkward words of Christ to the Pharisees he will but explain away; Christ meant something other than what his words apparently mean: there is no question of putting 'nature' above Christ's words in the Gospel. The most he can do is to allow exceptions to Paul's precept, 'wives, be subject to your husbands.'

Not but that particular exceptions may have place, if she exceed her husband in prudence and dexterity, and he contentedly yield: for then a superior and more natural law comes in, that the wiser should govern the less wise, whether male or female.[3]

The nature of Milton's belief in the Bible is indeed a puzzle. At one moment he seems to be a literalist, at another to interpret the mythology of the Old Testament as pure symbolism. Now he will rest on the authority of biblical precepts literally understood, and now he would subordinate them all to the higher sanctity of the good of man. In few men could the variance between radical and nominal beliefs have been so acute.

Colasterion is a dreary piece of invective, but a single passage deserves quotation. It is a fine example of lofty scorn and high intolerance of the inferior breed of men. Milton's sense of man's

1. Bohn, iii. 323–4.   2. ibid., 335.   3. ibid., 325.

dignity by now applies to what a few men may be, more might be, but most are not.

I have now done that, which for many causes I might have thought could not likely have been my fortune, to be put to this underwork of scouring and unrubbishing the low and sordid ignorance of such a presumptuous lozel. Yet Hercules had the labour once imposed upon him to carry dung out of the Augean stable. At any hand I would be rid of him: for I had rather, since the life of man is likened to a scene, that all my entrances and exits might mix with such persons only, whose worth erects them and their actions to a grave and tragic deportment, and not to have to do with clowns and vices. But if a man cannot peaceably walk into the world, but must be infested, sometimes at his face with dorrs and horseflies, sometimes beneath with bawling whippets and shin-barkers, and these to be set on by plot and consultation with a junto of clergymen and licensers, commended also and rejoiced in by those whose partiality cannot yet forego old papistical principles; have I not cause to be in such a manner defensive, as may procure me freedom to pass more unmolested hereafter by those encumbrances, not so much regarded for themselves, as for those who incite them?[1]

If the discovery that the presbyters could be as tyrannical as the bishops brought disappointment, no less did the way in which the divorce tracts were received. In the *Doctrine and Discipline of Divorce* Milton imagined himself the agent of untold good, the apostle of healing liberty. But the more he wrote and argued, the less headway his ideas made, the greater grew the opposition. The result in Milton was a bewildered disappointment that the truth, so plain and health-giving, should have been disregarded or opposed. He had once more misjudged the common fabric of human nature. This bewildered disappointment is expressed in the two sonnets, notable for the light which they shed on Milton's character, *On the detraction which followed upon my writing certain treatises*. These treatises are the divorce tracts. The first sonnet, beginning 'A book was writ of late call'd *Tetrachordon*', contains the bitter complaint against the illiteracy of his age:

> Thy age, like ours, O Soul of Sir *John Cheek*,
> Hated not Learning wors than Toad or Asp:

but the second deserves quoting in full.

> I did but prompt the age to quit their cloggs
> By the known rules of antient libertie,
> When strait a barbarous noise environs me
> Of Owles and Cuckoes, Asses, Apes and Doggs.

1. Bohn, iii. 460.

As when those Hinds that were transform'd to Froggs
    Raild at *Latona's* twin-born progenie
    Which after held the Sun and Moon in fee.
    But this is got by casting Pearl to Hoggs;
That bawle for freedom in their senseless mood,
    And still revolt when truth would set them free.
    License they mean when they cry libertie;
For who loves that, must first be wise and good;
    But from that mark how far they roave we see
    By all this wast of wealth, and loss of blood.

This is the earliest place where Milton confesses deep disappointment in his countrymen.

CHAPTER SEVEN
Interval in Pamphlet-Writing
1645–1649

Date	Milton's age	Writing or event in Milton's Life	Contemporary event
1645, July or Aug.	36	Reconciliation with wife	(June) Naseby. Decisive victory of Cromwell and New Model Army
1645, late	36–7	Publication of collected minor poems. About now begins *History of Britain* and collecting of material for *De Doctrina Christiana*	
1646, Jan.	37	*Ode to Rouse*	
1646, June	37		Fall of Oxford. End of first phase of war
1646, July	37	Receives ruined Powell family into his house	
		Sonnet, *On the New Forces of Conscience*	Intolerance of Parliament. Anglicanism proscribed. Then Bills to suppress sectarianism
1647, April	38	Letter to Dati of Florence	
1647, Aug.	38		New Model Army occupies London. Beginning of Cromwell's dictatorship. Growth of democratic opinion in army
1647, Nov.	38		Charles's flight to Carisbrooke
1648, May	39		Cromwell persuaded to extreme measures. Resolution to bring Charles to death. Second Civil War (Royalists and Presbyterians *v.* Independents). Sufferings of Charles begin to affect the people.
1648, Aug.	39	Sonnet to Fairfax	Defeat of Scots at Preston
1648, Dec.	39		Presbyterians expelled from Parliament

THE last divorce pamphlets were published in March 1645. In the same summer the immediate personal cause for their having been

written was removed by Mary's return. One episode in Milton's life
was closed. If I am right in thinking that about the time of *Areopagitica*, November 1644, he abandoned all thought of an epic of England, another episode would have closed not long before. He was
now thirty-six, at the close of youth and the beginning of middle age.
Knowing as one does Milton's habit of reviewing his past achievement, of counting up the interest he had earned on the talents
entrusted to him, one would expect something of the sort at this
time. And one can find it, I think, in the publication of his collected
poems at the end of 1645. There is no need to see in the preface of
Moseley, the publisher, a proof that but for his solicitations Milton
would not have published at all: the preface is no more than the
conventional Renaissance apology for going into print. The edition
was arranged and supervised by Milton with great care and has a
kind of stock-taking significance. Like *Epitaphium Damonis* the 1645
edition of the poems closes a phase of Milton's life.

The ode *Ad Joannem Rousium* is the most considerable poetic
interlude (apart from the unfortunate version of the Psalms) between *Epitaphium Damonis* and *Paradise Lost*. It is closely connected
with the 1645 edition of the poems. Milton had sent a copy to John
Rouse, Librarian of the Bodleian, but it either failed to reach him or
got lost. Rouse asked Milton for another copy, a request which
pleased Milton enough to procure not only the second copy but an
elaborate Latin poem telling Rouse something of his feelings about
the state of England and about his literary ambitions at the time
(January 1646). The ode, which casts a very pleasing light on
Milton's thought, has been so little noticed that I give here a prose
rendering of the whole. Cowper's elegant verse translation (which
he tells us cost him more trouble than any of the other translations
of Milton's Latin poems) is very free, and the interest of content may
excuse the ugliness inevitable in a prose version of a beautiful but
pleonastic piece of verse, Milton's last poem in the vein of stately
compliment.

*Ode to John Rouse, Librarian to the University of Oxford, concerning a lost book
of poems, a fresh copy of which he asked to have sent him to place with the rest of my
works in the public library.*
My twofold book, rejoicing in its single garb though double in content,[1]
gaily bound but with a simple elegance, which once a youthful hand brought
forth eagerly though guided by but modest genius, who sported at one time
in the Italian shades at another in the woods of Britain, unsoiled by the mob,
and in retirement gave scope to his native lute, but soon roused his comrades

1. That is, English and Latin.

with an alien strain on the Latin lyre, and almost trod on air – who, my little book, who stole thee away from all thy brothers, when, sent from the City at the continual requests of my learned friend, thou tookest thy glorious way to the source of blue Father Thames, where rise the clear fountains of the Muses and their sacred followers sing songs that will be known to the world through immense revolutions of time, nay even to perpetuity?

Now what god or son of a god, pitying the ancient virtue of our people (if we have expiated our former sins, and the degenerate luxury that corrupted our peace) may remove the crime of civil war and with his blessing recall the liberal arts and the Muses, now driven from their abodes and banished almost beyond the bounds of England; and may shoot as with Apollo's bow the foul threatening birds and drive away the plague of Harpies from the Muses' stream?

But thou, my book, though thou hast strayed from the array of thy brothers through the treachery of thy bearer or by carelessness, whether thou art imprisoned in some cellar or den to be taken thence and mangled by the hard hand of a boorish hawker, rejoice and be glad, for behold a second time there shines the hope of escaping deep oblivion, of mounting on oary wings to the courts of Jove above: for Rouse desires thee for his store, and complains that though promised to him thou art lacking from the full tale of my books, and he asks thee to come, Rouse, to whose care are given the glorious monuments of men; and he wishes to house thee in the inner shrine, his charge, faithful Keeper of deathless works, of treasure nobler than that which Ion guarded, Ion descendant of Erechtheus, in the rich temple of Apollo his father among the golden tripods and Delphic gifts, Ion son of Creusa.

Therefore thou wilt go to visit the pleasant woods of the Muses, once more thou wilt enter the divine home of Apollo which he inhabits in the valley of Oxford, preferring it to Delos and the twin peak of Parnassus; thou wilt go in glory, since it is to enjoy a noble fate that thou leavest, answering the propitious prayers of my friend. There thou shalt be read along with the famous writers of antiquity, the ancient glory of the Greeks and Romans and their true adornment.

You then my works, no longer vain, the sum of what this lean genius of mine has produced, I bid you expect a quiet though late repose free from envy, a fortunate home which kind Hermes and Rouse's shrewd care will give, whither the insolent noise of the mob shall not penetrate, while the common crowd of readers shall retire far off. But distant generations and a more judicious age shall perhaps (with impartial mind) give judgments that shall better answer merit: then with malice buried an unprejudiced posterity shall recognise any merit I deserve – thanks to Rouse.

However flat the abundant mythology may read in a prose translation it can sound noble in the original. There is a Pindaric nobility about the following description of Rouse and his books:

ipse praesidet
Aeternorum operum custos fidelis,
Quaestorque gazae nobilioris,
Quam cui praefuit Ion
Clarus Erechtheides
Opulenta dei per templa parentis
Fulvosque tripodas, donaque Delphica
Ion Actaea genitus Creusa.[1]

Can it be that this ode is not an isolated poem written for an occasion but an experiment in the style of what Milton in *Reason of Church Government* calls the 'magnific odes and hymns, wherein Pindarus and Callimachus are in most things worthy'? Not that the style is predominantly Pindaric: the ode is a mixture of stateliness and of half-humorous and urbane elegance. About this elegance there is something very pleasing, as there is not always about the elegance of men whose lives, unlike Milton's, have been sheltered and easy. Milton had by his entry into action earned the right to indulge in redundant graces. But though the tone of the poem may not be entirely Pindaric, the metrical scheme has no Latin original and seems to be modelled principally on Pindar. I venture no metrical comparison, but I may record a personal impression that Milton is complete master of his new medium, that he accommodates sound to sense with the greatest skill, and that if read with due quantitative emphasis the ode reveals itself as one of the greater Latin poems, less serious than *Mansus* and the *Epitaphium Damonis*, but in completeness of achievement worthy to rank with them.

There are a number of interesting details. First there is his loving reminiscence of the quiet days when he wrote his youthful poems, English and Latin, and of his ecstasy in the writing when 'humum vix tetigit pede'. He longs for the time when civil war may really cease, and culture, of whose expulsion from England he is only too conscious, may be brought back. Plainly the habit of controversy had not brought the appetite as well. But in this poem no less than in those *On the detraction which followed upon my writing certain treatises*

1. 53–60:
   He, therefore, guardian vigilant
   Of that unperishing wealth,
   Calls thee to the interior shrine, his charge,
   Where he intends a richer treasure far
   Than Ion (Ion, Erectheus' son
   Illustrious, of the fair Creüsa born)
   In the resplendent temple of his God,
   Tripods of gold, and Delphic gifts divine.

there is a criticism of his countrymen and a doubt whether they have been sufficiently punished for their sins. Still there is hope that the virtuous acts of their ancestors (in the Reformation of course) may prevail with God. His final wish that his poems may be read with those of Greece and Rome and his plea that a later and more judicious age may decide their merits are as temperately and ingenuously expressed as they have been happily fulfilled. Altogether the poem gives a charming picture of the more amiable Milton, of whom we see but too little during the years of the Commonwealth.

Why, it may be asked, was Milton in this period engaged neither in writing pamphlets nor in writing his great poem? Richard Garnett writes that at this time

he might have been the apostle of toleration in England, as Roger Williams had been in America. The moment was most favourable. Presbyterianism had got itself established, but could not pretend to represent the majority of the nation. . . . The Independents were for toleration, the Episcopalians had been for the time humbled by adversity, the best minds in the nation, including Cromwell, were Seekers or Latitude men, or sceptics. Here was invitation enough for a work as much greater than the 'Areopagitica' as the principle of freedom of thought is greater than the most august particular application of it. . . . But unfortunately no external impulse stirred him to action.[1]

It is certainly strange that the only protest Milton made against the intolerance of the Presbyterian majority in Parliament, which in the latter half of 1646 proscribed Anglicanism and passed Bills to suppress the very sects that had brought victory, was the *sonetto caudato* headed *On the New Forcers of Conscience under the Long Parliament*. This poem is without doubt a grand piece of savage invective aimed, as Milton thought satire should be, at the vices of eminent men; but it is an isolated poem and was not published till 1673. It may be Garnett is correct in supposing that Milton did not write because there was no personal stimulus; but there are other possibilities. For one thing *Areopagitica* is quite as much a defence of general liberty of thought as of the more restricted liberty of publishing: Milton had already had his say in the matter and was not likely to better his expression. For another, the reception of his divorce pamphlets may have made him chary of casting his pearls (as he estimated them) before swine. Lastly, he may have felt that it had become by now increasingly imperative to continue the main designs of his life.

1. *Life of Milton*, 99–100.

The other question remains: why did Milton in this period, if he was not engaged in pamphleteering, fail to make a beginning in writing his great poem? The answer is that he had been prevented by the trend of events from writing as he had meant, but that he was not ready for a new design. It was impossible to celebrate in a poem the doings of Parliament at a time when the Scots and their Presbyterian friends in England were in the act of establishing a tyranny as hostile to freedom of conscience as Laud's had been. On the other hand, Milton's opinions about mankind had changed; human nature had not come up to his hopes. He was more obsessed than he had been by the problem of evil, and was working towards some settled faith in the matter. All he could do was to watch history in the making, to study, and to await developments.

It is probable that Milton's studies at this time in preparation for his great poems consisted in amassing the material that later became his treatise *De Doctrina Christiana*. It looks as if he had determined to settle his philosophy by a gigantic digest of the Scriptures under all the relevant headings. A prodigious, heart-breaking task, which no sensitive man could have accomplished without the exercise of an inflexible will.

But besides studying in preparation for his great poem Milton began a work which in some measure must have meant relaxation, his *History of Britain*, the first four books of which were completed in these years. Hanford makes the following interesting comment:

> The *History of Britain* may be regarded as a sort of commutation of Milton's earlier projects for a drama or an epic on a British legendary theme. . . . More directly the *History* is the fruit of the course of historical reading recorded in the *Commonplace Book*. Milton reached in his program the British historians about 1641–42 and went carefully through Holinshed, Speed, Camden, Buchanan, together with a few older authorities like Bede.[1]

Hanford's suggestion may well be true. I should guess that Milton felt able and glad to commute the national poem he was compelled to abandon into the safer form of a prose history. The poem to satisfy his requirements must have included the present and the future, so troubled and undecided; but with the past it was safe to deal.

There may be too a more concrete reason for Milton's making no beginning with his great poem. His wife's family, ruined by the Royalist downfall at Naseby, then a year later by the fall of Oxford in June 1646, lodged themselves in his home in London. The burden

---

1. *Handbook*, 3rd ed., 115–16.

of these penniless and noisy refugees must have been heavy, for Milton writes pathetically to his friend Dati in Florence (21 April, 1647):

> Soon an even more depressing thought came into my mind, a thought which often makes me lament my fortune, namely that those who are closely bound to me by the fact of neighbourhood or by some other tie of no real importance, either by chance or by some legal claim, though they have nothing else to commend them to me, are with me every day, deafen me with their noise, and, I swear, torment me as often as they choose; while those who are so greatly endeared to me by sympathy of manners, disposition and tastes, are almost all separated from me either by death or by the cruel accident of distance.[1]

It was clearly impossible for Milton to begin his epic in the circumstances so described.

Any importance that Milton may have had as historian is outside the scope of this book; but the few non-narrative, homiletic passages in the first four books of the *History of Britain* (composed according to Milton's own statement in the *Defensio Secunda* during the period now under review) are interesting in revealing his opinions on contemporary politics. It is these passages, together with the sonnet to Fairfax, that show us how Milton despised and hated the religious intolerance, the self-seeking and the financial inefficiency of the Parliamentary government of England between the First and Second Civil Wars. He seems indeed at this time to have fallen into a more advanced political despondence than at any time before the complete ruin of his hopes in 1660, and he cannot refrain from comparing the initial promise of the Civil War with the lamentable way in which success has been used.

> They who of late were extolled as our greatest deliverers, and had the people wholly at their devotion, by so discharging their trust as we see, did not only weaken and unfit themselves to be dispensers of what liberty they pretended, but unfitted also the people, now grown worse and more disordinate, to receive or to digest any liberty at all. For stories teach us, that liberty sought out of season, in a corrupt and degenerate age, brought Rome itself to a farther slavery: for liberty hath a sharp and double edge, fit only to be handled by just and virtuous men; to bad and dissolute, it becomes a mischief unwieldy in their own hands: neither is it completely given, but by them who have the happy skill to know what is grievance and unjust to a people, and how to remove it wisely; what good laws are wanting, and how to frame them substantially, that good men may enjoy the freedom which they merit, and the bad the curb which they need. But to do this, and to know these

1. P. B. Tillyard, op. cit., 22.

exquisite proportions, the heroic wisdom which is required, surmounted far
the principles of these narrow politicians.[1]

And after a few lines, in a passage of very great interest, he goes on
to attack not only these politicians but the English in general as
lacking in real education and culture. The English are good fighters
but unphilosophical. He is in fact anticipating Arnold's strictures
on his countrymen by two hundred years.

For Britain, to speak a truth not often spoken, as it is a land fruitful
enough of men stout and courageous in war, so it is naturally not over-
fertile of men able to govern justly and prudently in peace, trusting only in
their mother-wit; who consider not justly,[2] that civility, prudence, love of
the public good, more than of money or vain honour, are to this soil in a
manner outlandish; grow not here, but in minds well implanted with solid
and elaborate breeding, too impolitic else and rude, if not headstrong and
intractable to the industry and virtue of executing or understanding true
civil government. Valiant indeed, and prosperous to win a field; but to
know the end and reason of winning: unjudicious and unwise: in good or
bad success, alike unteachable. For the sun, which we want, ripens wits as
well as fruits; and as wine and oil are imported to us from abroad, so must
ripe understanding, and many civil virtues, be imported into our minds from
foreign writings, and examples of best ages: we shall else miscarry still, and
come short in the attempts of any great enterprise.[3]

Considering that the more cultured portion of the population was
excluded from government altogether, Milton's criticism may be
somewhat partial, but what thoughtful person would deny that
the charge of provinciality is perspicacious and not without all
foundation?

One effect of Milton's changed opinion about his country's
leaders is that he did not think them worth celebrating in his own
writings any more. There is a significant passage near the beginning
of the *History*. He is inquiring into the causes why the acts of certain
ages remain unrecorded. One of his conjectures is:

Perhaps disesteem and contempt of the public affairs then present, as not
worth recording, might partly be in cause. Certainly ofttimes we see that

1. Bohn, v. 239–40.
2. *Who consider not justly, i.e.* who are not aware of the truth that . . .
Since this was written a MS. at Harvard, probably more trustworthy than the
early printed version, has been published. In this the word 'justly' does not occur
at this point (see the Columbia edition, x. 324, and Note at end of volume). It seems
unlikely that Milton would have used the word in a different sense from 'govern
justly' immediately before. [P.B.T.]
3. Bohn, v. 240.

wise men, and of best ability, have forborn to write the acts of their own days, while they beheld with a just loathing and disdain, not only how unworthy, how perverse, how corrupt, but often how ignoble, how petty, how below all history, the persons and their actions were; who, either by fortune or some rude election, had attained, as a sore judgment and ignominy upon the land, to have chief sway in managing the commonwealth.[1]

There is no doubt whatever, both from the tone and from the analogy of the other homiletic passages, that Milton is thinking partly of his own age. He does not deem the Long Parliament of the years 1646 to 1648 worthy of the best historical writing.

In contrast let me quote the opening of the second book, in which he celebrates the power of eloquence to perpetuate the memories of great men. It is one of the most dignified and weighty among the great passages of Milton's prose. As it is too little known I quote liberally.

I am now to write of what befel the Britons from fifty and three years before the birth of our Saviour, when first the Romans came in, till the decay and ceasing of that empire; a story of much truth, and for the first hundred years and somewhat more, collected without much labour. So many and so prudent were the writers, which those two, the civilest and the wisest of European nations, both Italy and Greece, afforded to the actions of that puissant city. For worthy deeds are not often destitute of worthy relaters: as by a certain fate, great acts and great eloquence have most commonly gone hand in hand, equalling and honouring each other in the same ages. It is true, that in obscurest times, by shallow and unskilful writers, the indistinct noise of many battles and devastations of many kingdoms, overrun and lost, hath come to our ears. For what wonder, if in all ages ambition and the love of rapine hath stirred up greedy and violent men to bold attempts in wasting and ruining wars, which to posterity have left the work of wild beasts and destroyers, rather than the deeds and monuments of men and conquerors? But he whose just and true valour uses the necessity of war and dominion not to destroy, but to prevent destruction, to bring in liberty against tyrants, law and civility among barbarous nations, knowing that when he conquers all things else, he cannot conquer Time or Detraction, wisely conscious of this his want, as well as of his worth not to be forgotten or concealed, honours and hath recourse to the aid of eloquence, his friendliest and best supply; by whose immortal record his noble deeds, which else were transitory, become fixed and durable against the force of years and generations, he fails not to continue through all posterity, over Envy, Death, and Time also victorious.[2]

It may well be that here we have an implied avowal of Milton's earlier desire to be at once the historian and the poet of the political

1. Bohn, v. 164. 2. ibid., 185.

heroes of 1640 who were to have created the new England. Largely with a view to this mission he had studied the sources of English history, for his praise of the present must be firmly grounded on a thoroughgoing knowledge of the past. Finding his intended theme impossible, he gives to the public the benefit of his researches. There is a pathetic and instructive passage in which Milton gives his reason for rehashing the arid chroniclers who were his main authority for Anglo-Saxon history:

> This travail [*i.e.* of reading these chronicles], rather than not to know at once what may be known of our ancient story, sifted from fables and impertinences, I voluntarily undergo; and to save others, if they please, the like unpleasing labour.[1]

He must have read them as he had read the Christian Fathers, sick to fury and tears at their distastefulness but urged on by his fierce desire for omniscience. Considering them (like all knowledge) but a means to an end, disappointed of the end he had first in view, he turns his researches to the pathetically humble one of saving smaller people than himself unnecessary trouble.

> And yet thy heart
> The lowliest duties on herself did lay.

The sonnet *On the Lord General Fairfax at the siege of Colchester* is at once an attack on the Presbyterian government ('While Avarice and Rapine share the land') and an appeal to the victorious general for reform.

> O yet a nobler task awaites thy hand;
>   For what can Warr, but endless warr still breed,
>   Till Truth, and Right from Violence be freed,
> And Public Faith cleard from the shamefull brand
>   Of Public Fraud. In vain doth Valour bleed
>   While Avarice, and Rapine share the land.

Fairfax was to fade into obscurity, but the triumph of the party he led was to give Milton's starved hopes something at least to feed on before they were finally extinguished.

1. Bohn v. 295.

CHAPTER EIGHT

First Pamphlets against Monarchy

Date	Milton's age	Writing or event in Milton's life	Contemporary event
1649, Jan.	40		Execution of Charles I
1649, Feb.	40	*Tenure of Kings and Magistrates*	*Eikon Basilike*
1649, Mar.	40	Appointment as Secretary for Foreign Tongues to Council of State. *Observations upon the Articles of Peace*	
1649, Oct.	40	*Eikonoklastes*	Salmasius's *Defensio Regia pro Carolo I.* Cromwell in Ireland
1650, Sept.	41		Dunbar. Recovery of sea power begins
1651, Mar.	42	*Defensio pro Populo Anglicano.* Total blindness not long after	

THE Tenure of Kings and Magistrates was published in February 1649, a fortnight after Charles's execution. As is well known, it is written with comparative moderation, and refers less to Charles than to troublesome kings in general. The arguments and citations by which Milton justifies the execution matter little to us, but the first few pages state with admirable clearness ideas, already indeed familiar, but central in the meaning of *Paradise Lost*.

Milton is perfectly aware that popular opinion has swung round in Charles's favour, and he makes no attempt to conceal his contempt for the fickleness of the men who could wage war against a perfidious king and then, when God had delivered him into their hands, hesitate to make safe by the only possible way the great freedom they had wrested.

It is true, that most men are apt enough to civil wars and commotions as a novelty, and for a flash hot and active; but through sloth or inconstancy, and weakness of spirit, either fainting ere their own pretences, though never so just, be half attained, or through an inbred falsehood and wickedness, betray, ofttimes to destruction with themselves, men of noblest temper joined with them for causes whereof they in their rash undertakings were not capable.[1]

And again:

But certainly, if we consider who and what they are, on a sudden grown so pitiful, we may conclude their pity can be no true and Christian commiseration, but either levity and shallowness of mind, or else a carnal admiring of that worldly pomp and greatness, from whence they see him fallen.[2]

Levity and shallowness of mind: this we shall see is of so great importance in the story of the Fall. A few lines further on he speaks of those who 'almost shiver at the majesty and grandeur of some noble deed, as if they were newly entered into a great sin'.

This levity is due to a double weakness – over-readiness to be excited by passion on the one hand and to be checked by custom on the other. Following blind instinct and convention, they are not ruled by reason. This is how the tract opens:

If men within themselves would be governed by reason, and not generally give up their understanding to a double tyranny, of custom from without, and blind affections within, they would discern better what it is to favour and uphold the tyrant of a nation.

Passion and reason make another of the themes of *Paradise Lost*.

But though Milton has by now a low opinion of most men, he has a high opinion of a few men. In contrast with the levity and shallowness of the many he is aware of the 'others for the deliverance of their country endued with fortitude and heroic virtue to fear nothing but the curse written against those "that do the work of the Lord negligently"'. These of course are the regicides, whom he praises as men worthy to be looked up to as benefactors by future ages, should these ages not prove too degenerate. In *Paradise Lost*, too, the fortitude founded on thought is contrasted with the levity that does not think. Henceforth it is on the deeds of a few just men that he fixes his hopes.

The *Observations upon the Articles of Peace with the Irish Rebels*, the next piece of political writing, is the first composition after Milton's appointment in March 1649 as Secretary for Foreign Tongues to the Council of State. It consists of dull invective against the Irish rebels and the Ulster royalists. In it for the first time Milton mentions Cromwell.[3]

Eikonoklastes, the answer to *Eikon Basilike,* written at the order of Parliament, has small interest outside the introduction. Here Milton

1. Bohn, ii. 3.   2. ibid., 4–5.   3. ibid., 186.

restates with considerable power some of the opinions already found in *The Tenure of Kings and Magistrates*. His contempt for the fickleness of his countrymen, contrasting so sharply with the praise he gave them five years before in *Areopagitica*, is now even more emphatic.

But now, with a besotted and degenerate baseness of spirit, except some few who yet retain in them the old English fortitude and love of freedom and have testified it by their matchless deeds, the rest, imbastardized from the ancient nobleness of their ancestors, are ready to fall flat and give adoration to the image and memory of this man, who hath offered at more cunning fetches to undermine our liberties and put tyranny into an art than any British king before him.[1]

Yet in the next sentence he blames not the natural disposition of an Englishman but the prelates who have taught servility. He cannot bring himself to distrust the bulk of his countrymen completely. But he has despaired of them as his hearers: 'fit audience though few' has by now become his utmost hope.

And though well it might have seemed in vain to write at all, considering the envy and almost infinite prejudice likely to be stirred up among the common sort, against whatever can be written or gainsaid to the king's book, so advantageous to a book it is only to be a king's; and though it be an irksome labour to write with industry and judicious pains that which, neither weighed nor well read, shall be judged without industry or the pains of well-judging, by faction and the easy literature of custom and opinion; it shall be ventured yet, and the truth not smothered but sent abroad, in the native confidence of her single self, to earn, how she can, her entertainment in the world and to find out her own readers: few perhaps, but those few of such value and substantial worth as truth and wisdom, not respecting numbers and big names, have been ever wont in all ages to be contented with.[2]

There is visible in this passage too, as in the opening sentences of the tract, a reluctance to write at all: he did not fancy the work assigned him by the government. And his being compelled to write against his will may provide some excuse for the lamentable passage in the body of the pamphlet sneering at Charles for being so uninventive of prayers that he had to resort to the profane pages of Sidney's *Arcadia* to find one during the last days of his life.[3] The whole passage,

1. Bohn, i. 309.

2. ibid., 309–10.

3. I omit the vexed question of Milton's responsibility for forging the insertion of this prayer in *Eikon Basilike* (see Liljegren, *Studies in Milton*, 39–44). J. S. Smart (*Review of English Studies*, 1925, 385–91) has done something to clear Milton of the charge.

utterly at variance with Milton's usual liberality of thought, is indefensible; and the kindest supposition is that it was done to order. As propaganda appealing to the most ignorant and bigoted section of Milton's readers it is known to have been effective, causing serious annoyance to his adversaries.

Although Milton may have written *Eikonoklastes* with small relish, there is every reason to believe that he trusted and admired his employers. These, it must be remembered, were not Parliament but the Council of State, the executive authority and a body of men contrasted in their integrity with the corrupt members of Parliament. Through the Council of State he sees the hand of God working and on it he focuses his hopes. Because he believes in it, he can once again speak of his country with enthusiasm when called on to answer the attacks of Salmasius on the regicides.

The years of the controversy with Salmasius and its sequels, 1650 to 1655, are very important in Milton's mental development, but turbulent, pathetic, and obscure: possibly the years of greatest trial in his life; for by 1660 he was partially prepared to face any disaster, whereas the shock of blindness and the danger of concomitant futility necessitated a violent adjustment of his mental balance. Milton's sight began seriously to fail about the time he got his government appointment: it is well known that he sacrificed the remnants of it to write his *Defensio pro Populo Anglicano*.[1] In doing this he doubtless thought that he was thereby forfeiting all chance of writing his great poem. When we read its many pages of dreary invective, the contrast between what was achieved and what might have been lost makes us ashamed and horrified at Milton's lack of judgment. And indeed in his whole estimate of the importance of the controversy there is a curious strain of megalomania, the motives of which it will be worth attempting to disentangle. But first in fairness it must be pointed out that the political situation may somewhat extenuate the error.

The year 1649, following Charles's death, was one of extreme danger to Cromwell and his party. Not merely were there rebellions in Ireland and Scotland, but the power of the government was so low abroad that English ambassadors were murdered. Salmasius's *Defensio Regia pro Carolo I* appeared in the early autumn of that year. Written by so distinguished a scholar, it was likely to depress English prestige still further. An immediate answer might conceivably have done a very little to re-establish this prestige: Milton doubtless thought it would do a very great deal. And it was not his fault that

1. For the original Latin see the Columbia edition, vii. [P.B.T.]

by March 1651, when his *Defensio* was published, Cromwell's victories in Ireland and at Dunbar and the recovery of naval strength had made it politically unnecessary. It was force alone that could affect the prestige abroad of a government whose domestic rule rested on force alone likewise. Politically the *Defensio* was ineffective, but it was written in circumstances that somewhat justify Milton's exaggerating its importance.

There are other reasons why Milton's enthusiasms should have fired at the task allotted him. He had at last become associated with a body of men he admired and with a cause which had a daring thoroughness in it that satisfied the needs of his nature. If the mob had shown shallowness and levity in their feelings about Charles, the ruling few had not shrunk from the logical and heroic deed of putting him to death. At last there had been swift, decided action; God had not been mocked by the refusal of his favours. And so Milton is inspired by an unqualified enthusiasm for the greatness of his cause. Thus in his preface to the *Defensio* he talks of 'almost the greatest task that ever was', 'this most noble cause and most worthy to be recorded to all future ages'. Besides justifying the cause, Milton could praise his masters. In so doing he could at last fulfil (not indeed in verse) his early-cherished wish of celebrating the heroes of a reformed England, of an England that they were seeking to reform in the right way. In the following passage from the *Defensio* he confesses as much. He speaks of the honour it is that those in authority

should pitch upon me before others to be serviceable in this kind of those most valiant deliverers of my native country; and true it is that from my very youth I have been bent extremely upon such sort of studies as inclined me, if not to do great things myself, at least to celebrate those that did.[1]

There was too another desire of his youth he could fulfil, not merely as a thing permitted but as a duty. He was called upon to address himself, not to his country alone, but to the whole of the educated Western world. To do this he must write in Latin. Years before in Italy he had decided to drop Latin and forgo the wider audience, in order to honour his country. But now he is more lucky: he is forced to write in Latin (and incidentally to be more profuse in the classical allusions he loved so well than he could be when writing for his Puritan compatriots) in order to do his duty in justifying his country before the eyes of the world.

The result is a species of intoxication: the love of fame, so long kept in check and unsatisfied, runs riot. It is not, of course, till the

1. Bohn, i. 5.

Defensio Secunda that this intoxication, inflamed by the vogue of his *Defensio* on the Continent, is fully expressed: in the *Defensio* he does no more than magnify the grandeur of the allotted work. Here is the extraordinary passage from the *Defensio Secunda*, in which he believes himself the God-inspired orator before a listening Europe. My eloquence, he writes,

has excited such general and such ardent expectation, that I imagine myself not in the forum or on the rostra, surrounded only by the people of Athens or of Rome, but about to address in this, as I did in my former Defence, the whole collective body of people, cities, states, and councils of the wise and eminent, through the wide expanse of anxious and listening Europe. I seem to survey, as from a towering height, the far extended tracts of sea and land, and innumerable crowds of spectators, betraying in their looks the liveliest interest, and sensations the most congenial with my own. Here I behold the stout and manly prowess of the Germans disdaining servitude; there the generous and lively impetuosity of the French; on this side, the calm and stately valour of the Spaniard; on that, the composed and wary magnanimity of the Italian. Of all the lovers of liberty and virtue, the magnanimous and the wise, in whatever quarter they may be found, some secretly favour, others openly approve; some greet me with congratulations and applause; others, who had long been proof against conviction, at last yield themselves captive to the force of truth. Surrounded by congregated multitudes, I now imagine that, from the columns of Hercules to the Indian Ocean, I behold the nations of the earth recovering that liberty which they so long had lost; and that the people of this island are transporting to other countries a plant of more beneficial qualities, and more noble growth, than that which Triptolemus is reported to have carried from region to region; that they are disseminating the blessings of civilization and freedom among cities, kingdoms, and nations.[1]

But there is another, deeper, cause for the inordinate store Milton set by the *Defensio*: his blindness. And not only was he half-blind when he wrote but in a state of sickness.

For myself I can boldly say that I had neither words nor arguments long to seek for the defence of so good a cause, if I had enjoyed such a measure of health as would have endured the fatigue of writing. And being but weak in

---

1. Bohn, i. 219–20. Even after Milton had begun *Paradise Lost* he retained his exaggerated estimate. In *The Ready and Easy Way to establish a Free Commonwealth* (1660) he wrote: 'Nor was the heroic cause unsuccessfully defended to all Christendom, against the tongue of a famous and thought invincible adversary; nor the constancy and fortitude, that so nobly vindicated our liberty, our victory at once against two the most prevailing usurpers over mankind, superstition and tyranny, unpraised or uncelebrated in a written monument, likely to outlive detraction, as it hath hitherto convinced or silenced not a few of our detractors, especially in parts abroad.' (Bohn, ii. 113.)

body, I am forced to write by piecemeal and break off almost every hour, though the subject be such as requires an unintermitted study and intenseness of mind. But though this bodily indisposition may be a hinderance to me in setting forth the just praises of my most worthy countrymen, who have been the saviours of their native country and whose exploits, worthy of immortality, are already famous all the world over; yet I hope it will be no difficult matter for me to defend them from the insolence of this silly little scholar.[1]

The sickness to which he alludes would be nervous exhaustion brought on by the strain of work done at high pressure with failing sight. And this nervous state would very easily upset his sense of proportion. Further, for the sake of some sort of mental peace it would be a necessity for him to consider very important the work upon which he had chosen, in exclusion of other possible works, to spend his last months of vision. To have to admit that the work was of little moment would, added to the bitterness of oncoming blindness, have been unendurable.

These are some of the considerations that make the *Defensio pro Populo Anglicano* such a pathetic work. It is the longest and one of the most ephemeral of Milton's pamphlets. His furious plungings into controversy are more ridiculous than impressive. And there is an unbalanced, feverish quality in his protestations that fills the reader not with admiration but with sorrow.

Of the exultations and agonies which occupied Milton's mind during the period under discussion we know only a little. That he at times fell into despair is undoubted, if only from the unnatural way in which he exaggerated the importance of his work. Apart from this, *Samson Agonistes* is evidence that at certain times of his life he was beset by this temptation.[2] The following passage from Samson's lament, when his spirit is at its lowest ebb, seems to be very pertinent to Milton's own case when his blindness was new:

> I was his nursling once and choice delight,
> His destind from the womb,
> Promisd by Heav'nly message twice descending.
> Under his special eie
> Abstemious I grew up and thriv'd amain;
> He led me on to mightiest deeds
> Above the nerve of mortal arm
> Against the uncircumcis'd, our enemies.

1. Bohn, i. 6.

2. See Hanford's article – perhaps his most important contribution to the study of Milton's mind – 'The Temptation Motive in Milton' in *Studies in Philology*, 1918, 176–94.

But now hath cast me off as never known,
And to those cruel enemies,
Whom I by his appointment had provok't,
Left me all helpless with th' irreparable loss
Of sight, reserv'd alive to be repeated
The subject of thir cruelty, or scorn.
Nor am I in the list of them that hope;
Hopeless are all my evils, all remediless;
This one prayer yet remains, might I be heard,
No long petition, speedy death,
The close of all my miseries, and the balm.[1]

If Milton is thinking of his own case here, he would be referring with more propriety to his first months of blindness than to the period of the Restoration, when his pen was by no means helpless. For after the *Defensio* ('mightiest deeds . . .'. against the uncircumcis'd') he thought himself helpless, unable to defend himself against the attacks he was certain would be made against him. This analogy is of course no more than conjectural, but some definite evidence is given by a too little known passage from the *Defensio pro Se*[2] and possibly from the sonnet on his blindness, 'When I consider . . .' The first refers to a definite date, the time when the *Regii Sanguinis Clamor*, the anonymous reply to *Defensio pro Populo Anglicano*, appeared. This was about August 1652, not long after Milton had become totally blind. In the following passage, written presumably late in 1655, Milton is addressing himself to Morus, the supposed author of *Regii Sanguinis Clamor*:

There appeared two years ago a disgraceful anonymous book entitled *The Cry of the Royal Blood to Heaven against the English Parricides*, in which the whole Commonwealth, and especially Cromwell (then Commander-in-Chief of our armies, now the head of the Republic), mentioning him by name, were attacked with all the insults that words could express. After Cromwell our anonymous author thought fit to hurl the greatest part of his slander at me. Scarcely was this book handed to me all complete in the Council than a second copy was sent me by the man who was then president of the Court. And it was notified that I was expected on behalf of the Republic to get to work in stopping the mouth of this importunate crier. But this was the time of my worst distresses, when very different troubles combined to oppress me: bad health, the grief of the deaths of two relatives, and the now utter failure of my eye-sight. Abroad too my former adversary[3] (far worthier than the

1. 633–51.

2. *Defensio pro Se* is not included in Bohn. (For the original Latin see the Columbia edition, ix [P.B.T.].) 3. Salmasius.

present one[1]) was hovering about, daily threatening to attack me with all his might. But he died suddenly. And so, seeing that I had been relieved of a portion of my labour, with health partly restored and partly lost beyond hope, strengthened thereby for one reason or the other, lest I should appear to disappoint the expectations of the most eminent men or in the midst of so many misfortunes to have abandoned all care for the esteem of others, I attacked this man as soon as I had the power to get any certain information about that anonymous crier.

Such is Milton's own testimony to his misfortunes soon after his total blindness and to his subsequent recovery. He says nothing of the nature of his thoughts, of the sort of misery he suffered or of the subsequent reaction towards happiness. These are best seen by comparing the sonnet on his blindness[2] with the passage quoted above from *Defensio Secunda* where he vaunts that Europe is awaiting his voice. In the first there is almost an acquiescence in passivity, in the second lust for action.

> When I consider how my light is spent
> Ere half my days, in this dark world and wide,
> And that one Talent which is death to hide
> Lodg'd with me useless, though my Soul more bent
> To serve therewith my Maker, and present
> My true account, lest he returning chide;
> Doth God exact day-labour, light deny'd,
> I fondly ask; But patience to prevent
> That murmur, soon replies, God doth not need
> Either man's work or his own gifts. Who best
> Bear his milde yoak they serve him best, his State
> Is Kingly. Thousands at his bidding speed
> And post o're Land and Ocean without rest:
> They also serve who only stand and waite.

Considered in relation to the rest of Milton's works this is an extremely difficult and strange poem. There is in it a tone of self-abasement found but once again in Milton. In a way the theme is that of *Lycidas*: the ranking of the state of mind above the deed. But the conception of the deed is quite different. In *Lycidas* the deed is personal, the exercise of Milton's creative faculty: in the sonnet it is the passive yielding to God's command; Milton crouches in humble expectation, like a beaten dog ready to wag its tail at the smallest

1. Morus.
2. For dating of this sonnet see Appendix G, p. 331.

token of its master's attention. In view of Milton's normal self-confidence, of his belief in the value of his own undertakings, I cannot but see in the sonnet the signs of his having suffered an extraordinary exhaustion of vitality. Yet for all this weakness the sonnet shows the nature of Milton's greatness and the promise of recovery. When he says that God does not need man's work or his own gifts, he is expressing less a moral generalization than a conviction applying to his own case: he is stating that his own deeds and genius are of less value than personal integrity. Now this in Milton was a permanent attitude of mind, an attitude which makes his egotism not a tyranny over others but an encouragement to fortitude, not a yoke but an inspiration. The promise of recovery lies in Milton's having (at least in this sonnet) overcome his despair. He has compounded with his afflictions, and, exacting less from life than at any other time, has made his bargain with fate. In an unusual lowliness he has found repose. That attained, it was but a question of time for recovery to follow. The whole mood of the sonnet is that of the opening of *Samson Agonistes*. Samson suffers from a terrible lassitude, and yet he is all the time a 'saved' man: he has fitted his mind to the terms of his abasement and, all unknowing, has prepared it for the regeneration to come.

CHAPTER NINE
Defensio Secunda

Date	Milton's age	Writing or event in Milton's life	Contemporary event
1651, Sept.	42		Worcester. End of fighting in England
1652, May	43	Sonnet to Cromwell	
1652, June	43	Death of Mary Powell	Dutch naval war, economically disastrous
1652, July	43	Sonnet to Vane	*Regii Sanguinis Clamor.*
1653	44		Cromwell dissolves the Rump. The nominated Puritan Barebones Parliament. The Protectorate
1654 (spring)	45	*Defensio Secunda*	
1655	46	*Defensio pro Se*	The rule of the Major-Generals

THREE years intervene between the *Defensio pro Populo Anglicano* and the *Defensio Secunda*. We can be fairly certain that Milton occupied them with his public duties and his general interest in politics, experiments with amanuenses till he devised some satisfactory methods of work, and perhaps with the preliminaries to his marriage with Katharine Woodcock. The sonnets to Cromwell and Vane, written not long after that on his blindness, show his ardent interest in public affairs and at the same time are a slight exploitation of 'that one Talent which is death to hide'; for in them he does a little to fulfil his duty of celebrating the glory of the rulers of England. It was in the *Defensio Secunda* that he fully carried out that duty. But whatever Milton's occupations during these three years, we can be certain that by the time of the *Defensio Secunda* he had fought with and beaten his despair.

The *Defensio Secunda*[1] is the greatest of Milton's prose works and one of the greatest of the world's rhetorical writings. It is also the

1. For the original Latin see the Columbia edition, viii.

turning-point of Milton's literary life, the work in which he found his true strength after his utmost weakness. It is further the one prose work that sprang directly from the mood which first conceived *Paradise Lost*. These are large claims to make, and will need substantiating.

I will take the second claim first: that in the *Defensio Secunda* Milton found his true strength after his utmost weakness. I have already quoted a long and very fine passage in which Milton imagines himself addressing a listening Europe. Applied to the *Defensio pro Populo Anglicano* and to the actual political influence Milton expected his pamphlets against Salmasius to have, it showed a species of megalomania. Applied on the other hand to Milton's state of mind when he wrote the *Defensio Secunda*, it is perfectly justified. Milton has projected his own personal magnificence into the immediate practical cause he was championing. Thinking quite mistakenly that he has deserved very greatly on account of the solid services he has done his countrymen, he forgets that he is benefiting posterity by revealing to it the wealth of his own nature.

The contrast between the two *Defensiones* is as striking as it can be. The first is the labour of a man sick in body and spirit, carried through by force of will. Before he wrote the second, Milton might have said with his own Samson,

> I begin to feel
> Some rouzing motions in me which dispose
> To something extraordinary my thoughts.

In it one feels the man's vitality flooding in and surging up to a level it has never attained before. He has experienced the worst that life can submit him to: he has passed safely through the Valley of the Shadow of Death. And now he has grown to the full stature of his manhood. So overpowering is the sense of his vitality that he sees himself more vividly than ever before a man inspired by God. His blindness is less an affliction than a proof that God has marked him out like the great men of old, Timoleon the virtuous King of Sicily, Appius Claudius the Roman Censor, for some remarkable work.

The result of this returning vitality and mental growth is that Milton now speaks in a fuller and more certain tone than ever before. Behind his exhortation to the English people there is a larger experience than behind the parallel passage in *Areopagitica*, and no danger of his being disappointed by events going against his hopes.

He has already faced the worst possibilities, and his exhortation has the calm that belongs to the fulness of knowledge. *Defensio Secunda* is thus the fourth *apex* in Milton's mental progress as revealed in his writing, fourth after the *Nativity Ode, Lycidas,* and *Areopagitica.*

Besides this, the mentality of *Defensio Secunda* is very largely the mentality of *Paradise Lost.* One can be more precise and say that *Defensio Secunda* and the first two books or so of *Paradise Lost* are closely akin in their temper. *Paradise Lost* as a whole is pervaded by a pessimism not found in the prose work, a pessimism which resulted (to anticipate a little) from the course of political events leading up to the Restoration. But the earlier books are less pervaded by this spirit than the later. I feel confident from internal evidence that they were shaping themselves in Milton's mind about the time of the *Defensio Secunda,* and that, however modified, they never quite lost the original brightness of the time of reviving hopes. But there is external evidence too connecting *Defensio Secunda* with *Paradise Lost,* nor is the internal evidence confined to a general similarity of tone. In July 1654, that is a couple of months after *Defensio Secunda* was published, Milton wrote a letter to Oldenburg about his controversy with Salmasius. He ends as follows:

It would not be difficult to persuade me to engage in other undertakings, though I doubt whether they would be nobler or more useful (for what human activity could be nobler or more useful than the vindication of liberty?), if only my health and the loss of my sight (which is a greater affliction than old age itself), and most of all if the 'cries' of such impostors as this will allow me to do so. For mere idleness, on the one hand, has never had any charm for me, and on the other, it was much against my will that I found myself obliged to take part in this unexpected contest with the enemies of liberty, at a time when I was engrossed in far different and more delightful occupations. At the same time I do not regret my action, since it was necessary, and I am far from thinking that I have wasted my time to no purpose, as you seem to suggest.[1]

What were the other undertakings, the more delightful occupations? The *History of Britain* or the *De Doctrina Christiana*? Hardly; when Milton speaks of delight in writing he probably means verse: he is thinking of *Paradise Lost.* Aubrey tells us that the writing of *Paradise Lost* was begun in 1658, according to what Phillips told him. Phillips is not so definite in his own written statement, but certainly implies that Milton got busy with *Paradise Lost* as soon as the

1. P. B. Tillyard, op. cit., 29–30.

Salmasius episode was ended, that is in 1655. Here is his statement:

> He wrote, by his amanuensis, his two *Answers to Alexander More*; who upon the last answer quitted the field. So that being now quiet from state adversaries and publick contests, he had leisure for his own studies and private designs; which were his foresaid *History of England* and a new *Thesaurus Linguae Latinae*. . . . But the heighth of his noble fancy and invention began now to be seriously and mainly employed in a subject worthy of such a Muse, *viz.* a heroick poem, entitled *Paradise Lost*.

Phillips's two statements do not conflict. Milton probably spent three years in meditating upon the plan of *Paradise Lost* and in composing passages in his head before he committed anything to writing. His written account would confirm Oldenburg's letter and the idea that the *Defensio Secunda* and *Paradise Lost* had their origin about the same time.

There is one striking piece of internal evidence. The Hymn to Light at the opening of *Paradise Lost*, Book Three, is a poetic version of part of the passage in *Defensio Secunda* on Milton's blindness:[1] or the other way about. It is likely that they were composed about the same time. Further, there is an analogy between the 'characters' of the Devils in Book One of *Paradise Lost* with those of Cromwell and his fellows in *Defensio Secunda*. I do not mean to imply any direct comparisons: merely that the 'character' idea, so strong in the seventeenth century, is present in both works and probably entered Milton's mind as an idea applicable to both forms of composition.

If, as I conjecture, the serious beginnings of *Paradise Lost* are to be found in the state of mind that prompted the *Defensio Secunda*, it may be legitimate to allow the ideas found in the *Defensio* to guide our search for the ideas that are of real importance in *Paradise Lost*. The *Defensio Secunda* is likely to be particularly useful in this quest because it is singularly little complicated by theological discussion or the hunting of texts. Milton seems to speak his mind unimpeded. We have a singular opportunity of looking into that volcano.

Saurat sees as the main idea of Milton's life the conflict of passion and reason, a conflict primarily personal and in important part concerned with sex, but projected from his particular case to the world in general. Passion is bad if allowed free play: if tempered by reason it is good and admits the only true liberty. I incline to think that Saurat exaggerates the importance of this theme in the earlier

1. Bohn, i. 236-9.

writings, possibly in *Paradise Lost*, but I am bound to admit that in the *Defensio Secunda* it is to the fore, conditioning all desirable action. In the character of Cromwell the highest praise is that he conquered himself: his heroic acts are derived from this conquest.

> When the sword was drawn, he offered his services, and was appointed to a troop of horse, whose numbers were soon increased by the pious and the good, who flocked from all quarters to his standard; and in a short time he almost surpassed the greatest generals in the magnitude and the rapidity of his achievements. Nor is this surprising; for he was a soldier disciplined to perfection in the knowledge of himself. He had either extinguished or by habit learned to subdue, the whole host of vain hopes, fears, and passions, which infest the soul. He first acquired the government of himself, and over himself acquired the most signal victories; so that on the first day he took the field against the external enemy, he was a veteran in arms, consummately practised in the toils and exigencies of war.[1]

Of Fairfax he says:

> Nor was it only the enemy whom you subdued, but you have triumphed over that flame of ambition and that lust of glory which are wont to make the best and greatest of men their slaves.[2]

And the whole of the appeal to England at the end is based on the doctrine that only those are free who have learnt to rule their own passions.

Areopagitica looked back to the once planned Arthuriad: it also contained hints of *Paradise Lost*. *Defensio Secunda*, though mainly pointing to the future, does yet fulfil one early pledge. Milton had in his first pamphlets expressed his wish to praise the benefactors of his country in some worthy way, as he then thought, in verse. From time to time he praised Parliament, but never with all his heart, for Parliament never fulfilled its promise. Now at last England was governed by a body of men in whom he believes, and who by their destruction of tyranny have to their credit a solid achievement; and he can let himself go. He praises the men and he praises their deeds with no uncertain voice. And he ends the pamphlet with the conviction of having fulfilled at last the duty of patriotism so long ago proposed.

> I have delivered my testimony, I would almost say, have erected a monument, that will not readily be destroyed, to the reality of those singular and mighty achievements which were above all praise. As the epic poet, who

1. Bohn, i. 285–6. 2. ibid., 287.

adheres at all to the rules of that species of composition, does not profess to
describe the whole life of the hero whom he celebrates, but only some particular action of his life, as the resentment of Achilles at Troy, the return of
Ulysses, or the coming of Aeneas into Italy; so it will be sufficient, either for
my justification or apology, that I have heroically celebrated at least one
exploit of my countrymen; I pass by the rest, for who could recite the achievements of a whole people?[1]

The reference to the epic in this passage should be clear. Milton hated
to abandon any project on which he had embarked. He is thinking
of the promised Arthuriad and the present fulfilment of it, the only
fulfilment it is in his power to accomplish. But the reference to epic
claims more. Milton says that he has in his *Defensio Secunda* 'heroically' done his work. Does this piece of prose really come up to this
exalted claim?

The question resolves itself really into one of style. The matter, as
we have seen, is serious and lofty enough. Is Milton's Latin a fitting
vehicle? I can do little more than record a personal impression
that it is, and submit one or two quotations to the judgment of those
readers who have sufficient interest, and patience of Latin, to read
them critically. By writing in a foreign tongue Milton has of necessity sacrificed the homeliness and freshness that enlivened the style
of his English prose. We are remote from the language of everyday
speech and frankly in the realms of rhetoric. But granted the rhetorical setting, the way Milton makes the Latin language obey him,
rousing it to eloquence, subduing it to plainness, hushing it to a
poetical serenity, or goading it to the brutalities of his satire, is
astonishing. He seems perfectly at ease in the sonorities of Latin and
puts them, regally, to whatever use he desires. Here is a passage
from the panegyric on Cromwell. Being a piece of formal and
elaborate rhetoric, it cannot suffer abbreviation. Amplitude is
essential to this mode of writing, which depends for its effect on a
gradual working up and frequent repetitions.

Tu igitur, Cromuelle, magnitudine illa animi macte esto; te enim decet:
tu patriae liberator, libertatis auctor, custosque idem et conservator, neque
graviorem personam neque augustiorem suscipere potes aliam; qui non
modo regum res gestas sed heroum quoque nostrorum fabulas factis ex-
superasti. Cogita saepius, quam caram rem, ab quam cara parente tua,
libertatem a patria tibi commendatam atque concreditam, apud te de-
positam habes; quod ab electissimis gentis universae viris illa modo ex-
pectabat, id nunc a te uno expectat, per te unum consequi sperat. Reverere

tantam de te expectationem, spem patriae de te unicam; reverere vultus et
vulnera tot fortium virorum, quotquot, te duce, pro libertate tam strenue
decertarunt; manes etiam eorum qui in ipso certamine occubuerunt: reverere exterarum quoque civitatum existimationem de nobis atque ser-
mones: quantas res de libertate nostra tam fortiter parta, de nostra republica
tam gloriose exorta, sibi polliceantur: quae si tam cito quasi aborta evanuer-
it, profecto nihil aeque dedecorosum huic genti, atque pudendum fuerit:
teipsum denique reverere, ut pro qua adipiscenda libertate tot aerumnas
pertulisti, tot pericula adiisti, eam adeptus violatam per te aut ulla in parte
imminutam aliis ne sinas esse.[1]

Very different, but not less masterly, is the opening of Milton's
account (so well known in its English version) of his own career. It is
quiet and simple, but the style with its unobtrusiveness and purity
has great charm.

Londini sum natus, genere honesto, patre viro integerrimo, matre
probatissima et eleemosynis per viciniam potissimum nota. Pater me
puerulum humaniorum literarum studiis destinavit; quas ita avide arripui
ut ab anno aetatis duodecimo vix unquam ante mediam noctem a lucu-
brationibus cubitum discederem; quae prima oculorum pernicies fuit,
quorum ad naturalem debilitatem accesserant et crebri capitis dolores.
Quae omnia cum discendi impetum non retardarent, et in ludo literario et
sub aliis domi magistris erudiendum quotidie curavit; ita, variis instructum

1. Bohn, i. 289–90, gives the following rather free translation. The translations
from the other passages to be quoted are from the same source:

Do you then, sir, continue your course with the same unrivalled magnanimity;
it sits well upon you; – to you our country owes its liberties; nor can you sustain
a character at once more momentous and more august than that of the author,
the guardian, and the preserver of our liberties; and hence you have not only
eclipsed the achievements of all our kings, but even those which have been
fabled of our heroes. Often reflect what a dear pledge the beloved land of your
nativity has entrusted to your care; and that liberty which she once expected
only from the chosen flower of her talents and her virtues, she now expects from
you only, and by you only hopes to obtain. Revere the fond expectations which
we cherish, the solicitudes of your anxious country; revere the looks and the
wounds of your brave companions in arms, who, under your banners, have so
strenuously fought for liberty; revere the shades of those who perished in the
contest; revere also the opinions and the hopes which foreign states entertain
concerning us, who promise to themselves so many advantages from that liberty
which we have so bravely acquired, from the establishment of that new government which has begun to shed its splendour on the world, which, if it be suffered
to vanish like a dream, would involve us in the deepest abyss of shame; and lastly,
revere yourself; and, after having endured so many sufferings and encountered so
many perils for the sake of liberty, do not suffer it, now it is obtained, either to be
violated by yourself, or in any one instance impaired by others.

linguis et percepta haud leviter philosophiae dulcedine, ad Gymnasium gentis alterum Cantabrigiam, misit.[1]

The next passage, which comes from Milton's discourse on his blindness, is a good example of his most poetical prose. It is simple rather than rhetorical, but its simplicity is not that of plainness but of high emotion adequately controlled.

Est quoddam per imbecillitatem, praeeunte Apostolo, ad maximas vires iter: sim ego debilissimus, dummodo in mea debilitate immortalis ille et melior vigor eo se efficacius exserat, dummodo in meis tenebris divini vultus lumen eo clarius eluceat. Tum enim infirmissimus ero simul et validissimus, caecus eodem tempore et perspicacissimus; hac possim ego infirmitate consummari, hac perfici, possim in hac obscuritate sic ego irradiari.[2]

Finally I quote what is perhaps the most diverting passage in all the many pages of Milton's personal scurrility. Morus, the object of his attack, had been accused of seducing a servant-girl. Neighbours had seen them together in a garden. Luckily for Milton his opponent's name *Morus* means mulberry-tree in Latin and provides him with the means of some extremely apt botanical innuendo. He fairly goes off into hoots of glee as he suggests the kind of botany lesson Morus gave the girl – harmless, of course; only, the presbytery saw fit to expel him from the ministry nevertheless.

Hospitis ancillam quandam forte adamaverat; eam paulo post etiam alteri nuptam sectari non destitit; tuguriolum quoddam intrare hortuli, solum cum sola, vicini saepe animadverterant. Citra adulterium, inquis;

1. Bohn, i. 254:
I was born at London, of an honest family; my father was distinguished by the undeviating integrity of his life; my mother, by the esteem in which she was held, and the alms which she bestowed. My father destined me from a child to the pursuits of literature; and my appetite for knowledge was so voracious, that, from twelve years of age, I hardly ever left my studies, or went to bed before midnight. This primarily led to my loss of sight. My eyes were naturally weak, and I was subject to frequent head-aches; which, however, could not chill the ardour of my curiosity, or retard the progress of my improvement. My father had me daily instructed in the grammar-school, and by other masters at home. He then, after I had acquired a proficiency in various languages, and had made a considerable progress in philosophy, sent me to the University of Cambridge.

2. ibid., 239:
There is, as the apostle has remarked, a way to strength through weakness. Let me then be the most feeble creature alive, as long as that feebleness serves to invigorate the energies of my rational and immortal spirit; as long as in that obscurity in which I am enveloped, the light of the divine presence more clearly shines, then, in proportion as I am weak, I shall be invincibly strong; and in proportion as I am blind, I shall more clearly see. O! that I may thus be perfected by feebleness, and irradiated by obscurity!

poterat enim quidvis aliud. Sane quidem poterat confabulari, nimirum de re hortensi, praelectiones quasdam suas sciolae fortasse foeminae et audiendi cupidae expromere de hortis, Alcinoi puta vel Adonidis; poterat nunc areolas laudare, umbram tantummodo desiderare; liceret modo ficui morum inserere, complures inde sycomoros quam citissime enasci, ambulationem amoenissimam; modum deinde insitionis mulieri poterat monstrare. Haec et plura poterat, quis negat? Verumtamen Presbyteris satisfacere non poterat, quin illum tanquam adulterum censura ferirent, et pastoris munere indignum prorsus judicarent.[1]

The letter to Philaras, the Athenian, written on 28 September, 1654, in reply to an offer to procure the aid of a famous French oculist, confirms the spirit of the *Defensio Secunda*: it is full of confidence and courage.

The *Defensio pro Se*, published in August 1655, completes the Salmasian controversy. It is personal and abusive, and chiefly interesting in showing that Milton would not allow any considerations for the pursuits he preferred, to prevent him from carrying through to the end the dispute to which he had committed himself.

1. Bohn, i. 225–6. I quote no translation, as the passage is amusing only in the original. The reference to the fig is interesting. Milton may have learnt something about the symbolism of the fig from his Italian friends. See D. H. Lawrence's poem 'Figs', in *Birds, Beasts and Flowers* (Collected Poems, ii. 129).

CHAPTER TEN
Interval in Pamphlet-Writing
1655–1659

Date	Milton's age	Writing or event in Milton's life	Contemporary event
1655	46	Sonnets to Lawrence and Skinner Salary reduced to life pension. Freedom from much official work. Begins again upon *History of Britain*. Begins *De Doctrina Christiana*	Wars with Spain Religious tolerance under Cromwell
1658, Sept.	49		Death of Cromwell
1658, Oct.	49	Second edition of *Defensio Prima*	

I T IS probable that from the completion of the Salmasian tracts to the death of Cromwell Milton enjoyed a mental calm greater than at any previous time since the civil troubles began. He had delivered his testimony to Cromwell and to the English people, and for the moment he need meddle with politics no longer. The two Horatian sonnets, one to Lawrence, the other to Cyriack Skinner, express the serenity of the period, while the second sonnet to Skinner, written three years after blindness had become total, is full of cheerful courage. It should be compared with the sonnet, so emptied of vitality, referring to the newly-fallen calamity.

> *Cyriack*, this three years day these eys, though clear
>   To outward view, of blemish or of spot,
>   Bereft of light thir seeing have forgot,
>   Nor to thir idle orbs doth sight appear
> Of Sun or Moon or Starre throughout the year,
>   Or man or woman. Yet I argue not
>   Against heavns hand or will, nor bate a jot
>   Of heart or hope; but still bear up and steer
> Right onward. What supports me, dost thou ask?
>   The conscience, Friend, to have lost them overply'd

> In libertyes defence, my noble task,
> Of which all Europe talks from side to side.
> This thought might lead me through the worlds vain mask
> Content though blind, had I no better guide.

It would be at this period, too, that Milton's fame abroad gave him most satisfaction. Aubrey tells how

He was visited much by the learned, more than he did desire. He was mightily importuned to goe into France and Italie. Foreigners came much to see him and much admired him, and offered to him great preferments to come over to them; and the only inducement of severall foreigners that came over into England, was chiefly to see Oliver Protector, and Mr J. Milton; and would see the house and chamber where *he* was borne. He was much more admired abrode than at home.

Even if Milton was overdone with foreign visitors, he loved fame enough to be more gratified than annoyed. Then the brief spell of happy marriage with Katharine Woodcock, his 'late espoused saint', falls within this epoch. Not only would Milton be calmer and more cheerful, but he had more leisure, for in 1655 his official duties were reduced and his salary commuted to a life pension. The four years must have been propitious to work.

He would have spent them, in the first place, on *Paradise Lost*. A passage from Phillips's *Life of Milton* was quoted in the last chapter suggesting that Milton busied himself with that poem as soon as the Salmasian controversy was finished. And this is not the only evidence. It cannot be thought that Milton would have begun writing before he had the plan of the poem, on which he spent the utmost care, complete in his mind: to have done so would have been to contradict his essential nature. Beginning to write *Paradise Lost* in 1658, it must have been long before this date that he began planning it in his mind. Again, Aubrey says that the poem, begun in 1658, was completed in 1663; Phillips that Milton composed only from the autumnal to the vernal equinox. Between 1658 and 1661 came a period of tract-writing and all the danger and harassment of the Restoration. Further, dictation would not make for speed. Unless the plan (and possibly some of the speeches) were in Milton's mind by 1658, it is difficult to see how he could, in the circumstances, have got his poem finished by 1663. The evidence, then, is that these years of calm must have been very important to the shaping of *Paradise Lost*.

There are some sentences in a letter to Emeric Bigot,[1] written 24 March, 1657, revealing Milton's state of mind and containing an interesting resemblance to a passage in *Paradise Lost*.

I am glad to find you convinced of my serenity in the great affliction of blindness, and of my friendly interest in foreigners and hospitality to them. I have indeed good reason for patience under the loss of my sight, in hoping that it is not so much lost as retired and withdrawn into myself, and that it serves to sharpen rather than dull the sight of my mind. Thus it is that I feel no resentment against books and have not altogether given up the study of them, great as is the price they have exacted. Against such pettiness I am warned by the example of Telephus, King of the Mysians, who did not refuse to be cured by the very weapon which inflicted the wound.[2]

The second sentence, like the passage in *Defensio Secunda*, reminds of the Hymn to Light in *Paradise Lost* and in particular of the lines:

> So much the rather thou Celestial light
> Shine inward, and the mind through all her powers
> Irradiate, there plant eyes.[3]

It is easy to see why Milton should harp on the notion that there was compensation for his blindness. Although a scholar and a poet, he had always been proud of physical soundness. Aubrey noted of him,

His harmonicall and ingeniose soul did lodge in a beautifull and well-proportioned body.
In toto nusquam corpore menda fuit. OVID.

He had resented the implication of effeminacy in the college nick-name of 'the lady'; he had exercised himself in fencing and habitually had worn a sword; in the early days of the Civil War he spoke of himself 'with useful and generous labours preserving the body's health and hardiness to render lightsome, clear, and not lumpish obedience to the mind'; and in the *Defensio Secunda* he had responded to the taunt of physical deformity with a vehemence that betrayed how deeply the charge had hurt him. Blindness must have been a humiliation as well as an inconvenience. His pride demanded some satisfaction, and he is forced to the notion that though now physically inferior to most men his mental powers have thereby become almost superhuman.

1. Bigot was a French scholar, who must have been among the many visitors from abroad Milton had in these years. See Masson, op. cit., v. 284.

2. P. B. Tillyard, op. cit., 39.   3. *Paradise Lost*, iii. 51–3.

His other work was to write two more books of the *History of Britain*, bringing it down to the Norman Conquest, and to begin his treatise *De Doctrina Christiana*. The second, probably not completed till soon after the Restoration, must be kept for discussion in the chapter on Milton's beliefs, but in passing one may mention that it perhaps had an international as well as a personal aim. Milton seems to have intended it both as a summary of his own beliefs and as a theological handbook, based on the Bible alone, for an international union of Protestant churches in England and abroad.[1] Hopes for such a union were alive while, under Cromwell, every variety of Protestant belief was allowed to flourish. Having this international aim, Milton, as in the Salmasian tracts, wrote in Latin. Thus even in this comparatively private period of his life Milton was planning for what he considered the practical welfare of mankind; was trying, while justifying the ways of God to men, to promote the heaven on earth of which he had not altogether despaired.

At about the time of Cromwell's death Milton was preparing a second edition[2] of the *Defensio Prima*. There is little new except a postscript, in which he reviews the work and hints of plans for the future. As this postscript is not included in editions of Milton's prose and is of considerable interest, I give a translation of the whole:[3]

Some years ago now I made haste to publish this work as the business of the State then demanded. But I thought that if leisure should ever enable me to take it up again, I might (as commonly happens) do a good deal in the way of polishing, expunging, or inserting. This I think I have accomplished, but with fewer changes than I expected. Such as it is, I see that it is a monument that will not easily perish. And if any man shall be found to have defended civil freedom more freely than I have, it would certainly be hard to find anyone who has done so in a greater or more notable example. Further, if one must believe that an example so difficult and so glorious could not have been so successfully attempted and accomplished without divine inspiration, does it not follow that it was by the same help and guidance that it was glorified and defended in this eulogy? a conclusion I would wish universally held rather than that I should get the credit of any personal merit, be it natural ability, good judgment, or diligence.

Only I must add this. As the famous Roman Consul in laying down his office swore that Rome had been kept safe by his care alone, so I, in putting the finishing touch to my work, while I call God and men to witness, dare make this claim: In this book of mine proofs have been given, and passages from the chief authorities on wisdom both human and divine have been

1. See Hanford, *Handbook*, 3rd ed., 120–1.
2. A rare volume: one copy in the British Museum.
3. It has since been published in the Columbia edition, vii. 555–9 [P.B.T.].

cited, by virtue of which I am confident the people of England have been defended in this cause to their deathless fame with posterity, and by virtue of which many men, formerly deceived by their ignorance of what they were entitled to and by the phantom of a religious scruple, have, unless they prefer and hence have merited slavery, won a sufficient measure of liberty. And as this most solemn oath of the Consul was confirmed by the unanimous vote of the whole Roman people met together, so, I have long been assured, this plea of mine has been approved with universal acclamation by the noblest, not only of my own citizens, but of mankind. That then has been the fruit of the efforts I have in my life set myself, and I rejoice in it. At the same time this is my most urgent thought: how I may best be able to prove, not only to my country (which I have served with all my strength) but to men of every nation and especially to the whole of Christendom, that my whole desire and thought is for their sakes, if I have the power, which God granting it I shall have, to accomplish even greater things than I have accomplished already.

The four and a half years that intervened between this piece of writing and the *Defensio Secunda* have by no means mitigated Milton's pride in the *Defensio Prima*. Nor is there the slightest hint that he doubted the permanence of the Commonwealth. Masson[1] assumes that the last sentence refers to *Paradise Lost*. I doubt it. The reference to the whole of Christendom reminds of the dedication of the *De Doctrina Christiana* 'to all the churches of Christ and to all who profess the Christian faith throughout the world'. In the preface to the same work Milton speaks of giving 'as wide a circulation as possible to what I esteem my best and richest possession'. He wrote the *Defensio Prima* in Latin in order that it might be read by the whole civilized world; he is addressing his second edition to the same audience: and when he speaks to them of a still greater accomplishment I believe he refers to his other great Latin work, at that time in progress, the *De Doctrina Christiana*. It is not in the least impossible that Milton at this time thought as highly of that work as of its poetic counterpart, *Paradise Lost*.

The last two books of the *History of Britain* have practically no bearing on Milton's opinions at this time.

---

1. *Life of Milton*, v. 574.

CHAPTER ELEVEN
Pamphlets preceding the Restoration

Date	Milton's age	Writing or event in Milton's life	Contemporary event
1659, Feb.	50	Civil Power in Ecclesiastical Causes	
1659, May	50		Richard Cromwell abdicates. Rump restored
1659, Aug.	50	Likeliest Means to remove Hirelings out of the Church	
1659, Oct.	50	On the Ruptures of the Commonwealth	
1660, Mar.	51	Ready and Easy Way to establish a Free Commonwealth	General Monk occupies London, declares for a free Parliament

CROMWELL's death in September 1658 must have ended this period of Milton's comparative mental serenity. He could no longer trust the rulers; for he *had* trusted Cromwell, however much he had disagreed with Cromwell's refusal to abolish tithes and Church Establishment in general. However, though Milton may have feared for England, he could at least argue with the new government on the matters of ecclesiastical liberty so dear to his heart and so impossible of realization while Cromwell was there to differ from him. Thus, during the year 1659 he addresses to Parliament the two tracts, *A Treatise of Civil Power in Ecclesiastical Causes* and *The Likeliest Means to remove Hirelings out of the Church.*

In the first Milton argues for the complete separation of civil and ecclesiastical control. It is not a great pamphlet, but it contains an interesting passage on what he understands by doctrinal authority[1] and a fine denunciation of Protestant persecutors. The only authority in doctrine is the Bible, and no man has the right to enforce on another his interpretation of the Bible. The passage on Protestant persecutors is worth quoting.

> How many persecutions, then, imprisonments, banishments, penalties, and stripes; how much bloodshed have the forcers of conscience to answer

1. Bohn, ii. 523.

for, and protestants rather than papists! For the papist, judging by his principles, punishes them who believe not as the church believes, though against the scripture; but the protestant, teaching every one to believe the scripture, though against the church, counts heretical, and persecutes against his own principles, them who in any particular so believe as he in general teaches them.[1]

The second tract shows Milton's break with almost any kind of religious organization. The clergy are to have no stipend except voluntary contributions and are to be encouraged to have other occupations. He plainly favours the Quakers and other newly-arisen sects rather than the state-paid Independents. In neither of these tracts is there any sign that Milton thought the Commonwealth to be nearly at an end or that he seriously interrupted his writing of *Paradise Lost*.

The last pamphlets are different. Milton suddenly awoke to the peril of the situation. In his letter to a friend *On the Ruptures of the Commonwealth* he recounts how he had been startled out of his security by the conversation they had had the evening before. Up till then his state had been one of

resigning myself to the wisdom and care of those who had the government; and not finding that either God or the public required more of me than my prayers for them that govern.[2]

Now he realized the perils of the military rule of contending generals into which the country had fallen, and wrote to put forward his own remedy. His ideas, which need not concern us, are briefly outlined in the letter. They were elaborated in his last pamphlet of any importance, *The Ready and Easy Way to establish a Free Commonwealth*, addressed to General Monk, then about to summon the Parliament that called back Charles II. A second edition was addressed to the Parliament itself shortly before its definitive act. It is one of the most interesting of Milton's pamphlets, one of the most earnest and dignified, and one of the least spoilt by contemporary methods of pamphleteering. Yet with all its earnestness and enthusiasm it has not quite the vehemence of his earliest prose. Milton is indeed hopeful – and at a time when hope was unreasonable – but the heady vehemence has been replaced by a fine Stoicism. He is just a little detached: the occupation with *Paradise Lost* has robbed the present hour of just a shade of its urgency. Or is it simply that Milton is now fifty-one years old? Anyhow, along with the typically san-

1. Bohn, ii. 532.   2. ibid., 102.

guine expectation that his scheme, if adopted, will work with the greatest ease is the full facing of the facts. He is perfectly aware that the monarchy may be restored and (as he thought) the fruits of reformation lost. The way he propounds is 'plain, easy, and open before us', but he talks too of the present as quite possibly 'a little shroving-time, wherein to speak freely and take our leaves of liberty'.

One of the most eloquent and significant passages is that in which he asks how the people once free can permit themselves to be again enslaved by a King. Only a kind of infatuation or a criminal inertia could cause such a disaster.

Certainly then that people must needs be mad or strangely infatuated, that build the chief hope of their common happiness or safety on a single person; who, if he happen to be good, can do no more than another man; if to be bad, hath in his hands to do more evil without check, than millions of other men. The happiness of a nation must needs be firmest and certainest in full and free council of their own electing, where no single person, but reason only, sways. And what madness is it for them who might manage nobly their own affairs themselves, sluggishly and weakly to devolve all on a single person; and, more like boys under age than men, to commit all to his patronage and disposal, who neither can perform what he undertakes; and yet for undertaking it, though royally paid, will not be their servant, but their lord! How unmanly must it needs be, to count such a one the breath of our nostrils, to hang all our felicity on him, all our safety, our well-being, for which if we were aught else but sluggards or babies, we need depend on none but God and our own counsels, our own active virtue and industry![1]

The old Miltonic antithesis: self-reliance and active virtue contrasted with dependence and sluggishness.

But the last paragraph is the finest of all. It is the fitting epilogue of the controversial pamphlets. By its inflexible resolution to hope on till ultimate disaster it not merely expresses Milton's courage but recalls the ardent hope of the earliest pamphlets. Nor is the courage founded on the senseless optimism that will not face the facts: he is perfectly aware of the desperate situation.

What I have spoken, is the language of that which is not called amiss 'The good old Cause': if it seem strange to any, it will not seem more strange, I hope, than convincing to backsliders. Thus much I should perhaps have said, though I was sure I should have spoken only to trees and stones; and had none to cry to, but with the prophet, 'O earth, earth, earth!' to tell the very soil itself, what her perverse inhabitants are deaf to. Nay, though what I have spoke should happen (which thou suffer not, who

1. Bohn, ii. 118–20.

didst create mankind free! nor thou next, who didst redeem us from being servants of men!) to be the last words of our expiring liberty. But I trust I shall have spoken persuasion to abundance of sensible and ingenuous men; to some, perhaps, whom God may raise from these stones to become children of reviving liberty; and may reclaim, though they seem now choosing them a captain back for Egypt, to bethink themselves a little, and consider whither they are rushing; to exhort this torrent also of the people, not to be so impetuous, but to keep their due channel; and at length recovering and uniting their better resolutions, now that they see already how open and unbounded the insolence and rage is of our common enemies, to stay these ruinous proceedings, justly and timely fearing to what a precipice of destruction the deluge of this epidemic madness would hurry us, through the general defection of a misguided and abused multitude.[1]

It has been suggested above that the disillusionment caused by the ruin of Milton's political hopes must have been enormous. Certainly the contrast in tone between the passage just quoted and the tremulous eagerness of hope that marked the first pages of *Reformation in England* is powerful enough: Milton is a changed man. But for all the stoicism he learnt since his blindness I cannot believe that he was completely prepared for the Restoration or that this event was not a very great shock. Unfortunately there is no prose work to inform us of the truth. We can only learn from *Paradise Lost*: and not from the scheme of *Paradise Lost*, which was fixed before the Restoration, only from the tone of say the last half, which cannot well date till after 1660. But if in these we do indeed find traces of a disillusionment deeper than anything in this his last significant pamphlet, we shall be justified in assuming that the ultimate destruction of those hopes on which he seemed at one time to have staked everything was indeed responsible.

1. Bohn, ii. 138.

INTERCHAPTER
Milton's Beliefs

THERE is good evidence for dating the *De Doctrina Christiana* from 1655 to 1660.[1] It will therefore be in place to insert here any remarks I have to make on Milton's religious beliefs. There is another reason too. It will be a good thing to clear the ground for discussing *Paradise Lost* by speaking of these beliefs beforehand. There is in all people's minds a discrepancy between professed and real beliefs – real in the sense of prompting a person's actions or attitudes. Such a discrepancy has been noted in Milton from the time of Blake at least, though not usually outside the person of Satan. There may still be room for another attempt to find the real meaning of *Paradise Lost*, and incidentally the relation of this real to the professed meaning of the poem; for the two may be widely different or they may overlap a very great deal. Now the *De Doctrina Christiana*[2] is of all the works of Milton (if we except such things as the Latin Grammar) the least emotional, the most guarded, hence the most likely to give his professed beliefs. The same is true, to a lesser extent, of all his prose compared with *Paradise Lost*. Conversely, only in the more emotional medium are we likely to get at the largest measure of unconscious truth. If then we have in our mind the main beliefs as revealed in the prose and particularly in the *De Doctrina Christiana*, we may be better able to detect anything fresh that has entered into the poem. Of course Milton's professed beliefs are found in *Paradise Lost* too, and it is quite possible to compare the professed and the real beliefs without reference to the *De Doctrina Christiana*. But the prose treatise is more definite and more convincing. Moreover it is good to refer to it in order to clear away the very considerable remnants of wrong ideas about Milton's professed beliefs as found in *Paradise Lost* : and the prose statement is likely to be more easily credited than the poetical; he would hardly have said what he did not pretty strictly profess, when he wrote in his soberest prose.

But quite apart from *Paradise Lost* it is useful to speak of Milton's beliefs. In spite of much good work in the last dozen years or so[3]

1. See J. H. Hanford in *Studies in Philology*, 1920, 309–19.

2. For the original Latin see the Columbia edition, xiv–xvii.

3. I refer especially to the work of Liljegren, Saurat, Hanford, and Greenlaw. But it must not be forgotten that as early as 1890 Richard Garnett, in his *Life of Milton*, put the emphasis very strongly on Milton's relation to the Renaissance. Raleigh, too, is free from the Puritan obsession. Grierson anticipated a good deal

pointing out that Milton's thought belongs primarily to the Renaissance, the idea still prevails widely that he held the conventional Puritan beliefs of his age; or, more accurately, he is credited with the beliefs which the nineteenth century understood the Puritans of the seventeenth century to hold. Writers on Milton should do what they can to destroy this fallacy.

In saying above that the *De Doctrina Christiana* was more definite and convincing than *Paradise Lost* in its exposition of Milton's professed doctrines, I do not wish to imply that it has more than a relative definiteness. The unprofessed element, though smaller, is by no means absent from the prose work. Indeed there has been the tendency (and Saurat is not quite free of it) of working out Milton's beliefs too precisely. It has usually been assumed that Milton was quite decided in his mind, that his beliefs, whether orthodox or not, were clear, but this assumption may turn out not to be justified.

Before giving an account of Milton's main doctrines in his theological treatise, it will be well to speak of two questions: first the authority for these doctrines, secondly the nature of belief in his mind. Although Milton announces in his Dedication, 'For my own part I adhere to the Holy Scriptures alone – I follow no other heresy or sect', it will be seen that this claim has to be modified. He may follow no sect, but he certainly follows something besides the Scriptures, even in the work compiled exclusively from them. Of the nature of belief in his own mind he speaks with equal confidence.

I so far satisfied myself in the prosecution of this plan as at length to trust that I had discovered, with regard to religion, what was matter of belief, and what only matter of opinion. It was also a great solace to me to have compiled, by God's assistance, a precious aid for my faith – or rather to have laid up for myself a treasure which would be a provision for my future life, and would remove from my mind all grounds for hesitation, as often as it behoved me to render an account of the principles of my belief.[1]

But I do not think the evidence bears out this extraordinary presumption of certainty, a presumption so extraordinary that it argues not a little conflict in the mind of the writer. Only a man – I mean a

---

of the more recent work in his article on Milton in *Hastings' Encyclopædia*: he there sums up Milton's creed as 'Protestant Christianity accommodated to the spirit of the classical Renaissance'. I should like to mention the same author's essay on Milton in the *Criterion*, Sept. and Dec. 1928, one of the most interesting modern sketches of Milton's character, career, and ideas.

1. Bohn, iv. 4.

man of Milton's stature – who had been perplexed and had longed for some fixed guide could have written those sentences. It will certainly become evident that this division of faith into matter of belief and matter of opinion argues a quite fallacious rigidity in Milton's mind.

The authorities for Milton's beliefs are three: nature, the Bible, and (in a very minor way) the writings of any wise men outside the Bible. Nature is also called reason or right reason. It has been noted already how in the pamphlets Milton came dangerously near upsetting the authority of Scripture by his exaltation of nature, particularly when in *Tetrachordon* he said 'no ordinance, human or from heaven, can bind against the good of man'; also that he fluctuated in the relative importance which nature is allowed. In the *De Doctrina* he is, as one would expect, more explicit. He explains what nature is, when speaking of divine providence.

> [God's] ordinary providence is that whereby he upholds and preserves the immutable order of causes appointed by him in the beginning. This is commonly, and indeed too frequently, described by the name of nature; for nature cannot possibly mean anything but the mysterious power and efficacy of that divine voice which went forth in the beginning, and to which, as to a perpetual command, all things have since paid obedience.[1]

This is what nature is generally: another passage explains its application to the mind of man.

> The Law of God is either written or unwritten. The unwritten law is no other than that law of nature given originally to Adam, and of which a certain remnant, or imperfect illumination, still dwells in the hearts of all mankind; which, in the regenerate, under the influence of the Holy Spirit, is daily tending towards a renewal of its primitive brightness.[2]

In other places he calls this law of nature reason. It is easy to see how personal such an authority could become and how well suited to Milton's independent spirit. In the *De Doctrina* he quite definitely makes it more important than Scripture, the written law of God.

> Under the gospel we possess, as it were, a twofold Scripture; one external, which is the written word, and the other internal, which is the Holy Spirit, written in the hearts of believers, according to the promise of God, and with the intent that it should by no means be neglected; . . . Hence, although the external ground which we possess for our belief at the present day in the written word is highly important, and, in most instances at least, prior in point of reception, that which is internal, and the peculiar possession of each believer, is far superior to all.[3]

1. Bohn, iv. 211–12.   2. ibid., 378.   3. ibid., 447.

And again a little further down:

> The external Scripture or written word, particularly of the New Testament, . . . has been liable to frequent corruption, . . . But the Spirit which leads to truth cannot be corrupted.[1]

Milton is puzzled at textual corruption of the Bible.

> It is difficult to conjecture the purpose of Providence in committing the writings of the New Testament to such uncertain and variable guardianship, unless it were to teach us by this very circumstance that the Spirit which is given to us is a more certain guide than Scripture.[2]

Personal insight, then, is the chief guide, but not in matters beyond human ken. Reason may tell us of the existence of God but nothing of his nature.

> No one, however, can have right thoughts of God, with nature or reason alone as his guide, independent of the word or message of God.[3]

And again:

> Let us be convinced that those have acquired the truest apprehension of the nature of God who submit their understandings to his word.[4]

This compromise between reason and Scripture is interesting, as it is the outcome of Milton's character. It gave him great liberty of thought in the matters of human destiny and conduct that fundamentally interested him, and it expressed his dislike for any claims a mystic might make to have intuitional knowledge of the nature of God. Such claims were absurd: be content with Scripture alone.

When we come to the Bible and the kind of authority Milton allowed it the difficulties are great. The reason seems to be that Milton changed his views in the course of his life and was never really settled in them. To some it may seem surprising that, having gone so far in freedom as the passages just quoted, exalting reason above Scripture, imply, he did not break loose from scriptural authority altogether, or at least reduce it to that of the classics. He might have gone along the road to rationalism as far as Lord Herbert of Cherbury without thereby becoming an absolute outcast from society. And it was not from any deficiency of knowledge that Milton could have clung to a real or nominal orthodoxy. For instance, it has been discovered[5] that he once possessed a copy of Bodin's *Heptaplomeres*, 'the most extensive account of those "atheistic" ideas which circu-

1. Bohn, iv. 447–8. 2. ibid., 448–9. 3. ibid., 16. 4. ibid., 19.

5. By L. I. Bredvold, 'Milton and Bodin's *Heptaplomeres*' in *Studies in Philology*, 1924, 399–402.

lated widely by secret and underground channels in Renaissance society, and which, when discovered, put their adherents in danger of a burning death for heresy'. This book, written in 1593, was not printed till the nineteenth century and was in Milton's day obtainable only with utmost difficulty in manuscript. Christina of Sweden tried for years before getting a copy. That Milton had one shows how well acquainted with the most advanced thought of his time he must have been. But, as it was, with all his knowledge and his instinct for liberty he retained a deference to the Bible as to no other book.[1] However much it may have on occasions to yield to man's (or rather Milton's) reason, it remains the unparalleled written authority of thought and conduct. Nor can the passage in *Paradise Regained*, Book Four, in which Milton exalts the political wisdom of the Prophets over that of classical oratory be explained but on the supposition of some uncommon impulse in his mind towards the Bible.

For this deference to the Bible several reasons can be conjectured. First there was the whole trend of his upbringing. At the end of the autobiographical passage in the *Apology for Smectymnuus* Milton writes how 'that care was ever had of me, with my earliest capacity, not to be negligently trained in the precepts of the Christian religion', and he goes on to speak of 'the doctrine of holy scripture with timeliest care infused'. Undoubtedly he had been brought up on the Bible in such a way that only a violent revolt could have dislodged it from a place of great fixity in his mind. Secondly, his anti-Catholicism must have made the Bible, the great Protestant weapon against ecclesiastical authority, almost indispensable to him. Thirdly, the Bible supplied Milton with a minimum of support, for even a Milton could not stand quite alone. It must be borne in mind that most men who depend little on dogma make up by depending on those who think like them: one agnostic will find support in the opinion of his fellows. Milton's career had consisted of one disappointment after another in the body of opinion he had trusted: the people of England, Parliament, the Presbyterians, Cromwell himself and the Independents, had failed to fulfil his expectations. Even an intellectual and sympathetic wife might have supplied, if not authority, at least a reassuring echo of the irreducible minimum of his ideas. Moreover the whole trend of education had been towards authority, for though the Renaissance had asserted the worth of the individual it by no means encouraged him to ignore the

1. It is scarcely necessary to quote texts in support of this. The introduction to the *De Doctrina Christiana* and the whole idea of that work are instances sufficient.

authority of the wider culture it had made accessible. It had rather widened the body of authoritative writing than abolished the idea of authority. If the Church had less authority, the Bible, Plato, Cicero had more. Thus in his controversial writings it is second nature to Milton to appeal to some sort of authority as well as to reason. Impelled then by the whole direction of contemporary learned thought and the fear of an isolation intolerable even to so proud a spirit as his, he must have some body of opinion to rely on. It may be asked why he should have narrowed this body of opinion to the Bible, or why he should have put the Bible in a different category from Plato, to whom he had owed not a little. His biblical upbringing, already mentioned, is a partial answer, but in addition this narrowing of authority expresses a rather desperate attempt to set a reasonable limit. It is pretty clear that he began his self-education with the intention of grappling with all that was worth knowing in the world; and he did grapple with a very great deal. Pride would make it hard to admit failure, but how could a single man succeed? Some limited territory he could subdue, or thought he could subdue, was necessary. And this leads to the fourth reason why the Bible provided him with necessary or congenial authority. It happened that the mythology and history of the Bible expressed for him certain ideas about life in which he believed. Largely because of the power he felt in his own mind Milton believed in the almost boundless possibilities of Man: in the Bible he found this expressed in the statement that God made Man in his own image. But he sees also, has had it forced upon him by his experience, that actually there is a perverseness in men that brings them to failure without there being any absolute need of their failing. The Fall is a myth at once recounting the perverse nature of men and attaching to them the responsibility. This perverseness is common to all men: through Adam all have fallen. But there is still that in the human mind which can live down this perverseness and lead on to these possibilities: a few take advantage of this possible good. This idea is expressed in Scripture by the possibility of regeneration in Christ. Finding in certain very important portions of the Bible necessary confirmations of his fundamental ideas, it is not surprising that he was heartened to endorse the Protestant allegiance to the whole body of Scripture.

But with what amazing masterfulness does Milton make Scripture mean what he wishes; how coolly does he disregard the plain sense of a passage or altogether omit what is for the biblical author of the first importance! An example has already been cited in discussing Milton's ideas about chastity. When Milton was young he had pondered and taken seriously St Paul's sentiments in *First Corinthians*, which plainly are that chastity is preferable to its opposite, however legitimate. Convinced later that the flesh is good, he twists St Paul's own words to support his new conviction. A modern may be inclined to accuse Milton of dishonesty, and some modern critics have done this with more or less moderation, Liljegren in particular with more and Mutschmann with none. But who is completely honest? and, if a moral judgment is being passed, should not allowance be made for the daring and the originality Milton did undoubtedly show in the ideas of his own for which he insisted on finding somehow a scriptural justification?

It would be easy to compare, to Milton's disadvantage, the way Shakespeare must have treated the epistles of St Paul. There would have been no illusions in Shakespeare's mind about the Pauline nature: he had little in common with that enemy of the flesh. But of what use to express his dislike? Better enjoy the maximum of liberty through a light conformity. And this self-admitted dishonesty we may guess at certainly appears less sinful than the unadmitted dishonesty of Milton in a matter with which he dealt so thoroughly. But we must remember the ages in which the two poets lived. It was not from theological or political agitation that Shakespeare could best draw his mental sustenance, whereas for Milton to have kept aloof from it would have been mental starvation. And if Milton was in some degree affected by the malady of that tract-writing age, the sin of soulless, humourless text-juggling to the neglect of what a writer, even an 'inspired' writer, clearly meant, need we pass on him a sentence so very severe?

When Milton says he believes something in the Bible, what does he mean? It is impossible to say precisely, but it is extremely important to be aware of the nature of this impossibility: for most writers on Milton's beliefs have assumed that he meant something quite precise when he said he believed, have in fact made the mistake of applying Victorian standards of belief to the seventeenth century. It is not at all easy to realize how peculiar these Victorian standards were, how dependent on an age of science, perhaps as transitory as it was sudden. At no time, probably, since savagery has belief been so purely scientific as in the Victorian Age, whereas in the early and middle seventeenth century scientific and poetic belief were mingled in a way which to many to-day would be incomprehensible.

Savages are said to believe in a purely scientific manner, never to separate their beliefs from literal concrete facts. Belief to them is the affirmation of an event, not the affirmation of a state of mind independent of the literal occurrence. Thus, when a savage calls a butterfly his grandfather he believes that the life-breath of his ancestor has entered the butterfly: his grandfather's life and the butterfly's life are the same material reality. Poetic belief is later: it betokens a complication of mind. The more sophisticated man may see a double meaning in the butterfly, which is a human soul not merely in the sense of having swallowed the human life-breath but in supplying an emotional correspondence with the human soul. The butterfly is bright, brittle, capricious in its flight: a good working symbol of the *animula vagula blandula*. Thus the next stage in belief after the purely scientific would be the blending, quite unconsciously, of the poetic with the scientific. Once blended the two forms of belief would become hopelessly confused, and it was not till an age of science that they were consciously distinguished. It is possible that in Europe scholasticism first attempted to establish a scientific notion of belief. Although unscientific in that it did not base its beliefs on experience, at least it recognized different grades of belief: those that had to be accepted without argument and those that had a scientific basis, granted certain premises, on reason. With the reaction against scholasticism and the return to classical antiquity there was a relapse for the moment to the earlier unconscious mix-up. But in the same period the modern notions of belief have their origin. Rational thinkers, as science extends its scope, tend to exclude more and more the possibility of poetic belief. But in the seventeenth century it was still easy for a kindly person with an intelligent and well co-ordinated mind to profess, for instance, a belief in Hell, because there was no need for him to sort out the measure of scientific and the measure of poetic belief in his mind. The one-tenth of scientific belief based on a simple faith that the Bible was literally true could be swamped by the nine-tenths of poetic belief in Hell as the symbol of rational and not vindictive justice. But as knowledge of the physical world grew and was more heeded, it became less and less possible for intelligent people to attach their poetic beliefs to religion. In the Victorian Age both belief and disbelief show this scientific trend carried to its extreme. For instance, if a Victorian literalist believed in Hell he would believe very definitely in material flames and a physical undying worm. Contrariwise a Victorian who doubted these material or living realities would feel the very grave importance of this doubt: he had not got the allegorizing faculty uppermost in his mind. In the seventeenth century it was far otherwise. Consider, for instance, the mixture of beliefs in the *Religio Medici*. Now Victorian standards of belief have nearly always been applied to Milton. He plainly believes in Adam and Eve and the Fall, but that does not mean that he is convinced throughout his mind that they had a physical existence as described in *Genesis*. To say that you disbelieved in Adam and Eve was of course a much worse thing in Milton's day than in Victoria's, but to say you did believe was not half so exacting. Nor is it necessary to argue by analogy from Thomas Browne: there is evidence enough in Milton himself for this greater flexibility of belief. The following passage from *Tetrachordon*, already quoted,[1] shows Milton to all appearances taking quite literally the story of Eve's creation out of Adam's rib:

> That there was a nearer alliance between Adam and Eve, than could be ever after between man and wife, is visible to any. For no other woman was ever moulded out of her husband's rib.[2]

But in the following passage from *Areopagitica* the legend of Psyche is mingled with the legend of the Fall and mentioned in exactly the same tone. Milton appears to believe the one legend as implicitly as the other, and yet would any one suggest that he understood the legend of Psyche as literally true?

> Good and evil we know in the field of this world grow up together almost inseparably; and the knowledge of good is so involved and interwoven with the knowledge of evil, and in so many cunning resemblances hardly to be discerned, that those confused seeds which were imposed upon Psyche as an incessant labour to cull out, and sort asunder, were not more intermixed. It was from out the rind of one apple tasted, that the knowledge of good and evil, as two twins cleaving together, leaped forth into the world. And perhaps this is that doom which Adam fell into of knowing good and evil; that is to say, of knowing good by evil.[3]

The six days of the Creation give another illustration of ambiguous belief. There is no passage in the whole *De Doctrina Christiana* dealing with the subject to suggest that Milton did not believe that God created the world in six days of twenty-four hours each. In his discussion on the Sabbath, for instance, though anxious to prove that the Jewish custom of resting on the seventh day has no modern application, he never argues that the account in *Genesis* should be taken figuratively. And yet when Raphael in *Paradise Lost* is describing the Creation he says:

> Immediate are the Acts of God, more swift
> Then time or motion, but to human ears
> Cannot without process of speech be told,
> So told as earthly notion can receave.[4]

1. p. 140.   2. Bohn, iii. 335.   3. Bohn, ii. 67–8.   4. *Paradise Lost*, vii. 176–9.

One cannot have a much plainer statement that Milton did not take *Genesis* literally; and a nineteenth (or twentieth) century 'fundamentalist' would consider him guilty of inconsistency. And yet in a manner he believed both the figurative and the literal account. Similarly Milton refuses to give any rigid belief to the accounts in Scripture of the nature of God.

> Our safest way [*sc.* of knowing God] is to form in our minds such a conception of God, as shall correspond with his own delineation and representation of himself in the sacred writings. For granting that both in the literal and figurative descriptions of God, he is exhibited not as he really is, but in such a manner as may be within the scope of our comprehensions, yet we ought to entertain such a conception of him, as he, condescending to accommodate himself to our capacities, has shewn that he desires we should conceive. For it is on this very account that he has lowered himself to our level, lest in our flights above the reach of human understanding, and beyond the written word of Scripture, we should be tempted to indulge in vague cogitations and subtleties.[1]

The accounts, therefore, of God in Scripture are at once true and untrue: true according to our limited capacity, untrue because partial and inadequate.[2] And we feel that Milton always holds himself free to believe a story figuratively if it should suit him to do so. His main method, however, in dealing with the inconvenient is to omit. And Milton, like Aeschylus, may mean much by his silences. A good example of this is in his treatment of miracles. He cannot omit the subject altogether, but he confines it to half a page. In his citations from Scripture not a single one of Christ's miracles is mentioned. Later in the treatise he says, 'Miracles have no inherent efficacy in producing belief, any more than simple teaching.' Now Milton profoundly disliked any supernatural alteration of the divine order of things once established: miracles are distasteful to his nature. He is as silent about them as he dare be, yielding them a grudging and superficial belief. We cannot even be sure that he allowed them historical verity. Luckily there was no need for Milton to be perfectly clear on this point.

Another question is involved in Milton's beliefs: how much did he change them? If the *De Doctrina* was finished about 1660, can we be certain that here is Milton's final position? Firm and clear though the main lines of his nature had been from early years, his dogma had changed. In his anti-episcopal pamphlets he expressed not only

1. Bohn, iv. 16–17.

2. For a more detailed analysis of Milton's process of faith see Saurat's excellent chapter, op. cit., 169–77.

a general belief in the Trinity, but called attention to the co-eternity of the Son by addressing him as the 'ever-begotten light and perfect image of the Father': he also followed Protestant orthodoxy in believing in predestination. If in the interval he became an Arian and an Arminian, can we be certain that his dogma did not later undergo still further changes? It may be said here that there is little evidence; we cannot be certain either way. Though there is little dogma in *Paradise Regained* and *Samson Agonistes*, the argument from silence is not convincing.

To give a fair summary in a few paragraphs of the main doctrines of the *De Doctrina Christiana* would be very difficult. It is almost impossible not to deal with that work as Milton dealt with the Bible: lay the stress on what one would like to see stressed. At any rate, I shall not attempt a summary so much as an account of what seems to me in the treatise to be of importance for understanding Milton.

As the reader forces his way through the jungle of texts that form the bulk of the treatise he begins to see how expressive and personal a work it is. It is a wonder how efficiently Milton has impressed on Scripture the forms of the beliefs that were essential to his nature, has approximated what he felt to what he was bound to profess. Thus, though the treatise may be a lamentably biassed criticism of the Bible, it is a work not unworthy of a great man and a great poet.

Milton begins by discussing the nature of God; and there is in this discussion at once humility and pride. He is humble because he considers God unknowable: 'that those have acquired the truest apprehension of God who submit their understanding to his words', and that man should not be tempted to 'indulge in vague cogitations and subtleties' on the subject of God. He is proud because he dislikes any avoidable interference on the part of God with the order of things as originally established. God is perfectly just, and there is nothing wrong in the scheme of human affairs. Man must make the best of things out of his own resources. One of the arguments for the existence of God is the order of the world:

> There can be no doubt but that every thing in the world, by the beauty of its order, and the evidence of a determinate and beneficial purpose which pervades it, testifies that some supreme efficient Power must have pre-existed, by which the whole was ordained for a specific end.[1]

Milton never admitted going back on this belief: how far he actually went back remains to be seen. The other main reason for the existence of God lies in the human mind.

1. Bohn, iv. 14.

The existence of God is further proved by that feeling, whether we term it conscience, or right reason, which even in the worst of characters, is not altogether extinguished. If there were no God, there would be no distinction between right and wrong; the estimate of virtue and vice would entirely depend on the blind opinion of men; none would follow virtue, none would be restrained from vice by any sense of shame, or fear of the laws, unless conscience or right reason did from time to time convince every one, however unwilling, of the existence of God, the Lord and ruler of all things, to whom, sooner or later, each must give an account of his own actions, whether good or bad.[1]

These two arguments for the existence of God, however commonplace theologically, are interesting in Milton because they express the two notions concerning humanity on which he relied: the notion of a beneficent scheme of things and a sufficient standard of conduct in his own mind. Whatever became of the first support, the second never failed him.

After speaking of God, Milton does not, as might be expected, treat of the Trinity. As if by his arrangement he meant to make his Arianism the more emphatic he interposes a long discussion of the Divine Decrees and Predestination. Milton's position is well enough known to any reader of *Paradise Lost*. God in his omniscience has foreknowledge of man's fate but he leaves his will free. No one has been pre-elected to salvation or damnation. All have the chance of salvation. But certain men have been singled out for special eminence, good or bad. The whole discussion proves, what to some readers the parallel parts of *Paradise Lost* alone do not, that the whole question was to Milton not at all academic but belonged to the very essence of his nature. He is in fact fighting for the individualism which he had inherited from the Renaissance and without which life was not worth while. A life in which man was not responsible for his own actions was meaningless. The Miltonic doctrine of the elect shows interestingly how Milton could make use of what suited him in an authority and reject what did not. Liljegren[2] has pointed out how well in harmony with the Renaissance idea of the great individual was the Calvinistic doctrine of election. But this doctrine was bound up with predestination. Milton rejects predestination but keeps the idea that God singled out certain men for special distinction.

Milton prefaces the chapter on the Son by a claim to have as much right as any human being to interpret the Scriptures, a dignified apology for his major heresy. After much close and, I think one

1. Bohn, iv. 15.   2. *Studies in Milton*, xv.

may say, passionate argument Milton concludes that the Son is of a different essence from the Father, and that he did not exist from the beginning. He is the agent of the unknowable God and quite definitely inferior to him. About the Holy Ghost Milton can say little. He is definitely inferior to the Son.

Discussing the Creation Milton expounds one of his most heretical and characteristic doctrines: his materialism. Even God cannot create out of nothing: the orthodox doctrine that man was created out of nothing is false. God created man out of matter, and matter is good, part of God himself. When Taine complained that Milton lived too early to have created God pantheistically he was exactly wrong. Milton hovers over the question of evil. Arguing with the hypothetical supporter of the orthodox idea he says:

> And if it be asked how what is corruptible can proceed from incorruption, it may be asked in return how the virtue and efficacy of God can proceed out of nothing. Matter, like the form and nature of the angels itself, proceeded incorruptible from God; and even since the fall it remains incorruptible as far as concerns its essence.[1]

Milton does not allow his adversary to push him to the unavoidable position of admitting that there is latent evil in God; there was nothing in Scripture to call for this extreme admission: but Saurat[2] gives good reasons for thinking that such an admission Milton elsewhere did indeed make.

Believing in the essential goodness of matter, Milton refuses to separate body and soul.

> Man is a living being, intrinsically and properly one and individual, not compound or separable, not, according to the common opinion, made up and framed of two distinct and different natures, as of soul and body – but the whole man is soul, and the soul man, that is to say, a body, or substance individual, animated, sensitive, and rational; and the breath of life was neither a part of the divine essence, nor the soul itself, but as it were an inspiration of some divine virtue fitted for the exercise of life and reason, and infused into the organic body.[3]

Hence in a later chapter Milton is with the Mortalists in believing that at death the soul perishes with the body to await a common resurrection. And it is with this belief in the essential goodness of matter that his belief in the essential goodness of the flesh is to be connected. This belief is one of those that separates him so far from St Paul and contemporary Puritanism and makes him, as in some ways he was, so curiously modern.

1. Bohn, iv. 180.   2. op. cit., 110.   3. Bohn, iv. 188.

As well as man the angels are spoken of in the chapter on the Creation. Milton also devotes a chapter to them entirely. He was interested in them as he was not in Christ's miracles and gives them a good deal of attention. The angels were interesting to him because they fitted in well with his materialism. They were material but of a more airy matter than man. If the goodness of the body was to be believed in, a kind of ladder of matter ranging from gross to tenuous was a desirable explanation: the angels were beings high up on this material ladder. The angels were created before man, and like him they possess the gift of free will.

In the same chapter Milton advances his very characteristic belief that God did his soul-creating once for all with Adam. The soul is contained in the seed of the father, and thus God is spared the 'servile task' of creating souls daily. Why Milton felt strongly on this matter is easy to explain. He wishes the least possible interference with man after the initial act of creation. Man must be allowed every possible responsibility. If God created each soul afresh, the responsibility incurred through Adam would be somehow impaired.

On the other hand, Milton has absorbed the Old Testament so thoroughly that he cannot deny the interference of God in carrying out his purposes. But he interferes in such a way as in no wise to affect human responsibility.

God . . . may instigate an evil agent, without being in the least degree the cause of the evil. . . . For example, – God saw that the mind of David was so elated and puffed up by the increase of his power, that even without any external impulse he was on the point of giving some remarkable token of his pride; he therefore excited in him the desire of numbering the people; he did not inspire him with the passion of vain glory, but impelled him to display in this manner, rather than in any other, that latent arrogance of his heart which was ready to break forth.[1]

Even so Milton does not wrestle with complete success against the jealous God of the Hebrews, the Great Taskmaster whose terrible anthropomorphic eye was ever fixed on the world. It was in such a God that he must have been brought up to believe, and the substitution of a less personal God must have been a slow process. Relics of the Hebrew God there certainly are in this chapter on the Providence of God. And yet, in view of Milton's early statement that nothing in Scripture told of God must be taken literally, we may be wrong in assuming any direct act of God in for instance the case of David quoted above. Milton may well believe that for David to

1. Bohn, iv. 204.

number the people was to act merely according to the initial decrees of God and that the specific interference is but figurative. It is certainly true that the examples of God's acts that he gives all concern men's thoughts, they are instigations and temptations: and these he seems to include in the ordinary providence of God 'whereby he upholds and preserves the immutable order of causes appointed by him in the beginning'.[1] The extraordinary providence of God is that 'whereby God produces some effect out of the usual order of nature':[2] that is a miracle. The grudging admission of these extraordinary interferences has already been mentioned. So even the chapter on God's Providence ultimately suggests that Milton wished mankind to be left to its own devices.

Marriage and divorce are the subject of a long chapter. Milton concludes that polygamy is not forbidden by Scripture and restates his ideas about divorce.

In writing of the Fall Milton is orthodox. He believes in original as well as in personal sin. This orthodoxy he could hardly help, for, as has been pointed out, the Fall was a myth typifying that proneness of man to error in which Milton had come to believe. But the Hebrew doctrine that this proneness was not merely a regrettable fact but a personal crime, that the sin of Adam had incriminated all his posterity, that it is perfectly just for the sins of the father to be visited on the children, Milton seems to have found not quite easy to accept, though accept it fully he does. He takes refuge in Pagan authority and example, as if he felt the weakness of the biblical doctrine.[3] The death that followed sin is, according to Milton, far more than mere mortality. It consists first 'in the loss or at least in the obscuration of that right reason which enabled man to discern the chief good and in which consisted as it were the life of the understanding'.[4] But Milton goes on to insist that 'some remnants of the divine image still exist in us, not wholly extinguished by this spiritual death'.[5] Hence the wisdom and holiness of many of the heathen. Further, there is sufficient will left to do good 'to deprive us of all excuse for inaction'. To have postulated sufficient will for virtue would have deprived Milton of the reason of his theology: he could then have dispensed with regeneration. But he cannot relinquish the qualified self-sufficiency of man, even after the Fall and without the intervention of Christ.

This brings us to the subject of regeneration. And first it must be remembered that 'under the name of Christ are also comprehended Moses and the Prophets'. Regeneration is as old as Adam. The

1. Bohn, iv. 211. 2. ibid., 212. 3. ibid., 258. 4. ibid., 265.
5. ibid., 210.

prophetical function of Christ is twofold, the promulgation of divine truth and the illumination of the understanding: and it began with the creation of the world and will continue to the end of all things. The sacrifice of Christ 'may be abundantly sufficient even for those who have never heard of the name of Christ and who believe only in God'.[1] In its plain form Milton looked on Christian regeneration as a mental state able to be superimposed on the original perverseness of all mankind. However that may be, his exposition of redemption, renovation, regeneration, faith, justification, is orthodox and Pauline enough. It should be noted, however, that Milton is completely separated from the Evangelicalism that makes much of Christ's blood. Redemption at the price of Christ's blood is mentioned, but little more. It is remarkable how closely Milton follows St Paul and how little weight he gives to the Gospels, in writing of Christ. The Crucifixion is hardly mentioned, most of the events of Christ's life are passed over in silence. Far from being in danger of making Christ mere man he tends to make him divine indeed, though less than God, but a divine abstraction; a tendency which apparently grew into the dimness of *Paradise Regained*.

One very important idea is placed at the very beginning of the chapters just discussed:

The restoration of Man is the act whereby man, being delivered from sin and death by God the Father through Jesus Christ, is raised to a far more excellent state of grace and glory than that from which he had fallen.[2]

This is an essential of Milton's nominal beliefs. The Fall was an evil leading to a good greater than without it could have happened.

It is in his chapters on regenerate man that Milton developes his individualism and his demand for liberty. Regenerate man can reach in this life a state of glory, albeit imperfect, while under the Gospel the widest liberty is allowed. Not only the ceremonial but the total Mosaic law has been abolished by the Gospel. The unwritten law of the individual conscience is of enormous weight.

In matters of the sacraments and of Church organization Milton approximates to the Quakers. 'The sacraments are not absolutely indispensable.' 'Any believer is competent to act as an ordinary minister.'[3] There was to be autonomy of individual churches.

In the last chapter of the First Book the end of the world and the judgment are described. Milton follows *Revelation* quite literally. From the context one would judge that he believed that Satan would be bound for exactly one thousand years to the day. He needed the

1. Bohn, iv. 321.   2. ibid., 284.   3. ibid., 432-3.

mythology for *Paradise Lost*, but the precise nature of his belief who can tell?

The Second Book concerns not dogma but the duties of man. Its chief interest consists in the great debt to classical ethics. Virtues are placed between their respective extremes. Self-government is one of the supreme virtues.

Righteousness towards ourselves consists in a proper method of self-government. I Cor. ix. 27: 'I keep under my body, and bring it into subjection.' From this, as from a fountain, the special virtues in general derive their origin; inasmuch as under the head of righteousness towards ourselves are included, first, the entire regulation of the internal affections; secondly, the discriminating pursuit of external good, and the resistance to, or patient endurance of, external evil.[1]

'The entire regulation of the internal affections': this is the nearest mention in the *De Doctrina Christiana* of the fight between reason and passion, so important in the later pamphlets. The debt to the classics is nicely shown by the inclusion among the virtues of urbanity:[2] it is not usually reckoned either a Jewish or a Protestant virtue.

Interesting points of detail are Milton's conclusions that there is no theological authority for the Sabbath – to keep it is merely a matter of human expedience – and that a good deal of falsehood is legitimate. Milton seems to justify almost any falsehood that is supposed ultimately to bring good results. Both conclusions would have scandalized his Puritan contemporaries.

Most of Milton's mental qualities or impulses noticed in discussing the early poems or pamphlets can be found in the *De Doctrina Christiana*. Even ambition is evident in the sanguine address to 'All the Churches of Christ'. He dedicates to the world at large 'what I esteem my best and richest possession'. The belief in action is indeed not expressed unless it be implicit in the laborious zeal that carried through the curious mixture of argument and quotation which makes up the *De Doctrina Christiana*.

It is probable that this account of Milton's creed may seem vague and inconclusive. I should be sorry if it did not, for it is an error to tidy up Milton's beliefs. Rather I hope to have pointed out how curiously mixed and personal this so-called system of Milton's turns out upon investigation to be.

This chapter may end aptly with a quotation from a later English poet who, as has been pointed out before, had so much in common

1. Bohn, v. 79.   2. ibid., 125.

with Milton. In the preface to *Prometheus Unbound* Shelley wrote as follows:

We owe the great writers of the golden age of our literature to that fervid awakening of the public mind which shook to dust the oldest and most oppressive form of the Christian religion. We owe Milton to the progress and development of the same spirit: the sacred Milton was, let it ever be remembered, a republican, and a bold inquirer into morals and religion.

PART III

THE LATER POEMS

CHAPTER ONE

Paradise Lost: Introductory

It is strange how little, till quite recently, critics have concerned
themselves with the meaning of *Paradise Lost*. The style, the versification, the celestial geography, the thought, who is the hero: all
these have concerned the critics far more than what the poem is
really about, the true state of Milton's mind when he wrote it.
Perhaps to those of earlier generations the meaning appeared too
simple to need discussion: does not Milton himself tell us all we need
to know about it in his opening lines? But such simple-mindedness
can ill satisfy a generation which is sceptical of professed motives
and which suspects the presence of others, either concealed or not
realized by the author. It is not surprising, then, that in the last ten
years or so there has been more discussion of the subject than in all
the rest of the time during which *Paradise Lost* has been in print.
From the differences of opinion it may be judged that the question
has by no means been settled, and another attempt to answer it may
well be pardoned.

Not that it is possible to define precisely what the 'real' meaning
of the poem is, just as it is impossible to say where the real heart of
an onion begins. There may easily be the danger of stripping the
onion of so many integumentary layers that by the time the real
onion is reached there is little of it left. It is folly to discount a motive
merely because it is professed. But that the apparent or professed
meaning of a poem or passage can be very different from its deeper
meaning is very easily proved. Milton, owing to his free use of
mythology and of proper names, can supply an unusual number of
such passages. Take one of the most famous:

> The hasty multitude
> Admiring enter'd, and the work some praise
> And some the Architect: his hand was known
> In Heav'n by many a Towred structure high,
> Where Scepter'd Angels held thir residence,
> And sat as Princes, whom the supreme King
> Exalted to such power, and gave to rule,
> Each in his Hierarchie, the Orders bright.
> Nor was his name unheard or unador'd
> In ancient *Greece;* and in *Ausonian* land
> Men call'd him *Mulciber;* and how he fell

From Heav'n, they fabl'd, thrown by angry *Jove*
Sheer o're the Chrystal Battlements; from Morn
To Noon he fell, from Noon to dewy Eve,
A Summers day; and with the setting Sun
Dropt from the Zenith like a falling Star,
On *Lemnos* th' *Aegaean* Ile.[1]

The mood of the first eight lines is not complicated. Milton intends
grandeur and achieves it completely. But what of the fall of Hephaestus on to Lemnos, so much more thrilling to the imagination? How
much of the thrill is connected with the professed meaning, the myth
of Zeus in a temper pitching the Fire God out of heaven and the
excellent joke of a broken leg and a limp ever afterwards? Are we
meant to think of Milton's original, the passage in the *Iliad*, Book
One, where Hera is in a dudgeon with Zeus and her son Hephaestus
comforts her?

Cheer up, mother, and give in, though you are feeling sore; because I
am very fond of you and do not want to see you damaged. If that happens,
I shall not be able to help it however much I mind, for the Olympian is a
dreadful being to fight against. I proved it once before, when, though I
tried hard to save myself, he caught me by the foot and threw me from the
sacred threshold. All day I was carried along and with the setting sun I
fell on Lemnos: and there was little wind left in me, I can tell you.[2]

Nothing could be further from Milton than this richly comic
'source' in the *Iliad*: it does nothing at all to explain what it is in
the later passage that moved us so. The myth is a blind: if we think
it the real meaning or even an important part we are mistaken.
There is something very different behind it, something which no
critic has ventured to define and which need not be sought for here.
Enough that the passage illustrates the frequent importance in
Milton of the covert meaning. The whole question is usually settled
or rather cut short by the statement that Milton is a musical poet,
that a rather high proportion of his meaning is conveyed through
sound as against statement. This may be perfectly true, but it does
not exonerate the critic from the task of trying to extract a meaning
from the Miltonic music. The meaning of a poem is not the story
told, the statements made, the philosophy stated, but the state of
mind, valuable or otherwise, revealed by the sum of all the elements
of the poem, of which the sound of the words happens to be an
important one; and the only way to arrive at this meaning is to
examine our own minds as we read. The best a critic can do is, after

1. i. 730–46.   2. *Iliad*, i. 586–93.

discarding what he feels is personal prejudice, to record the dominant sensations a work of art arouses in him, in the hope that these sensations may be some indication of the author's own experience. If he finds them little related to, or at variance with, the professed meaning of the poem, he cannot help himself; his own experience may be fallible, but in the last resort it is all he can trust.

In dealing with *Paradise Lost* I shall try first to give the outlines of Milton's professed plan, then to ask what modifications the reader's experience forces him to make in that plan, and finally to suggest what the poem can most truly be said to mean.

Although contemporary novelists and short-story writers construct their writings more carefully than their predecessors, critics are still apt to forget how important a part of the meaning of a work of literature the construction may be. The close construction of *Othello*, compelling the mind to dwell unremittingly on the terrible story, befits the almost purely domestic tragedy that the play is and forms an essential part of the tragic meaning. The looser construction of *Antony and Cleopatra,* not necessarily bad because it is loose, gives the feeling of great happenings in wide space contrasted with the pair who found their best empire in each other; and this feeling cannot be spared from the meaning of the play. Now Milton, bred in the classical tradition and naturally gifted with a powerful mental control, can hardly have done other than impose a rigorous unity on his great poem. This unity would be perfectly conscious and thus a very important element of the professed meaning. It is with the construction of the poem that I propose to begin my enquiry. But construction has another significance, for the impression of greatness given by a work of art is very largely due to the sense of control implied by good construction. We feel that the mind which for all its heat of excitement can shape the material into a harmonious order must be mighty indeed. As Longinus might have said, for what is greatly planned we keep our astonishment. The reason why of all Shelley's lyrics the *Ode to the West Wind* is the most powerful is that as well as containing the qualities common to most of Shelley's other ambitious lyrics it is much more masterfully shaped. On the construction, then, of *Paradise Lost* depends not only the professed meaning but much of the power of the poem.

These questions of construction may, in Milton of all poets, seem too simple not to have been answered long ago. Yet none of the better known critics has added much to Addison's brief comment on the Fable and how it is evolved. Let me enlarge a little on this surprising deficiency.

Matthew Arnold, in his Preface to the 1853 volume of his poems, laments that whereas to the Greeks the total effect of a poem was all-important, the English care only for the separate parts. He laments further that, as a natural result, the English poets of the Romantic Revival lack unity and what, following Goethe, he calls architectonic power. Unfortunately, when he comes to criticize Milton,[1] he insists on showing his patriotism by failing to apply the architectonic test. He does indeed say that it *would* be possible to point out the masterly construction of *Paradise Lost*, but he leaves the matter at that and proceeds to air his pet obsession, the Grand Style. Other critics of Milton, too, are disappointingly reticent on matters of construction. A number of them note the constructional mastery, but without entering into details. Lamb, for instance, from whom it would be unfair to demand systematic criticism, objecting to Johnson's remark that no one ever wished *Paradise Lost* longer, wrote as follows:

'We read the Paradise Lost as a task', says Dr Johnson. Nay, rather as a celestial recreation, of which the dullard mind is not at all hours alike recipient. 'Nobody ever wished it longer'; – nor the moon rounder, he might have added. Why, 'tis the perfectness and completeness of it, which makes us imagine that 'not a line could be added to it, or diminished from it, with advantage. Would we have a cubit added to the stature of the Medicean Venus? Do we wish her taller?[2]

John Bailey in his *Milton* remarks the grandeur of the scheme but does not describe the details; and Raleigh makes the following emphatic statement, which, had it been expanded, might have made my next chapter superfluous:

A prerogative place among the great epics of the world has sometimes been claimed for *Paradise Lost*, on the ground that the theme it handles is vaster and of a more universal human interest than any handled by Milton's predecessors. It concerns itself with the fortunes, not of a city or an empire, but of the whole human race, and with that particular event in the history of the race which has moulded all its destinies. Around this event, the plucking of an apple, are ranged, according to the strictest rules of the ancient epic, the histories of Heaven and Earth and Hell. The scene of the action is universal space. The time represented is Eternity. The characters are God and his creatures. And all these are exhibited in the clearest and most inevitable relation with the main event, so that there is not an incident, hardly a line of the poem, but leads backwards or forwards to those central lines in the Ninth Book:

1. In his essays on Milton in *Essays in Criticism*, ii., and *Mixed Essays*.
2. *Table-Talk* (Oxford Edition), i. 448.

> So saying, her rash hand in evil hour
> Forth-reaching to the fruit, she plucked, she eat.
> Earth felt the wound, and Nature from her seat,
> Sighing through all her works, gave signs of woe
> That all was lost.

From this point radiates a plot so immense in scope, that the history of the world from the first preaching of the gospel to the Millennium occupies only some fifty lines of Milton's epilogue.[1]

Raleigh may not have wished to devote the space to pointing out exactly how every event leads up to the central lines in the Ninth Book: or perhaps he may have felt that the proposition was too evident to require proof or explanation. But to many the proposition is not evident at all. Here, for instance, is Saurat's brief account of the way *Paradise Lost* is constructed:

Paradise Lost is built round two great themes which are harmoniously balanced: the fall of the angels and the fall of man. The first books describe the state of the fallen angels; in contrast to this, after an interval in Heaven, the following books picture man before his fall, in Paradise; then comes the fall of the angels, and the creation of the world which compensates it; and finally, the fall of man and the history of the world which will make up for it. The dramatic interest in the first half is in Satan's efforts; in the second, in the human drama between Adam and Eve. The two parts are linked, Satan's efforts being the cause of the human drama. The scheme is simple, clear and grand, and bears the imprint of Milton's mind.[2]

This is a very different account from Raleigh's. Instead of every-thing being subordinated to the single theme of the Fall of man, whose climax is the eating of the apple by Eve, there are two themes, neither of which is the theme which Raleigh considers of chief im-portance. I happen to agree with Raleigh; but when a critic like Saurat holds entirely different views with firm conviction, one cannot treat Raleigh's proposition as too obvious to need any proof.

How astonishingly the construction of *Paradise Lost* has been mis-understood in the past is made clear by the comments that have been passed on the four great personal passages, the preludes to the First, Third, Seventh, and Ninth Books. For a long time they were considered blemishes, perhaps excusable for their beauty, but faulty because they are accretions.[3] Johnson is often thought to have

---

1. *Milton,* 81-2.   2. op. cit., 178.

3. Landor provides a notorious example of this misunderstanding. In his *Southey and Landor* (first conversation) he writes: 'Beautiful as are many parts of the Invocation at the commencement of the Seventh Book, I should more gladly have seen it without the first forty lines', and, 'We are come to the Ninth Book, from which I would cast away the first forty-seven verses.'

justified them for good in the following very characteristic passage:

The short digressions at the beginning of the third, seventh, and ninth books might doubtless be spared; but superfluities so beautiful who would take away? or who does not wish that the author of the *Iliad* had gratified succeeding ages with a little knowledge of himself? Perhaps no passages are more frequently or more attentively read than those extrinsick paragraphs; and, since the end of poetry is pleasure, that cannot be unpoetical with which all are pleased.

Johnson is beside the mark: he does not realize that Milton might have had very definite reasons for putting prologues to these particular books rather than to others; that they may be organic as well as beautiful in themselves.[1] In point of fact they are a most valuable guide to the way the poem is constructed.

Seeing then that the construction of *Paradise Lost* has been so misunderstood or has been so little treated, I may be permitted to give some account of it. Let me repeat that in my account I shall have two matters in view: the evidence for Milton's professed subject and the constructional unity.

1. Verity in his edition of *Paradise Lost* (Cambridge) has a note at the beginning of Book Seven saying that these passages mark each a significant stage in the development of the story. But he is very brief and goes into no detail.

CHAPTER TWO

Paradise Lost: the Construction

IN DESCRIBING the construction of *Paradise Lost*, as I see it, I shall have to sketch, as briefly as possible, the outline of the poem from beginning to end.

The opening needs little comment. It is natural that Milton, believing in the high seriousness of his purpose, should invoke the Holy Spirit to be his help and that he should outline the scope of his plan. Homer had done much the same before, invoking the Muse and putting forward the wrath of Achilles as his theme. Man's disobedience is the main theme. There is nothing in Milton's opening to suggest two great contrasted themes. Satan is mentioned as the instrument of Man's fall, not as the subject of half of the poem. Being the chief instrument, he is to be described first; and as his machinations against Man begin after he has been thrown into Hell, it is fitting that Hell and its inhabitants should first be described. Hell, then, is the subject of the first movement of the poem. Milton's opening is at once the prologue to the whole poem and the prologue to the first movement.

In the first movement we are shown Hell: the terrors, the hopelessness, of the place. The worst terror is inaction, the futility of any possible course of action; for the fallen angels are still full of a divine energy. Then Satan thinks of Man, and the outlet of energy is provided. Man is at present distant, dim, uncertain; but he and his new habitation supply the hope and motives of the inhabitants of Hell. Till Satan goes on his journey, the reader imagines himself in Hell, a spectator of its contents and a listener to the council held within it: he does not contemplate Hell from without. And here it may be remarked that the location of the reader is of the highest moment for understanding the construction of the poem, for the centre of importance will be where the reader imagines himself to be situated, and not necessarily where the action is taking place. Then Satan, the reader accompanying him, struggles up through Chaos to the first glimmerings of light that penetrate Chaos from Heaven; and at this point, the end of Book Two, the first movement of the poem closes.

Addison considered the invocation of light at the beginning of Book Three 'rather . . . as an Excrescence, than as an essential part of the poem': but it is (and this has been noticed before) a singularly beautiful and very necessary transition from one movement to another. The Second Book ends as follows:

> But now at last the sacred influence
> Of light appears, and from the walls of Heav'n
> Shoots farr into the bosom of dim Night
> A glimmering dawn; here Nature first begins
> Her fardest verge, and *Chaos* to retire
> As from her outmost works a brok'n foe.
> With tumult less and with less hostile din,
> That *Satan* with less toil, and now with ease
> Wafts on the calmer wave by dubious light
> And like a weather-beaten Vessel holds
> Gladly the Port, though Shrouds and Tackle torn;
> Or in the emptier waste, resembling Air,
> Weighs his spread wings, at leasure to behold
> Farr off th' Empyreal Heav'n, extended wide
> In circuit, undetermined square or round,
> With Opal Towrs and Battlements adorn'd
> Of living Saphire, once his native Seat;
> And fast by hanging in a golden Chain
> This pendant world, in bigness as a Starr
> Of smallest Magnitude close by the Moon.
> Thither full fraught with mischievous revenge,
> Accurst, and in a cursed hour he hies.[1]

Satan has struggled up to the light, and the Third Book begins with perfect aptitude

> Hail, holy Light.

Not only is this transition apt, but within the invocation the thought moves with perfect aptitude to the description of Heaven, the theme of the second movement. After calling on light, Milton naturally thinks of the deprivation of it in himself, of his kinship in blindness with Homer and Thamyris, and of his need for celestial illumination of his inner mind to compensate for the loss of physical vision. And when celestial light has been mentioned, what more natural than to proceed to speak of God, its author? And so in line 56 the second movement begins:

> Now had the Almighty Father from above,
> From the pure Empyrean where he sits
> High Thron'd above all highth, bent down his eye,
> His own works and their works at once to view:
> About him all the Sanctities of Heaven
> Stood thick as Starrs, and from his sight receiv'd
> Beatitude past utterance.

I. ii. 1034-55.

The picture of Heaven corresponds to that of Hell, and gains greatly in beauty by the contrast. Saurat is wrong in calling the scenes in Heaven an interlude and making the contrast between Hell and Paradise. Paradise is not contrasted with Hell; it stands in contrasted relationship to Hell and Heaven. The correspondences and contrasts between Hell and Heaven are easily seen. Divine beatitude is described, but more shortly than Hell's concrete miseries. Far below, Adam and Eve, in blissful solitude, are the unconscious cause in Heaven, as they had been in Hell, of debate and deliberation. As in the council in Hell Satan alone accepts the perilous journey through Chaos to Earth, so in the council in Heaven the Son alone dares sacrifice himself for the redemption of Man. Compare the two passages:

> This said, he sat; and expectation held
> His look suspence, awaiting who appeerd
> To second, or oppose, or undertake
> The perilous attempt; but all sat mute,
> Pondering the danger with deep thoughts; and each
> In others count'nance red his own dismay
> Astonisht: none among the choice and prime
> Of those Heav'n-warring Champions could be found
> So hardie as to proffer or accept
> Alone the dreadful voyage; till at last
> *Satan,* whom now transcendent glory rais'd
> Above his fellows, with Monarchal pride
> Conscious of highest worth, unmov'd thus spake.[1]

> He askd, but all the Heav'nly Quire stood mute,
> And silence was in Heav'n: on Mans behalf
> Patron or Intercessor none appeerd,
> Much less that durst upon his own head draw
> The deadly forfeiture, and ransom set.
> And now without redemption all mankind
> Must have bin lost, adjudg'd to Death and Hell
> By doom severe, had not the Son of God,
> In whom the fulness dwels of love divine,
> His dearest mediation thus renewd.[2]

Another intentional contrast is between the divided occupations of the fallen Angels in Hell when the council is over and the common hymn of praise in Heaven when the issue of the heavenly council has been decided. Though Hell and Heaven and their inhabitants are described, Man is always the theme of activity; and Man, though better known in Heaven, remains to the reader minute,

1. ii. 417–29.　　2. iii. 217–26.

distant, and ignorant of the great events of which he is becoming the cause. The second movement ends with line 415 of the Third Book.

We are now taken back to Satan, who in the remaining lines of the book traverses the universe, deceives Uriel, and reaches the Earth. At the beginning of the Fourth Book there are twelve introductory lines beginning

> O for that warning voice,

whose significance in the construction may be asked. Milton apparently wishes to mark some new feature, but he does not wish to stress it very strongly, for the prologue is slight compared with the four other prologues, to Books One, Three, Seven, and Nine. The answer seems to be that it marks an important new stage in the story, the extension of the field of events to the Earth, but without marking a vital change of atmosphere. As will be pointed out shortly, the definite transference of interest from Heaven and Hell to Earth is marked by the long introduction to the Seventh Book. It is not till this book that the reader definitely feels himself on Earth; in the earlier books he watches Adam and Eve from without, or is rather a visitor in Paradise than lives there. Moreover, from Book Three, 416, to Book Five, 561, where Raphael begins his narrative, there is much shifting of scene: the reader lives, if anywhere in particular, in the firmament or in the spaces between the universe and Heaven. I think if one compares the impressions derived from the descriptions of Paradise in Books Four and Nine respectively, the difference of location will be clear. In the earlier book Paradise is described with such a remote beauty that we feel it to be a colony of Heaven, not real Earth; we see it from without, suffused with an unearthly glow; at any rate we do not for any length of time enter the minds of Adam and Eve.

> Millions of spiritual Creatures walk the Earth
> Unseen, both when we wake, and when we sleep,[1]

says Adam, and we feel the nearness of Paradise to Heaven; while the lines

> So passd they naked on, nor shunnd the sight
> Of God or Angel,[2]

and

> Sleep on,
> Blest pair,

illustrate the usual point of view. But in the later book Paradise is familiar enough to be the scene of a struggle in which living human

1. iv. 677–8. 2. iv. 319–20.

beings take part. In this gradual familiarizing of Paradise Milton shows consummate skill, and through it he cunningly gives an impression of progress and action. But though the reader may not yet inhabit Paradise, the Fourth Book introduces the third motive, that of Paradise and its inhabitants, which gains in importance when Hell and Heaven begin to fight over them. For the battle begins when Satan in the form of a toad inspires Eve with the evil dream and the Angels by their vigilance and Gabriel by his courage counter this the fiend's first attack. Let it be noted that Eve, when first tempted, does not have to rely on herself: she is saved by heavenly intervention. Gabriel and his guard are as effective in the Fourth Book as they are useless in the Ninth. Man is not yet a free agent, and consequently not yet the full centre of attention. In Book Five the same atmosphere prevails, but we are made more familiar with Paradise, we begin to see it from within, when Adam and Eve sing their morning hymn, go about their tasks, and see Raphael approaching. Satan having been so recently foiled, we are not yet ready for another attempt, which was bound to be somewhat similar to the first. We therefore welcome the episode of Raphael's visit, which occupies most of Book Five and the whole of Books Six, Seven, and Eight. It has more than one function. First and most obviously it describes the history of the universe previous to the fall of the Angels and during their period of stupor in Hell. This description was necessary to Milton's plan of narrating the events of the complete course of time. He made it episodic, to minimize the inevitable distraction from the central theme, the story of the Fall. This arrangement makes it most improbable that Greenlaw[1] and Saurat are right in thinking that *Paradise Lost* is composed round two equipollent themes. But the episode fulfils another function: it effects the final transfer of interest from Heaven and Hell to Earth, thus preparing for the catastrophe. A consummate stroke of constructive genius was to effect this change *within* Raphael's visit, thus preventing the 'unresolved duality' that would have resulted had there not been some powerful continuity carrying us across the gap. The prologue to the Seventh Book marks the change; the continuity of Raphael's narrative bridges the gap: and the compromise is triumphant.

The words with which the Seventh Book begins,

Descend from Heav'n *Urania*,

are sometimes misinterpreted: are made to refer to the Seventh

1. 'A Better Teacher than Aquinas', in *Studies in Philology*, 1917, 204.

Book alone and to mean that the poet, having finished the war in Heaven, will proceed to tell the creation of the world. That they apply to all the rest of the poem is proved by lines later in the prologue:

> Half yet remaines unsung, but narrower bound
> Within the visible Diurnal Spheare;
> Standing on Earth, not rapt above the Pole,
> More safe I Sing with mortal voice.[1]

The words *standing on Earth* confirm the idea that the location of the reader (implied by that of the writer) is of importance in understanding the course of the epic.

Though this opening of the Seventh Book marks the final change of scene to Earth, the transition is not abrupt. The last lines of the Sixth Book, Raphael's application of Satan's fall to Adam's own case, point forward, while the world's creation in the Seventh Book is described first from without, the reader being gradually introduced into Earth the centre of the universe, and into the centre of the Earth, Paradise. In the Eighth Book the process is made complete by Adam's astronomical enquiries. The reader finds himself fixed on Earth and looking away from it to the sun and stars. Further, Raphael's answer, though putting forward the Copernican astronomy as a possibility, speaks of the Ptolemaic, the system on which the poem is based, as not unfitting the high nature of Man. Here is how Raphael justifies the subservience of the great luminaries to the smaller Earth:

> consider first, that Great
> Or Bright inferrs not Excellence: the Earth
> Though, in comparison of Heav'n, so small,
> Nor glistering, may of solid good containe
> More plenty then the Sun that barren shines,
> Whose vertue on it self workes no effect,
> But in the fruitful Earth; there first receavd
> His beams, unactive else, thir vigor find.
> Yet not to Earth are those bright Luminaries
> Officious, but to thee Earths habitant.[2]

This well marks the centring of attention on Man. Just as the Earth is tiny yet the *omphalos* of all creation, so the struggle in the garden, though its actors are small in stature compared with the warring Angels, is yet the central event in the history of things. Adam's own account of his creation (lines 250–559) fixes us with added certainty

1. vii. 21–4.   2. viii. 90–9.

to Earth. Instead of watching Satan going to Earth, we watch, with Adam, God coming there. Adam's last words and Raphael's admonitory reply are (as Addison noticed) a most effective premonition of the events of the Ninth Book, rich in irony. As the climax of all the wonders he has experienced, Adam ends his speech with his famous praise of Eve, in which occur the fatally prophetic lines,

> All higher knowledge in her presence falls
> Degraded, Wisdom in discourse with her
> Looses discount'nanc't, and like folly shewes.[1]

No wonder, when, Adam ceasing, we read

> To whom the Angel with contracted brow.
>   Accuse not Nature, she hath don her part;
> Do thou but thine, and be not diffident
> Of Wisdom, she deserts thee not, if thou
> Dismiss not her, when most thou needst her nigh,
> By attributing overmuch to things
> Less excellent,[2]

we think of the catastrophe coming. Raphael's final warning (lines 633–43) and departure complete, with a boding solemnity it is impossible to overpraise, the preparations for the ensuing tragedy. For hitherto Heaven has never remitted its guard over Paradise. But with the departure of Raphael Heaven's vigilance is withdrawn; Gabriel's honest watch is quite ineffective; Man is left to his own resources; and the stage is empty for the three chief actors, Adam, Eve, and the Serpent.

The prologue to the Ninth Book, which as a functional portion of the construction I incline to think the finest of all the prologues, effects a double change of atmosphere. It suggests the blackness of storm clouds after the treacherous beauty of a dazzling sky, and it takes the action from the Garden of Eden into its final scene, the mind of Man. Though in the Eighth Book the reader feels himself to be on Earth, he is not on ordinary soil. But, says Milton,

>   I now must change
>   Those Notes to Tragic,

and in very truth this prologue does mark the entrance of the dramatic element and of the more potent human passions (bating Satan's in the early books) into the poem. The conversations between Adam and Eve and between Eve and Satan in the Ninth and Tenth Books,

---

1. viii. 551–3.   2. viii. 560–6.

fragments of which Milton may have had in his mind from the time
when he intended to treat the Fall in a play, are more dramatic
than any others in the poem. One touch before the catastrophe
illustrates the dramatic tone – a touch quite unlike anything that has
gone before. Satan hopes to find Eve alone, and *by a lucky chance* he
does so. This introduction of chance, but of chance that does not
disagree with character, belongs eminently to the drama. The
prologue has one more function: it marks a return from the great
central episode to the main theme. Milton in the opening lines refers
back to the opening of the whole poem, thereby reminding us that
the episodic books, Five to Eight, should be put back into their
proper sequence of time and that Man's disobedience is the main
theme. He refers back by the simple expedient of repetition.

> No more of talk where God or Angel Guest
> With Man, as with his Friend, familiar us'd
> To sit indulgent, and with him partake
> Rural repast, permitting him the while
> Venial discourse unblam'd: I now must change
> Those Notes to Tragic; foul distrust, and breach
> Disloyal on the part of Man, revolt,
> And disobedience: On the part of Heav'n
> Now alienated, distance and distaste,
> Anger and just rebuke, and judgement giv'n,
> That brought into this World a world of woe,
> Sinne and her shadow Death, and Miserie
> Deaths Harbinger.[1]

The line,

> That brought into this World a world of woe,

echoes the third line of the poem,

> Brought Death into the World, and all our woe.

And after the prologue to the Ninth Book Milton does more than
merely proceed to the catastrophe. He refers back to each of the
main earlier motives, as if to point out how they all lead, in subservience, to the supreme scene that is to follow. It is significant that
these references back are in the order in which the motives were
presented in the earlier books: Hell, Heaven, and Paradise. (1) He
repeats the Hell motive by putting into Satan's mouth the one great
tortured speech (lines 99–178) he utters in the last seven books. We
are inevitably taken back to Hell and the passions Satan displays

1. ix. 1–13.

there. (2) Adam in his speech (lines 343–75) echoes God's discourse on Free Will uttered in Heaven (Book Three, lines 80–134). This speech is the first spoken in the description of Heaven. Again we are brought back to an earlier motive – Heaven. Of course it is Adam, not God, who speaks. God has retired for the time being from the action. Adam is here the mouthpiece of Heaven for the benefit of Eve. (3) Immediately before the Serpent begins his wiles (and there is the most poignant beauty in the contrast) Eve is described in a way that brings back to our senses all the unearthly glory of the first description of Paradise:

> Thus saying, from her Husbands hand her hand
> Soft she withdrew, and like a Wood-Nymph light
> *Oread* or *Dryad*, or of *Delia's* Traine
> Betook her to the Groves, but *Delia's* self
> In gate surpassd and Goddess-like deport,
> Though not as shee with Bow and Quiver armd,
> But with such Gardning Tools as Art yet rude,
> Guiltless of fire had formd, or Angels brought.
> To *Pales*, or *Pomona*, thus adornd,
> Likest she seemd, *Pomona* when she fled
> *Vertumnus*, or to *Ceres* in her Prime,
> Yet Virgin of *Proserpina* from Jove.[1]

The last line (which roused the wrath of Bentley to perhaps its most ridiculous sublimity) recalls by its mention of Proserpine the more famous but not more beautiful lines in the first description of Paradise,

> Not that faire field
> Of *Enna*, where *Proserpin* gathring flours
> Herself a fairer Floure by gloomie *Dis*
> Was gatherd.[2]

The reference back is made quite certain by the lines a little later where Eve, busied with the flowers, is like Proserpine compared with them,

> Her self, though fairest unsupported flower,
> From her best prop so farr, and storm so nigh.[3]

The triple recalling of the earlier books is of the greatest value in tightening the construction of the poem and in adding significance to the central theme. Milton plainly wishes to imply that the eating of the apple was an act in which not Man alone but the destinies of Heaven, Hell, and Paradise were closely concerned.

1. ix. 385–96.   2. iv. 268–71.   3. ix. 432–3.

The climax comes with the words

> So saying, her rash hand in evil hour
> Forth reaching to the Fruit, she pluckd, she eat:
> Earth felt the wound, and Nature from her seat
> Sighing through all her Works gave signs of woe,
> That all was lost.[1]

The rest of the Ninth Book describes the immediate effect of the forbidden fruit on Adam and Eve, and ends with their futile quarrelling.

Much still remained for Milton to do. He had, according to his gigantic plan, to outline the scheme of the world to the end of time: he had to describe the effects of the Fall, the central event of all time, on Hell, Heaven, Paradise, and the mind of Man: he had also to enlarge the scene from the narrow tragic stage of the Garden to the measure of the world as he knew it, that what he wished to convey by his story might acquire a human reality. In the Tenth Book are described the effects of the Fall. Hell is let loose and apparently triumphs. In reality its triumph is more than balanced by the Grace called forth in Heaven. So potent is this effluence of Grace that redeemed mankind will be more excellent than ever in his days of happy ignorance. Thus the Fall led to greater good than it occasioned evil. Meanwhile the Earth is made subject to death and mutability, and Adam and Eve to all the woes of common humanity. But already by the end of Book Ten Grace has softened their hearts to repentance. When at the beginning of Book Eleven God accepts their prayers and we are assured that the world is not doomed to immediate destruction, a place of comparative rest has been reached; and Milton takes advantage of it to insert episodically the history of mankind from Cain and Abel to the end of time. Not only did he choose the right place for the episode, but he had the happy idea of narrating events in the form of pageants presented to the eyes of Adam. This is a fine piece of craft. There had been nothing of the sort before, and the novelty was exactly what was wanted to prevent the interest flagging. Unfortunately the pictorial method took much space and could not be applied to the whole of history. Milton has to abandon it in the Twelfth Book and to scramble too hastily in straightforward narrative through the ages. But the episode fulfils its functions. History is recorded to the end of time in close relation to the Fall, and the reader, confined in the Ninth and Tenth Books within the leafy bounds of Paradise, sees wide across

1. ix. 780-4.

the world. In the mouth of Michael, Milton puts his weightiest pronouncements on the art of living in the world with which he is familiar.

Many have praised the end of the poem, but often as if it could be detached. However beautiful in itself, its full grandeur can only be felt if one realizes what has led up to it. The action, that has started in Hell, shifted to Heaven, narrowed to the firmament, to Earth, to the Garden of Eden and its tenants, has broadened once again to Earth but to a different Earth; and brings itself to a close in showing us two minute human creatures erring and uncertain like their descendants, and with all the world before them in which to exercise their hazardous and momentous power of choice.

CHAPTER THREE
Paradise Lost: the Conscious Meaning

IF THE foregoing account of the way *Paradise Lost* evolves is correct in the main, it becomes plain that everything was meant to be subordinate to the human drama. Whatever the actual result, Milton intended neither Satan nor the picture of paradisaical bliss nor the descriptions of heavenly beatitude to detract from the struggle that took place in the hearts of Adam and Eve. The thorough-going Satanists will have to sacrifice both Milton's conscious intention and the structural unity to their belief. Such a sacrifice might conceivably be necessary, but it is too drastic to be made lightly. Further, if we are to discover the main structure of Milton's conscious idea we shall best do it by examining that part of the poem round which everything else revolves.

In passing it may be pointed out that for Milton with the beliefs he professed the Fall was necessarily the most pregnant event in the history of the world. The only event that could seriously compete with it was the entrance of sin into Heaven, but the direct effect of this was limited to expulsion and irrevocable condemnation: there was no evocation of Grace. But the Fall of man, occasioned by the sinful angels, instead of bringing unmitigated perdition called forth Grace in addition and was the reason of regeneration and the incarnation of the Son. It is thus both effect and cause of the highest moment: of higher moment than the incarnation itself, which without the sin of Adam would simply not have taken place.

But the nature of the Fall is a very different problem from its comparative importance, and it is this we must examine in order to find the centre of Milton's conscious intention. Unfortunately the problem presented by the Ninth Book of *Paradise Lost* is not quite simple. There is one radical difficulty: that it is not always clear for what Adam and Eve stand. Do they stand for humanity or for man and woman? When Eve in evil hour stretches forth her rash hand for the fruit, does Milton intend her rashness to be universally human or specifically feminine? The answer may make a good deal of difference. As a matter of fact Milton seems to mix the two meanings, while ultimately his old grudge against the female sex gets the upper hand of his conscious intentions, of which more presently. Let it suffice to say that this complication makes it difficult for me to accept any very simple explanation of the meaning of the

Fall, like that of Addison or of Greenlaw and Saurat. Addison considers the Fall simply a matter of disobedience and is content with this rather vague explanation:

> The great Moral . . . which reigns in Milton is the most universal and most useful that can be imagined: it is in short this, *that Obedience to the Will of God makes Men happy, and that Disobedience makes them miserable.* This is visibly the Moral of the principal Fable which turns upon Adam and Eve, who continued in *Paradise* while they kept the Command that was given them, and were driven out of it as soon as they had transgressed.

Milton could hardly have demurred, but mere unmotivated disobedience does not get us very far. We would know to what motive Milton consciously attributed that sin. Greenlaw[1] combines a theory of what *Paradise Lost* means with a comparison of that poem with the adventures of Guyon in the second book of *The Faerie Queene*. He opposes the Satanists and stresses the Platonic rather than the Biblical influences. The theme of *Paradise Lost* is less that of obedience to God than of obedience to *sophrosyne*, to temperance, to the rational against the irrational part of human nature. There are two conflicts: one between Satan and the two intemperate vices, ambition and lust for power; the other between Adam and sensuality. These conflicts correspond to Guyon's adventures first with Mammon and then in the Bower of Bliss, and were indeed suggested by them.[2] The Fall then will be the yielding of reason to passion, and in particular to the passion of sensuality. Saurat agrees entirely with this interpretation of the Fall. That it contains much truth I do not deny, but as a complete explanation it seems to me to disregard a large portion of Milton's text; which it may now be well to examine.

The last words of Raphael to Adam in the Eighth Book, when at sunset he departs, are prophetic of the struggle that is to come, and merit close attention.

> But I can now no more; the parting Sun
> Beyond the Earths green Cape and verdant Isles
> *Hesperean* sets, my Signal to depart.
> Be strong, live happie, and love, but first of all
> Him whom to love is to obey, and keep
> His great command; take heed least Passion sway
> Thy Judgement to do aught, which else free Will
> Would not admit; thine and of all thy Sons

1. In 'A Better Teacher than Aquinas', in *Studies in Philology*, 1917, 196–217.
2. For the question of Spenser's influence on Milton see Appendix H, p. 332.

The weal or woe in thee is plac't; beware.
I in thy persevering shall rejoyce,
And all the Blest: stand fast; to stand or fal
Free in thine own Arbitrement it lies.
Perfet within, no outward aid require;
And all temptation to transgress repell.[1]

From this it would seem that the struggle was to be between passion and reason, but it must be remembered that Raphael is speaking to Adam alone: his words need not refer to the prior temptation of Eve. Coming to the Ninth Book we find Eve leaving Adam to garden alone, fully warned and confident in her own strength to overcome any temptation, anxious even to prove her individual worth. She utters the very Miltonic sentiment:

And what is Faith, Love, Vertue unassaid
Alone, without exterior help sustaind?[2]

But when the actual temptation occurs, her mind quite belies her apparently sober preparedness. Nor is there any need of a great wave of passion to overwhelm her resolution. Eve shows little strength of feeling: it is not so much excess of passion as triviality of mind that is her ruin. She is a prey to a variety of feelings, but it is always this triviality that allows her thus to be preyed on. First comes susceptibility to flattery. After Satan's first speech follow the lines:

So gloz'd the Tempter, and his Proem tun'd;
Into the Heart of *Eve* his words made way,[3]

Then she is unwary:

So talk'd the spirited sly Snake; and *Eve*
Yet more amaz'd unwarie thus reply'd.[4]

Just before following Satan to the Tree she is called 'our credulous Mother'. Confronted by the Tree for a moment she recollects herself and makes a faint resistance: but a single long speech of Satan is enough to overcome it. Well aware of Eve's shallowness he says:

will God incense his ire
For such a petty Trespass?[5]

And when he ceases speaking, Milton writes:

He ended, and his words replete with guile
Into her heart too easie entrance won.[6]

1. viii. 630–43.   2. ix. 335–6.   3. ix. 549–50.   4. ix. 613–14.   5. ix. 692–3.
6. ix. 733–4.

In other words, Eve's resistance was inexcusably trivial. The sin of greed is added next:

> Meanwhile the hour of Noon drew on, and wak'd
> An eager appetite, rais'd by the smell
> So savorie of that Fruit, which with desire,
> Inclinable now grown to touch or taste,
> Sollicited her longing eye.[1]

But this is the only form of sensuality that sways her mind and cannot compare in power with the other motives. To say that Eve's fall expresses the struggle between reason and sensuality is to go clean contrary to the bulk of the text. Once Eve has eaten, her judgment is thoroughly upset: it is the fruit itself that is passion rather than the motives that led to eating it. Inflamed by passion she commits the *hubris* of imagined godhead and gorges herself unrestrainedly with the fruit. But mental triviality is still to the fore, for Eve imagines light-heartedly that God may not notice her act:

> And I perhaps am secret; Heav'n is high,
> High and remote to see from thence distinct
> Each thing on Earth; and other care perhaps
> May have diverted from continual watch
> Our great Forbidder, safe with all his Spies
> About him.[2]

In sum, Eve's prime sin is a dreadful unawareness, despite all warnings, of the enormous issues involved.[3]

Adam is initially better aware. He is horrified when he hears Eve's story:

> *Adam*, soon as he heard
> The fatal Trespass done by *Eve*, amaz'd,
> Astonied stood and Blank, while horror chill
> Ran through his veins, and all his joints relaxd;
> From his slack hand the Garland wreath'd for *Eve*
> Down drop'd, and all the faded Roses shed.[4]

But what is his first thought? It is comradeship: to forsake Eve cannot for an instant be contemplated. Adam's speech, his first comment on Eve's fall, must be momentous and had better be quoted entire:

1. ix 739–44.   2. ix. 811–16.

3. In his first mention of the Fall in *Paradise Regained* (i. 51) Milton speaks of '*Adam* and his facil consort *Eve*'. Eve's mental triviality seems to have remained in his mind as her dominant characteristic.

4. ix. 888–93.

O fairest of Creation, last and best
Of all Gods works, Creature in whom excelld
Whatever can to sight or thought be formd,
Holy, divine, good, amiable, or sweet!
How art thou lost, how on a sudden lost,
Defac't, deflourd, and now to Death devote?
Rather how hast thou yeelded to transgress
The strict forbiddance, how to violate
The sacred Fruit forbidd'n? som cursed fraud
Of Enemie hath beguil'd thee, yet unknown,
And mee with thee hath ruind, for with thee
Certain my resolution is to Die;
How can I live without thee, how forgoe
Thy sweet Converse and Love so dearly join'd,
To live again in these wilde Woods forlorn?
Should God create another *Eve,* and I
Another Rib afford, yet loss of thee
Would never from my heart; no, no, I feel
The Link of Nature draw me: Flesh of Flesh,
Bone of my Bone thou art, and from thy State
Mine never shall be parted, bliss or woe.[1]

This seems simple enough: the heart of any normal reader warms with sympathy at these exquisitely tender words of Adam refusing to forsake Eve in her extremity. And yet how can Milton at this of all places in the poem have given Adam his conscious approval? Unconscious approval even is difficult to accept, for the issues at stake are so absolutely clear. Had Milton unconsciously approved of Adam's sense of comradeship he would have described it far less obtrusively. Now if he disapproves, what is Adam's sin? It is certainly not sensuality. Adam's passions are in no wise roused: he merely voices the natural human instinct of comradeship with his kind. Adam cannot face solitariness, 'to live again in these wilde Woods forlorn'. He does not for a moment hesitate to sacrifice the course of action he knows to be right to his gregariousness. Ordinary man is far too weak to live alone. Milton makes the accusation with all tenderness, but I believe he meant to make it; and when we remember his own extraordinary self-sufficiency, we need not be surprised at this strange arraignment of essential human nature.

Once Adam has put gregariousness above what he fully knows to be right, he is open to every kind of weakness. He quickly falls into a mental levity similar to Eve's, arguing that perhaps God will withhold his doom, and into an infatuation that dreams of Godhead. His

1. ix. 896–916.

final sin is uxoriousness. Eve has lavished praise on him for his
fidelity and Milton writes:

> So saying, she embrac'd him, and for joy
> Tenderly wept, much won that he his Love
> Had so enobl'd, as of choice to incurr
> Divine displeasure for her sake, or Death.
> In recompence (for such compliance bad
> Such recompence best merits) from the bough
> She gave him of that fair enticing Fruit
> With liberal hand: he scrupl'd not to eat
> Against his better knowledge, not deceav'd,
> But fondly overcome with Femal charm.[1]

The last line is curiously inconsistent with what went before. Adam
had made up his mind before Eve exercised her charms on him: her
caresses were superfluous. The fruit acts on Adam as on Eve:

> As with new Wine intoxicated both
> They swim in mirth, and fansie that they feel
> Divinitie within them breeding wings
> Wherewith to scorn the Earth.[2]

Adam reaches the height of criminal levity when he says

> If such pleasure be
> In things to us forbidd'n, it might be wisht,
> For this one Tree had bin forbidd'n ten.[3]

(Milton's grim humour never showed more dramatic power than in
these lines. We can hear Eve's hectic, infatuate giggles at Adam's
words.) But it is now sensuality that comes to the fore: sensuality the
effect rather than the cause of the Fall. Inflamed by the fumes of
the fruit the pair fall into lust, impure in itself and the more criminal
as yielded to so frivolously at the most terribly fateful hour of mankind's whole history.

   When the first intoxicating effect of the fruit has passed, Adam
and Eve fall to quarrelling; and Milton makes it perfectly plain
that he means the effect of the Fall to signify the victory of passion
over reason:

> They sate them down to weep, nor onely Teares
> Raind at thir Eyes, but high Winds worse within
> Began to rise, high Passions, Anger, Hate,
> Mistrust, Suspicion, Discord, and shook sore

1. ix. 990–9. 2. ix. 1008–11. 3. ix. 1024–6.

Thir inward State of Mind, calme Region once
And full of Peace, now tost and turbulent:
For Understanding rul'd not, and the Will
Heard not her lore, both in subjection now
To sensual Appetite, who from beneathe
Usurping over sovran Reason claimd
Superior sway.[1]

In this strife at the end of Book Nine and in the Tenth Book the
emphasis gets laid on Adam's folly in yielding to Eve's advances,
on the theme of 'fondly overcome with Femal charm'. Adam
generalizes bitterly on the relations of the sexes:

Thus it shall befall
Him who to worth in Woman overtrusting
Lets her will rule; restraint she will not brook,
And left to her self, if evil thence ensue,
Shee first his weak indulgence will accuse.[2]

When the Son comes to the Garden to deliver judgment, his chief
ground for blaming Adam seems to be his uxorious yielding. But
we must remember that Adam's defence was that Eve gave him of
the tree and he did eat. The Son replies to this defence:

Was shee thy God, that her thou didst obey
Before his voice, or was shee made thy guide,
Superior, or but equal, that to her
Thou did'st resigne thy Manhood, and the Place
Wherein God set thee above her made of thee,
And for thee, whose perfection farr excell'd
Hers in all real dignitie: Adornd
Shee was indeed, and lovely to attract
Thy Love, not thy Subjection, and her Gifts
Were such as under Government well seem'd,
Unseemly to beare rule, which was thy part
And person, had'st thou known thy self aright.[3]

The last line seems to show that Milton recognizes a prior cause of
Adam's fall, lack of self-knowledge, itself implying a kind of triviality
of mind. But still Milton cannot leave alone the theme of woman's
delusiveness and indulges in a heartfelt outburst before Adam and
Eve become reconciled.

O why did God,
Creator wise, that peopl'd highest Heav'n
With Spirits Masculine, create at last
This noveltie on Earth, this fair defect

1. ix. 1121-31.   2. ix. 1182-6.   3. x. 145-56.

Of Nature, and not fill the World at once
With Men as Angels without Feminine,
Or find some other way to generate
Mankind? this mischief had not then befall'n,
And more that shall befall, innumerable
Disturbances on Earth through Femal snares,
And straight conjunction with this Sex: for either
He never shall find out fit Mate, but such
As some misfortune brings him, or mistake,
Or whom he wishes most shall seldom gain
Through her perversness, but shall see her gaind
By a farr worse, or if she love, withheld
By Parents, or his happiest choice too late
Shall meet, alreadie linkt and Wedlock-bound
To a fell Adversarie, his hate or shame:
Which infinite calamitie shall cause
To Humane life, and household peace confound.[1]

This prophetic outburst of Adam, so entirely uncalled for, is very illuminating. It is of course Milton's own voice, unable through the urgency of personal experience to keep silent. And it may help to explain the curious shift, mentioned above, of the motive that prompted Adam's fall: the shift from gregariousness to sensuality. The qualities that ruin most men were not shared by Milton: he has no part in their levity and their terror of standing alone. But he cannot for long keep himself out of the poem. The one occasion when he allowed passion to gain the mastery over reason was when he made his first marriage: for him personally sex was the great pitfall. And so he cannot refrain from grafting sex onto the scheme of the Fall. The story in *Genesis* is too good an excuse to be missed for uttering his ancient grievance. Even in writing of the Fall, therefore, Milton is not exempt from the sin of sacrificing reason to passion.

The question remains: how many of the motives attributed to Adam and Eve are common to humanity, how many peculiar to one sex? Mental levity is common to both Adam and Eve, but stronger in Eve. It is the besetting sin of all humanity; fear of standing alone or gregariousness is of course common to it too, but it is a sin only in the man, for it is not woman's function to stand alone. Uxoriousness is a purely masculine failing.

To sum up, Milton seems to mean by the Fall the following. There is in man a 'levity and shallowness of mind', as he calls it in

The Tenure of Kings and Magistrates, or, with varied metaphors, a 'numb and chill stupidity of soul, an unactive blindness of mind', in *Reason of Church Government*, which makes him unaware of the important issues of life. Not knowing himself properly, he allows his passions to deceive and get the better of his judgment. For Milton (there is no proof that he thought it true for all men) it is through the female sex that this deception is likely to happen. Once the passions have got the upper hand, chaos ensues, all peace of mind is gone, man has fallen from true liberty to mental anarchy.

Milton connects the loss not merely of mental but of political liberty with the Fall, in a very important passage of the Twelfth Book where Michael comments on Nimrod, the first monarch. Michael says to Adam:

> Justly thou abhorr'st
> That Son, who on the quiet state of men
> Such trouble brought, affecting to subdue
> Rational Libertie; yet know withall,
> Since thy original lapse, true Libertie
> Is lost, which alwayes with right Reason dwells
> Twinn'd, and from her hath no dividual being:
> Reason in man obscur'd, or not obeyd,
> Immediately inordinate desires
> And upstart Passions catch the Government
> From Reason, and to servitude reduce
> Man till then free. Therefore since hee permits
> Within himself unworthie Powers to reign
> Over free Reason, God in Judgement just
> Subjects him from without to violent Lords;
> Who oft as undeservedly enthrall
> His outward freedom: Tyrannie must be,
> Though to the Tyrant thereby no excuse.[1]

The rest of the conscious meaning of the poem is easier to state. First may be added the doctrine of free will, without which any kind of obedience had for Milton no meaning. This he insists on so frequently and emphatically that we need not question the conscious store he set by it. Moreover the construction, by which at the end of the Eighth Book Heaven withdraws itself, leaving Adam and Eve completely free, brings the doctrine home to us more emphatically at the climax than anywhere else, and thus stresses its conscious importance in Milton's mind. No other idea is mentioned so often in the other parts of the poem also: too often according to the com-

1. xii. 79–96.

mon view; and Pope was largely thinking of the pronouncements in
Heaven on free will and foreknowledge when he accused Milton's
God the Father of turning School Divine. But it is well to heed these
passages if we can and try to gauge their weight in Milton's mind.
I think the doctrine of free will had for him a double meaning. It was
a condition of significant action and it expresses his belief in the
value of the conscious will. If action was controlled beyond the
power of choice by an outside force, it became separated from the
mind and its value disappeared. Secondly, the kind of action or
state of mind Milton felt desirable was one perfectly controlled by
the conscious will. He had little belief in any deed, however seem-
ingly great, performed instinctively or with the full significance of
the issues unrealized. Part of the sin of Adam and Eve is that they
fail most lamentably to realize the full issue and to make full use of
the will-power that is the great weapon for good in their natures.
They are not worthy of the great gift of free will. Milton's feelings
about the conscious will can be well illustrated by a contrast. He
would have been utterly out of sympathy with those stanzas of
Wordsworth that most clearly describe the virtue of suspending
completely the operations of the conscious will.

> The eye – it cannot choose but see;
> We cannot bid the ear be still;
> Our bodies feel, where'er they be,
> Against or with our will.
>
> Nor less I deem that there are Powers
> Which of themselves our minds impress;
> That we can feed this mind of ours
> In a wise passiveness.
>
> Think you, 'mid all this mighty sum
> Of things for ever speaking,
> That nothing of itself will come,
> But we must still be seeking.
>
> – Then ask not wherefore, here, alone
> Conversing as I may,
> I sit upon this old grey stone
> And dream my time away.

Meditation and the exercise of the imagination in calling up

> Such sights as youthfull Poets dream
> On Summer eeves by haunted stream

were modes of activity Milton believed in, and the spirit that urged him to create poetry might work in a mysterious way; but the idea of cultivating a vacancy, a wise passiveness, on the assumption that all sorts of things happened without or against one's will, would have been abhorrent.

It may be surmised that if Milton belonged to the present generation he would have distrusted profoundly the idea that a good deal should be yielded to our subconscious desires. He would have felt that the danger of encouraging latent barbarity by fostering them was far greater than the dangers following their repression. Progress in evolution he would have liked to think had resulted from the creative power of the conscious will. Man said I *will* walk and he did walk. And instead of following Wordsworth he would have agreed with Shelley's words at the end of *Prometheus Unbound* to the effect that Hope may create by hoping the thing it contemplates.

Conscious control is so much a part of Milton's nature, so inseparable from the cadence of his verse, that illustration is almost superfluous. Two passages, however, are particularly illuminating. The first is from *Comus*. Comus, having heard the Lady's song, says in comment:

> But such a sacred, and home-felt delight,
> Such sober certainty of waking bliss
> I never heard till now.[1]

Waking bliss is most significant. The Lady, following not blind instinct but fully conscious of her own mind, had attained a felicity more powerful than Comus has ever dreamed of. The other passage is the description of the fiends mustered on the plains of Hell:

> Anon they move
> In perfect *Phalanx* to the *Dorian* mood
> Of Flutes and soft Recorders; such as rais'd
> To hight of noblest temper Hero's old
> Arming to Battel, and in stead of rage
> Deliberate valour breath'd, firm and unmov'd
> With dread of death to flight or foul retreat,
> Nor wanting power to mitigate and swage
> With solemn touches, troubl'd thoughts, and chase
> Anguish and doubt and fear and sorrow and pain
> From mortal or immortal minds.[2]

Deliberate valour, the valour of the hero who knows himself and knows what he is fighting, of Homer's Ajax praying that, if he must

1. *Comus*, 262-4. 2. *Paradise Lost*, i. 549-59.

die, it may be in the light, not the sudden flare-up of ignorant reck-
lessness, was what Milton believed in. In this passage if anywhere
Milton is on the Devil's side.

Mankind, in Milton's conscious thought, was not only perverse:
it had a natural nobility and dignity. All the strength of his conscious,
traditional humanism comes out in his first description of the human
pair:

> Two of far nobler shape erect and tall,
> Godlike erect, with native Honour clad,
> In naked Majestie seemd Lords of all,
> And worthie seemd, for in thir looks Divine
> The image of thir glorious Maker shon,
> Truth, Wisdom, Sanctitude severe and pure,
> Severe, but in true filial freedom plac't;
> Whence true autoritie in men.[1]

And again in his description of Adam going to meet Raphael:

> Mean while our Primitive great Sire, to meet
> His god-like Guest, walks forth, without more train
> Accompani'd then with his own compleat
> Perfections, in himself was all his state,
> More solemn then the tedious pomp that waits
> On Princes.[2]

Such then is man in *Paradise Lost*: noble by nature; owing obedience to his Creator; free to choose and hence capable of action,
morally good or bad, for which he alone is responsible; beset by a
strange mental perverseness or levity which thwarts his native en-
dowment and opens him to the rule of passion over reason.

That Satan and Christ in some sort represent passion and reason
cannot be doubted. Such clearly was Milton's conscious intention.
Satan is meant to typify those bad passions that entered man at the
Fall. In the mental levity that marked the human pair he has no
part. Generally he seems to express a turbulent, unreasoning energy,
aiming at the impossible and dissatisfied with what it attains. His
crowning folly is to imagine that he and his companions are self-
created. In reply to Abdiel's opposition in the rebels' council in
Book Five he says:

> That we were formd then saist thou? and the work
> Of secondarie hands, by task transferd
> From Father to his Son? strange point and new!
> Doctrin which we would know whence learnt: who saw

1. iv. 288–95. 2. v. 350–5.

When this creation was? rememberst thou
Thy making, while the Maker gave thee being?
We know no time when we were not as now;
Know none before us, self-begot, self-rais'd
By our own quick'ning power, when fatal course
Had circl'd his full Orbe, the birth mature
Of this our native Heav'n, Ethereal Sons.
Our puissance is our own.[1]

When Satan arrives on earth with good hope of success he gets no
satisfaction at the prospect of his

> dire attempt, which nigh the birth
> Now rowling, boils in his tumultuous brest,
> And like a devillish Engine back recoiles
> Upon himself; horror and doubt distract
> His troubl'd thoughts, and from the bottom stirr
> The Hell within him, for within him Hell
> He brings, and round about him, nor from Hell
> One step no more then from himself can fly
> By change of place.[2]

And when success is achieved its bitter taste is symbolized by the
ashy fruit chewed by the devils in the serpentine form forced on
them. There is not the slightest reason to doubt that Milton intended Satan to be a terrible warning embodiment of the unre-
strained passions, inspiring horror and detestation rather than
sympathy.

If Satan is unreasoning energy, Christ is intended to be energy as
well as reason. He is the creator while Satan is but the destroyer.
Milton means to express as much energy in his description of the
world's creation in Book Seven as in any of the exploits of Satan. He
does his utmost too to attribute energy to the good angels, and he
sometimes succeeds. There is a fine military keenness about Gabriel
and his guard in Book Four, and they have the satisfaction, rare
among the celestial troops, of effecting something. But Milton
seemed to connect Christ with reason above all. God the Father,
praising Abdiel for his fortitude, speaks of the rebel angels,

> who reason for thir Law refuse,
> Right reason for thir Law, and for thir King
> *Messiah*, who by right of merit Reigns.[3]

This conjunction of the Messiah and reason can hardly be fortuitous.
But Christ is more than an allegory of reason: he is the divine

---

1. v. 853–64.   2. iv. 15–23.   3. vi. 41–3.

Redeemer of mankind. (There has been no intention to imply that Milton intended either his Christ or his Satan to be purely allegorical figures. To say that they in some sort represent reason and passion does not mean that their functions stop here.) From beginning to end of *Paradise Lost* Milton adheres to the orthodox idea of guilt and redemption. It is as important to the poem as the Fall itself. God the Father states the position with the utmost clarity in the first conversation in Heaven:

> Man disobeying,
> Disloyal breaks his fealtie, and sinns
> Against the high Supremacie of Heav'n,
> Affecting God-head, and so loosing all,
> To expiate his Treason hath naught left,
> But to destruction sacred and devote,
> He with his whole posteritie must dye,
> Dye hee or Justice must; unless for him
> Som other able, and as willing, pay
> The rigid satisfaction, death for death.[1]

And along with the redemption of man by Christ is a professed optimism. Regenerate man, man with his reason reillumined by Christ, will rise to a more excellent state than that from which he has fallen. Thus in the end Satan's schemes have turned to good, and Adam, though himself sinning, did an ultimately beneficial act. This professed optimism is constant. We are carefully informed that Satan would never have risen from the lake of fire, had not God intended him to be the instrument of ultimate good. When at the beginning of Book Eleven Christ presents the prayers of Adam and Eve to the Father, he exalts them above anything they were capable of producing in their state of innocence. The new earth revealed to Adam by Michael near the end of the poem will be far happier than the original Eden, and Adam exclaims:

> O goodness infinite, goodness immense!
> That all this good of evil shall produce,
> And evil turn to good; more wonderful
> Then that which by creation first brought forth
> Light out of darkness! full of doubt I stand,
> Whether I should repent me now of sin
> By mee done and occasiond, or rejoyce
> Much more, that much more good thereof shall spring.[2]

Such are the main lines of the conscious plan. It may be added that *Paradise Lost* confirms the idea that matter is good. All things

1. iii. 203–12.   2. xii. 469–76.

are created pure, the body as well as the soul of man. Milton feels this so strongly that he inserts in the long and moving speech of Adam in his despair an argument for the inseparability of soul and body and of their common mortality:

> Yet one doubt
> Pursues me still, least all I cannot die,
> Least that pure breath of Life, the Spirit of Man
> Which God inspir'd, cannot together perish
> With this corporeal Clod; then in the Grave,
> Or in some other dismal place who knows
> But I shall die a living Death? O thought
> Horrid, if true! yet why? it was but breath
> Of Life that sinn'd; what dies but what had life
> And sin? the Bodie properly hath neither.
> All of me then shall die.[1]

And he delights to describe the material nature of the angels, better and airier than of men but material still.

To sum up the conscious meaning: Man was created of matter; pure, noble, but curiously fallible, having freedom of will. His mental levity and gregariousness expose him to the assaults of passion, which, while it sways reason, robs him of liberty and subjects him to slavery both within and without; but by the operation of Christ he may establish reason once again in his mind and reach a higher state than that from which he fell.

Before leaving Milton's conscious intention I should like to mention, not to discuss, one of the chief ideas in Saurat's book. After discussing Milton's idea of God, Saurat writes:

From the Absolute nothing can proceed. As Milton says, He has neither reason nor power to change into a less perfect state. How is it possible, then, to derive from the Absolute, the only necessary cause of all that is, the existence of limited individual beings? . . . Milton saw the problem. He found no solution that could be drawn from scripture or theology. So he boldly took a passage out of the *Zohar* and made it the very centre of his metaphysics:

> . . . I uncircumscribed Myself retire,
> And put not forth My goodness, which is free
> To act or not.

According to His eternal plans, God withdraws His will from certain parts of Himself, and delivers them up, so to speak, to obscure latent impulses that remain in them. Through this 'retraction', matter is created; through this retraction, individual beings are created. The parts of God thus freed from His will become persons.[2]

1. x. 782-92.   2. op. cit., 102-3.

It has been objected that three lines provide small ground on which
to found the centre of Milton's metaphysics. But they occur in a
very emphatic place – God is himself explaining his own intentions
in creation – they are striking in themselves, and Milton did not
write lines lightly. I incline to think that Saurat is right in stressing
them and in reading into them as much as he does, all the more
because in the course of the poem I have felt the 'retraction' of God
from Paradise, the gradual freeing of the wills of Adam and Eve till
by the time of uttermost trial the process is complete.

This retraction of God has a definite object. I will quote Saurat's
fascinating conjecture of what it is, but without comment, for
Milton's thought is not the subject of this book. I wish merely to
bring to the notice of any readers who imagine that Milton's
philosophy was conventional or jejune, the daring speculations
that may have occupied his mind.

God has drawn from Himself a perfectly organized society of free spirits,
an expression of and a witness to His glory. . . . Evil, Sin, Suffering, end in
this. There existed in the Infinite a sort of latent life which God has liberated,
given over to its own forces, and which developed and expressed itself, in the
good towards joy eternal, in the evil towards pain eternal. God has intensified His own existence, raising to glory the good parts of Himself,
casting outside of Himself the evil parts of Himself, too, because

> Evil into the mind of God or man
> May come and go. . . .

Terrible words, applied to God: and Satan confirms them with his 'The
Son of God I also am.' For God is the One Being, and all is in Him. This is
as near as we can get to Milton's idea of God's aims: to drive away the evil
latent in the Infinite, to exalt the good latent also.[1]

1. op. cit., 110.

CHAPTER FOUR
Paradise Lost: the Unconscious Meaning

A CLOSE study of the text would reveal many instances of Milton's betraying what he will not admit or does not realise he feels. An instance was given in the last chapter: his unconscious betrayal of a personal spite against the enticements of women. To set out all the instances would be a matter of very arbitrary criticism; different people attempting the task would end with very different results: further, a whole book would be needed to record the work. So I propose to confine myself to the four chief themes in which to my thinking Milton's unconscious meaning is betrayed: Satan, Christ, Paradise, and pessimism.

There is no need to trace the growth of the Satanic school of Milton's critics: they are the best known and still, in England, the most popular. Blake perhaps made the neatest statement of their case when in the *Marriage of Heaven and Hell* he said that Milton was of the Devil's party without knowing it. Lascelles Abercrombie has put the case for Satan in its extreme form with considerable power in his short book on the Epic. Here is the gist of his idea:

> It is surely the simple fact that if *Paradise Lost* exists for any one figure that is Satan; just as the *Iliad* exists for Achilles, and the *Odyssey* for Odysseus. It is in the figure of Satan that the imperishable significance of *Paradise Lost* is centred; his vast unyielding agony symbolises the profound antinomy of the modern consciousness.

There is one very important objection to all purely Satanic explanations. The grandeur of Satan is confined to the first half of the poem; if we risk the total significance on him, the second half contributes nothing to the whole: it is an accretion, however excellent in itself. To this matter I shall return when dealing with the question of unity in the next chapter. On the other hand, I do not see how one can avoid admitting that Milton did partly ally himself with Satan, that unwittingly he was led away by the creature of his own imagination. However much the romantic critics may have been biassed in favour of passion and against reason, it is hardly likely that the strong balance of nineteenth-century feeling should be completely false. And it is not enough to say with Saurat that Satan represents a part of Milton's mind, a part of which he disapproved and of which he was quite conscious. The character of Satan expresses, as

234

no other character or act or feature of the poem does, something in which Milton believed very strongly: heroic energy. Not that this quality is confined to Satan; how could it be, when it is the very essence of Milton's nature? It is expressed, for instance, in the technical features of Milton's verse that have been so often (and sometimes so well) described: the sustained music, the domination over words that twists them from their normal English order into a highly individual expressiveness, or any other features that go to make up his sublimity or the 'gigantic loftiness of port' praised by Johnson. For sublimity, though giving the appearance of calm, can only subsist on vast energy directed by an equally vast control. Then there is the deliberate attempt, mentioned in the last chapter, to infuse energy into the acts of Christ and of the faithful angels; and sometimes the attempt succeeds. Take, for example, the description of the Son overwhelming the rebel angels, who at the first taste of his power lose all resistance:

> Full soon
> Among them he arriv'd; in his right hand
> Grasping ten thousand Thunders, which he sent
> Before him, such as in thir Soules infix'd
> Plagues; they astonisht all resistance lost,
> All courage; down their idle weapons drop'd;
> O're Shields and Helmes, and helmed heads he rode
> Of Thrones and mighty Seraphim prostrate,
> That wish'd the Mountains now might be again
> Thrown on them as a shelter from his ire.
>
> .   .   .   .   .
>
> Yet half his strength he put not forth, but check'd
> His Thunder in mid Volie.[1]

Or take the first beginning of creation in the Seventh Book:

> On heav'nly ground they stood, and from the shore
> They view'd the vast immeasurable Abyss
> Outrageous as a Sea, dark, wasteful, wilde,
> Up from the bottom turn'd by furious windes
> And surging waves, as Mountains to assault
> Heav'ns highth, and with the Center mix the Pole.
>   Silence, ye troubl'd waves, and thou Deep, peace,
> Said then th' Omnific Word, your discord end:
>   Nor staid, but on the Wings of Cherubim
> Uplifted, in Paternal Glorie rode
> Farr into *Chaos*, and the World unborn;
> For *Chaos* heard his voice.[2]

1. vi. 834–43, 853–4.   2. vii. 210–21.

Such descriptions are as impressive as descriptions of strength and energy can be without the added interest of a struggle. We certainly feel the enormous reserves of divine power: before it the angels simply fall astonished; the tumult of chaos is stilled in a moment. But there is only one figure in *Paradise Lost* whose strength is shown through conflict and endurance. This is Satan, and it is through him that Milton's own heroic energy is most powerfully shown. Just as *Lycidas*, the outcome of struggle, is a more powerful poem than *Comus*, which rather expresses a habit of mind, so Satan is a more powerful figure than the Son. The odds are against him, but still he struggles, and wins our profoundest sympathy and admiration. It is of no avail to retort that Satan's energies are evil. Nominally they are either evil, or only good in so far as they are a relic of his former glory. But in reading we are perfectly certain, in spite of all arguments to the contrary, that Satan showed a noble and virtuous energy in rousing himself from the fiery lake and inspiring his fellows with his own desire for action, the one thing that could make their existence tolerable. In sum it is Satan who in *Paradise Lost* best expresses that heroic energy of Milton's mind, best hitherto expressed in *Areopagitica*, which undoubtedly, though in very different form, would have been the master emotion of the projected Arthuriad.

On Milton's treatment of Christ I cannot argue, I can only dogmatize. The matter depends on the tone of Milton's verse: his professed belief presents a solid enough front. The impression I get is that Milton had no profound belief in the incarnate Christ. He happened to believe in the idea of spiritual regeneration: certain selected mortals were able to live down their innate perverseness and reach a high degree of virtue. It so happened that the story of the incarnate Christ could be made to fit this belief, and to the story Milton forced himself to give a cold, intellectual adherence. A distinction must here be made between the Son, the vicegerent of the Father, and Christ the Redeemer of mankind. In describing the first Milton could spend whole-heartedly his powers of sublime writing: in describing the second he can indeed give an impression of dignity and mercifulness, as in Christ's speech beginning 'Father, thy word is past, man shall find grace',[1] but his descriptions of the Jesus of the Gospels are relatively scanty and lack the fervour of conviction. This is particularly true of the lines in the Twelfth Book: lines which, had Milton felt profoundly, would necessarily have been the very height of Michael's account of the history of the world. As an example here is the account of the crucifixion:

1. iii. 227.

The Law of God exact he shall fulfill
Both by obedience and by love, though love
Alone fulfill the Law; thy punishment
He shall endure by coming in the Flesh
To a reproachful life and cursed death,
Proclaiming Life to all who shall believe
In his redemption, and that his obedience
Imputed becomes theirs by Faith, his merits
To save them, not thir own, though legal works.
For this he shall live hated, be blasphem'd,
Seis'd on by force, judg'd, and to death condemnd
A shameful and accurst, naild to the Cross
By his own Nation, slaine for bringing Life;
But to the Cross he nailes thy Enemies,
The Law that is against thee, and the sins
Of all mankinde, with him there crucifi'd,
Never to hurt them more who rightly trust
In this his satisfaction; so he dies.[1]

It may be possible to gauge the nature of this passage better by a comparison. Take this passage from Traherne:

That Cross is a tree set on fire with invisible flame, that illuminateth all the world. The flame is Love: the Love in His bosom who died on it. In the light of which we see how to possess all the things in Heaven and Earth after His similitude. For He that suffered on it was the Son of God as you are: tho' He seemed only a mortal man. He had acquaintance and relations as you have, but He was a lover of Men and Angels. Was He not the Son of God; and Heir of the whole world? To this poor, bleeding, naked Man did all the corn and wine, and oil, and gold and silver in the world minister in an invisible manner, even as He was exposed lying and dying upon the Cross.[2]

However various the feelings aroused by this passage in different readers, it will be agreed that Traherne believed in the crucifixion very much more profoundly than Milton: the belief has entered into the intimacies of his mind. Milton could have spared it without inconvenience. Another comparison also is significant. The first council in heaven, described in the Third Book, ends with the angels' hymn to Father and Son. There is an evident contrast in the tones in which they hymn the Father Infinite and Christ the Redeemer. And the contrast is between conviction and intellectual acceptance. Although Milton was no mystic and disapproved of speculation concerning the unknowable, he was humbled and awed

1. xii. 402–19.   2. *Centuries of Meditations* (Dobell), 43.

PARADISE LOST

by that illimitable hinterland. Thus when he writes of God, the
Unknowable not the School Divine, he writes with full conviction.

> Thee Father first they sung Omnipotent,
> Immutable, Immortal, Infinite,
> Eternal King; thee Author of all being,
> Fountain of Light, thy self invisible
> Amidst the glorious brightness where thou sit'st
> Thron'd inaccessible, but when thou shad'st
> The full blaze of thy beams, and through a cloud
> Drawn round about thee like a radiant Shrine,
> Dark with excessive bright thy skirts appeer,
> Yet dazle Heav'n, that brightest Seraphim
> Approach not, but with both wings veil thir eyes.[1]

Then, after hymning the Son as Creator, the angels sing thus of
him as the Redeemer of man:

> No sooner did thy dear and onely Son
> Perceive thee purpos'd not to doom frail Man
> So strictly, but much more to pitie enclin'd,
> He to appease thy wrauth, and end the strife
> Of Mercy and Justice in thy face discern'd,
> Regardless of the Bliss wherein hee sat
> Second to thee, offerd himself to die
> For mans offence. O unexampl'd love,
> Love no where to be found less then Divine!
> Hail Son of God, Saviour of Men, thy Name
> Shall be the copious matter of my Song.[2]

This is pallid, set by the brightness of the first passage. If a contrast
is admitted between Milton's beliefs in the Father and Christ, it
amounts to this. He humbled himself before the unknowable, putting
godhead far from his thoughts, unlike Satan and Adam and Eve in
their infatuation. He admits a perverseness native to Man; he believes in free will. He would like to believe that Man, once created
and set in his surroundings, has it in him to work out unaided his
own salvation. But such a belief was so utterly incompatible with
Christianity that it was out of the question for Milton to admit it –
even to himself. We can only guess it by the reluctant tone in which
he deals with what to most Christians are the central facts of their
religion.

I did not mention Paradise among the themes that make up the
main plan of Milton's conscious meaning, not because it is without

1. iii. 372–82.   2. iii. 403–13.

all conscious meaning, but because much of that meaning breaks down. It is not very difficult to distinguish the two elements. The actual Paradise in Book Four consciously expresses Milton's yearning for a better state of things than this world provides: all the idealism of his youth is concentrated in that amazing description. Conscious and unconscious are at one in it. But when Milton attempts to introduce people into the picture, to present his age of innocence, he can be no more successful than any other human being in an attempt to imagine a state of existence at variance with the primal requirements of the human mind. He fails to convince us that Adam and Eve are happy, because he can find no adequate scope for their active natures.

> They sat them down, and after no more toil
> Of thir sweet Gardning labour then suffic'd
> To recommend coole *Zephyr*, and made ease
> More easie, wholsom thirst and appetite
> More grateful, to thir Supper Fruits they fell.[1]

Milton cannot really believe in such a way of life. Reduced to the ridiculous task of working in a garden which produces of its own accord more than they will ever need, Adam and Eve are in the hopeless position of Old Age Pensioners enjoying perpetual youth. Of course Milton makes it clear that he believed a state of regeneration arrived at after the knowledge of good and evil to be superior to a state of innocence, but he does not convince us, as he means to do, that a state of innocence is better than an unregenerate state of sin. On the contrary, we feel that Milton, stranded in his own Paradise, would very soon have eaten the apple on his own responsibility and immediately justified the act in a polemical pamphlet. Any genuine activity would be better than utter stagnation. I do not think these flippant thoughts about Paradise intrude in the Ninth Book, when Adam and Eve have turned into recognizable human beings, even before the Fall: we instinctively associate their characters with life as we know it, not with the conditions of life that prevailed in the Garden of Eden.

Here may be mentioned an interesting essay by Paul Elmer More[2] in which he seeks for the central significance of *Paradise Lost*. Assuming that the poem has a permanent interest, that a successful epic must contain 'some great human truth, some appeal to universal human aspirations, decked in the garb of symbolism', although

---

1. iv. 327–31.   2. *Shelburne Essays*, fourth series, 239–53.

'the poet himself may not be fully conscious of this deeper meaning', he concludes that the essence of *Paradise Lost* is Paradise itself:

> Sin is not the innermost subject of Milton's epic, nor man's disobedience and fall; these are but the tragic shadows cast about the central light. Justification of the ways of God to man is not the true moral of the plot: this and the whole divine drama are merely the poet's means of raising his conception to the highest generalisation. The true theme is Paradise itself; not Paradise lost, but the reality of that 'happy rural seat' where the errant tempter beheld
>
> > To all delight of human sense exposed
> > In narrow room nature's whole wealth, yea more,
> > A heaven on earth.

Milton's paradise is his presentation of that aspiration after a Golden Age that has existed at all times among all peoples. Set between the description of Hell and the description of the world after the fall it occupies the central position of the epic and commands our highest attention.

That Milton's Paradise (I mean Paradise itself, not the life of Adam and Eve in it) is described with passion no one can possibly deny. As I said, his lifelong search for perfection, for something better than the world can give, finds its fullest expression here. But More has not really finished his essay: he omits to say by what this passionate desire for a golden age is conditioned, of what profounder feeling it is really the expression. One of his sentences might easily have supplied him with the necessary sequel. Let us not forget, he writes,

> that the greatest period of our own literature, the many-tongued Elizabethan age, where the very wildernesses of verse are filled with Pentecostal eloquence and
>
> > airy tongues that syllable men's names,
>
> let us not forget that the dramas and tales, the epics and lyrics, of that period, from Spenser to Milton, are more concerned with this one ideal of a Golden Age wrought out in some 'imitation of the fields of bliss', than with any other single matter.

And the reason, he might have added, lay in the very activity of the Elizabethan age. Only an active man can create a living picture of sedentary bliss. Similarly the poignant sweetness of Milton's descriptions of Paradise and his ardent desire for perfection have less an existence of their own than express the enormous energy of Milton's mind. The description of Paradise then, without being the centre, is in harmony with the main trend of the poem. It is only in the daily life of Adam and Eve that Milton's conscious intention breaks down.

It was noted in the chapter on Milton's beliefs that he accepted in all apparent literalness the eschatology of *Revelation*. He repeats his acceptance in *Paradise Lost* and bases his optimism largely on it. The millennium and the final reception of the elect in Heaven will put right all the woes that shall have beset mankind from Adam to the second coming of Christ. There is no professed belief which Milton holds with less sincerity than this. I do not see how any honest reader can fail to detect the underlying pessimism of the poem. To enumerate all the passages where it betrays itself would take far too much space: a few examples must suffice. Pessimism betrays itself in Satan's anguished impotence at the beginning, in the warning lines at the beginning of Book Four; it is implicit in the description of Paradise, which has in it the hopeless ache for the unattainable. But it comes out strongest of all in the last four books. There is a dreadful sense of the wrongness of the order of things in the first approach of the action in the Ninth Book:

> O much deceav'd, much failing, hapless *Eve*,
> Of thy presum'd return! event perverse!
> Thou never from that houre in Paradise
> Foundst either sweet repast, or sound repose;
> Such ambush hid among sweet Flours and Shades
> Waited with hellish rancor imminent
> To intercept thy way, or send thee back
> Despoild of Innocence, of Faith, of Bliss.
> For now, and since first break of dawne the Fiend,
> Meer Serpent in appearance, forth was come,
> And on his Quest, when likeliest he might finde
> The only two of Mankinde, but in them
> The whole included Race, his purposd prey.[1]

The woes of Adam and Eve are typical of humanity; and they never should have happened: such is, one feels, what Milton thought in the bottom of his heart. The same sense is present even more powerfully in the incomparable description in Book Eleven of the corruption of eternal spring and the entry of discord into the animal world. The whole is too long to quote, but here are the last lines:

> Thus began
> Outrage from liveless things; but Discord first
> Daughter of Sin, among th' irrational,
> Death introduc'd through fierce antipathie:
> Beast now with Beast gan war, and Fowle with Fowle,

1. ix. 404–16.

And Fish with Fish; to graze the Herb all leaving,
Devourd each other; nor stood much in awe
Of Man, but fled him, or with count'nance grim
Glar'd on him passing: these were from without
The growing miseries, which *Adam* saw.[1]

But, it may be said, such quotations prove no more than that Milton had a lively sense of the miseries of life. He may yet believe that these are made more than worth while by the possibility of regeneration in Christ. Without the Fall there would have been no special effusion of Grace, the Incarnation would never have been required. Certainly Milton says very plainly that in its ultimate effects the Fall was a good thing. The idea was no new one in poetry. Here is a medieval version, which may provide an instructive comparison:

> Adam lay ibounden
>   Bounden in a bond;
> Four thousand winter
>   Thoght he not too long;
> And all was for an appil,
>   An appil that he tok,
> As clerkes finden
>   Wreten in here book.
> Ne hadde the appil take ben,
>   The appil taken ben,
> Ne hadde never our lady
>   A ben hevene quene.
> Blessed be the time
>   That appil take was.
> Therefore we moun singen
>   *Deo gracias.*

But such light-heartedness is for airier natures than Milton. Nor was it a joyous Mariolatry that he put in the scales: the actual effects of the Fall in Milton's poem have very little joy in them. If Christ were destined really to transform the world, we might accept Milton's assertions of hope. But in his scheme the proportion of mankind, the true elect, who are to be saved through Christ is so miserably small. From the wreck of a world corrupt to the very end a few shall be rescued but the great bulk cast out into eternal torment. The crucial passage is in the Twelfth Book where Michael describes the state of the world after Christ and the end of all things: almost the end of the poem. Let the reader judge whether the

1. x. 706–15.

account of the world 'under her own waight groaning' does not quite overshadow the vision of eternal bliss at the end.

> What will they then
> But force the Spirit of Grace it self, and binde
> His consort Libertie; what, but unbuild
> His living Temples, built by Faith to stand,
> Thir own Faith not anothers: for on Earth
> Who against Faith and Conscience can be heard
> Infallible? yet many will presume:
> Whence heavie persecution shall arise
> On all who in the worship persevere
> Of Spirit and Truth; the rest, farr greater part,
> Will deem in outward Rites and specious formes
> Religion satisfi'd; Truth shall retire
> Bestuck with slandrous darts, and works of Faith
> Rarely be found: so shall the World goe on,
> To good malignant, to bad men benigne,
> Under her own waight groaning till the day
> Appeer of respiration to the just,
> And vengeance to the wicked, at return
> Of him so lately promis'd to thy aid,
> The Womans seed, obscurely then foretold,
> Now amplier known thy Saviour and thy Lord,
> Last in the Clouds from Heav'n to be reveald
> In glory of the Father, to dissolve
> *Satan* with his perverted World, then raise
> From the conflagrant mass, purg'd and refin'd,
> New Heav'ns, new Earth, Ages of endless date
> Founded in righteousness and peace and love,
> To bring forth fruits Joy and eternal Bliss.[1]

The comfort is nominal, the fundamental pessimism unmistakable. Milton seeks to comfort himself in an imagined new order, but it is not by any such distant possibility that his wound can be healed. For from his youth on Milton had nursed the hope that mankind would improve out of its own resources. Just as he, by his will and energy, had cultivated his own mind, so could the rest of mankind, if it did but bend itself to the task, increase in mental well-being and happiness. His hopes, elated for a time by political events, were dashed far below their former lowest point, never to recover. Mankind would never in this world be any better; and Milton cannot be comforted.

1. xii. 524–51.

This pessimism must not be misunderstood. It must not be thought that Milton blamed God for an unsatisfactory world. What he did was to blame mankind for having hopelessly thrown away their chances: they could have made the world a second paradise, and it was utterly their own fault that they failed to do so. Never for a moment does Milton disbelieve in this significance of the Fall. And in the sense that Milton believed God to be just he does not lose his faith in him. It will be remembered that in the *De Doctrina Christiana* Milton advanced two main arguments for the existence of God. This was the first:

> There can be no doubt but that every thing in the world, by the beauty of its order, and the evidence of a determinate and beneficial purpose which pervades it, testifies that some supreme efficient Power must have pre-existed, by which the whole was ordained for a specific end.[1]

The second argument was from conscience or right reason convincing every one 'of the existence of God . . . to whom, sooner or later, each must give an account of his own actions, whether good or bad'. The first argument he came to doubt, the second he never did. He always felt within himself a standard, and a peculiarly exacting standard, of conduct which he believed to come from outside him and which he had to obey. Some people will like to call it God, others some other name. But of Milton's belief in it – and he himself preferred to call it God – there can be no doubt. However much of the rebel in himself Milton may reveal when he created Satan, his obedience to the principle that guided his mind, to his *daimon*, is stronger still. It will be seen that only by considering this obedience and the pessimism together do we get at the meaning of *Paradise Lost*.

1. Bohn, iv. 14.

CHAPTER FIVE

Paradise Lost: Possible Inconsistency[1]

By examining the construction of the poem it became plain that a rigorous conscious unity had been imposed on it. The question remains how far the unconscious meaning affects this conscious unity. That Milton's belief in the redeeming Christ was held with small conviction makes little difference, because he did believe in some sort of regeneration, quite apart from Christian theology, and some sort of mythology is convenient for building up an epic. Anyhow there is no upsetting of balance. When we come to Satan the case is different. I have said that Satan best expresses the heroic energy which was a part of Milton's nature. If it appears that the treatment of the Fall, round which the rest of the incidents are grouped and which consequently should express all the more important feelings in the poem, has no connection with what Satan expresses, it will have to be admitted that the unity of the poem has been very badly impaired by this insubordinate creature of Milton's imagination.

I have tried to show that in his treatment of the Fall Milton meant to condemn the mental levity of Man, who is prone to forget the importance of his every action. His condemnation is the more weighty because of the solemnity with which by the art of his construction he invests the struggle. He clears the stage, gives us all heaven for audience, and the wretched human actors have hardly begun to grasp the fateful significance of their parts. Feebly they commit what they imagine is a trifling error, for which they are punished with a doom out of all apparent proportion to their crime. To their crime, yes; but not to the mental triviality that accompanied it: by their miserable inadequacy before the issues of life mankind have deserved their fate. Milton's treatment of the Fall yields the obvious meaning that it is the first business of man to understand the issues of life, and to be aware of the importance of every trivial act. This he believed, because not only his own nature but the trend of Puritan thought fostered this awareness. The present life, and the right use of every moment of it, were Milton's principal concern. Now, a belief that every moment is critical, that every action is irrevocable and determining, must heighten the pressure at which life is lived. Life will have nothing of routine in it, but will consist of one gala performance, never to be repeated. A man

1. See Appendix I, p. 333.

holding such beliefs will be in the temper to do heroic deeds. This is the strenuous Western temper at its height, the temper of the discoverers and of the other great men of the Renaissance. Thus it is that the immense weight of emphasis put on the eating of the apple does imply the heroic temper expressed most powerfully by Satan.

Satan then does not go counter to the meaning of *Paradise Lost* as implied by the construction, but he does somewhat upset the balance. He gives us the positive statement: the Fall the negative only, the implication. The negative is the weaker, and occurs just where from motives of balance we crave the greatest emphasis. Milton prepares with perfect craft for the climax, and when the climax comes, though sincere and in harmony with the rest of the poem, it does not come up to our expectations. Indeed it could not. Adam and Eve have no power of heroic action. They are hopelessly limited to inactive virtues. The myth Milton chose was of too intractable a stuff to allow of a perfect climax: he is forced to the method of negative implication; and the most powerful expression of heroic energy is found elsewhere.

We now see what it was that Milton sacrificed by abandoning his Arthuriad. He sacrificed a subject whose climax might easily have expressed his own energy, for one which had wider scope, but whose climax could not express that energy in a straightforward way. It is possible that the weakness inherent in the myth of the Fall as a subject impelled him to write his two last poems: the first a clear-cut struggle between opposing forces, with good victorious; the second a drama exhibiting the rebirth of heroic energy.

Milton's unadmitted pessimism also affects the unity. It is present in some degree throughout, but far more strongly in the last four or five books. And this difference is much more than a relative frequency of passages in which pessimism is latent: it amounts to a change of attitude. In the last books pessimism has got somehow into the texture of the verse, causing a less energetic movement. Not that energy is ever absent: in particular the Ninth Book shows a rise over the Eighth, perhaps because it may contain relics of the projected tragedy. It is also true that as the scene is more confined in the last books the verse movement will naturally be less expansive. But that is not enough to account for the change of tone. The only explanation is that Milton himself had altered during the writing of the poem. The change is very clear. In the first four books Milton gives energy out: in the last four or five he turns it inward into himself. In the first it is active: in the last books it has been converted into a stoical resistance. Satan aspiring after a new world is Milton, the Renaissance man seeking after experience and truth: Michael is equally Milton, but a different Milton, when he adapts the words of Seneca the Stoic into

> Nor love thy Life, nor hate; but what thou livest
> Live well, how long or short permit to Heav'n.[1]

It is in the last books that Milton most speaks of reason contending with passion and of the necessity of imposing limits on the desire for knowledge. Control has become more important than energy. When we remember Milton's early lust for knowledge and that he thought such a lust no bad thing, if we can trust the tone of his *Tractate on Education*, we must admit that the later books of *Paradise Lost* show a change from his earlier beliefs. And if we admit, as I think we should, that the variety and range of the first four books, as well as Satan himself, express this love of knowledge which Milton did not think bad, another discrepancy of tone between the beginning and the end of the poem will have been detected. This is how Raphael ends his account of the creation and constitution of the universe:

> Sollicit not thy thoughts with matters hid,
> Leave them to God above, him serve and feare;
> Of other Creatures, as him pleases best,
> Wherever plac't, let him dispose: joy thou
> In what he gives to thee, this Paradise
> And thy fair *Eve*; Heav'n is for thee too high
> To know what passes there; be lowlie wise:
> Think onely what concernes thee and thy being.[2]

But most important of all for the doctrine of self-limitation and self-sufficiency are Adam's words to Michael near the end of the poem when the history of the world has been brought to a close, and Michael's reply. These two speeches sum up, with a simplicity whose impressiveness one cannot describe but can merely note with profound admiration, Milton's mature, one may say middle-aged, philosophy of life. They must be quoted in full.

> He ended; and thus Adam last reply'd.
> How soon hath thy prediction, Seer blest,
> Measur'd this transient World, the Race of time,
> Till time stand fixt: beyond is all abyss,

1. xi. 553–4. For the reference to a passage in Seneca see A. H. Gilbert in *Modern Languages Notes*, 1919, 120–1.

2. viii. 167–74.

Eternitie, whose end no eye can reach.
Greatly instructed I shall hence depart,
Greatly in peace of thought, and have my fill
Of knowledge, what this Vessel can containe;
Beyond which was my folly to aspire.
Henceforth I learne, that to obey is best,
And love with fear the onely God, to walk
As in his presence, ever to observe
His providence, and on him sole depend,
Merciful over. all his works, with good
Still overcoming evil, and by small
Accomplishing great things, by things deemd weak
Subverting worldly strong, and worldly wise
By simply meek; that suffering for Truths sake
Is fortitude to highest victorie,
And to the faithful Death the Gate of Life;
Taught this by his example whom I now
Acknowledge my Redeemer ever blest.
    To whom thus also th' Angel last repli'd:
This having learnt, thou hast attained the summe
Of wisdome; hope no higher, though all the Starrs
Thou knewst by name, and all th' ethereal Powers,
All secrets of the deep, all Natures works,
Or works of God in Heav'n, Air, Earth, or Sea,
And all the riches of this World enjoydst,
And all the rule, one Empire; onely add
Deeds to thy knowledge answerable, add Faith,
Add vertue, Patience, Temperance, add Love,
By name to come call'd Charitie, the soul
Of all the rest: then wilt thou not be loath
To leave this Paradise, but shalt possess
A Paradise within thee, happier farr.[1]

All is turned inwards: the inner paradise is the only paradise that
matters. It is a different Milton from the one who wrote the *Defensio
Secunda* and such lines as

                But first whom shall we send
In search of this new world, whom shall we find
Sufficient? who shall tempt with wandering feet
The dark unbottom'd infinite Abyss
And through the palpable obscure find out
His uncouth way, or spread his aerie flight
Upborn with indefatigable wings
Over the vast abrupt.[2]

1. xii. 552–87.   2. ii. 402–9.

The conclusion I would draw is that Milton was in some respects a changed man after the Restoration. In dealing with the prose I said that we could not be certain how the Restoration affected him, how far he had reconciled himself to what should have appeared to be inevitable. *Paradise Lost* gives the answer. He had not reconciled himself: he could not believe that the dreaded event would really come. And when it did come, his activity turned itself into resistance. What we know of the composition of *Paradise Lost* is in keeping with this supposition. If Milton had begun to plan the poem in 1655, to write it in 1658, and finished it in 1663, it is probable that by the Restoration he had written the first four books; in unrevised form at least. The middle books concern us less. Much of them Milton may have had in his head before the Restoration, or he may have written them while still in doubt what the Restoration would mean and how permanent it was. The last four or five would probably belong to the Restoration period alone.

That the Restoration should have been the greatest shock Milton received during his life was almost inevitable. Always sanguine by temper and joining tenacity to hope, he could not have persuaded himself that the Parliamentary cause could fail, until its ruin was quite complete. For all the forebodings and disillusion of the last pamphlets, a great store of hope must have remained. We need not be so surprised that he turned his energies inward as that he did not fall into despair and inertia. It must be remembered too that Milton was at one with Aristotle in exalting the political virtues, and to exercise them political liberty was necessary. Cut off from freedom of speech by the Restoration, no wonder if like the Romans under the Empire he sought a stoical comfort in the fortitude of his own mind.

The pessimism, then, causes a change of tone and thereby somewhat impairs the unity of the poem. But it calls forth Milton's courage, the courage of resistance, and courage is the link with the more active form of that virtue displayed in the early books. Nor do I think that the dominance either of Satan in the earlier, or of pessimism in the later, books altogether impairs the design. The gradual working out of the action on to earth and into the heart of man remains the expression of one of the most powerful of human wills.

CHAPTER SIX

Paradise Lost: Summary of the Meaning

SINCE Milton himself changed during the writing of *Paradise Lost*, it is the more difficult to attach any one broad general meaning to the poem. Instead we shall do better to look on it as summing up most of what he had been expressing in the prose and as looking forward to the consistent and settled reasonableness of *Paradise Regained*. But the main convictions it expresses in these two functions have already been stated. Predominant on the whole in the pamphlets was reforming energy, call it if you will the desire to do great deeds, based on the assumption that the world would be made a better place. This is the feeling that dominates too in the first half of *Paradise Lost*. There is much else, including a good deal of the courage of resistance that gathers force in the second half. During the writing of the poem Milton's hopes of the future of man are broken, the main ambition of his youth has gone. He loses faith in everything except what he called God, and what some men might call himself. Personal peace is all that remains for him to accomplish, and by his constant method of generalizing from personal experience inward peace becomes the chief aim of man. The 'paradise within' is the substitute for the paradise on earth, now proved to be impossible of achievement. As 'deliberate valour', the will to do, powerfully controlled and directed, were to have been the means to the earthly paradise, so the defeat of the passions by reason (always a condition of the earthly paradise but insufficient in itself) has become the main object in a man's life, for only through the victory of reason can true liberty and inward peace be attained. Again, the chief meaning of the first part is to be found in the second, but only in a subordinate and negative form.

Further still, and perhaps most important of all, Milton has no personal complaint against life, although he sees mankind taking the road to ruin. He has found his own inward paradise. The saving thing about life is that such a paradise is within the reach of others; their destiny is in their own power. The tragedy is that so few attain to it. The most extraordinary thing about Milton is that having been more disappointed by life than most people, having less humour and human sympathy than some great poets to help him to tolerance, he has a fund of courage sufficient to reconcile him to the life that has fallen so far short of his expectations.

CHAPTER SEVEN

Paradise Regained: its Relation to Paradise Lost

THE mistaken idea that *Paradise Regained* is a sequel to *Paradise Lost* rests partly on the titles of the two poems and the opening lines of *Paradise Regained,* partly on the statement of Thomas Ellwood. When Milton writes

> I who e're while the happy Garden sung,
> By one mans disobedience lost, now sing
> Recover'd Paradise to all mankind,

he might appear to mean that he will now complete *Paradise Lost* by a supplementary poem. But he cannot really mean this, because the recovery of Paradise is an essential part of *Paradise Lost,* treated at considerable length in that poem. All he can mean is that he is now going to write a poem in which the recovery of Paradise is to be the principal not the second subject. It is unnecessary to press the point further, as Raleigh[1] has turned his wit with considerable effect on the old heresy and may have done something to scotch it. He also makes excellent fun of poor Ellwood. But the whole passage in Ellwood's autobiography gives such an amusing picture of Milton in his middle age and has been usually understood in so humourless a fashion, that I cannot help quoting the whole and adding my comments.

Some little time before I went to Aylesbury prison I was desired by my quondam master, Milton, to take a house for him in the neighbourhood where I dwelt, that he might go out of the city, for the safety of himself and his family, the pestilence then growing hot in London. I took a pretty box for him, in Giles Chalfont, a mile from me, of which I gave him notice, and intended to have waited on him, and seen him well settled in it, but was prevented by that imprisonment. But now being released and returned home, I soon made a visit to him, to welcome him into the country. After some common discourses had passed between us, he called for a manuscript of his; which being brought he delivered to me, bidding me take it home with me, and read it at my leisure; and when I had done so, return it to him with my judgment thereupon. When I came home, and had set myself to read it, I found it was that excellent poem which he entitled 'Paradise Lost'. After I had with the best attention read it through, I made him an-

---

1. *Milton,* 161.

other visit, and returned him his book, with due acknowledgment of the favour he had done me in communicating it to me. He asked me how I liked it and what I thought of it, which I modestly but freely told him, and after some further discourse about it, I pleasantly said to him, 'Thou hast said much here of "Paradise Lost", but what hast thou to say of "Paradise Found"?' He made me no answer, but sat some time in a muse; then brake off that discourse, and fell upon another subject. After the sickness was over, and the city well cleansed and become safely habitable again, he returned thither. And when afterwards I went to wait on him there, which I seldom failed of doing whenever my occasions drew me to London, he showed me his second poem, called 'Paradise Regained', and in a pleasant tone said to me, 'This is owing to you, for you put it into my head by the question you put to me at Chalfont, which before I had not thought of.'

This is tediously written stuff. Ellwood may have been honest and kindly, but he was not at all intelligent. Milton, we know, was given to satire and irony. Aubrey noted of Milton:

Extreme pleasant in his conversation, and at dinner, supper etc. but satirical. . . . He pronounced the letter R very hard (*littera canina*). A certain sign of a satirical wit. From John Dryden.

And then there is the story of Milton and his servant, told by Jonathan Richardson in his *Life of Milton*, a story there is no reason to doubt.

Milton had a servant who was a very honest, silly fellow and a zealous and constant follower of those teachers [*sc.* sectaries]. When he came from the meeting, his master would frequently ask him what he had heard, and divert himself with ridiculing their fooleries, or it may be the poor fellow's understanding: both one and t'other probably. However, this was so grievous to the good creature that he left his service upon it.

Further, irony is one of the few human qualities Milton allows God the Father in *Paradise Lost*; and Milton was not exempt from the law of making God in his own image. How can one doubt that he was making fun of Ellwood when remarking 'pleasantly' that Ellwood had put *Paradise Regained* into his head? It is a misfortune that Ellwood's 'modest and free' discourse on *Paradise Lost* has not survived: doubtless it was to elicit this that Milton lent him his manuscript. And Ellwood's final remark – is it not the instinct of every critic of a friend's dubious verses to take refuge in 'But I do hope you will not stop here but write some more'? And in so doing he blundered into the subject that had ranked second in importance in *Paradise Lost*, the subject fully discussed and settled by God the Father in heaven, and dominating the last two books. Well might

Raleigh imagine Milton in his 'muse' considering the abysses of human stupidity.

Still, though Milton doubtless wrote *Paradise Regained* not at the chance suggestion of one of his less intelligent friends but as the result of mature deliberation, he had *Paradise Lost* in his mind when he wrote it. For one thing, he assumes, in the first book especially, some knowledge of the earlier poem. The councils of heavenly and infernal beings, for instance, would be abrupt and disturbing, had we not been made familiar with them before. A line, too, like

> And Eden rais'd in the waste wilderness,

the seventh in the poem, loses some of its point unless we think of the reverse process in *Paradise Lost*: the Garden of Eden first reduced from immortality to mortality by Adam's sin and finally by the Flood (itself the effect of sin) into

> an Iland salt and bare,
> The haunt of Seales and Orcs, and Sea-mews clang.[1]

And when the beasts in the wilderness grow mild at Christ's approach, we are meant to remember how in Paradise they grew hostile when sin had entered in. But there are different and closer links. *Paradise Regained* seems to be not a continuation – that was impossible, as *Paradise Lost* has taken history down to the destruction of the world and the division of all things into heaven and hell – but a corrective to features of *Paradise Lost* that Milton had come by that time to disapprove of. The change of tone during the course of the earlier poem has been noticed. Milton's opinions changed, but to rewrite the first half or so of his great poem was out of the question: all he could do was to write a new poem that would be entirely to his liking and express unequivocally the ideas that held his mind about the sixth year of the Restoration.

Milton must have realized that homogeneity is exceedingly difficult of attainment in a long poem, for there is always the danger that the poet may change in the years that must be spent in the actual composition of an epic. Dissatisfied with the change of tone in *Paradise Lost*, he may well have taken up his old idea of the brief epic on the model of the Book of Job. And homogeneity he does most certainly achieve. Another defect he put right was that of balance. We found that the climax of *Paradise Lost* could not quite sustain the weight imposed on it. The emphasis is too strongly on the first books. In *Paradise Regained* the beginning is of the quietest,

---

1. *Paradise Lost*, xi. 834-5.

and there is a most carefully planned rise of power sustained nearly to the end. The characters too are thoroughly kept in hand: Satan is not allowed to usurp too much sympathy; while it is Christ, not his adversary, who exhibits the greatest vigour. And of the issue at stake there is no doubt: the fight is perfectly plain, straightforward, and unembarrassed. The possibilities of action in Christ are as wide as the earth: he is not hedged in like Adam with an ignorant innocence.

There is the further evidence of subject-matter. The theme is very closely connected with the last books of *Paradise Lost*. I can only infer that Milton, having after the Restoration modified his opinions, wished to devote a whole poem to expressing them and to put right the balance which in *Paradise Lost* had hung in doubt. For in *Paradise Regained* it is the struggle of reason against passion that is presented; and the virtue of the 'paradise within', of the proper rule of the kingdom of the mind, is exalted over the impulse to do great deeds.

Another connection is that of method. *Paradise Regained* gets its effects largely by its pageantry; and I should guess that Milton was encouraged in this method by the success of his tableaux in the Eleventh Book of *Paradise Lost*. Spenser of course has a good deal to do with both, but without the example of the earlier poem Milton might have made the pageantry less organic or chosen some subject of which pageantry was not so obvious a part. The connection then of *Paradise Regained* with the last books of *Paradise Lost* is very close: far closer than with *Samson Agonistes*, with which from the accident of joint publication it is usually associated; for in the interval between *Paradise Regained* and *Samson Agonistes* Milton had regained some of his old desire for heroic action.

Paradise Regained then does not continue the existence of *Paradise Lost*, which is complete and final, admitting no extension. It is rather a colony, linked by first tradition to its mother-city, but autonomous and with a character entirely its own. It should stand alone, untwinned with any other creature of the poet's brain and perhaps the most fairly proportioned of them all.

CHAPTER EIGHT

Paradise Regained: its Subject and Characters

IN *Paradise Regained* there is no difficulty in detecting the subject; for it is stated and restated with the greatest clarity, and there is small sign of any discrepancy between admitted and unadmitted meaning. Moreover there is hardly any theological discussion. Milton was completely dominated by the thought that a man must rule his mind before his actions can avail anything. Probably the whole of the struggle between King and Parliament presented itself to him as a dreadful example of ill-regulated actions, of men attempting to rule others before they had learnt to rule themselves. If this is so, it is easy to see why Milton chose the Temptation rather than any other incident in the Gospels as summing up the life of Christ on earth. It was in the quiet of the wilderness that Christ gained the final dominion over his mind: once that was done, his right actions were inevitable and in a way subsidiary. Further, the Temptation took place before Christ had begun his ministry. He is the antithesis of the hasty idealist or the opportunist politician. Mary recounts how his life has been hitherto

> Private, unactive, calm, contemplative.[1]

And yet the temptation to premature action had not been absent. After describing his desire to become perfect in the Law of God, Christ says in his soliloquy:

> Yet this not all
> To which my Spirit aspir'd, victorious deeds
> Flam'd in my heart, heroic acts, one while
> To rescue *Israel* from the *Roman* yoke,
> Thence to subdue and quell o're all the earth
> Brute violence and proud Tyrannick pow'r,
> Till truth were freed, and equity restor'd:
> Yet held it more humane, more heavenly first
> By winning words to conquer willing hearts,
> And make perswasion do the work of fear.[2]

And he goes out into the desert to think things over finally before beginning his work.

1. ii. 81.   2. i. 214–23.

Mean while the Son of God, who yet some days
Lodg'd in *Bethabara* where *John* baptiz'd,
Musing and much revolving in his brest,
How best the mighty work he might begin
Of Saviour to mankind, and which way first
Publish his God-like office now mature,
One day forth walk'd alone, the Spirit leading;
And his deep thoughts, the better to converse
With solitude.[1]

Satan is clever enough to know that the strongest temptation to Christ will concern not the senses but the desire for action. He rejects with scorn Belial's advice to seduce him with women, and points out that he is framed for action, speaking of his 'amplitude of mind to greatest Deeds',[2] and again,

But he whom we attempt is wiser far
Than *Solomon*, of more exalted mind,
Made and set wholly on the accomplishment
Of greatest things.[3]

And so, after the obvious bait of food to a hungry man, Satan turns all his energies into luring Christ to do actions, good in themselves, but bad unless preceded by the fullest self-mastery and performed at the dictates of reason.

Money brings honour, friends, conquest, and realms, says Satan, and Christ replies that the true conquest and realm is inward:

Yet he who reigns within himself, and rules
Passions, Desires, and Fears, is more a King;
Which every wise and vertuous man attains:
And who attains not, ill aspires to rule
Cities of men, or head-strong Multitudes,
Subject himself to Anarchy within,
Or lawless passions in him which he serves.[4]

And Christ's whole attitude to Satan urging him to action is summed up in the lines,

who best
Can suffer, best can do; best reign, who first
Well hath obey'd.[5]

The pageants of earthly pomp presented as temptations to wrong action are reduced to insignificance by comparison with the human

1. i. 183–91.   2. ii. 139.   3. ii. 205–8.
4. ii. 466–72.   5. iii. 194–6.

mind striving in the wilderness with its very self. Satan grasps Christ's feelings and with admirable subtlety suggests that a study of the Stoic and other Greek philosophies will help in the acquiring of the indispensable self-control. He ends his speech on them:

> These here revolve, or, as thou lik'st, at home,
> Till time mature thee to a Kingdom's waight;
> These rules will render thee a King compleat
> Within thyself, much more with Empire joyn'd.[1]

Christ replies by rejecting all outward aids. The inner light is all that is needed for mental well-being.

> he who receives
> Light from above, from the fountain of light,
> No other doctrine needs, though granted true.[2]

Catholics, Quakers, and Agnostics would comment differently on these lines, but they are the essence of Milton's religion when he wrote *Paradise Regained*. They sum up his extreme individualism and his dislike of all authority except what comes directly from God to the human being.

Satan, on his side, stands for passion, the passion that rushes to ill-grounded and ill-considered acts. And it is the passion that fails. He is one who had aimed, against reason, at glory, and who

> Insatiable of glory had lost all.[3]

Satan is of course much more: he is one of Milton's most successful characters, and so different from his namesake in *Paradise Lost* that it is a pity he cannot be given another title. I will speak of him at the end of the chapter, but the character of Christ is more closely bound up with the thought of the poem and must be discussed at once.

I have already mentioned that there is little theological discussion. This is most strikingly true in the treatment of Christ; for the plain fact is that Christ is no longer in the main the Redeemer of man. He merely typifies the way in which the human soul can be regenerated. The Pauline fabric of fall, grace, redemption, and regeneration, seems to have crumbled. Only in one place does Milton seem to pull himself up and assert with suspicious truculence the dogmas he had worked into the fabric of *Paradise Lost*. In the great speech where Christ deals with ancient philosophy, after the lines quoted concerning the inner light, Milton inserts an abrupt

---

1. iv. 281–4.   2. iv. 288–90.   3. iii. 148.

attack on the Greek philosophers for being ignorant of true doctrine:

> Alas what can they teach, and not mislead;
> Ignorant of themselves, of God much more,
> And how the world began, and how man fell
> Degraded by himself, on grace depending?[1]

The tone of this passage is curiously out of keeping with the rationalistic moralizing of most of the poem.

And if Christ has almost ceased to be the Redeemer, how strange a figure Milton has made of him. In the last two lines of the poem alone,

> hee unobserv'd
> Home to his Mothers house private return'd,

does he bear any relation to the Jesus of the Gospels. His classical education and contempt for the people (he calls them 'a herd confus'd, a miscellaneous rabble') do not sit well on the carpenter's son who had compassion on the multitude. Christ in fact is partly an allegorical figure, partly Milton himself imagined perfect. Christ's description of his own childhood has often been considered as a bit of covert autobiography:

> When I was yet a child, no childish play
> To me was pleasing, all my mind was set
> Serious to learn and know, and thence to do
> What might be publick good.[2]

But some of the sequel might have as clear a personal reference. I mean the passage, quoted in part above, when Christ speaks of his youthful ambitious dreams:

> victorious deeds
> Flam'd in my heart, heroic acts, one while
> To rescue *Israel* from the *Roman* yoke,
> Thence to subdue and quell o're all the earth
> Brute violence and proud Tyrannick pow'r,
> Till truth were freed, and equity restor'd:
> Yet held it more humane, more heavenly first
> By winning words to conquer willing hearts,
> And make perswasion do the work of fear.[3]

'To rescue *Israel* from the *Roman* yoke': I do not think Milton wrote this line without thinking of his own youthful efforts to free his own

1. iv. 309-12.   2. i. 201-4.   3. i. 215-23.

native country from the yoke of the Romanizing prelates. Nor when he speaks of quelling 'proud Tyrannick power' has he his own case less in mind. But Christ only thought of doing these things, holding it better to persuade human hearts than to attack institutions. I cannot help thinking that Milton had come to regret the part he played in the Civil War. The desire for action had carried him away before he had learnt to know himself fully and to distrust the achievements of soldiers and politicians, however well-intentioned.

Another quite personal feature is introduced, with consummate adroitness, by means of the argument between Belial and Satan in Book Two: Milton's susceptibility to female charm. To hint the possibility that Christ could have felt such a sensation would have been out of keeping with the Gospel narrative, as well as irreverent; but the blundering Belial may fittingly propose the temptation, to be scouted forthwith by the more intelligent Satan. Thus Milton can satisfy his desire of self-expression as well as invite a contrast with the yielding to female charm which had its place in undoing Adam.

But of all the autobiographical passages grafted on to the figure of Christ the most patent, the most interesting, and the most puzzling, is Christ's long speech on Greek philosophy and literature. In spite of its length I quote the whole, for it cannot be properly discussed piecemeal.

> Think not but that I know these things, or think
> I know them not; not therefore am I short
> Of knowing what I aught: he who receives
> Light from above, from the fountain of light,
> No other doctrine needs, though granted true;
> But these are false, or little else but dreams,
> Conjectures, fancies, built on nothing firm.
> The first and wisest of them all profess'd
> To know this only, that he nothing knew;
> The next to fabling fell and smooth conceits,
> A third sort doubted all things, though plain sence;
> Others in vertue plac'd felicity,
> But vertue joyn'd with riches and long life,
> In corporal pleasure he, and careless ease,
> The Stoic last in Philosophic pride,
> By him call'd vertue; and his vertuous man,
> Wise, perfect in himself, and all possessing
> Equal to God, oft shames not to prefer,
> As fearing God nor man, contemning all

Wealth, pleasure, pain or torment, death and life,
Which when he lists, he leaves, or boasts he can,
For all his tedious talk is but vain boast,
Or subtle shifts conviction to evade.
Alas what can they teach, and not mislead;
Ignorant of themselves, of God much more,
And how the world began, and how man fell
Degraded by himself, on grace depending?
Much of the Soul they talk, but all awrie,
And in themselves seek vertue, and to themselves
All glory arrogate, to God give none,
Rather accuse him under usual names,
Fortune and Fate, as one regardless quite
Of mortal things. Who therefore seeks in these
True wisdom, finds her not, or by delusion
Far worse, her false resemblance only meets,
An empty cloud. However many books
Wise men have said are wearisom; who reads
Incessantly, and to his reading brings not
A spirit and judgment equal or superior,
(And what he brings, what needs he elsewhere seek)
Uncertain and unsettl'd still remains,
Deep verst in books and shallow in himself,
Crude or intoxicate, collecting toys,
And trifles for choice matters, worth a spunge;
As Children gathering pibles on the shore.
Or if I would delight my private hours
With Music or with Poem, where so soon
As in our native Language can I find
That solace? All our Law and Story strew'd
With Hymns, our Psalms with artful terms inscrib'd,
Our Hebrew Songs and Harps in *Babylon*,
That pleas'd so well our Victors ear, declare
That rather *Greece* from us these Arts deriv'd;
Ill imitated, while they loudest sing
The vices of thir Deities, and thir own
In Fable, Hymn, or Song, so personating
Thir Gods ridiculous, and themselves past shame.
Remove their swelling Epithetes thick laid
As varnish on a Harlots cheek, the rest,
Thin sown with aught of profit or delight,
Will far be found unworthy to compare
With *Sion's* songs, to all true tasts excelling,
Where God is prais'd aright, and Godlike men,
The Holiest of Holies, and his Saints;
Such are from God inspir'd, not such from thee;

Unless where moral vertue is express't
By light of Nature not in all quite lost.
Thir Orators thou then extoll'st, as those
The top of Eloquence, Statists indeed,
And lovers of thir Country, as may seem;
But herein to our Prophets far beneath,
As men divinely taught, and better teaching
The solid rules of Civil Government
In thir majestic unaffected stile
Then all the Oratory of *Greece* and *Rome*.
In them is plainest taught, and easiest learnt,
What makes a Nation happy, and keeps it so,
What ruins Kingdoms, and lays Cities flat;
These only with our Law best form a King.[1]

It is beside the mark to attribute, as Saurat does, some of the sentiments to a mood of fatigue. The whole speech is a masterpiece of restrained eloquence, whose rise and fall hint at the stores of power that lie all ready beneath the surface. There is no question but it expresses Milton's considered opinions, perhaps his most keenly felt opinions, at the time. The mood which it expresses (after the first few lines) is one of mortification or masochism[2] rather, not fatigue. He goes out of his way to hurt the dearest and oldest inhabitants of his mind: the Greek philosophers, his early love Plato included, the disinterested thirst for knowledge, the poets and orators of Greece and Rome. Against these he defiantly puts the orthodox scheme of sin and salvation, the poetry and political wisdom of the ancient Hebrews. Even granting his undoubted admiration of the *Psalms,* we have reason to be astounded at his assertions. I can only conclude that Milton had before *Paradise Regained* undergone some important mental experience, whose nature can be conjectured from a hint given before. It was suggested that Milton had come to doubt the wisdom of his action during the Civil War. For all his accumulation of knowledge he had been led into a course of action which had apparently achieved nothing. He had been led to influence men's deeds instead of enlightening their minds. For the second time in his life (the first had been in his earliest divorce tract) he admits himself to have been in the wrong. In spite of his growing distaste for dogma it was in the Bible, especially in the *Psalms,* that he found expressed what for him was of all things most important, the communion of the isolated human

1. iv. 286–364.

2. I use the word without sexual connotation, if this is permissible.

being with God. Hence and not from mere Stoic passivity was derived the 'paradise within' which alone made life worth while. In the anguish of admitting himself to be wrong he turns against his old supports, as if *they* had been responsible for his error of judgment. His very affection for them, their power over him, makes him the fiercer. He must not be their slave; only if he subjects them to what is of genuine value will it be legitimate for him to enjoy them again. For in many passages of the poem enjoy them he does. He has not cast out the love of knowledge and of the humanities: only he cannot allow them to usurp a place to which they are not entitled.

The above is conjectural. But I may plead that none of the explanations of this puzzling speech with which I am acquainted have seemed to me in the least adequate. The usual one is that Milton in some sort did not mean what he said. But is it really likely, is it even possible, that Milton should have inserted, in the longest speech occupying the most prominent of all positions in a poem on which he lavished every care to construct and to execute without blemish, a series of opinions he had hastily adopted in a spirit of irresponsible pique?

Such then are the main lines of thought in *Paradise Regained*. It remains to speak of the character of Satan. He, as I have said, stands for ill-regulated passion. Not only has he the primal sin of inordinate ambition, but he cannot even control himself when carrying out his evil intentions. In the first council of devils he announces that the danger which Christ constitutes must have opposed to it,

> Not force, but well couch't fraud, well woven snares;

and yet, when his schemes fail, he forgets his good intentions and resorts to terrorism, afflicting Christ with a storm and a purely physical trial on the pinnacle of the temple. It is this weakness in evil-doing that separates him so widely from his more steadfast namesake in *Paradise Lost*.[1] The earlier Satan, though at times subject to despair, hate, and other passions, gives the impression of having as strong a self-control as Milton himself. Further, he would never have resorted to such a variety of allurements as did the Satan of *Paradise Regained*: he would have staked everything on the utmost he could devise and have accepted his defeat with restraint. However, though the later Satan is weaker, he is more human and quite as clever. Indeed he is too clever: his restless brain cannot stay

---

1. That the two Satans should be different characters is yet another argument that *Paradise Regained* is not a continuation of *Paradise Lost*.

content with a clear single issue, but must ever be advancing secondary reasons to persuade Christ to act in a certain way. I think Milton's dislike of politicians had entered into his conception of Satan, as his earlier admiration for the more impressive of their kind had entered into the council of devils in *Paradise Lost*, Book Two. Another piece of cleverness is Satan's power of taking a hint and turning his arguments to suit what seems to be passing in Christ's mind. He is also very ingenious in excuses, whenever accused. A few illustrations must suffice out of many possible. When Satan opens his attack by suggesting that Christ might turn stones to bread to satisfy his hunger, he gives the additional reason that by this act not Christ alone but the half-starved inhabitants of the wilderness will be relieved: ingenious, but a tactical error. Later, in exhibiting the power of Parthia with the primary intention of perverting the desire for action so strong in Christ's nature, he insinuates the virtuous argument that Christ may thereby free the Temple from Roman violation. And he subtly cites the case of Judas Maccabaeus, who, like Christ, retired to the desert but with arms.[1] Satan never presses a plea too long. Seeing that Christ is quite unaffected by the empty pomp of material riches, he at once guesses that the subtler pomp of glory will entice more powerfully.[2] And when, almost at the end of his resources, he finds to his astonishment that Christ is unmoved by political ambition, he has the quickness of wit to shift his ground and to tempt Christ to reach the preferred inward peace of mind through the illicit means of Greek philosophy.[3] Perhaps Satan's most brilliant counter-attack occurs in the discussion of glory. Christ has exalted Job and Socrates, who lived inglorious, over Alexander and Caesar, and Satan retorts that Christ in not seeking glory is unworthy of his Father who

> not content in Heaven
> By all his Angels glorifi'd, requires
> Glory from men, from all men good or bad.[4]

The most human characteristic of Satan is his habit of complaining that he is not being treated fairly, not being given a chance. He almost descends to a whine in his last speech in Book One, where he complains that misery has forced him to tell lies and that Christ cannot refuse access to one so down-trodden and unfortunate. Later, when the crowning offer of Rome has been rejected, the whine is dropped and the tone becomes bullying:

1. iii. 166. 2. ibid., opening. 3. iv. 195 ff. 4. iii. 112–14.

> To whom the Tempter impudent repli'd.
> I see all offers made by me how slight
> Thou valu'st, because offer'd, and reject'st:
> Nothing will please the difficult and nice,
> Or nothing more then still to contradict.[1]

This tone is very true to human nature, to the hawker who, having tried to pass off his trash by begging, demands 'a civil answer to a civil question', or to the disappointed politician who complains of the ingratitude of the country in refusing to accept something it does not want and demands angrily that his nostrum should be given a chance. For all his subtlety, there is a streak of coarseness in Satan, and we are made to feel that he is more at home with the crude ambitions of the worldling than with the subtler selfishness of the scholar or philosopher.

1. iv. 154–8.

CHAPTER NINE

Paradise Regained: its Literary Character

I T is not surprising that if *Paradise Regained* is not allowed a separate existence of its own, it should be frequently judged by wrong standards; that is, not by internal, but by the external standards of *Paradise Lost* on the one hand and *Samson Agonistes* on the other.

The usual explanation of the frigidity of *Paradise Regained* is that it is the effect of age – it betrays the feebleness of senility and has one of the most certain marks of that stage of authorship, the attempt to imitate himself in those points in which he was once strong. Or it is an *œuvre de lassitude*, a continuation, with the inevitable defect of continuations, that of presenting the form and wanting the soul of the original.[1]

A more erroneous series of statements it would be difficult to make. *Paradise Regained* is not a continuation; after the first two hundred lines it has little to do with the form of *Paradise Lost*; it does not want the soul of that work because it has one of its own; it has very great underlying vigour; it makes no attempt to imitate the most powerful points of its supposed model. Such is the result of demanding from a work of art not its 'proper pleasure' but some other pleasure.

Others, Landor and Saurat for instance, allow many 'beauties' in the poem but consider it to lack vitality in general. Their assumption would be that, if he had been able, Milton would have written the whole poem as grandly as he wrote these excepted passages. In other words, the normal style of the poem is other than he wished it, and he had not the power to summon his sublimity at will. I can only deny this completely and say that the normal style of the poem is deliberately chastened or dimmed, and that Milton has complete command over his sublimity: he is not always sublime, simply because he does not wish to be. When he wrote the first two books of *Paradise Lost* he aimed at a continuous sublimity: but is that any reason for assuming that he never changed his aim? He probably thought it might be well for a change to economize in grandeur and to contrast it with a quieter mode of writing. But the power over grandeur is never absent. Even in the subdued parts he will let drop a line or two to remind one of this; and when he wishes, he can

1. Pattison, *Milton*, 192.

266

astonish in a way which makes the accusation of lassitude ridiculous.
Here are three lines near the beginning which show how easily he
can summon up his older grand manner:

> and led thir march
> From Hell's deep-vaulted Den to dwell in light,
> Regents and Potentates, and Kings, yea gods
> Of many a pleasant Realm and Province wide.[1]

And in the following five lines the fourth suddenly reveals all the
hidden power:

> So spake the Son of God; and here again
> Satan had not to answer, but stood struck
> With guilt of his own sin, for he himself
> Insatiable of glory had lost all,
> Yet of another Plea bethought him soon.[2]

Surely from a passage of this kind it is clear that Milton is employing
a method quite different from the frontal attacks of the first books of
Paradise Lost, and with all deliberateness. The fourth line would
hardly have stood out in the earlier setting: here it gains enormously
by the extreme simplicity of the rest. And when he sees good to
write greatly, he does it, with less amplitude than formerly it is true,
but with an ease and mastery unmatched in our literature.

> To whom thus Jesus: also it is written,
> Tempt not the Lord thy God, he said and stood.
> But Satan smitten with amazement fell
> As when Earths Son *Antaeus* (to compare
> Small things with greatest) in *Irassa* strove
> With *Joves Alcides,* and oft foil'd still rose,
> Receiving from his mother Earth new strength,
> Fresh from his fall, and fiercer grapple joyn'd,
> Throttl'd at length in the Air, expir'd and fell;
> So after many a foil the Tempter proud,
> Renewing fresh assaults, amidst his pride
> Fell whence he stood to see his Victor fall.
> And as that *Theban* Monster that propos'd
> Her riddle, and him, who solv'd it not, devour'd;
> That once found out and solv'd, for grief and spight
> Cast her self headlong from th' *Ismenian* steep,
> So strook with dread and anguish fell the Fiend,
> And to his crew, that sat consulting, brought
> Joyless triumphals of his hop't success,
> Ruin, and desperation, and dismay,
> Who durst so proudly tempt the Son of God.[3]

1. i. 115–18.   2. iii. 145–9.   3. iv. 560–80.

The style of *Paradise Regained* has however had its admirers. Its deliberate austerity and bareness have been well described and praised, not unqualifiedly, but at least as an astonishing technical achievement. John Bailey[1] for instance describes well how near to prose it can go without incurring the charge of prosiness. But it is very easy to exaggerate this alleged bareness. Undoubtedly Milton has simplified his language and cut down his unit of rhythm. But if he has simplified his language, he has introduced in compensation subtleties of verbal emphasis not found in the main in *Paradise Lost*. Here is a passage chosen at random: a fair sample of the normal style.

> But why should man seek glory? who of his own
> Hath nothing, and to whom nothing belongs
> But condemnation, ignominy, and shame?
> Who for so many benefits receiv'd
> Turn'd recreant to God, ingrate and false,
> And so of all true good himself despoil'd,
> Yet, sacrilegious, to himself would take
> That which to God alone of right belongs;
> Yet so much bounty is in God, such grace,
> That who advance his glory, not their own,
> Them he himself to glory will advance.[2]

These lines form a complete unit of rhythm, a short unit judged by the standards of *Paradise Lost*. Their motion does not urge forward, and yet how cunningly do they invite close scrutiny and meditation! To enumerate every delicacy of emphasis would take too long, or every speeding up or relaxing of tempo. Let me point only to the stressing of the two 'nothings' and of 'sacrilegious'. Nor is the passage unemotional; as it should be if its excellence is confined to mere technical cleverness: emotion, however straitly controlled, throbs through it. Only it is a peculiar emotion, relevant to the mood of inwardness that pervades the poem. And this indicates another defect in the criticism of *Paradise Regained*: it has made no effort to relate the very unusual and strange style with the other features of the poem: its thought, its atmosphere, its form. As if Milton was likely to have evolved a highly wrought manner of writing for no further reason than to display the accomplishment of his technique.

It is not difficult to extract the main thoughts from *Paradise Regained* or to point out where the critics have fallen short, but to speak of the meaning of the poem – 'meaning' in any sense that is

1. *Milton*, 208–10.   2. iii. 134–44.

not quite superficial – in other words to criticize it, is very much more difficult. But the attempt is worth making, if only because it seems new.

Perhaps the best way of approach is to point out two of the things which *Paradise Regained* does not resemble. It is not an epic, it does not try to be an epic, and it must not be judged by any kind of epic standard. There is practically no action, the characters (Satan excepted) do not live, and there is the smallest relation to normal life. All this does not mean that Milton wrote a bad poem, it merely shows one of the things he was not trying to do. The bulk of the poem consists of speeches, suggesting an analogy with the drama; but the speeches are void of dramatic interest. The issue of what little action takes place is a foregone conclusion. Any chance Milton had of creating a dramatic situation he deliberately passes over. The unmasking of Satan was such a chance: but Christ sees through his disguise in a moment, and Satan abandons the attempt at conceal-ment without a struggle. Again, the characters are not such as would add life to any of the developed forms of drama. In nature *Paradise Regained* is equally remote from *Samson Agonistes* and *Paradise Lost*. And yet the language of the speakers, which has at times a simplicity almost conversational and, as we saw, a delicacy of em-phasis far from undramatic, does suggest some sort of dramatic analogy.

In discussing *Comus* I conjectured that Milton was experimenting in more than one kind of dramatic style: the normal Elizabethan, the Pastoral, and the Greek. There is evidence that when he came to contemplate writing a play on some highly serious theme after his return from Italy he had considered not only these forms but the Morality. The third draft of *Paradise Lost* in the Trinity Manuscript is particularly full of analogies with that form of drama.[1] Quite

1. R. L. Ramsay, 'Morality Themes in Milton's Poetry', in *Studies in Philology*, 1918, 123–58, points to a number of places where the influence of morality themes is found. He sees no direct influence of any single Morality Play. The influence gradually diminishes. There is a good deal in the minor poems, very little in *Paradise Lost* or *Paradise Regained*, and none in *Samson*. This may be true for the influence of the themes (though the debate between Christ and Satan in *Paradise Regained* could be compared with the struggle between the Virtues and the Vices), but as far as the more important analogy of atmosphere goes the minor poems do not resemble the Morality Play in the least, while *Paradise Regained* resembles it in a very important way. Ramsay compares the third draft of *Paradise Lost* with the *Castle of Perseverance*, and writes (p. 148): 'These early drafts demonstrate that what Milton began in 1640 was not an epic, not even, except in external form, a classical tragedy, but a morality play.' For the third draft of *Paradise Lost* see Masson, *Milton's Poetical Works* (1890), ii. 45–6; Hanford, *Handbook*, 3rd ed., 183–4.

apart from such concrete evidence, it is pretty certain that Milton would have made himself acquainted with every type of religious drama produced in England before settling the mode of his own projected play. He must have been acquainted with the prevailing tone of the Morality. Now the form of *Paradise Regained* with its long dialogues was probably taken from the *Book of Job*. This book is mentioned several times in the poem and had already, in *Reason of Church Government*, been called the model of the brief epic. It is also probable that Milton felt at this time particularly drawn to it as something that suited his own case. But here the resemblance ceases. There is nothing in common between the patriarchal setting of *Job* and the allegorical twilight of *Paradise Regained*. The re-semblance is really closer with the other writer to whom Milton has several direct debts in the poem: Spenser. And the debt is not merely one of phrases. Greenlaw[1] is probably right in seeing some connection, more or less close, between the book of Guyon, the second of the *Faerie Queene*, and *Paradise Regained*. The temptations in each are pretty similar and it is quite likely that Archimago sug-gested Satan's first disguise.[2] More important still, the allegorical twilight in Milton might be compared with the dimness of Mam-mon's Cave, and the banquet in the wilderness to the Bower of Bliss. But Spenser himself owes much to the instinct for allegory from which the Morality arose; and I would suggest that to this form too *Paradise Regained* shows the truest resemblances. Not that it can be said to owe anything concrete to the Morality or to any other type of medieval or pre-Elizabethan play. The supposed analogy with Bale's *Temptacyon of our Lorde by Sathan in the Desart* (1538)[3] amounts to nothing. But the long homiletic speeches set in an air of abstrac-tion and unreality give the prevailing tone to both objects of our comparison.

Paradise Regained may be narrower in scope than the other great works of Milton, but I do not wish to suggest by what I have just said that it can be narrowed to the compass of the Morality. The unearthly dialogue between Reason on the one hand and Passion in very subtle and sophisticated form on the other in the enchanted wilderness may indeed suggest some dramatized contest of virtues and vices for the possession of the human soul. But such dialogues are only part of *Paradise Regained*, for into the dimness are projected,

1. 'A Better Teacher than Aquinas', in *Studies in Philology*, 1917, 196–217.

2. It is equally likely that Giles Fletcher (*Christ's Victory on Earth*, stanza 15) gave Milton the suggestion.

3. See Todd's edition of Milton, v. p. xv.

like a sudden vision in a dream, the dazzling pageants of fair women, gorgeous banquet, and earthly pomp. And it is this contrast between brown shades and brilliant light that gives the poem its strong fascination. Nor is the contrast distracting, for its two parts are united by the common element of unnaturalness.

It looks as if Milton had deliberately divested his poem of all relation to ordinary life, just as in Books Nine and Ten of *Paradise Lost* he had done his best to be dramatic. And he has done this because he wishes to say that the business of the human mind with itself and its Creator counts for more than all its relations with human beings. The dim wilderness stands for the loneliness of the individual mind, cut off from the experiences of every day and from the support of its fellows in its struggle for self-mastery, while the dreamlike and artificial brilliance of the spectacles that tempt the mind expresses at once the glamour of worldly success and its essential insubstantiality.

Two of the best known lines of the poem,

> Knights of *Logres,* or of *Lyones,*
> *Lancelot* or *Pelleas,* or *Pellenore,*

may help to a further comparison. Milton was thinking in these lines of the 'lofty fables and romances' (the reading of his early youth, as he tells us in the *Apology for Smectymnuus*) and of Malory's *Morte d'Arthur* in particular. It is in Malory's account of the quest of the Grail that we get a resemblance, not very strong perhaps but certain enough, to *Paradise Regained*. In this episode Malory uses allegory very freely (as he does not use it elsewhere in his book), and corresponding to this freedom is a greater unreality of setting. The waste lands which the questing knights traverse and the shows fabricated by the fiends to entice them are not without their kinship to the wilderness and the pageants of *Paradise Regained*; and indeed the whole Grail episode might be said to stand in the same relation to the rest of *Morte d'Arthur* as *Paradise Regained* to *Paradise Lost*.

Finally let me mention the charming hints on the nature of *Paradise Regained*, given by Charles Lamb in his essay on *Grace before Meat*, where he speaks of the banquet in the Second Book.

The severest satire upon full tables and surfeits is the banquet which Satan, in the Paradise Regained, provides for a temptation in the wilderness:

> A table richly spread in regal mode,
> With dishes piled, and meats of noblest sort
> And savour; beasts of chase, or fowl of game,

In pastry built, or from the spit, or boiled,
Gris-amber-steamed; all fish from sea or shore,
Freshet or purling brook, for which was drained
Pontus, and Lucrine bay, and Afric coast.

The Tempter, I warrant you, thought these cates would go down without the recommendatory preface of a benediction. They are like to be short graces where the devil plays the host. I am afraid the poet wants his usual decorum in this place. Was he thinking of the old Roman luxury, or of a gaudy day at Cambridge? This was a temptation fitter for a Heliogabalus. The whole banquet is too civic and culinary, and the accompaniments altogether a profanation of that deep, abstracted holy scene. The mighty artillery of sauces, which the cook-fiend conjures up, is out of proportion to the simple wants and plain hunger of the guest. He that disturbed him in his dreams, from his dreams might have been taught better. To the temperate fantasies of the famished Son of God, what sort of feasts presented themselves? – He dreamed indeed,

                    – As appetite is wont to dream,
          Of meats and drinks, nature's refreshment sweet.

But what meats? –

          Him thought, he by the brook of Cherith stood,
          And saw the ravens with their horny beaks
          Food to Elijah bringing, even and morn;
          Though ravenous, taught to abstain from what they brought:
          He saw the prophet also how he fled
          Into the desert, and how there he slept
          Under a juniper; then how awaked
          He found his supper on the coals prepared,
          And by the angel was bid rise and eat,
          And ate the second time after repose,
          The strength whereof sufficed him forty days:
          Sometimes, that with Elijah he partook,
          Or as a guest with Daniel at his pulse.

Nothing in Milton is finelier fancied than these temperate dreams of the divine Hungerer. To which of these two visionary banquets, think you, would the introduction of what is called the grace have been the most fitting and pertinent?

Lamb misunderstood Satan, who was tempting not only Christ's hunger but his sense of brilliance and luxury: but in a phrase or two he gets nearer to the nature of *Paradise Regained* than any critic I have read. 'Deep, abstracted, holy scene'; 'nothing in Milton is finelier fancied than these temperate dreams of the divine Hungerer': these with their subdued rhythms are true aids, if only broken hints suggesting rather than informing, to the right understanding of Milton's most neglected great poem.

CHAPTER TEN

Paradise Regained: the Construction

WHY was it that Milton divided his poem into four books, thus cutting through the main lines of his construction? For only the division between Books One and Two corresponds to a main division in the fable, namely the end of the first temptation: the second temptation, beginning in Book Two and not ending till nearly half-way through Book Four, ought, as far as structure goes, to have remained intact. Possibly Milton had in mind the most erudite and admired of recent epics, published ten years earlier in four books, the *Davideis* of Cowley. But he must have known that these four books were but a portion of a projected full-size epic in the traditional twelve. A better reason may be found in his opening. 'I who e're while . . .' he begins, just as Spenser had begun his introduction to the *Faerie Queene* with 'Lo, I the man whose Muse whylome. . . .' Both poets are imitating the 'Ille ego qui quondam . . .' of the *Aeneid*. Spenser had indeed the better right, for he could claim a comparison between his own early pastorals and Virgil's. But Milton is probably claiming an analogy of bulk though he cannot one of order. There are 2070 lines in *Paradise Regained*, 2188 in the *Georgics*. Like Virgil's too his own chief poetical output has been one brief, one long poem. To hint the Virgilian analogy he divides his short poem, like the *Georgics,* into four books and begins with an imitation of the *Aeneid*. In fairness one must remember that the books of *Paradise Lost* ran in the first edition to the un-Virgilian number of ten, but Milton may well have resolved on the later twelve at the time he was making the divisions in *Paradise Regained*. These divisions need not be contemporary with the poem's composition; they may have been made at any later date before the publication in 1671.

However this may be, in studying the structure of *Paradise Regained* we should forget the division into books and remember the story of the Temptation as told in the *Gospel of St Luke*. Milton treats the first temptation, to turn stones into bread, as a prelude; the second temptation, the vision of the kingdoms of the world, is the body of the poem; the third temptation, when Christ is set on the pinnacle of the temple, is less a temptation than the brief and sudden rout of Satan. The following table will show the poem's proportions:

Division of Poem	No. of Lines in Division	Reference to Text
Preludes	182	i. 1–182
First (introductory temptation) . .	320	i. 183–502 (end of Book i.)
Prelude to second (main) temptation .	241	ii. 1–241
Second (main) temptation . .	1081	ii. 242–iv. 393
Third temptation	187	iv. 394–580
Epilogues	59	iv. 581–639 (end of poem)
	2070	

From this table it may be seen how much the second temptation preponderates. In structure the poem might be likened to an imaginary church. The preludes would correspond to an elaborate doorway at the west end leading to an ante-chapel (the first temptation). A second doorway (the prelude to the second temptation) leads from the ante-chapel to the body of the church. This, opening into transepts, corresponds to the second temptation with its visions expanding to Parthia and Rome. The chancel is the third temptation and the apse the epilogues.

Such is the general structure; to describe the details I will run over the development of the poem. After references to *Paradise Lost* and a short invocation to the Holy Spirit Milton begins his narrative with the baptism of John:

> to his great Baptism flock'd
> With aw the Regions round, and with them came
> From *Nazareth* the Son of *Joseph* deem'd
> To the flood *Jordan,* came as then obscure,
> Unmarkt, unknown.[1]

Milton had ended *Paradise Lost* on the note of common humanity: he wished to show that the poem had a universal human application. He begins *Paradise Regained* with the above lines concerning the man Jesus and brings the poem to a close on the same theme:

> hee unobserv'd
> Home to his Mothers house private return'd.

Once again he seeks to relate his poem, however dehumanized in its main substance, to ordinary life. After the account of Christ's baptism we are shown councils: the devils' in the air, God the

---

1. i. 21–5.

Father's in his Heaven. Milton thus keeps to the scheme of *Paradise Lost* with its division of Hell, Heaven, and Earth: but with one great difference. The reader never shifts his position from the earth. Milton means to fix his attention on the conflict in the wilderness. The result is that he cannot afford to make the prologue too interesting: indeed he has damped down his fires till they are almost in danger of extinction.

With the beginning of the first temptation (i. 183) comes a change. Our eyes as it were become used to the dim light and begin to see. Christ walks in his holy trance into the wilderness and utters an enormous unnatural prologue, which we feel to be perfectly fitting. One thinks of the 'Moses *prologizei*' of the third draft of *Paradise Lost* in the Trinity Manuscript, the draft that owes so much to the Morality Play. The prologue spoken, Christ is in mid desert and the prevailing twilight of the poem has settled in. Satan approaches and lays his first snare, the temptation to turn stones into bread. His object is to suggest to Christ a distrust of God for having left him without food for forty days,[1] for Christ says to him (i. 355):

> Why dost thou then suggest to me distrust?

But the temptation is subsidiary to Satan's main object: to gain information and leave of access. The first temptation is thus made introductory to the second temptation, which occupies the bulk of the poem.

To emphasize the main temptation Milton interrupts the story and gives us a picture of Mary, Andrew, and Peter in their distress at Christ's prolonged absence and in their trust in God's promises. The style is subdued as in the opening of the poem, but the effect is that of common day, quite different from the desert dimness. Then for a moment (ii. 109-14) we return to the wilderness: I think in order that we may not forget it and its atmosphere during the council of devils which follows. This council with its restless passions balances the serenity of Mary and the two Apostles, but in tone it is far more spirited than anything hitherto in the poem. Belial,

> the dissolutest Spirit that fell
> The sensuallest, and after *Asmodai*
> The fleshliest Incubus,[2]

deserves to be called a character, and when he begins his speech on the best means to tempt Christ with the words,

1. See A. H. Gilbert, 'The Temptation in *Paradise Regained*', in *Journal of English and Germanic Philology*, 1916, 599–611.
2. ii. 150-2.

Set women in his eye and in his walk,

we see his dreadful, vulgar leer. In what follows Milton gives us the first specimen of the third kind of style used in *Paradise Regained*, the style in which he describes the visions of worldly splendour. As pointed out above, there were difficulties in the way of making his vision of fair women a part of the second temptation: in the mouths of Belial and Satan there could be no objection to it. It was probably to gain his contrast between brilliance and dimness that he inserted, before the council of devils, his few lines about Christ in the wilderness. Anyhow the speeches of Belial and Satan on women have an admirable glamour about them.

The council of devils over, we are taken deeper than ever into the wilderness. Christ's hunger grows and he dreams at night of the frugal meals of Daniel and Elijah. Then Satan approaches and the second temptation begins. First there is the banquet (ii. 289–403), another piece of pageantry. Gilbert[1] would have it that the temptation is not one of hunger (already tried in vain) but of earthly pomp. Satan invites Christ to use the ministering spirits as his own servants. I agree that earthly pomp is part of the temptation, but I cannot see that hunger does not enter in too. Christ counters the offer of ministering spirits by saying that he could command the angels to attend him. But he adds (ii. 389):

And with my hunger what hast thou to do?

Then follow (all parts of the second temptation) the temptations of riches (ii. 404–86), glory (iii. 1–148), empire (iii. 149–iv. 194), and vain learning (iv. 195–363). These are carefully graded according to the subtlety and inwardness of their appeal. The bait of riches is comparatively crude. Glory is more refined but purely selfish. Empire has a subtler appeal, for Satan insinuates (iii. 160–70) that through empire Christ may free Israel from Roman sacrilege and imitate the noble example of his compatriot, Judas Maccabaeus. Christ's unexpected retort to the vision of Parthia and to the suggestion that by ruling the Parthians he may free the Jews is that the Jews are not worth a special act of rescue. Satan is badly cast down at finding Christ so unparochial, but gathers all his forces and presents Christ with the vision of Rome. That this vision is the climax Milton makes clear not merely by the prodigious descriptive power he displays but by the long series of similes (opening of Book Four) which he inserts as a prelude. Into the temptation of Rome Satan inserts the refined plea of superior civilization: Rome

1. loc. cit.

> whose wide domain
> In ample Territory, wealth and power,
> Civility of Manners, Arts, and Arms,
> And long Renown thou justly may'st prefer
> Before the Parthian.[1]

Satan finally sees that Christ has no political ambition, and, though by now almost desperate, makes a last appeal to Christ's inwardness of ambition by offering the philosophy of Greece, whose

> rules will render thee a King compleat
> Within thy self.[2]

When Christ has rejected this too, Satan has spent all his cunning and no real hope remains:

> So spake the Son of God; but Satan now
> Quite at a loss, for all his darts were spent,
> Thus to our Saviour with stern brow reply'd.[3]

And he proceeds, not to tempt further, but to foretell the sufferings Christ will have to undergo.

The third temptation is strongly contrasted with the second. Satan has despaired and turns from the subtle tempter of mind to a crude physical bully. Night intervenes between the second and third temptations, and in it Satan manufactures a storm with which to terrify the Son of God. Finding it to have had no effect, he is 'swoln with rage' and loses his judgment. He claims equality with Christ ('The Son of God I also am' he says) and hurries him to the pinnacle of the temple to see whether by physical test Christ is indeed what he claims to be. Christ is to fall from the pinnacle; if he is the Son of God the angels will save him. But something greater happens. Christ does not fall: he stands; and it is Satan, his period of power ended, who falls. The third temptation is not really a temptation at all but the rout of Satan. We have left the desert, and the style has become freer and more vigorous, as in the descriptions of earthly pomp.

The poem ends with the ministry of the angels and Christ's return to his home.

1. iv. 81–5.   2. iv. 283–4.   3. iv. 365–7.

CHAPTER ELEVEN

Samson Agonistes: its Origin

WE DO not know the exact date of *Samson Agonistes*. It was published in 1671, and we may be reasonably certain that it was written after *Paradise Regained*. Why did Milton write it? There is no one answer, but the chief is that whether months or years separate his two last poems, he had changed in the interval and sought to express what probably was his final phase of mind. *Paradise Regained* has the narrowest scope of Milton's three long poems: it concerns itself with a single idea, namely that action is to be distrusted and that what matters almost exclusively is that inner paradise which it is in the power of every individual to attain. But Milton seems to have changed and by the time of *Samson* to have regained his faith in action. He makes a deed, not a thought, the centre of his drama. Not that he omits the inner paradise: he makes it the essential preliminary to the heroic deed. It is only because Samson has proved his mental wholesomeness that he is allowed to carry out God's vengeance on the Philistines. *Samson Agonistes*, then, was written to express Milton's final adjustment of the two ideas that had dominated his mind with fluctuating sway for so many years.

But there are other reasons. A wonderful thing about *Samson Agonistes* is that with all its massiveness it is very varied. In a way it is the most objective of all Milton's long poems; it can be read as the tragedy of Samson and nothing more. To be enjoyed it need be related to its author no closer than the *Oedipus Rex* to Sophocles or the *Medea* to Euripides. At the same time it is the most political and the most personal. All three characteristics, personal, political, and objective, may suggest their corresponding reasons why the play was written.

It appeared that in *Paradise Regained* Milton was not far from personal suffering. A mood of masochism was detected, all the more likely to be near because not avowed. By the time of *Samson Agonistes* Milton was far enough removed from his worst agonies to be able to survey them more calmly and to desire to express them with a directness on which he had not hitherto ventured. Samson's despair is far more personal than anything in *Paradise Lost* or *Paradise Regained*. And it was probably a relief to utter his own past miseries through Samson's mouth. When in his preface he speaks of the Aristotelian purgation he may well have been transferring what

278

Aristotle meant to apply to the audience from them to the author. Tragedy would be the outlet of the excessive emotions that harassed the mind of the poet.[1]

As a political manifesto Milton must have enjoyed writing *Samson Agonistes*. It is nothing less than stark defiance of the restored government and a prophecy that it will be overthrown. And yet there is scarcely a word in the play that could not be referred quite plausibly to the story of Samson as narrated in the Old Testament. The controversial side of Milton's nature must have got rich satisfaction.

The reason why Milton wrote an objective drama is less clear. He probably began (as after all most authors must begin) with the desire of personal expression and succeeded in becoming interested in Samson as Samson, not merely in Samson as himself. But Hanford[2] has the interesting idea that with *Samson Agonistes* Milton fulfilled his early literary programme as outlined in *Reason of Church Government*. In this pamphlet Milton had mentioned 'that epic form whereof the two poems of Homer, and those other two of Virgil and Tasso, are a diffuse, and the book of Job a brief model' and had gone on to wonder 'whether those dramatic constitutions, wherein Sophocles and Euripides reign, shall be found more doctrinal and exemplary to a nation'. Hanford[3] concludes that *Paradise Lost* is Milton's fulfilment of the 'diffuse model', *Paradise Regained* (a good deal reminiscent of

1. See J. H. Hanford, *Samson Agonistes*, in University of Michigan Publications (Language and Literature), i. 181. I do not however agree with him in making the statement of this the main object of the preface. Milton's main objects there are two: (*a*) To justify himself in writing tragedy at all, when his own party has suppressed stage-plays. Hence his citations from Scripture and the Fathers and his disavowal of any intention of getting the play acted. (*b*) To show how completely Aristotelian he is, how he reverences the correct idea of a tragedy. Even in the text of the play (166–175) he slips in a hint that his hero, even though of not quite the same high birth as Oedipus and Thyestes, whom Aristotle cites, is yet eminently 'one who is highly regarded and prosperous' (*Poetics*, xiii.).

> The rarer thy example stands,
> By how much from the top of wondrous glory,
> Strongest of mortal men,
> To lowest pitch of abject fortune thou art fall'n.
> For him I reckon not in high estate
> Whom long descent of birth
> Or the sphear of fortune raises;
> But thee whose strength, while vertue was her mate,
> Might have subdu'd the Earth,
> Universally crown'd with highest praises.

2. loc. cit., 167–8.   3. et seq.

the *Book of Job*) of the 'brief model', and *Samson Agonistes* of 'those dramatic constitutions, wherein Sophocles and Euripides reign' – all according to plan. This suits admirably with Hanford's larger theory, held by him too rigidly, that Milton's mind was settled and stopped growing at an early age and that his writings are a fulfilment alone, not a development. This is not the place to dispute this larger theory. I must confine myself to casting doubt on the supposed relation of *Reason of Church Government* to Milton's subsequent poems. First it must be pointed out that other projects (which Hanford ignores) are mentioned in *Reason of Church Government*: a pastoral drama on the model of the *Song of Solomon*, a tragedy on the model of *Revelation*, 'magnific odes and hymns, wherein Pindarus and Callimachus are in most things worthy'. Surely it would be more reasonable to add these to the programme and argue that Milton failed to complete it, than to omit their mention altogether and argue from the more convenient items. But there is little probability of any fixed programme beyond the intention of writing an epic. At one time Milton may have intended an epic, a pastoral drama, and a brief epic; at another an epic, a tragedy on the model of *Revelation*, and a series of Pindaric Odes. Once he had committed himself to writing, he would frame his programme by what he had not yet succeeded in expressing. It happened that the myth of Samson and the classical form of tragedy were suited to expressing something he had yet to express after he had completed his two epics. As W. P. Ker[1] put it, '*Samson Agonistes* was not written merely as an experiment in Greek poetic form. It was written because the Greek form was the right form for something that Milton wanted to say.' I refuse to believe that, if Milton had found in the Pindaric Ode (for instance) a more suitable means of expressing what he wanted to say, he would have discarded that form for one that suited him worse, in order to carry out a supposed programme of work drawn up nearly thirty years before.

But if Milton was not unduly influenced by the abstract idea of writing a tragedy, it is possible that he wished to improve in one important dramatic particular on his previous poems. In neither *Paradise Lost* nor *Paradise Regained* had there been a normal hero.[2] Adam, if the hero, was in a situation too far removed from ordinary human conditions to be quite satisfactory as normal man: further, he did not have the opportunity of effecting anything that could be

1. *The Art of Poetry*, 57.
2. See W. P. Ker, ibid., 53–71; J. H. Hanford, loc. cit., 171–2.

called worthy of the highest abilities of mankind. Christ in *Paradise Regained* cannot be said to correspond to fallible humanity: his victory is a foregone conclusion and his struggle, as struggle, has little interest. Samson is different: human, fallible, and yet exhibiting to what heroism humanity can rise. Milton may well have rested unsatisfied till he had achieved his creation.

CHAPTER TWELVE

Samson Agonistes: its Quality

To many readers *Samson Agonistes* is the most simple, direct, and moving of all Milton's poems. Nothing could be more appropriate, if they are right: we should here see Milton not only winning through to a fresh and definitive peace of mind but crowning all his earlier attempts at self-expression with a final perfection. But I have to confess that for all its merits *Samson Agonistes* appeals to me least of the three long poems. I do not know any single certain reason. All I can do is to make some hesitating suggestions, admitting meanwhile that there may be no explanation to seek beyond a personal lack of susceptibility.

The great merits of the play must be acknowledged. It expresses Milton's state of mind at the time of writing more adequately than any of the other poems did the corresponding state. There is in it practically no evidence of any discrepancy between admitted and unadmitted thought. Milton as it were empties the vessel of his mind with a single turn of the hand, and there is no sediment left behind. The adequacy of statement is beyond praise. Nor is there anything wrong with the plotting and shaping. Johnson erred in asserting that there was a beginning and an end, but no middle. He failed to detect the clear and sufficiently interesting growth in Samson's mind throughout the middle episodes of Manoa, Dalila, and Harapha, connecting beginning and end. There may be a few errors in detail; Samson's revival of spirit between the two appearances of the Officer may be a little abrupt or Dalila may usurp slightly too much space: but broadly it is difficult to see how the shaping could be bettered. The mental power displayed is huge: there is no relaxing in hold, rarely any weakening in the verse; not the slightest sign that age had impaired the vigour of Milton's mind. On the contrary, that he was able to regain his faith in action and in the political future of his country in spite of the Restoration, that his courage, lately forced into resistance, could press outwards once more into political defiance (and that too in his old age) is perhaps the most astonishing example of his indomitable spirit.

Nor is it true that *Samson* is not tragic, that it ends too happily. Hanford[1] has disposed of this accusation very successfully. Referring

1. loc. cit., 182-3.

to the last Chorus he writes:

> The pronouncement 'All is best' is of scarcely more avail than the identical formula which brings Greek plays to their conclusion and from which this one is derived. The consolation which is offered of 'what can quiet us in a death so noble' is not enough. Samson should have gone on from one glad triumph to another and emerged unscathed.

This is true. There is a sense of waste in the play which arouses the tragic feelings, though it would certainly be greater if we could feel more enthusiasm for Samson's tedious butcheries and if his blindness did not make death a merciful release. Similarly the *Oedipus Colonaeus* may arouse the tragic feelings, but we do not feel the death of the blind Oedipus to be as tragic and wasteful as his downfall in the *Oedipus Rex*.

So much for some of the merits. There is little need to dwell on them, as they have been freely acknowledged. But the merit of unimpaired strength may suggest a possible defect. If age has not impaired the vigour of Milton's mind, it may have checked its power of growth. From *Samson Agonistes* I get, as I do not from *Paradise Regained*, a depressing sense of the end of all development. But perhaps it is not really the fact of ended development, but the state of mind development has ended in, which is depressing. There had always been a vein of ferocity in Milton, but it had been mixed with other mitigating qualities: ingenuousness, a quick response to kindness, urbanity, even self-distrust for the moment. In *Samson* there appears a settled ferocity, not very lovely. This is how Manoa (kind father) receives the news of the Philistines' destruction.

> *Manoa.* Tell us the sum, the circumstance defer.
> *Messenger. Gaza* yet stands, but all her Sons are fall'n,
> All in a moment overwhelm'd and fall'n.
> *Man.* Sad, but thou knowst to *Israelites* not saddest
> The desolation of a Hostile City.
> *Mess.* Feed on that first, there may in grief be surfet.
> *Man.* Relate by whom. *Mess.* By *Samson.*
> *Man.* That still lessens
> The sorrow, and converts it nigh to joy.[1]

The cool, ironical gloating of Manoa's answers is a fine dramatic rendering of the spirit of 'that infuriate people', the Jews of the Old Testament: but I cannot help feeling that Milton expresses a personal sympathy with them and that if King Charles II with his

---

1. 1557–64.

Court and counsellors had been similarly overwhelmed Milton would have experienced a not less savage jubilation.

Another way of pointing out the less amiable qualities of *Samson Agonistes* is to contrast it with the *Nativity Ode*. No poem, not even *Paradise Regained*, is so far removed from the qualities that especially endear the early poem. There, the children were invited to play on the grass; in *Paradise Lost*, even in *Paradise Regained*, there were prohibitory notices, but still a certain number of children disregarded them unchecked; in *Samson Agonistes* the park is perfectly ordered with notices complete and the children have departed for good. Even if you compare Milton's tragedy with his Greek models, you will see that it outdoes them in austerity. He seems to have attempted to reconcile two types of Greek drama (and not quite succeeded): the simpler Aeschylean and the Sophoclean. Unlike Aeschylus's Prometheus, Samson's overwhelming figure is not softened by a romantic setting or a strain of true lyric. The Chorus's odes do nothing to universalize the individual's suffering. Neither does any Sophoclean subtlety mitigate the starkness of the fable. Not that Milton's minor characters are unskilfully drawn, but they exact too little of the reader's attention to take his mind at all from the protagonist. Milton's Samson resembles less the tragic figures of the Attic dramatists than a statue of the Peloponnesian school portraying some powerful and sombre athlete, mathematically proportioned and yet appealing in some queer way to the emotions: the Diadumenus of Polyclitus, for instance. For all their power there is something a little starved about them both.

A very much smaller matter is an occasional lapse in style. The 'tame villatic Fowl' is often cited. The following lines are curiously uncouth, and particularly evident in their uncouthness as being almost the last in the play:

> Oft he seems to hide his face,
> But unexpectedly returns
> And to his faithful Champion hath in place
> Bore witness gloriously; whence *Gaza* mourns
> And all that band them to resist
> His uncontroulable intent.[1]

Worst of all is the opening of one of Dalila's speeches:

> Yet hear me *Samson;* not that I endeavour
> To lessen or extenuate my offence,
> But that on th' other side if it be weigh'd

1. 1749–54.

> By it self, with aggravations not surcharg'd
> Or else with just allowance counterpois'd
> I may, if possible, thy pardon find
> The easier towards me, or thy hatred less.
> First granting, as I do, it was a weakness
> In me, but incident to all our sex,
> Curiosity, inquisitive, importune
> Of secrets, then with like infirmity
> To publish them, both common female faults:
> Was it not weakness also to make known
> For importunity, that is for naught,
> Wherein consisted all thy strength and safety?[1]

No analogy with Euripidean dialectic can justify such inhuman speech in a play. But these lapses are exceptional (Dalila on the whole is not unconvincing), and count for little in comparison with the hardness or ferocity to which I have pointed.

1. 766–80.

CHAPTER THIRTEEN

Samson Agonistes: the Dramatic Motive

SAMSON AGONISTES is a drama of temptation and its conquest.[1] Much of the temptation took place before the action begins.
I do not refer to the actual yielding to Dalila but to the temptation
to blame God for the ensuing disasters of blindness and slavery. The
fact is that Samson is from the very beginning of the play a 'saved'
man: he has only to persist to make sure of his regeneration. The
reader of the opening soliloquy should not be too absorbed by the
pathos of Samson's laments to miss the lines in which he accepts full
responsibility for his deed and admits to the sin of pride:

> Yet stay, let me not rashly call in doubt
> Divine Prediction; what if all foretold
> Had been fulfilld but through mine own default,
> Whom have I to complain of but my self?[2]

and

> But what is strength without a double share
> Of wisdom, vast, unwieldy, burdensom,
> Proudly secure, yet liable to fall
> By weakest suttleties.[3]

The sin of pride is mentioned again. It was the primal cause of
Samson's fall; sensuality was secondary, powerful only when pride
has weakened the moral sense: for this is how Samson later speaks
of his past career:

> when in strength
> All mortals I excell'd, and great in hopes
> With youthful courage and magnanimous thoughts
> Of birth from Heav'n foretold and high exploits,
> Full of divine instinct, after some proof
> Of acts indeed heroic, far beyond
> The Sons of *Anac*, famous now and blaz'd,
> Fearless of danger, like a petty God
> I walk'd about admir'd of all and dreaded
> On hostile ground, none daring my affront.

---

1. See J. H. Hanford, 'The Temptation Motive in Milton', in *Studies in Philology*,
1918, especially pp. 190–1.
2. 43–6.   3. 53–6.

> Then swoll'n with pride into the snare I fell
> Of fair fallacious looks, venereal trains,
> Softn'd with pleasure and voluptuous life.[1]

Any temptation to pride, to putting the blame on God, has been thoroughly overcome, before the action begins. Milton keeps the spirit as well as the letter of Greek tragedy in beginning the play at so late a stage of the story.

The first temptation Samson undergoes in the play is the very opposite to pride. He bewails to the Chorus his folly in telling his secret to Dalila, and is naturally met with the answer that perhaps it was not too wise for him to marry outside his own nation. Samson replies that he married his first wife at the prompting of God, even though he had no similar reason for marrying Dalila. The Chorus is sceptical and remarks (240):

> Yet *Israel* still serves with all his Sons.

But Samson will not be driven from his position. He will not yield so far to self-abasement as to lose his intellectual integrity. He knows he committed a sin in yielding to Dalila, but that is no reason why he should mistrust the earlier promptings of God. He admits that he deserves his afflictions for this yielding, but he is clear-headed enough to refuse to think himself punished for his country's servitude, the cause of which is not his own acts but his countrymen's inertia.

> Had *Judah* that day join'd, or one whole Tribe,
> They had by this possess'd the Towers of *Gath*,
> And lorded over them whom now they serve.[2]

Samson has not only humility but reasonableness and self-knowledge. Moreover, by a skilful dramatic touch, he unconsciously reveals great latent energy in his reply to the Chorus's incredulity, an energy which prepares us for his subsequent revival.

> Mean while the men of *Judah* to prevent
> The harrass of thir Land, beset me round;
> I willingly on some conditions came
> Into thir hands, and they as gladly yield me
> To the uncircumcis'd a welcom prey,
> Bound with two cords; but cords to me were threds
> Toucht with the flame: on thir whole Host I flew
> Unarm'd, and with a trivial weapon fell'd
> Thir choicest youth; they only liv'd who fled.[3]

1. 522-34.   2. 265-7.   3. 256-64.

The Chorus is impressed and admits that Samson may after all have been right (293–325).

With the entrance of Manoa the temptation to blaspheme God is added. Manoa is a well-drawn character: the rather weak and affectionate father of a stronger son. Milton may well have had his own father in mind. Manoa had always been opposed to his son's marrying into the Philistines, and now he cannot restrain himself from saying 'I told you so':

> I cannot praise thy Marriage choises, Son,
> Rather approv'd them not; but thou didst plead
> Divine impulsion.[1]

Nor can he refrain from rubbing it into Samson that his situation is even worse than had been supposed, announcing with a certain satisfaction that Samson will have to appear at the feast of Dagon and glorify that idol by his shame. Having depressed his son thoroughly, he hopes to make more important his offers of mediation with the Philistine lords. Finally, when he has succeeded in depressing Samson beyond his expectations, he grows a little alarmed, tries to comfort him, and hurries off to see about the ransom:

> Believe not these suggestions which proceed
> From anguish of the mind and humours black,
> That mingle with thy fancy. I however
> Must not omit a Fathers timely care
> To prosecute the means of thy deliverance
> By ransom or how else: mean while be calm,
> And healing words from these thy friends admit.[2]

But to return to the temptation to which Manoa subjects Samson. First he suggests that God was to blame: God should not (like the gods of Greece, Milton may have been thinking) have given so double-edged an answer to his prayers for a son. Even for the sake of consistency God ought not to have abased his chosen warrior:

> Alas methinks whom God hath chosen once
> To worthiest deeds, if he through frailty err,
> He should not so o'rewhelm, and as a thrall
> Subject him to so foul indignities,
> Be it but for honours sake of former deeds.[3]

To this temptation Samson is proof: he is perfectly convinced that he has only himself to blame. But the mention of the Philistines'

1. 420–2.   2. 599–605.   3. 368–72.

triumph and the feast to Dagon and the possibility of surviving to a useless old age (as he might if ransomed) summon up what must have been the hardest of all temptations: that of loss of intellectual integrity in unreasoning despair. He resists, keeps a hold on his reason, but falls into a dejection of spirit which comes out in lines of the highest beauty. This is his final answer to Manoa's offer to obtain his ransom:

> Here rather let me drudge and earn my bread,
> Till vermin or the draff of servil food
> Consume me, and oft-invocated death
> Hast'n the welcom end of all my pains.[1]

And to Manoa's hopes for a miraculous recovery of sight:

> All otherwise to me my thoughts portend,
> That these dark orbs no more shall treat with light,
> Nor th'other light of life continue long,
> But yield to double darkness nigh at hand:
> So much I feel my genial spirits droop,
> My hopes all flat, nature within me seems
> In all her functions weary of herself;
> My race of glory run, and race of shame,
> And I shall shortly be with them that rest.[2]

And the lyric lament into which Samson breaks is followed by the bewildered questionings of the Chorus concerning the sufferings of man.

The bright picture of Dalila in her finery breaks effectively into the gloom. She comes with a double dramatic function: to tempt, but more lightly than Manoa: and to rouse Samson from his dejection. She does the second immediately. When the Chorus announces her arrival, we feel him wince and start sweating, as he says (725):

> My Wife, my Traytress, let her not come near me.

The temptations Dalila brings are of mere unreasoning surrender to the blandishments of a pretty woman, luxury, and lust. She argues and excuses herself in order to display her charms and overwhelm Samson's judgment. Samson counters with more vigour and cogency than Dalila has succeeded in conveying charm. Then she offers him comparative luxury: the comforts of a home in exchange for the prison. All she does is to rouse his spirit. She has provided the

1. 573–6.   2. 590–8.

best possible tonic for his misery; for he realizes that to be looked
after by Dalila would be a worse fate than his present. He has now
some fragments of mental liberty: dependent on her he would have
none. And he cries out:

> This Gaol I count the house of Liberty
> To thine whose doors my feet shall never enter.[1]

Finally she would touch his hand, plainly to arouse physical passion,
whose force in himself Samson betrays by his sudden fury; but he
gives it no possible chance. Dalila leaves Samson with his nerves on
edge but roused. As a person Dalila is credible: a fine woman impelled by cruelty and curiosity to visit Samson. A good touch is
the hint that the finery in which she appears was bought with the
gold she received for betraying her husband. Her power is conveyed by Samson's intense resolution to counter every plea abruptly
and finally: he cannot afford the slightest initial hesitation. Her
beauty is conveyed not only by the Chorus's description of her as
she enters but by their reverie after she has left. Ignoring Samson's
valedictory curses, they say:

> Yet beauty, though injurious, hath strange power,
> After offence returning, to regain
> Love once possest, nor can be easily
> Repuls't, without much inward passion felt
> And secret sting of amorous remorse.[2]

They recall Homer's old men speaking of Helen.

Harapha's function (and what remains of the action) needs little
comment. Samson has resisted all temptations: and indeed his
regeneration has already begun. But now he needs a less hard task,
by successfully dealing with which he can gain confidence without
exhaustion. Harapha is easy game, and Samson's spirit rises when he
has routed him. His despair has been conquered and he believes
that God may yet pardon and employ him. But he is quite exempt
from pride in all his defiance of Harapha. He is truly regenerate.
And this true regeneration is made plain during the rest of the play.
For instance, Samson speaks to the Philistine officer of the 'internal
peace' (1334), to which presumably he has now attained. And,
most notable instance of all, in his last great act he lets the Philistine
lords know that he is a man who acts with intellectual control. The
messenger tells how Samson

1. 949–50.   2. 1003–7.

At last with head erect thus cryed aloud,
Hitherto, Lords, what your commands impos'd
I have perform'd, as reason was, obeying.[1]

Who but Milton in English literature could have slipped in this 'as reason was' at the very height of excitement?

There is a dramatic improbability about Samson's final regeneration. His sudden resolution, due to an inner prompting, to obey after all the lords' summons is too abrupt to be convincing: it seems to be taken too lightly.

There is effective irony near the end of the play. Manoa is full of hope about ransoming Samson at the very moment when Samson's death is at hand, and the Chorus comment on the mad desire of the Philistines to invoke their own destruction in the person of Samson.

This use of irony suggests the analogy of Greek tragedy, an analogy which, though often made, has not been exhausted. It may be conveniently approached through Milton's treatment of Aristotle. How seriously and intelligently Milton had studied him may be seen by his use in *Samson* of *peripeteia* or at least of that device as interpreted in a certain way. F. L. Lucas[2] has revived Vahlen's interpretation and, I hope, given it the vitality it deserves. He points out that Aristotle[3] himself has given a perfectly lucid explanation, ignored by most commentators. One of Aristotle's examples of *peripeteia* is from the *Oedipus Rex,* where 'the messenger comes to cheer Oedipus and free him from his alarms about his mother, but by revealing who he is, he produces the opposite effect'. A *peripeteia* happens, not when there is a mere change of fortune, but when an intention or action brings about the opposite of what was meant. Now Milton made *Samson Agonistes* answer so closely to this interpretation of *peripeteia* that I believe it was his own interpretation too and that he chose to make his action depend on *peripeteia* in order to range his play under the heading of 'complex', preferred by Aristotle to the simple form. For by 'complex' Aristotle[4] tells us he means 'with *peripeteia* and *anagnorisis*'. The essence of the plot in *Samson* is that nearly all the actions should lead whither they had not seemed to lead. Jebb pointed out how everything in the plot narrows Samson's prospects into greater and greater chance of ignominy: Samson always seems to choose the course that will exaggerate his misery.

1. 1639-41.
2. *Classical Review*, Aug.-Sept. 1923; *Tragedy*, 91–105.
3. *Poetics*, xi.   4. ibid., x.

Samson, crushed by despair and shame for himself and Israel, has rejected
the proposal of Manoah to treat for his release; has made the intercession
of Dalila impossible; finally, by bitter defiance of Harapha, has prepared
for himself some crowning ignominy at the hands of his captors.[1]

This is a partial account of the action, taking no heed of Samson's
revival, but it is true as far as it goes. The *peripeteia* consists in this
choice of apparent ignominy inevitably leading to triumph. The
same *peripeteia* is applied to the Philistines in a choric passage,
already noted by Hanford as having references to the other Greek
ideas of *Ate* and *Hubris*:

> While thir hearts were jocund and sublime,
> Drunk with Idolatry, drunk with Wine,
> And fat regorg'd of Bulls and Goats,
> Chaunting thir Idol, and preferring
> Before our living Dread who dwells
> In *Silo* his bright Sanctuary:
> Among them he a spirit of phrenzie sent,
> Who hurt thir minds,
> And urg'd them on with mad desire
> To call in hast for thir destroyer;
> They only set on sport and play
> Unweetingly importun'd
> Thir own destruction to come speedy upon them.[2]

The *peripeteia* consisted in the fact that by calling Samson in to make
them sport they were really calling him in to destroy them. As to
anagnorisis, or recognition of the *peripeteia*, there is a partial recognition in Samson's mind when he feels that he is tending to something
great and mysterious, while the actual recognition must be supposed
as taking place after Samson has addressed the Philistines or in the
brief interval between his tugging at the pillars and the catastrophe.
The broader recognition by the audience is brought about by the
messenger's speech.

It is interesting to have found that not only in the matter of
katharsis, as is well known, but in that of *peripeteia*, Milton was more
enlightened than some modern commentators.

There are two very curious reminiscences of the Elizabethan
literature near the end: the lines,

> Abortive as the first-born bloom of spring
> Nipt with the lagging rear of winters frost,[3]

1. Sir Richard Jebb, '*Samson Agonistes* and the Hellenic Drama', in *Proceedings
of the British Academy*, 1907–8, 342.

2. 1669–81.   3. 1576–7.

are much more like early Shakespeare than the latest Milton. And when the Chorus speaks of the Phoenix they fall (whether with voluntary or involuntary reminiscence I do not know) into the metre and style of *The Phoenix and the Turtle*:

> Like that self-begott'n bird
> In the *Arabian* woods embost,
> That no second knows nor third,
> And lay e're while a Holocaust.[1]

1. 1699–1702. Noted also by Middleton Murry at the end of his *Problem of Style* (147–8).

CHAPTER FOURTEEN

Samson Agonistes: its Relation to Milton's Experience and Thought

WHATEVER the value of *Samson Agonistes* as a work of art, there can be no doubt of its value in illuminating Milton's life and thought. It seems to refer to the main emotional crises in his life and to epitomize the permanent elements of his thought. Granting that Milton is a remarkable enough person to be remembered, *Samson Agonistes* deserves preservation as a personal document.

Quite enough has been made of the personal references, and there is of course the ever-present danger of seeing them when they are not there. But they are usually, and I think mistakenly, confined to Milton's case after the Restoration. Their scope seems to me to be wider and to include the earlier crises in his life. Take the first crisis, the failure of his marriage with Mary Powell. There is small analogy indeed between her and Dalila,[1] but between Samson's and Milton's wounded pride, the consciousness that they have made themselves ridiculous, there is a close one indeed. Take this passage:

> tell me Friends,
> Am I not sung and proverbd for a Fool
> In every street, do they not say, how well
> Are come upon him his deserts? yet why?
> Immeasurable strength they might behold
> In me, of wisdom nothing more then mean;
> This with the other should, at least, have paird,
> These two proportiond ill drove me transverse.[2]

These words would suit Milton's thought in 1643 to perfection. 'Immeasurable strength' would be his own estimate of himself the smiter of Bishops, but lack of wisdom in allowing his senses to prevail over his reason he must have admitted in thinking of his foolish

---

1. There is one place, however, in which he may have been thinking of Mary's sin in preferring her Cavalier parents to his Puritan self (882–6):
> Why then
> Didst thou at first receive me for thy husband?
> Then, as since then, thy countries foe profest:
> Being once a wife, for me thou wast to leave
> Parents and countrey.

2. 202–9.

marriage. To a passage,[1] already quoted, which seemed to refer to the first shock of blindness I will add another which may well do the same. In fact, one may guess that all the bitterest agony must have been felt at that time, rather than when Milton had found that he was still able to write. The true analogy of Samson, a prisoner and helpless, is with Milton when in his first blindness he believed himself to be helpless too.

> Since light so necessary is to life,
> And almost life itself, if it be true
> That light is in the Soul,
> She all in every part; why was the sight
> To such a tender ball as th' eye confin'd?
> So obvious and so easie to be quench't,
> And not as feeling through all parts diffus'd,
> That she might look at will through every pore?
> Then had I not been thus exil'd from light;
> As in the land of darkness yet in light,
> To live a life half dead, a living death,
> And buried.[2]

By referring what personal application there is in the above passages to the life of Milton before the Restoration, I do not wish to say that many do not refer to his later feelings; or to imply that the Restoration was not the greatest shock of his life. The great Chorus beginning 'Many are the sayings of the wise' (652) is filled with the despairing questions Milton must have put when his political hopes were disappointed. He cannot understand the ways of God towards his saints,

> such as thou hast solemnly elected,
> With gifts and graces eminently adorn'd
> To some great work, thy glory,
> And peoples safety, which in part they effect:
> Yet toward these thus dignifi'd, thou oft
> Amidst thir highth of noon,
> Changest thy countenance, and thy hand with no regard
> Of highest favours past
> From thee on them, or them to thee of service.[3]

Such must have been Milton's turbulent thoughts at the Restoration, thoughts which caused him to distrust the value of action and to turn all his efforts of courage to attain an inner peace of mind. Another passage directly expresses the same mood: the passage where Samson goes so far as to rejoice that he is out of the struggle,

1. See pp. 159–60 above.   3. 90–101.   3. 678–86.

which is now between God and Dagon alone.

> This only hope relieves me, that the strife
> With me hath end; all the contest is now
> 'Twixt God and *Dagon*.[1]

Such self-abasement could only have been a passing mood in
Milton, but I believe he experienced it.

Turning from Milton's special experiences to his general attitude
to life, I should like to reinforce with an illustration the reconcile-
ment of action with the inner paradise, to express which may have
been his main motive in writing. When Samson has defied Harapha
and once again feels himself capable of doing, the Chorus sings the
glory of the 'plain Heroic magnitude of mind' leading to action, but
not without mentioning the other state when action is denied and
every saint must be his own deliverer merely. It is a passage which
not only sums up the main thought of the play, but which gives in
brief the thought that was most characteristic of Milton's whole
mind. It is therefore quoted in full.

> Oh how comely it is and how reviving
> To the Spirits of just men long opprest!
> When God into the hands of thir deliverer
> Puts invincible might
> To quell the mighty of the Earth, th' oppressour,
> The brute and boist'rous force of violent men
> Hardy and industrious to support
> Tyrannic power, but raging to pursue
> The righteous and all such as honour Truth;
> He all thir Ammunition
> And feats of War defeats
> With plain Heroic magnitude of mind
> And celestial vigour arm'd,
> Thir Armories and Magazins contemns,
> Renders them useless, while
> With winged expedition
> Swift as the lightning glance he executes
> His errand on the wicked, who surpris'd
> Lose thir defence distracted and amaz'd.
> But patience is more oft the exercise
> Of Saints, the trial of thir fortitude,
> Making them each his own Deliverer,
> And Victor over all
> That tyrannie or fortune can inflict,
> Either of these is in thy lot,

1. 460-2.

> *Samson,* with might endu'd
> Above the Sons of men; but sight bereav'd
> May chance to number thee with those
> Whom Patience finally must crown.[1]

There remains the question of the beliefs Milton held when he wrote *Samson Agonistes.* Excellent in many ways as is Saurat's analysis[2] of them, I cannot but think that he carries the argument *ex silentio* too far. Because there is no mention of Christ or vicarious atonement, Saurat would have it that Milton has ceased to believe in them. I see no reason for going that far, unless by belief Saurat means something more than professed belief, a genuine influence on action. But already in the *De Doctrina Christiana* Milton had showed that he had little sympathy with vicarious atonement, and I cannot see that in *Samson* there is the slightest proof that he has gone any further. His latest pamphlet, *Of True Religion,* written after *Samson,* suggests no change from the *De Doctrina.* But if it is dangerous to argue from what Milton omits, it is reasonable to suppose that what doctrines he does utter he believes in profoundly; even that he believes in them more profoundly than any he has failed to utter. Let me therefore try to pick out the chief doctrines from *Samson Agonistes,* on the supposition that they were the doctrines that mainly occupied Milton's thoughts in the last years of his life.

To begin with, Milton still believes in the Fall: but, as Saurat points out, without any suggestion of original sin. Samson's fall seems to typify a human tendency to fall during life from the estate in which men find themselves, a natural perverseness. As in dealing with *Paradise Lost,* so here Saurat unduly narrows the nature of the Fall to sensuality and the more general triumph of passion over reason. On the contrary, Samson's fall, as pointed out above, was primarily due to pride, only secondarily to sensuality; while the motive which bulked so largely in *Paradise Lost,* mental slackness, is found in *Samson Agonistes* too. Samson, the strenuous man, is 'fearless of danger' (529), that is, in the context, criminally slack and negligent, before his fall. But it is of the enslaved Israelites that this quality is the special sin. It was their slackness, their refusal to see the issue and seize their chance, that caused their slavery.

> *Chorus.* Yet *Israel* still serves with all his Sons.
> *Samson.* That fault I take not on me, but transfer
> On *Israel's* Governours, and Heads of Tribes,
> Who seeing those great acts which God had done

1. 1268–96. 2. op. cit., 197–203.

Singly by me against their Conquerours
Acknowledg'd not, or not at all consider'd
Deliverance offerd: I on th' other side
Us'd no ambition to commend my deeds,
The deeds themselves, though mute, spoke loud the dooer;
But they persisted deaf, and would not seem
To count them things worth notice.[1]

And later in the same speech, after describing his slaughter of the
Philistines when he had broken the cords that bound him, he says:

Had *Judah* that day join'd, or one whole Tribe,
They had by this possess'd the Towers of *Gath*,
And lorded over them whom now they serve.[2]

It would almost seem as if Milton had come to believe in two forms
of Fall: one for the 'common rout', the other for the potential elect.
The 'common rout' have minds so trivial that their reason is easily
enslaved by the passions: the potential elect cannot be accused of
mental triviality, it is the sheer strength of their passions that may
lead them astray; sensuality would be one of those powerful,
deluding passions.

If Milton believes in the Fall, he still believes in regeneration, and
from Samson's case we may learn the process through which regeneration was effected. Humility, intellectual clarity, and self-
knowledge are the means. Man must recognize his own responsibility
for his fall, he must not put the blame on Fate, he must have a clear
intellectual grasp of his own weaknesses: then he may get help from
outside. Regeneration consists of an inner peace, which may or may
not find issue in action. By making pride (*hubris*) that which precedes
disaster, and self-knowledge the means of averting it, Milton is one
with the Greeks. I do not think he was merely inserting Greek
habits of thought because he had chosen the Greek form of tragedy.
He has a true kinship, and one which takes us back to the pamphlet
which shows most fully the influence of Greek thought: *Reason of
Church Government*.[3] There, it is true, the emphasis was on self-
reverence: know to what a high state mankind is called, and you
will have a proper self-confidence. In *Samson* the lesson is: know and
admit your utmost fault, and you may find peace and regeneration.
But the need of self-knowledge is common to both. It is admirable
in Milton that nothing should have shaken his belief in intellectual
integrity.

1. 240–50.   2. 265–7.   3. See p. 115 above.

Corresponding to Milton's renewed belief in action is a change in his belief in God. As I have pointed out, in the *De Doctrina Christiana* he advanced two main arguments for the existence of God: one, the beauty of the order of the world; the other, man's inward conviction. It seems too that in the later books of *Paradise Lost* he came to distrust the first, but never abandoned the second. In *Samson Agonistes* he seems to revert unconsciously as well as consciously (for he had never admitted his distrust) to his original position. He has brought himself once more to believe that the world of experience may after all have a beauty of order; that there is yet hope for its betterment.

> All is best, though we oft doubt,
> What th' unsearchable dispose
> Of highest wisdom brings about,
> And ever best found in the close.
> Oft he seems to hide his face,
> But unexpectedly returns.[1]

The change was as it should be. Milton had a natural belief in an evolutionary theory of man, and he was maiming his nature as long as he was forced to reject it. I do not mean that Milton had become a pronounced optimist or that 'simple faith' had displaced the Stoicism which was so plainly his support at the time when he wrote the last books of *Paradise Lost*. He had troubles enough, and he still needed his Stoicism as well as any sparks of renascent hope, to enable him to support them. As Hanford well points out, the Stoic and Christian strains are found in *Samson Agonistes* side by side.

There remains an irreducible element in the midst of Milton's faith – a sense as keen as Shakespeare's of the reality of suffering which neither the assurance of God's special favours to himself nor his resolute insistence on the final triumph of righteousness can blot out. The antique strain in Milton's experience and thought stands side by side with the Christian, and the two alternate or combine in their domination of his artistic moods. It is vain that he repudiates stoicism as a futile refuge and a false philosophy; he is betrayed by the vehemence of his declarations against it, and he instinctively adopts its weapons.[2]

Milton's belief in the inward standard of conduct, derived from God direct, remains very strong. Samson obeys without hesitation the 'rouzing motions' in him certain they are sent by God. The Chorus too admits, in accordance with Milton's teaching in the

1. 1745–50.   2. Hanford, op. cit., 183.

divorce pamphlets and in the *De Doctrina Christiana,* that the inner prompting overrides all other authority. God, says the Chorus,

> made our Laws to bind us, not himself,
> And hath full right to exempt
> Whom so it pleases him by choice
> From National obstriction, without taint
> Of sin, or legal debt;
> For with his own Laws he can best dispence.
>   He would not else who never wanted means,
> Nor in respect of the enemy just cause
> To set his people free,
> Have prompted this Heroic *Nazarite,*
> Against his vow of strictest purity,
> To seek in marriage that fallacious Bride,
> Unclean, unchaste.[1]

And he makes the inner prompting the excuse of an exceedingly dangerous political doctrine, the right of the individual to rebel. To Harapha's accusation of being a league-breaker and a private rebel, Samson replies:

> I was no private but a person rais'd
> With strength sufficient and command from Heav'n
> To free my Countrey; if their servile minds
> Me their Deliverer sent would not receive,
> But to thir Masters gave me up for nought,
> Th' unworthier they.[2]

It is good that Milton survived till he was able to give concrete proof of his renewed belief in action by engaging once more in controversy. In 1673 he wrote *Of True Religion, Heresy, Schism, Toleration, and what best means may be used against the Growth of Popery,* directed against the new Declaration of Indulgence, the object of which had been to emancipate not so much the Non-Conformists as the Roman Catholics. At last, after thirteen years, here was a subject on which he could safely write, and he joins his own voice to the chorus of Protestants who wished to see the Roman worship in England suppressed. There is nothing very remarkable about the pamphlet. As we should expect, Milton advocates the widest toleration among Protestants while wishing to suppress the Catholics. It is characteristic of his sense of international courtesy that he should expressly exempt from his proposals 'foreigners, privileged by the

1. 309–21.   2. 1211–16.

law of nations'.[1] He advocates the intense private study of the Scriptures: evidence that he has not departed far from the *De Doctrina Christiana*. And he dares to end with a reproof of the evil ways of his countrymen:

> The last means to avoid popery is, to amend our lives. It is a general complaint, that this nation of late years is grown more numerously and excessively vicious than heretofore; pride, luxury, drunkenness, whoredom, cursing, swearing, bold and open atheism everywhere abounding: where these grow, no wonder if popery also grow apace.[2]

It is both pathetic, and a pleasing sign of Milton's optimism, that he believed to the last that some good might be done by scolding. In sum it is not the pamphlet but his writing it that matters.

1. Bohn, ii. 514.   2. ibid., 518.

EPILOGUE
Milton To-day

FOR two hundred years Milton has been allowed, in spite of suppressed murmurs, a secure position on an exalted pedestal. It is extremely salutary that the present age should have begun questioning his right to such an eminence. If this right is allowed, it will be based henceforth on a more reasonable and less superstitious appreciation; if it is disallowed, the sooner Milton is put on his proper level the better.

The more obvious and popular attack, to which I will revert, accuses his professed doctrines of being antiquated. More important are the attacks, covert as yet or half-formulated, that are connected with the revived taste for the Metaphysical poets and the growing reaction against the romantic verse of the nineteenth century. Milton made a strong appeal both to the Augustan and the Romantic ages. His sense of form, his vision of life as the struggle between reason and passion, were perfectly congenial to the eighteenth century; while his belief in a qualified perfectibility, in the virtue of action, was in full accord with the temper of the Romantics. But it has now become clear that because an author has appealed very strongly to ages as different as the Augustan and Romantic ages in England he does not necessarily command a variety sufficient to satisfy the requirements of every possible epoch. Both ages are now accused of a common deficiency, and Milton has been included in, has indeed been made partly responsible for, the accusation.

The accusation belongs to a wider theory; and this theory, initiated by T. S. Eliot (if by any one man), is perhaps the most suggestive and influential that has been recently propounded in the sphere of English literary history. If I attempt partially to dissociate Milton from it, I do not wish to imply that I necessarily impugn its general validity. Eliot had made his statement in his *Homage to John Dryden* (p. 30):

The poets of the seventeenth century, the successors of the dramatists of the sixteenth, possessed a mechanism of sensibility which could devour any kind of experience. They are simple, artificial, difficult, or fantastic as their predecessors were; no less nor more than Dante, Guido Cavalcanti, Guinizelli, or Cino. In the seventeenth century a dissociation of sensibility set in, from which we have never recovered; and this dissociation, as is natural, was due to the influence of the two most powerful poets of the century, Milton and Dryden. Each of these men performed certain poetic functions so magnificently well that the magnitude of the effect concealed the absence of others. The language went on and in some respects improved; the best verse of Collins, Gray, Johnson, and even Goldsmith satisfies some of our fastidious demands better than that of Donne or Marvell or King. But while the language became more refined, the feeling became more crude. The feeling, the sensibility, expressed in the 'Country Churchyard '(to say nothing of Tennyson and Browning) is cruder than that in the 'Coy Mistress'.

The second effect of the influence of Milton and Dryden followed from the first, and was therefore slow in manifestation. The sentimental age began early in the eighteenth century, and continued. The poets revolted against the ratiocinative, the descriptive; they thought and felt by fits, unbalanced; they reflected. In one or two passages of Shelley's 'Triumph of Life', in the second 'Hyperion', there are traces of a struggle toward unification of sensibility. But Keats and Shelley died, and Tennyson and Browning ruminated.

Speaking only of what in this passage concerns Milton, I would say that there is here a mixture of truth and falsehood. Some sort of dissociation of sensibility in Milton, not necessarily undesirable, has to be admitted; but that he was responsible for any such dissociation in others (at least till this general dissociation had inevitably set in) is untrue.

When Milton began writing, the chief poetic vitality was with the lyric poets of the school of Donne, not with the dramatists or with the writers of narrative. And it is certainly true that the great merit of these lyric poets was their varied sensibility. Donne was able to apply his sensibility to any object or event that came his way: a storm, a flea, a flower. Or, to mention his prose, has any writer relished an illness so keenly as he does that described in his *Devotions upon Emergent Occasions*? Milton was of a different nature: his experiences must be of a certain sort before he would allow his sensibility to deal with them. His description of himself watching the 'young divines' at Cambridge acting in comedies is only too true a self-revelation. He sees them

unboning their clergy limbs to all the antic and dishonest gestures of Trinculoes, buffoons, and bawds; prostituting the shame of that ministry, which either they had, or were nigh having, to the eyes of courtiers and court ladies, with their grooms and mademoiselles. There, while they acted and overacted, among other young scholars, I was a spectator; they thought themselves gallant men, and I thought them fools; they made sport, and I laughed; they mispronounced, and I misliked; and, to make up the atticism, they were out, and I hissed.[1]

Milton allowed but a portion of his sensibility to deal with this experience of play-watching: he had hardly touched its emotional potentialities. Take too the attitudes of Milton and Donne to the scholastic philosophy. Milton, as was pointed out early in this book, hated it because it seemed to him to lead nowhere; just as he hated the unrelated fact generally. But for Donne there was no such thing as the unrelated fact, and the scholastic philosophy did not need to lead anywhere: it was sufficiently exciting in itself apart from results.

Compared with Donne, then, Milton allowed himself a less varied and adaptable sensibility. But few poets can indulge their full sensibility without sacrificing strength or order to that indulgence. Shakespeare sacrificed comparatively little to his versatility: he could digest his experience. But Donne, although he devours experience, cannot always digest it. He suffers from surfeits: his mind rejects the strange mixtures of food to which he submits it. He does not really know what he wants: or rather he wants everything and cannot harmonize his wants. Hence, with all the eagerness of sensibility, the curious stagnancy of some of Donne's poems. His mind goes in circles, turning back upon itself. The prodigious power of the two *Anniversaries* does much to stir up the mind, little to order it. I do not mean to deny Donne's successes, but their relative frequency is less than those who know him chiefly from Professor Grierson's *Metaphysical Lyrics and Poems of the Seventeenth Century* are aware. Milton's mind, on the contrary, presses forward to some end. He will have none of what does not subserve his purposes. Power, order, stability must come first, and sensibility be sacrificed if need be. Thus we saw how Milton deliberately narrowed, as he grew older, the comparatively varied sensibility shown in the *Nativity Ode*. And although he would have been a greater poet had he united his strength with a wider variety of feeling, it is not at all certain that he was wrong, in view of his achievement, in limiting himself as he did; we must be circumspect in blaming him. He did not have it in him to be a Homer or a Shakespeare, but by concentrating the most powerful and individual elements of his mind he may have had a better chance of reaching the plane of an Aeschylus.

Milton's temperamental antagonism to Donne, the only metaphysical poet early enough in date and of sufficient stature to be likely to attract his attention, will help to excuse, if it needs excusing, his breach with the most vital literary tradition of his age. But,

1. *Apology for Smectymnuus*, Bohn, iii. 114–15.

really, to speak of a 'breach' with contemporary tradition is incorrect. Milton was not concerned with continuing any living tradition. Spenser, the one English poet to whom he professed allegiance, was already archaic, a classic. Virgil or Tasso were to him as alive as Jonson or Donne, and more relevant. Not only did he accept a personal necessity by ignoring the Metaphysicals: there was no revolt against a tradition, because there had been no allegiance. Though deeply susceptible to the political events, to the phases of thought of his age, in literary tradition Milton chose and rightly chose to stand apart: he was a big enough man to fashion his own literary tools.

It follows (and this brings me to the second point raised by Eliot's statement) that Milton was not responsible for the dissociation of sensibility that took place during the seventeenth century. Owing no allegiance, not seeking to influence any writers or to found any poetic school, he cannot be held responsible for the turn that poetry may have happened to take. Nor, in actual fact, did he have any appreciable effect on the poetry of the last half of the seventeenth century. Eliot[1] speaks of the Chinese Wall of Milton's blank verse, but it must have been an ineffective wall, for *Venice Preserved*, *All for Love*, and similar plays in blank verse were not confined by it; they owe nothing to Milton's versification. And if the eighteenth century was insensate enough to begin imitating a verse so isolated and personal as that of *Paradise Lost* instead of the more imitable medium of Otway and Dryden, can Milton be held responsible? But the main point is that the old metaphysical synthesis of divers sensibilities had broken up long before Milton was the object of imitation, or at all a powerful literary influence. He did not affect the issue. Nor indeed could any isolated personality, or group of writers even, have affected the issue. The demand for simplicity at the end of the seventeenth century was not merely a literary demand; it was too general to be resisted. The country wished for this dissociation of sensibility, and to attach the blame to any single author is to see things in false perspective.

But there is another implication in Eliot's statement that cannot be passed by. The poets who succeeded the Metaphysicals 'thought and felt by fits, unbalanced; they reflected'. I do not know whether Eliot means to accuse Milton of the same fault, but such an accusation would not be quite groundless; and it follows from the narrowing of sensibility already admitted. Milton was a thinker, but he was not specially sensitive to thought for its own sake. He thought, in order

1. In *The Sacred Wood* (2nd edition), 87.

to fit himself for action. And this lack of interest in thought comes out in his poetry. He is deeply concerned with the doctrine of free will: he must establish the doctrine in order to make life worth living. But his interest in the actual argument is lukewarm. Hence at once the passion and the dullness of the passages that concern this theme. Let it be admitted that Milton would have been a better poet if he could have given those passages a double not a single animation. Again this lack of interest in thought tempts him sometimes to a ruminative kind of beauty, a type of poetry in which the unconscious element is dangerously strong:

> Untwisting all the chains that ty
> The hidden soul of harmony.
> That *Orpheus* self may heave his head
> From golden slumber on a bed
> Of heapt *Elysian* flowres, and hear
> Such strains as would have won the ear
> Of *Pluto*, to have quite set free
> His half regain'd *Eurydice*.

There is the hint in this passage, for all its enchantment, of the day-dream and other psychologists' bugbears: a faint suspicion of the dreadful unconsciousness of *Epipsychidion*. It is a passage which those for whom the word 'romantic' has an evil significance might readily fasten on. But is it realized what an astonishing reaction Milton exhibited against this type of writing, how thoroughly he outgrew it? Present to some extent in the first half of *Paradise Lost,* it diminishes in the second half, and disappears altogether in *Paradise Regained* and *Samson Agonistes.* Milton would not rest satisfied till he had purged himself of every weakness. Less picturesque than his early poems and *Paradise Lost,* his two last poems show a new and sounder fusion of thought and emotion.

If Milton was guilty of a certain narrowing of sensibility, he was free from the narrowing of the scope of literature that has been apt to beset it since the advent of literary professionalism. If he narrowed the scope of his poems, it was because he had narrowed the scope of his own life. This is a very different thing from what the eighteenth century did, namely to exclude from poetry things which from life they could not possibly exclude. Milton's poetry lacks wit, because he was not witty by nature; and tenderness, because he thought fit to suppress that quality in himself: but Pope suppressed or disguised his own delicate sensibilities, because the conventions of the narrow literary circle to which he belonged had excluded them from poetry.

Indeed Milton's whole theory of the nature of literature is utterly opposed to the 'professional' ideas that arose in the Augustan ages and have continued to exercise considerable power ever since. Milton draws no line between literature and life: literature is simply a species of action, dependent primarily for its virtue on the character and motives of the person who creates it. Milton believed that

he who would not be frustrate of his hope to write well hereafter in laudable things, ought himself to be a true poem; that is, a composition and pattern of the best and honourablest things; not presuming to sing high praises of heroic men, or famous cities, unless he have in himself the experience and the practice of all that which is praiseworthy.[1]

Similarly with the historian:

My opinion is as follows: one who would be a worthy historian of worthy deeds must possess as noble a spirit and as much practical experience as the hero of the action himself, in order that he may be able to comprehend and measure even the greatest of these actions on equal terms.[2]

And Milton succeeds in living up to his own theory: his life, his prose, his verse are all of a piece.

In this he is in general accord with the Elizabethan dramatists before Fletcher, and strongly contrasted with Spenser. Spenser's *View of the State of Ireland* (too little known as one of the most beautiful and lucid pieces of Elizabethan prose) reveals him as an extremely clear-headed, even hard-headed, practical man. The *Faerie Queene* shows a very different person, a fastidious idealist who makes up for his dissatisfaction with the world as it is, by creating a fairyland better suited to his tastes. True, there is a great deal more than this in the poem, by way of detail; but the above I take to be the significance of the fairy setting, of the enchanted atmosphere of the whole poem. It is something of a shock to realize both from his life and, still more clearly, from the *View of the State of Ireland* how well Spenser knew the way to get on in the world he found so unsatisfactory. There is then in Spenser a divorce between poetry and life. His poetry is high contemplation; his practical life is a separate and inferior function. Once, however, in *Epithalamion*, he unites the two; and that is why this poem has a fullness unique in Spenser. In Milton, on the other hand, there is no separation between contemplation

1. *Apology for Smectymnuus*, Bohn, iii. 117–18. (The Stoic notion – 'It is impossible for anyone to be a good poet, unless he be first of all a good man.' Strabo I. 2, 5).

2. Letter to Henry de Brass. P. B. Tillyard, op. cit., 42.

and practice, between literature and life. A pamphlet like *Reason of Church Government* contains meditation as well as doctrine, *Paradise Lost* contains doctrine as well as meditation. And in his life Milton expresses, as far as was humanly possible, the thoughts he utters in his written works.

If Milton considered literature mainly as a species of action, Dryden considered it as an instrument of culture. Living when he did, after an age when culture had been threatened by fanaticism, Dryden may have been justified. But I fancy that this notion, which becomes associated with the coffee-house, Grub Street, and literary professionalism in general, constituted a narrowing of literature quite as potent as the general dissociation of sensibility. It is possible that the average educated man of the year 1625 had a more varied sensibility than the corresponding man of 1725 or 1825 (at any rate I do not wish to argue the point); but undoubtedly the rise of literary professionalism did a good deal to prevent the whole of what sensibility a man had from getting turned into poetry. Take the case of Gray. His poems and letters together reveal a sensibility less wide perhaps than (for instance) Andrew Marvell's, but pretty considerable; yet how lamentably do his poems fail to express this total sensibility! And the reason was the current ideas about the nature and the limits of poetry. If Gray could have looked on literature with Milton's eyes instead of indulging in a few unimportant verbal borrowings, the result would have been very different.

A considerable reason why Eliot and his associates have reacted against Milton is that they consider him irrelevant to modern poetic production. To Sir Herbert Read, for instance, Milton appears to be among the authors who 'have no immediacy, no impelling influence, no sympathetic power' at the present time; and he omits him almost entirely from his *Phases of English Poetry*. It is of course for the poets to say to what authors they owe the most; and it is probably true that the majority of modern poets find little in Milton to help their production. The fault, however, is not necessarily on Milton's side. Nor is the influence of an author on the poetry of a particular age more than a very partial indication of his value. It does not follow that Marlowe is worthless because Gray and his contemporaries owed to him nothing whatever. There is ever the double tendency in criticism to judge an author in himself (whatever that may mean) and as an influence on current literary production. Pater, with his desire to separate the 'virtue' of an author from its adjuncts, exemplifies the first tendency. Arnold, when he is nervous lest So-and-so should not be a sound model, exemplifies the second. Eliot, in more ways than this the critical Arnold of to-day, is chiefly interested in the second tendency. But the first cannot be ignored. The main literary public does not consist of craft-conscious authors, and the major value of most poets is their use, potential or realized, in the lives of all sorts and conditions of men.

The idea that Milton's theology is outworn and that his views on life have no modern relevance is still very widespread. It is particularly insidious too, because most of those who hold it praise Milton on other grounds, professing to be his admirers. They believe that the sweetness of *Comus,* the descriptions in the early books of *Paradise Lost,* the grandeur of Satan as an isolated figure, more than make up for the fault of theological staleness. But there is no need for this kind of argument: the theology itself may have a sufficient function. The fact is that one cannot separate Milton's theology from his general philosophy and from his attitude to life. If either of these has a modern relevance, the theology as their vehicle has its modern relevance too. Saurat has certainly established the daring nature of Milton's speculations and his fundamental independence of judgment. But I think he goes too far when he claims for Milton high distinction or originality as a thinker. Milton's thought, his intellectual setting, were very similar to those of the Cambridge Platonists. He is no greater as a thinker than Whichcote or Smith, if as great. And if one may reasonably value the Cambridge Platonists rather for their tolerance and the amiability of their natures than for their philosophy, much more may one subordinate Milton's philosophy to his character or reaction to life. And it is Milton's reaction to his experience of life, which, forming the very substance of his great poems, animates the theological framework.

I have tried in the course of this book to point out certain fundamental and simple ideas which, founded on his experience, dominated Milton's mind and which to some extent were symbolized by his theology. It remains here to point out that they are of more than temporary relevance, that they constitute a permanently credible attitude to life. Milton saw humanity free, in a way capable of guiding its fate, and with a certain instinct towards virtue; yet subject to a curious levity of disposition or sloth, which prevented most men from taking advantage of their powers. Passion only too often usurped reason's sway, and some sort of enslavement followed. Yet the possibility of self-mastery, of regeneration, remained; and a few prospered in self-betterment. Generally speaking, the world could be improved almost indefinitely, but in fact use was not made of the great opportunity. Now whether Milton was right or not, at least his notion has nothing specifically to do with the seventeenth century; it is as applicable to-day. His notion of the Fall would for some people fit in perfectly with the spectacle of modern humanity equipped with the mechanical power to obtain decent living for all, in a way desirous of using it, and yet apparently incapable of turning this power to use. Similarly the late war[1] might well be attributed to the laziness of mankind in failing to find an alternative solution of the problems of which war provided a horrible one. The men who fought did not want, the great majority of them, to fight; in a way they need not have fought; but they were the victims of their own original sin of political sloth. Further, Milton's belief, in spite of his disappointments, that man had it in him to become regenerate has obvious analogies with such belief in human progress as has survived the recent world upheaval. Even those who deny the possibility of progress apart from special acts of divine grace would admit that the opposite idea is credible in a modern. Probably the belief in progress has still an enormous vogue, being the main substitute for much vanished faith. Milton then has a plain relevance to-day by his belief, fluctuating, it is true, from extravagant hope to almost total despair and yet persisting to the end, in the power of man to improve his destiny out of his own endowments.

Further, the personal application of Milton's ideas is as fresh as ever it was. It will indeed appeal primarily to those who see life as a struggle, whether against outside things or against certain elements in their own natures. Such people exist in all ages and in most nations. The view is not in the least confined to any theology. By those who seek self-betterment through the conscious exercise of the will there must ever be experienced the round of sin, forgiveness, and regeneration, or, put more baldly, of the sense of failure, renewed resolve, and success; as much by the rationalist who seeks to decide between conflicting appetencies as by the convert to the Salvation Army. Nor is it easy to see how these simple elements in Milton's thought can ever be out of date.

The ideas described above, commonplace enough in themselves, do not make Milton a great poet, but as a basis on which to erect poetry they are of the utmost value. They provide a firmer basis than that possessed by Dryden or Wordsworth, for instance; they correspond to the more comprehensive views of life possessed by Virgil or Homer. For whatever his deficiencies in sensibility, however many of the details he ignored, Milton underwent varied

1. *i.e.* the 1914–18 War.

experiences and did not shrink from any of the major problems of life. It was through personal experience that he wrote:

> No man apprehends what vice is as well as he who is truly virtuous; no man knows hell like him who converses most in heaven.

And the accent of bewilderment that from time to time creeps into the assurance of his verse betrays how sensitively he brooded on the major problems; as in these words which Satan in *Paradise Regained* addresses to Christ:

> Thy Father, who is holy, wise and pure,
> Suffers the Hypocrite or Atheous Priest
> To tread his Sacred Courts, and minister
> About his Altar, handling holy things,
> Praying or vowing.

Dryden (who is nearer Milton in sublimity than most English poets) confines himself pretty well to the idea that culture, based on reason and honest pains, is a good thing. It is the basis of the magnificent fifteenth stanza of *Threnodia Augustalis*, a poem whose nominal subject, a fulsome funeral lament on Charles II, has obscured its underlying nobility.

> A Warlike Prince ascends the Regal State,
> A Prince, long exercis'd by Fate;
> Long may he keep, tho he obtains it late.
> Heroes in Heaven's peculiar Mold are cast,
> They and their Poets are not formed in hast;
> Man was the first in God's design, and Man was
>   made the last.
> False Heroes made by Flattery so,
> Heav'n can strike out, like Sparkles, at a blow;
> But e're a Prince is to Perfection brought
> He costs Omnipotence a second thought.
>   With Toyl and Sweat,
>   With hardning Cold, and forming Heat,
>   The Cyclops did their strokes repeat,
> Before the impenetrable Shield was wrought.
>   It looks as if the Maker wou'd not own
>   The Noble work for his,
> Before 'twas try'd and found a Masterpiece.

There is no finer passage in Dryden, and it marks the limits of his criticism of life. He was chiefly concerned in advancing the craft of literature, in which as an instrument of culture he passionately believed. Milton quite transcends these limits and is, potentially, a poet of greater stature. He has the materials for competing with the very greatest poets.

How far Milton makes use of his materials, with what success he communicates his vision of life, has been discussed in the body of this book. His success was not complete, but I believe sufficient to put him in a rank superior to all English poets except Shakespeare.

This is not, however, the final plea for Milton's greatness as a poet, for the success with which he communicates his vision will fluctuate very greatly from reader to reader. In the last resort Milton's importance is simply that of his own personality. Coleridge has made the best pronouncement on the subject:

> While Shakespeare darts himself forth, and passes into all forms of human character and passion, the one Proteus of the fire and the flood; the other attracts all forms and things to himself, into the unity of his own ideal. All things and modes of action shape themselves anew in the being of Milton; while Shakespeare becomes all things, yet for ever remaining himself.

One of the results of this egotism is that we are apt to feel personally about Milton: he rouses our personal admiration or dislike. You cannot hate Shakespeare, because if you begin, Proteus-like he changes into the form of what you love the best. But Milton in his greater works offers the unchanging front of his colossal personality. Hence such a personal tribute as the following:

> This little book presents my attempt to discharge the 'debt of endless gratitude' that from my youth up I owe to Milton, whose property is to fortify the mind against 'paralysing terrors' and false admirations; who is himself a far more romantic figure than Napoleon.[1]

Hence too the intense repugnance that Milton is bound to create in some natures. But you cannot ignore him, any more than you can ignore Alexander the Great, or Cromwell, or Napoleon. He is too extraordinary a person to shut out from our notice; and he is perhaps the only man of this type who has translated his mental urge into literature and not into action. I do not mean that he is a mere Tamburlaine. His was no uncontrolled lust for mere conquest. Rather he typifies the controlled energies of the great explorers and inventors. He stands thus as the perpetual monument of the pioneering spirit in man, a spirit which may have destroyed much as well as created, have caused misery as well as happiness, but to which human civilization is largely indebted and which we cannot condemn unless we condemn civilization itself.

1. E. H. Visiak, *Milton Agonistes*, 7.

APPENDICES

APPENDIX A

THOMAS YOUNG

It is a pity we do not know a little more about Thomas Young,[1] Milton's tutor. I rather suspect he had a considerable influence in forming the less pleasant side of Milton's Puritanism. Young was the son of a Scottish minister in Perthshire, who in 1606 joined with forty-one others to sign the protest offered to Parliament against introducing Episcopacy into Scotland. He probably inherited the anti-prelatical animus, and carried it with him to Milton's home. Later, after having been chaplain to the British merchants at Hamburg, Young was given the living of Stowmarket, whence he emerged into publicity by becoming in 1641 one of the joint authors of the anti-episcopal tract signed 'Smectymnuus'. It is quite possible that without Young's persuasions Milton would not have used his pen against the Bishops. This is conjecture, but it is not improbable that in the four years (1618–22) during which Young was Milton's tutor he obtained something of an ascendancy over him, an ascendancy Milton's father seems never to have had. Milton's two extant letters to him show a deep respect for his scholarship (which appears to have included Hebrew[2]) and his powers of teaching; and Milton was not given to praising lightly. If there was any such ascendancy, whatever remained of it must have disappeared when Young became one of the Presbyterian divines who in 1643 sat in the assembly at Westminster, and when Milton not very long after discovered that the Presbyterians were no more to his taste than had been the Episcopalians.

1. For the history of Thomas Young see (as well as Masson) David Laing, *Biographical Notices of Thomas Young*, Edinburgh, 1870.

2. See H. F. Fletcher, *Milton's Semitic Studies*, 27–31.

APPENDIX B

THE DATING OF THE 'SONG ON MAY MORNING', OF THE SONNET, 'O NIGHTINGALE', AND OF THE FIVE ITALIAN SONNETS AND THE CANZONE

IT may now be taken for granted that these poems are pretty close in date, and that they were written before Milton's sonnet on reaching the age of twenty-three (see D. H. Stevens in *Modern Philology*, 1919, 25–33; J. S. Smart, *The Sonnets of Milton*, 133–44; J. H. Hanford, *Modern Philology*, 1921, 482–3). There is the further question whether they were written before or after the *Nativity Ode*. Hanford puts them between the *Fifth Elegy* (April 1629) and the *Nativity Ode* (December 1629). Grierson (*Poems of Milton*, i. pp. xvii, xviii, xxi) suggests May 1630 for the *May Song*, and some date soon after for the rest. I do not think the matter can be proved either way, but I slightly favour the later date. Most of the arguments suggested are of small weight, but there is one serious argument for, and one serious argument against, assigning the poems to 1629. The first is given by Hanford in his *Youth of Milton*, 122–3. In his autobiographical passage in the *Apology for Smectymnuus* Milton, after describing how he came to prefer Dante and Petrarch to the Latin elegists, says:

And long it was not after, when I was confirmed in this opinion, that he who would not be frustrate of his hope to write well hereafter in laudable things, ought himself to be a true poem; that is, a composition and pattern of the best and honourablest things; not presuming to sing high praises of heroic men, or famous cities, unless he have in himself the experience and practice of all that which is praiseworthy.[1]

The close analogy between this passage and the *Sixth Elegy*, written in December 1629 as a covering letter to the *Nativity Ode*, has been admitted (p. 35), and I agree with Hanford that about Christmas 1629, and after he had turned his attention to Dante and Petrarch, Milton made his ascetic resolution. Further, if there were no other considerations, we might take it that Milton wrote his Italian sonnets at the time when he first studied the Italian sonneteers. But there is nothing to prove that Milton stopped reading Italian sonneteers by Christmas 1629, or that he would not have written in their style a little later. There is no hint in the *Sixth Elegy* that Milton meant to cut himself off from all literature but the heroic.

The one serious argument against dating the group of poems before the *Nativity Ode* is the style of the English pieces. I should like to agree with Hanford; his theory tidies up Milton's development beautifully: but I find it difficult to think that the style of the *May Song* and the *Nightingale Sonnet* is not maturer than that both of the *Fifth Elegy* and of the *Nativity Ode*. A new accent of certainty has entered in, for which I cannot account but by a fresh mental development.

1. Bohn, iii. 117–18.

Hanford's other most cogent argument is that the first lines of the *Nightingale Sonnet*,

> O Nightingale, that on yon bloomy Spray
> Warbl'st at eeve, when all the Woods are still,

are translated from lines 25–6 of the *Fifth Elegy* –

> Jam, Philomela, tuos foliis adoperta novellis
> Instituis modulos, dum silet omne nemus.

The English *may* be a translation, though the sentiment is commonplace enough for a young poet to have hit on twice independently. But even if it is, Milton with his excellent memory may have translated the lines a year, just as well as a week, after they were written.

Arguments, about as inconclusive, can be found for the later date. For instance in his third sonnet (*Qual in colle aspro*), after speaking of his having begun to write in Italian on the inspiration of love, he ends by saying,

Ah! were but my slow heart and hard bosom as good soil to him who plants from Heaven!

Such a sentiment would be peculiarly apt soon after Milton's failure to complete *The Passion*. Again in the *canzone* he speaks of the young men and women being aware of his grand poetical designs. It is slightly more likely that these designs should have been thus known after than before the writing of the *Nativity Ode*. I do not want to stress such arguments: only the two major pleas deserve serious consideration.

APPENDIX C

THE DOCTRINE OF CHASTITY IN MILTON

WHETHER or not Milton's personal ideas about chastity are the most important part of the meaning of *Comus*, such ideas had been exercising his mind, and were to exercise it for some years to come. No book that takes note of Milton's poetic development can very well escape enquiring what these ideas were; and as neither Saurat nor Hanford, who have dealt most fully with the matter, settle it quite to my satisfaction, I feel that a fresh discussion is worth while. I hope too that it may cast fresh light on Milton's conception of himself as a being set apart to do great things, and on some passages in his early poems.

Saurat[1] is explicit. Milton was deliberately chaste from his early years 'like the great ascetics of primitive magic in order to acquire supernatural powers'. By the year 1642 he had admitted the distinction between love commanded and love forbidden, but not till his marriage (based solely on the urgency of physical need) did he conclude that the desires of the flesh were good, provided they were controlled by reason. I suspect that Saurat has made the matter too simple. He says practically nothing of any transition of idea from *Comus* to the time of Milton's marriage, and throws all the emphasis on that event.

Hanford[2] elaborates with much ingenuity Milton's own statement in the *Apology for Smectymnuus* of how the writers of romance, Plato, St. Paul, and the author of the *Book of Revelation*, impressed the doctrine of chastity on his mind, and has certainly added a new chapter to the history of Milton's mental growth from *Comus* till the *Epitaphium Damonis*. He seems to believe, contrary to Saurat, that Milton never attributed magical powers to chastity. My own conclusions are that at the time of writing *Comus* Milton did hold some such belief; that the belief was imposed and discordant with his real nature; and that this imposition partly accounts for *Comus* not being a completely sound whole.

Milton doubtless began by accepting the rule, taken for granted in his Puritan household, of premarital strictness. When during his early college years he mentions chastity, he may mean by it no more than this; and the early love poems indicate that he did not, when writing them, contemplate on principle any necessarily prolonged postponement of marriage. But at some time the idea grew in his mind that if he was to be a great poet he must remain, either for some period or for life, chaste and unmarried.[3]

1. op. cit., 7–8, 38–9, 41–9.   2. *Youth of Milton*, 136 ff.

3. There is strong evidence for such a change in the lines, unfortunately not dated, attached to the Latin elegies in the 1645 edition beginning *Haec ego mente olim laeva* (quoted above, p. 23). These lines, clearly written much later than the elegies, state that his Platonic studies have quenched the vain desires of his youth, and that his heart is now icy cold and able to withstand the arrows of love. It will be seen that the reference to Plato is significant.

318

APPENDIX C

Precisely when this time was is uncertain. The beginnings of the idea are
seen in the *Sixth Elegy*, written just after the *Nativity Ode* at the age of twenty-
one. In it he says that *casta juventus* is necessary in the writer of epic poetry.
But *casta juventus* is but one among several conditions, and again it may mean
no more than premarital chastity, as indeed the word *juventus* might seem to
imply. There is better evidence in the letter to the unknown friend enclosing
the sonnet *How soon hath Time,* and probably written soon after the move to
Horton. Here Milton, as mentioned above,[1] implies that he has considered
marriage but rejected or postponed it, because he cannot spare the time
from his task of self-preparation, for the profession that marriage would
make necessary. There is no hint that he believed in any magical properties
of chastity.

Still the seed of the strange mixture of Platonic and Apocalyptic mysticism
with which he later invested the subject was already in his mind. While at
Cambridge, at what precise date is unknown, he wrote an academic exercise
De Sphaerarum Concentu, on the music of the Spheres. The idea of this music
goes back to Plato, to whom Milton refers in the exercise.[2] According to
passages in Plato's *Timaeus,* and in the vision of Er at the end of the *Republic,*
the Sun, the Moon, the five planets, and the heaven of the fixed stars, were
each tenanted by a Siren, who singing in monotone their proper note
together formed a scale or octave. That octave has its counterpart in the
immortal soul of each of us; for the circular motions of the soul of man only
reproduce on a smaller scale the mightier revolutions of the soul of the world,
which are the planetary orbits. Were it not for the earthy and perishable
nature of the body, our souls would sound in perfect accord with the soul
of the world. But Milton in his academic exercise adds something of his own
to the familiar Platonic mythology.

The fact that we are unable to hear this harmony seems certainly to be due to
the presumption of that thief Prometheus, which brought so many evils upon·men,
and robbed us of that happiness which we may never again enjoy so long as we
remain buried in sin and degraded by brutish desires, . . . But if our souls were pure,
chaste, and white as snow, as was Pythagoras' of old, then indeed our ears would
ring and be filled with that exquisite music of the stars in their orbits.[3]

The gist of the last sentence is repeated in the Genius's speech in *Arcades,*
probably the next poem in point of time which continues this strain of
Platonism.

> But els in deep of night when drowsines
> Hath lockt up mortal sense, then listen I
> To the celestial *Sirens* harmony,
> That sit upon the nine enfolded Sphears,
> And sing to those that hold the vital shears,
> And turn the Adamantine spindle round,

1. p. 51.
2. See the account in the very interesting pamphlet of the English Association,
(no. 45), *The Greek Strain in English Literature,* by Professor Burnet, of which I have
made free use here.
3. P. B. Tillyard, op. cit., 67.

319

On which the fate of gods and men is wound.
Such sweet compulsion doth in Musick ly,
To lull the daughters of *Necessity*,
And keep unsteddy Nature to her law,
And the low world in measur'd motion draw
After the heavenly tune, which none can hear
Of human mould with grosse unpurged ear.[1]

The mythology, Sirens, adamantine spindle, the daughters of Necessity, comes from the Vision of Er; and the theory that the gross ear of humanity cannot catch the music is Platonic. But I fancy Milton half identifies himself with the Genius, who *can* hear the music, and is thinking of his own 'nightward thoughts' when writing of the Genius's nocturnal reverie. He thinks of himself as a being privileged to hear, or not without hope of hearing, things unrevealed to ordinary humanity.

But it is in the lines *At a Solemn Music*[2] that the doctrine of the planetary music takes a new and more complicated form with the entry of Biblical mythology into what had been mainly Platonic. Here we get a hint of the doctrine that chastity is the means of hearing the celestial music.

The relevance of much of the poem to the doctrines of the *Timaeus* and of the *Republic* is plain. We have the mention of the Sirens of the Vision of Er, and in the 'Song of pure concent' *concent* has reference to the singing together of the celestial sirens. When Milton speaks of the inhabitants of the earth answering with undiscording voice the melodious noise of heaven, he is thinking of the repetition in the Soul of Man of the music in the Soul of the World. But interwoven with the Platonism there is the mythology and mysticism of the Old and New Testaments. The fall of Adam is interpreted Platonically: before it occurred, all creatures in perfect diapason responded to the celestial music. And the Platonic music of the spheres is identified with the song sung before the throne in the *Book of Revelation*. True, the epithet 'sapphire-colour'd' is from *Ezekiel*, but the impressive vagueness of 'him that sits thereon' is taken from *Revelation* v. 1: 'him that sat on the throne'. But more important than the throne is the song sung before it, the 'undisturbed Song of pure concent' once more; which as well as being the music of the planets is the song mentioned as sung before the throne in the *Book of Revelation*.[3] Now this song in *Revelation* is not only referred to several times in Milton's poems, but is cited in the *Apology for Smectymnuus* as one

1. 61–73.   2. Quoted on p. 55 above.

3. If further proof is wanted of this identity see *Ad Patrem*, 35–7,
    Spiritus et rapidos qui circinat igneus orbes
    Nunc quoque sidereis intercinit ipse choreis
    Immortale melos et inenarrabile carmen,
'And the spirit which circles through the swift-moving spheres is singing even now among the dances of the stars his immortal melody and unexpressive song.' I translate 'unexpressive' because the 'unexpressive nuptial song' of *Lycidas* is clearly a translation of the Latin phrase. But the nuptial song in *Lycidas* is of course the song in *Revelation*. The 'spirit' in *Ad Patrem* is the Soul of the World of the *Timaeus*.

of the passages which particularly affected him in his practice of chastity.
It is worth while quoting it in full:

> And I looked, and, lo, a Lamb stood on the mount Sion, and with him an
> hundred forty and four thousand, having his Father's name written in their fore-
> heads. And I heard a voice from heaven, as the voice of many waters, and as the
> voice of a great thunder: and I heard the voice of harpers harping with their harps:
> and they sung as it were a new song before the throne, and before the four beasts,
> and the elders; and no man could learn that song but the hundred and forty and
> four thousand, which were redeemed from the earth. These are they which were
> not defiled with women; for they are virgins. These are they which follow the Lamb
> whithersoever he goeth. These were redeemed from among men, being the
> firstfruits unto God and to the Lamb. And in their mouth was found no guile: for
> they are without fault before the throne of God.[1]

The 'just spirits' in line thirteen of *At a Solemn Music* are these 'men without
fault before the throne of God'. It is this making of chastity the condition of
hearing and learning the song before the throne that gives a new turn to
the ideas we are discussing. Milton had supposed that a heart of snowy
purity could hear the music of the Spheres, but this music is no other than
the song sung by the one hundred and forty-four thousand men in heaven,
and chastity was the condition of their learning it. It follows then that
chastity is the magic means of hearing the planetary music likewise, the
means of supernatural powers in this life.

We should remember these implications in *At a Solemn Music* when we
consider *Comus,* for if *Comus* stood alone it would be hazardous to guess at
Milton's personal beliefs. With the examples of the third book of the *Faerie
Quene* and of the *Faithful Shepherdess* what more natural than to profess a
temporary poetic allegiance to the cult of virginity in the somewhat irresponsible medium of the masque? But when it is remembered that an uncommon
theory of virginity can be deduced from a previous poem, and that in the
Apology for Smectymnuus Milton states quite plainly that he was personally
concerned with such theories at about the time *Comus* was written, it is
impossible not to give weight to the sage and serious doctrine of virginity
expounded in that poem. And the doctrine as stated in *Comus* is that
chastity gives supernatural powers. It is a 'sublime notion and high mystery'.[2] It is a hidden strength and protection against all perils.

> So dear to Heav'n is Saintly chastity,
> That when a soul is found sincerely so,
> A thousand liveried Angels lacky her,
> Driving far off each thing of sin and guilt,
> And in cleer dream, and solemn vision
> Tell her of things that no gross ear can hear,
> Till oft convers with heav'nly habitants
> Begin to cast a beam on th' outward shape,
> The unpolluted temple of the mind,
> And turns it by degrees to the souls essence,

1. *Revelation*, 14. 1–5.   2. 785.

Till all be made immortal: but when lust
By unchaste looks, loose gestures, and foul talk,
But most by leud and lavish act of sin,
Lets in defilement to the inward parts,
The soul grows clotted by contagion,
Imbodies, and imbrutes, till she quite loose
The divine property of her first being.[1]

The passage about the soul's degeneracy is Platonism from the *Phaedo*, and the mixture with it of the angels carries on the example of *At a Solemn Music*. 'Gross ear' too reminds us of *Arcades* and

the heavenly tune, which none can hear
Of human mould with grosse unpurged ear.

But chastity is now by very explicit statement the essential means by which the human soul reaches out to divinity. The question whether marriage dissipates the magic power is not raised: but it is worth remembering that in the *Faithful Shepherdess*, to which, with all his heed of Spenser, Milton is greatly indebted in *Comus*, Chlorin the lifelong virgin is altogether more sacred and powerful than even the most respectable of the pairs of lovers who presumably live happily ever after in Arcadia; only to her does the rough Satyr do instinctive obeisance. She has 'a hidden and private power', possessed by no other character.

Milton's own statement in the *Apology for Smectymnuus* can now be examined.[2] After speaking of the way in which the writers of romance affected him, he turns to Plato and Xenophon, and finally to the Bible.

Last of all, not in time, but as perfection is last, that care was ever had of me, with my earliest capacity, not to be negligently trained in the precepts of the Christian religion: this that I have hitherto related, hath been to shew, that though Christianity had been but slightly taught me, yet a certain reservedness of natural disposition,[3] and moral discipline, learnt out of the noblest philosophy, was enough to keep me in disdain of far less incontinences than this of the bordello. But having had the doctrine of holy scripture unfolding those chaste and high mysteries, with timeliest care infused, that 'the body is for the Lord, and the Lord for the body'; thus also I argued to myself, that if unchastity in a woman, whom St. Paul terms the glory of man, be such a scandal and dishonour, then certainly in a man, who is both the image and glory of God, it must, though commonly not so thought, be much more deflouring and dishonourable; in that he sins both against his own body, which is the perfecter sex, and his own glory, which is in the woman;

1. 453–69.

2. It must be remembered that Milton's statement is a direct answer to the charge of sexual laxity, and that it must not be taken to give a complete account of what was going on in his mind. He had to speak to the point and to omit the irrelevant. It is only too easy to exaggerate the extent to which Milton occupied his mind with questions of sex and chastity during the Horton period. Milton's object was to make himself as fine a person as possible in preparation for some great literary work, and chastity was but one element in the process of preparation.

2. This is a very typical piece of independence on Milton's part: an indication that he ranked his own bent above all authority.

and, that which is worst, against the image and glory of God, which is in himself. Nor did I slumber over that place expressing such high rewards of ever accompanying the Lamb, with those celestial songs to others inapprehensible, but not to those who were not defiled with women, which doubtless means fornication; for marriage must not be called a defilement.[1]

The end refers of course to the song sung in *Revelation* by the one hundred and forty-four thousand men who were not defiled with women, the song already identified in Milton's poetry with the music of the planets. The last sentence would seem to prove that Milton did not arrogate special powers to lifelong chastity. Certainly he did not in 1642 when he wrote the *Apology for Smectymnuus*, but eight years separate this work from *Comus*, during which his opinions may have changed; a change suggested by his reference to St. Paul. If Milton had meditated honestly on the chapter concerning marriage in *First Corinthians*, he must have concluded that St. Paul's bias was towards lifelong chastity: 'It is good for a man not to touch a woman', he begins, and nothing he says afterwards really alters this opinion. When Milton was writing *Comus*, he was particularly concerned with the question of chastity; I believe that at that time the bias of St. Paul would confirm what from *Comus* itself seems probable, that Milton intended his celibacy to last his life.

After *Comus* there is little in the poems[2] concerning chastity, but the lines speaking of Diodati's reception in heaven from the *Epitaphium Damonis* show that the earlier ideas were still alive.

> Quod tibi purpureus pudor, et sine labe juventus
> Grata fuit, quod nulla tori libata voluptas,
> En etiam tibi virginei servantur honores.[3]

Thus far I have spoken of Milton's opinions on sex. It remains briefly to relate these professed opinions to his life down to the time of *Comus*. There is nothing unusual in his feelings up to the *Nativity Ode*. He holds the Puritan code of morality, but by no means cuts himself off from female society. In the *Ode* was detected (among other feelings) a singularly healthy sexual excitement. About the time of the *Ode* he dedicates himself to an austere manner of life, holding the opinion

that he who would not be frustrate of his hope to write well hereafter in laudable things, ought himself to be a true poem; that is, a composition and pattern of the best and honourablest things; not presuming to sing high praises of heroic men, or famous cities, unless he have in himself the experience and the practice of all that which is praiseworthy.[4]

1. Bohn, iii. 122.
2. Hanford (*Youth of Milton*, 159), adduces evidence from the entries in the Commonplace Book that in the later Horton period Milton was 'satisfying himself that marriage is no defilement even for a priest, and, inferentially, that his own inferior priesthood of poetry does not demand a state of celibacy'.
3. For Cowper's translation see below, p. 325, where the whole passage is quoted.
4. *Apology for Smectymnuus*, Bohn, iii. 118.

Premarital chastity is but one, and not necessarily the most important, part of this austere mode of life. On finishing his college course Milton had to choose between going into the Church and going on with his education to be a poet. To have chosen the first would have made marriage possible, the inclination to which 'about this time of a man's life solicits most'. He rejects a profession, and with it matrimony, in order to have time to give to his greater project, and retires to Horton. Happy though he must have been in the main at being able to bend all his powers unimpeded to furthering his great object in life, he must have been more subject to sexual unrest than when living in the busier centres of Cambridge and London. Intense study was the only outlet at the time to Milton's furiously active nature, and this seems to have been insufficient to keep quite healthy his normal desires. He meditates on the doctrine of chastity and turns it, we do not quite know when, from something partly utilitarian and partly moral into a mystery. Hitherto he had considered fornication a sin, and marriage something for which he cannot spare the time; but now there is 'something in' chastity; it gives unique powers. In Milton the doctrine seems to me distinctly morbid.

Such briefly was Milton's mental state up to *Comus*. But there is evidence of a second sign of repressed desires. It is contained in the passage from the *Apology for Smectymnuus* immediately preceding the references to St. Paul and *Revelation*.

Thus, from the laureat fraternity of poets, riper years and the ceaseless round of study and reading led me to the shady spaces of philosophy; but chiefly to the divine volumes of Plato, and his equal Xenophon: where, if I should tell ye what I learnt of chastity and love, I mean that which is truly so, whose charming cup is only virtue, which she bears in her hand to those who are worthy; (the rest are cheated with a thick intoxicating potion, which a certain sorceress, the abuser of love's name, carries about;) and how the first and chiefest office of love begins and ends in the soul, producing those happy twins of her divine generation, knowledge and virtue. With such abstracted sublimities as these, it might be worth your listening.[1]

Hanford[2] relates this passage to Milton's letter to Diodati of September 23, 1637, and argues that Milton was affected by the homosexual theories of Plato's *Symposium* so dear to the Italian Renaissance. In this letter Milton describes how, urged by Plato, he seeks to cultivate afresh and with a new intensity the friendship of a noble spirit, Diodati, with the deliberate intention of thereby making his own nature more virtuous. But I cannot give the importance to this profession that Hanford does. Anxious to prove that it dominated Milton's thoughts till the time of the *Epitaphium Damonis*, he writes as if *Lycidas* and *Epitaphium Damonis* (both elegies to dead friends) were the only important poems written in the years 1637 to 1639, and as if *Lycidas* was primarily concerned with a Platonic friendship. He omits *Mansus*, the best of all Milton's Latin poems, and fails to take account of the pro-

1. Bohn, iii. 119-21.   2. *Youth of Milton*, 144 ff.

found effect of Milton's Italian tour. But it is true that the final lines of the *Epitaphium* dwell on the mystic orgies of the heavenly marriage with a religious eroticism that for a moment joins Milton to Giles Fletcher in the more delirious moments of *Christ's Triumph after Death*, if not to one kind of seventeenth-century Catholic.

> Quod tibi purpureus pudor, et sine labe juventus
> Grata fuit, quod nulla tori libata voluptas,
> En etiam tibi virginei servantur honores;
> Ipse caput nitidum cinctus rutilante corona,
> Laetaque frondentis gestans umbracula palmae
> Aeternum perages immortales hymenaeos;
> Cantus ubi, choreisque furit lyra mista beatis,
> Festa Sionaeo bacchantur et Orgia thyrso.[1]

From what little we know of the Italian tour any morbidity in Milton's mind must have been dissipated by the novelty of the experience and the enjoyable social activity he entered into. On resuming his studies in England he seems to have given up the idea of lifelong celibacy, and his marriage and the attendant complications must have made the heart-searching of *Comus* seem very remote.

The fact is that the magical idea of virginity was really repugnant to Milton's nature. He believed in the flesh and, so far from desiring to etherialize mankind should it attain to a superior state in heaven, he materializes the angels so that they can enjoy some higher kind of physical love. In his reply to Adam's question Raphael answers:

> Whatever pure thou in the body enjoy'st
> (And pure thou wert created) we enjoy
> In eminence, and obstacle find none
> Of membrane, joint, or limb, exclusive barrs:
> Easier than Air with Air, if Spirits embrace,
> Total they mix, Union of Pure with Pure
> Desiring; nor restrain'd conveyance need
> As Flesh to mix with Flesh, or Soul with Soul.[2]

This is the true Milton. There is something quaint and primitive in the idea that reminds one of those very qualities in the *Nativity Ode*. Still it is not sur-

1. Lines 212 to end:
> Thy blush was maiden, and thy youth the taste
> Of wedded bliss knew never, pure and chaste,
> The honours, therefore, by divine decree
> The lot of virgin worth, are given to thee;
> Thy brows encircled with a radiant band,
> And the green palm-branch waving in thy hand,
> Thou in immortal nuptials shalt rejoice
> And join with seraphs thy according voice,
> Where rapture reigns, and the ecstatic lyre
> Guides the blest orgies of the blazing quire.

2. *Paradise Lost*, viii. 622–9.

prising that for a spell, when his energies had hardly sufficient outlet, he played with an idea which certainly appeals to a very large number of people, the idea of chastity as an active principle, not a negation. For example, a recent writer on Spenser states that 'all Spenser's virtues are positive fighting virtues, and Chastity among them'. To some people's minds, however, chastity is in itself and apart from its effects no more than a negation, possibly good, possibly bad, but not an activity like love, hate, or ambition. It is to this class of mind that Milton really belongs. Again and again it has been remarked that he is no mystic, and, with the reservation that in matters of sex he was so for a short period, I should like to add my agreement.

APPENDIX D

THE DATE OF 'AD PATREM'

MASSON (op. cit., i. 2nd ed., 334) and Hanford (*Youth of Milton*, 130–1) associate the poem with the letter written by Milton to an unknown friend[1] enclosing the sonnet *How soon hath Time*, and date it therefore late in 1632. Both compositions have to do with Milton's refusal to take up a profession, but this is not the slightest evidence for a common date, as during the whole period of Milton's stay at Horton he was open to the charge that he ought to be finding a profession. I believe Grierson right (*Milton's Poems*, i. p. xxii) in putting *Ad Patrem* after *Comus* in date. He justly points out that 'the sonnet and the letter accompanying it are an apology for waiting and learning; the Latin poem is an apology for poetry'; and that it would be after *Comus* had made clear Milton's poetical purpose that so emphatic an apology for poetry would be apt. Stronger almost to my mind is the argument from style. *Ad Patrem, Mansus*, and *Epitaphium Damonis* make an inseparable group. They show a common sureness of touch that belongs to the period round *Lycidas*. *Inenarrabile carmen* of *Ad Patrem* is related to the *unexpressive nuptial song* of *Lycidas* (as has been often noted). Two lines of *Ad Patrem* – *Victrices hederas inter, laurosque sedebo* and *Heroumque actus, imitandaque gesta canebat* – are repeated in *Mansus*. As well as the sureness of touch there is confidence of future poetic greatness in all three Latin poems.

Here is another though small piece of evidence for late date. In talking of the languages his father had him taught Milton writes (lines 82–4):

> Addere suasisti quos jactat Gallia flores,
> Et quam degeneri novus Italus ore loquelam
> Fundit, barbaricos testatus voce tumultus.[2]

This gratuitous mention of the barbarian invasions having left their mark on the Italian tongue suggests recent interest in that part of history. On 23 September, 1637, Milton tells Diodati about his studies and writes: 'I have spent much time on the obscure history of the Italians under the Lombards, Franks, and Germans.' The probability is that *Ad Patrem* and this letter are not very many months separated in time.

1. See above, pp. 50–1.
2. Thyself didst counsel me to add the flow'rs,
   That Gallia boasts, those too, with which the smooth
   Italian his degen'rate speech adorns,
   That witnesses his mixture with the Goth.

APPENDIX E

PARAGRAPHING IN 'LYCIDAS', LINES 23-4

MOST editors of Milton, including Warton, Todd, Masson, and Aldis Wright, begin a new paragraph with the lines:

> For we were nurst upon the self-same hill,
> Fed the same flock, by fountain, shade, and rill.

This paragraphing has no authority in the early editions, and impairs the sense. It should certainly be discarded. The following are some of the reasons why these lines should end, not begin, a paragraph:

(1) The earliest readings are as follows: The Trinity Manuscript ends the second paragraph of the poem with lines 23-4 quoted above, and begins a new paragraph with line 25:

> Together both, ere the high Lawns appear'd

The first edition of *Lycidas* (1638) has no paragraphing either before or after lines 23-4. Some editors follow this edition. The first collected edition of Milton's minor poems (1645) reverts to the paragraphing of the Trinity Manuscript, and is followed by the second and third editions in 1673 and 1695. The 1638 edition is not only carelessly paragraphed (there are but six paragraphs indicated in the whole poem), but it cannot be considered to be as authoritative as the 1645 edition, which embodies Milton's own alterations. Further, the agreement of the Trinity Manuscript with the 1645 edition greatly strengthens the authority of this edition. The textual evidence is strong that Milton intended lines 23-4 to belong to the second paragraph of the poem and a new paragraph to begin with line 25.

(2) The evidence of the metre clearly favours the paragraphing of the Trinity Manuscript and the 1645 edition, and not Masson's. According to the one, the second paragraph will agree with six others in ending with a couplet; according to the other, the second paragraph will be unique in ending with one of the few unrhymed lines of the poem, and the third will be unique in beginning with a rhymed couplet. It is inconceivable that Milton should have begun with a couplet any paragraph not itself composed of couplets, or that without some very good reason (not apparent here) for creating an effect of incompleteness he should have ended a paragraph with an unrhymed line.

(3) The evidence of the meaning is less clear, but to my thinking favours the paragraphing of the Trinity Manuscript; if one accepts which, the connection between lines 23 and 24 and the rest of the poem will be as follows. Milton calls on the Muse for a song about Lycidas in the hope that some kind poet ('gentle Muse') may write an epitaph on Milton when Milton in his turn is dead ('with lucky words favour my destin'd Urn').

This is only fitting, he implies,

> For we were nurst upon the self-same hill,
> Fed the same flock, by fountain, shade, and rill.

'If', says Milton, 'Lycidas is favoured with an elegy, then I, brought up with him, his equal, should be favoured too.' Those who dislike this interpretation would follow Keightley (the only editor I have found to trouble to explain the connection of lines 23 and 24 with what goes before) in regarding lines 19–22 as parenthetic, and in taking lines 23 and 24 as referring to line 18. Whatever the interpretation, the third paragraph, which gives details of the common pursuits of Milton and Lycidas, would follow with a pleasing transition from the last words of the paragraph before, which mention the pursuits in general. Taking Masson's paragraphing, one is forced to regard lines 19–24 as parenthetic, and to forgo the pleasing transition from one paragraph to another. 'For', too, does not make a natural opening of a new paragraph.

In sum, I think the evidence is strongly against the liberty that some eminent editors have taken with the text of *Lycidas*.

APPENDIX F

THE 'TWO-HANDED ENGINE' IN 'LYCIDAS'

I DO not pretend to know all the explanations offered of the 'two-handed engine at the door', and the passage quoted below has possibly been employed already. Certainly it seems to me as if Milton had the *Lycidas* passage in mind when he wrote it, for the pastoral language in general, and the word 'sheephook' in particular, suggest the analogy quite apart from the avenging instrument. The sentence is from *Reformation in England* (Bohn, ii. 412).

First constitute that which is right, and of itself it will discover and rectify that which swerves, and easily remedy the pretended fear of having a pope in every parish, unless we call the zealous and meek censure of the church a popedom, which whoso does, let him advise how he can reject the pastorly rod and sheephook of Christ, and those cords of love, and not fear to fall under the iron sceptre of his anger, that will dash him to pieces like a potsherd.

The reference in this passage is to *Psalms* ii. 7–9: 'I will declare the decree: the Lord hath said unto me, Thou art my Son; this day have I begotten thee. Ask of me, and I shall give thee the heathen for thine inheritance, and the uttermost parts of the earth for thy possession. Thou shalt break them with a rod of iron; thou shalt dash them in pieces like a potter's vessel.' The 'two-handed engine' will be the iron sceptre or rod of Christ's anger: 'two-handed' for nothing further than its size and weight. The 'door' is the door of the sheepfold, which was well fenced round, since the bad shepherds have had to climb into it.

APPENDIX G

ON THE DATING OF THE SONNET 'WHEN I CONSIDER . . .'

HANFORD (*Modern Philology*, 1921, pp. 475–83) and Grierson (*Milton's Poems*, i. pp. xxiii–v) date this sonnet 1655, because it follows *Avenge O Lord* in the 1673 edition, and therefore presumably did in the Trinity Manuscript, from which both these sonnets are missing. There is no actual proof that this was the order in the manuscript. Hanford however does not trust the evidence of order entirely: he believes that Milton rearranged his sonnets in preparing them for the press. In view of this 'it now becomes necessary to set aside the assumption that their designated order in the press transcript (with the corresponding scribal numbering of Milton's originals) can be trusted for purposes of chronology'. Hanford does not, however, extend his doubt to *When I consider* . . . Grierson argues for the order indicating the dates. 'At least the *onus probandi* rests on any one who proposes to disturb that order.'

On grounds of internal evidence I find it difficult to believe that the sonnet was written in 1655. Smart, the closest of all students of Milton's sonnets, says that it was written in the early days of blindness; and the whole tone of it points that way. Milton believes that through blindness he is useless for his life's work ('that one Talent . . . lodg'd with me useless'). Could he possibly have uttered that belief after writing *Defensio Secunda* (1654) in spite of his blindness? 'When I consider how my light *is* spent, e're half my days'. *Is*, not *was*: he is referring to the time of writing. In 1652 Milton was forty-three years old. To refer to this age as less than half his days is optimistic enough; but to refer to it thus in 1655 when he was forty-six is outrageous. If Milton made his amanuensis copy the sonnet into the manuscript in 1655 (which is by no means certain), he composed it in 1652 or very little later.

APPENDIX H

SPENSER'S INFLUENCE ON MILTON

I record here my general impressions only.

(1) That Milton was very greatly influenced by details in Spenser is undoubted. The influence was lifelong, and as strong in *Paradise Lost* as anywhere. Milton must have had Spenser almost by heart. I therefore agree entirely with Greenlaw[1] and other American critics that Raleigh in his *Milton* was wrong in minimizing Milton's debts to Spenser.

(2) I cannot agree with Greenlaw that Dryden's remark in his *Preface to the Fables*, 'Milton has acknowledged to me that Spenser was his original', implies that there was a deep and intimate relation of spirit between them. Milton grew up in the same literary nursery as Spenser, and had the same ideas concerning the nature of poetry. Milton's remark may well imply no more than a recognition of this, and a disclaiming of other English influence. It might imply some technical debt also. Spenser in his own stanza, in parts of *Colin Clout,* in *Epithalamion*, may have been Milton's model for sustaining his verse, for constructing the long verse paragraph.

Greenlaw understands Milton to have made the above remark on the occasion when Dryden visited him to get leave to use *Paradise Lost* for writing his *State of Innocence*: hence that the remark has direct reference to *Paradise Lost*. This is uncertain. Milton's remark may have had a different reference even if made during this visit; or Dryden may have made more than one visit to Milton. Without the certainty that the remark did refer to *Paradise Lost*, Greenlaw's analogy between Guyon and Adam, plausible though it is, remains but a conjecture.

(3) I am readier to see a general Spenserian influence in *Paradise Regained* than in any other of Milton's poems. (See p. 270 above.)

1. op. cit., 197–8.

APPENDIX I

(From the Preface to the Sixth Impression)

PARADISE LOST: POSSIBLE INCONSISTENCY

IN the chapter called 'Possible Inconsistency' (pp. 245–9) I debated whether there was any inconsistency in *Paradise Lost* between Milton's ideas about action as expressed first through Satan and secondly through the conduct of Adam and Eve leading to the Fall. The question seemed important, because if Satan's journey and Adam's disobedience – the main active episodes, as I thought – should point different ways, the unity of the poem would suffer. I argued that though Satan's journeys best expressed Milton's belief in heroic energy, the condemnation of triviality implicit in his version of the Fall was in keeping with this belief. Satan indeed gave the positive version, Adam and Eve the negative or oblique.

I have now come to see that my premises were false and that the actual Fall is not (as usually assumed) the climax of the poem but is only an important point in a culminating episode that comprises the whole of Books Nine and Ten. The regeneration of Adam and Eve after the Fall, which includes their active efforts to extricate themselves from the despair into which they have fallen, is as much the climax as the Fall itself with the incidents leading up to it. These efforts are positively heroic and more than balance the earlier doings of Satan. No apology therefore for Milton's treatment of the Fall was needed.

I saw further that, with the climax comprising the whole of Books Nine and Ten, Milton constructed his poem round a great central irony. Satan thought that, if he could persuade Adam and Eve to disobey God's command, they would be lost forever. He expected their Fall would be their end; and Satan's expectation has been exactly duplicated in the reader's common habit of making the Fall the sole climax of the poem. But Satan had not seen that his case and Adam's were different: *he* fell on his own initiative, Adam on that of another. Thus for Adam there is a chance of regeneration; and the great irony is that, through the workings of God's grace, Adam is regenerate at the very time when Satan and Adam himself think he is ruined.

I have thought it wise to state these new conclusions in a separate study rather than to rewrite portions of the present book. I would therefore ask the reader to correct the chapter referred to above and a number of other statements by my essay called 'The Crisis of Paradise Lost' published in my *Studies in Milton*, pp. 8–52.

Index

Manso, 62, 77–8, 79.

Mansus, 62, 75, 77–9, 82, 87, 92, 101, 102, 146, 324, 327.

Marchioness of Winchester, Epitaph on, 38, 46, 78.

Marini, 77, 78.

Marlowe, 17, 308.

Martin, Burns, 120.

Marvell, 308.

Masson, D., 10, 12, 20, 29, 49, 76, 120, 174, 176, 269, 315, 327, 328, 329.

May Morning, Song on, 38, 40, 316–17.

Medievalism, 13, 24, 48.

Meredith, George, *Modern Love*, 86.

Metaphysical poetry, 28, 32–3, 39, 45–6, 98, 302, 305.

Milton, Christopher, 112.

Milton, the elder, 7, 50, 69.

Miracles, Milton's idea of, 190, 195.

Monk, General, 177, 178.

Montaigne, 112.

Morality Play, 62, 269–70, 275.

More, Henry, 47.

More, Paul Elmer, 239–40.

More, Sir Thomas, 104.

Mortalists, 193.

Morus (Alexander More), 113, 160–61, 170–71.

Moseley (publisher), 144.

Mulcaster, 9, 80.

Murry, J. Middleton, 293.

Mutschmann, H., 187.

Nativity Ode, 18, 20, 28, 30, 31–7, 38, 39, 42, 43, 64, 98, 133, 165, 284, 304, 316, 317, 319, 323, 325.

Naturam non pati Senium, 22, 24–5.

Nature, idea of, 127–9, 139–40, 183.

Neo-classicism, 129.

Newton (edition of Milton), 61.

Nicolson, Marjorie H., 47.

Observations upon the Articles of Peace, 153, 154.

Of True Religion, 78, 297, 300–1.

On the Death of a Fair Infant, 12, 16–18.

On Time, 38, 51, 53, 54–5, 56.

Otway, 305.

Ovid, 9, 10, 17, 18, 28, 34, 68.

Paradise Lost, 1, 3, 48, 50, 53, 54, 74, 92, 93, 96, 97, 103, 107, 117, 122, 133, 136, 137, 144, 153, 154, 158, 164–7, 173–4, 176, 178, 180, 181, 182, 189, 201–51, 252, 253–5, 258, 263, 264, 266, 267, 268, 269, 271, 274, 275, 279, 280, 284, 297, 299, 305, 306, 308, 309, 332.

Paradise Regained, 3, 48, 93, 97, 185, 191, 196, 221, 250, 252–78, 283, 284, 306, 311, 332.

Paradise, significance of, in *Paradise Lost*, 238–40.

Passion, The, 38–40, 42, 45, 53, 65, 73, 317.

Passionate Pilgrim, 17.

Pater, 308.

Pattison, Mark, 43–4, 120, 121, 266.

Peripeteia, 291–2.

Pervigilium Veneris, 29.

Pessimism in Milton, 241–4, 249.

Petition of Rights, 22, 23.

Petrarch, 35, 80, 83, 316.

Phillips, Edward, Milton's nephew, 91, 92, 111, 112, 113, 119, 120–1, 165–6, 173.

Pindar, 34, 84, 145–6, 280.

Plato, 47, 48, 104, 134, 186, 262, 318–22.

Pléiade, 80, 81, 83.

Polyclitus (Greek sculptor), 284.

Pope, 95, 306.

Powell, Mary, 112, 144, 163.
  Milton's marriage with, 119–23, 294.

Powells, the, the family of Milton's first wife, 120, 143, 148–9, 294.

Powicke, F. J., 47.

Predestination, 47, 136, 191, 192.

Prelatical Episcopacy, 98, 100, 110.